PRICES, INCOME, AND PUBLIC POLICY

PRICES, INCOME, AND PUBLIC POLICY

Clark Lee Allen
PROFESSOR OF ECONOMICS
SOUTHERN ILLINOIS UNIVERSITY

James M. Buchanan
PROFESSOR OF ECONOMICS
UNIVERSITY OF VIRGINIA

Marshall R. Colberg
PROFESSOR OF ECONOMICS
FLORIDA STATE UNIVERSITY

Second Edition

McGRAW-HILL BOOK COMPANY, INC.

NEW YORK
TORONTO | **1959**
LONDON

PREFACE

The first edition of *Prices, Income, and Public Policy* appeared five years ago. The authors had tried to write a book which they themselves would like to teach, and, although they felt that they had accomplished this objective, they presented the text to the public with certain misgivings. The book was less than half as long as some of those currently in use. It made relatively stringent demands on the intellectual capacity of the student. It sacrificed descriptive and institutional material in order to concentrate on analysis. It devoted approximately half of its pages to price theory at a time when in some quarters price theory was considered to be old hat. And it turned out to be one of almost a dozen elementary economics textbooks, new or revised, to be issued that year.

The response of economists generally to the first edition has been a source of genuine satisfaction. In the present revision the authors have attempted to retain the features which made the book a differentiated product, and they have attempted to refine and improve it wherever they could. Every chapter has been rewritten, sometimes changing only a phrase here and there in the interests of clarity or style, but frequently redoing the whole exposition. A few chapters which proved to be less than indispensable to a mastery of the fun-

damentals of economics have been dropped; five new chapters have
been added: Economic Growth (21), the Nature of Economic Analysis (22), Location of Economic Activity (28), Personal Income
Distribution (31), and Economic Aid for Underdeveloped Areas
(36).

The principal change in the second edition is in the organization
of the chapters. This change was made in order to solve a particular
problem which appears to have become troublesome on many cam-
puses, and we hope this arrangement may prove to be more satisfactory for all. Many colleges and universities have both a one-
semester and a two-semester introductory economics course. Students
in some curricula take the two-semester course, and those in other
programs take the one-semester course. But what is to be done with
the student who starts out in a curriculum which calls for the one-
semester course and then after one semester of economics shifts to
a curriculum which calls for the two-semester course? If he has already surveyed the whole field in a one-term course, the last half of
the conventional two-term course is not appropriate. It may not be
feasible to put him in an advanced course, and, clearly, it would not
be appropriate to reduce his economics requirement from two se-
mesters to one.

To solve this problem the following sequence of topics has been
set up: Book One, which consists of two parts: Part 1, Introduction
to Price Theory, and Part 2, Elements of Income Theory, is designed to serve as the text in the one-term survey course, and it also
serves as the first half of the two-term course. In Part 1 of Book Two
a more intensive study is made of price theory, and this is followed
in Part 2 by a consideration of selected topics in public policy,
where tools of both microeconomics and macroeconomics are employed.

The advantages of this organization are two: it solves some
knotty administrative problems, and it should make for more effective teaching. By combining the first half of the two-semester course
with the one-semester course the total number of sections required
in the elementary economics course can be reduced, conserving
one of our most scarce resources, the professor of economics. It is
also believed that the teaching of economic principles will be improved. One of the common complaints among teachers of courses
in intermediate theory is that their students appear to have learned
so little price theory as sophomores. By giving them a bird's-eye
view of economics in the first semester and then picking up price
theory again during the second semester and carrying the analysis

a bit further, it is hoped that the students will have assimilated it better than by the traditional one-shot approach. The limited experience of the authors seems to indicate that this is true.

For those who wish to retain the more conventional organization, Book One, Part 1, and Book Two, Part 1, may be used to comprise a semester's work in price theory, and Book One, Part 2, and Book Two, Part 2, could comprise a semester's work in macroeconomics.

Those who have made stimulating suggestions—both students and teachers—for the improvement of this book are literally too numerous to mention. To all of them the authors express their warmest thanks for their interest and help.

Clark Lee Allen
James M. Buchanan
Marshall R. Colberg

CONTENTS

BOOK TWO. ALLOCATION OF RESOURCES

Part 1. The Market Economy

Part 2. Political Economy

Book One

The ABC's of Economics

Part 1

INTRODUCTION TO PRICE THEORY

1

CONSUMER SOVEREIGNTY:
THE ORGANIZING PRINCIPLE

An old German fable describes a beautiful world where wants are
satisfied with a minimum of effort. Some of the rivers in this fabulous
land are filled with the best old wine, and others flow with fresh
milk. Along the streams grow trees that bear fresh rolls daily. The
fish swim on top of the water near the land; they are roasted and
ready to eat, and, when called, they jump promptly into one's hands
or mouth. Chickens, ducks, and turkeys sit in the trees. They, too,
are ready to eat and at the slightest beckon fly slowly into one's
mouth. The roasted pigs which roam the forests come equipped
with knives and forks on their backs. Cheeses hang in the trees in
such profusion that all the people in the world could never eat them
all. The stones and the snow are sugar, and the rain is honey. One
has but to shake a tree, and silver and gold, diamonds and pearls,
and beautiful dresses and shoes come tumbling down. If one bathes
in the water, he is cured of all sickness, and old people are made
young again. A gold piece is paid for every hour that one sleeps, and
the one who is the most stupid and who can sleep the longest and
eat the most is made king of the country.

The stories of the Garden of Eden, Aladdin and his wonderful lamp, the travels of Marco Polo, the Big Rock-Candy Mountain, and Li'l Abner's Shmoo all recount places and circumstances where wants are satisfied with virtually no effort. Contemplation of a world where one's every desire is promptly and effortlessly satisfied is a fit subject for reverie while one is stretched out on the beach on a warm summer afternoon, and perhaps we shall be able to enjoy such a listless and useless existence when we all get to heaven. But life in the Western world in the twentieth century is not like that. All of us are confronted with the stark fact that our wants exceed our means to satisfy them. There are just not enough goods and services to satisfy all our wants. The first and fundamental economic fact that we must face is the reality of *scarcity*. We cannot satisfy all our wants. Some may, at least temporarily, be fully satisfied, but others can be only partially satisfied, and some cannot be satisfied at all.

Scarcity and the Necessity to Economize

If the scarcity of economic goods necessitates less than the complete satisfaction of all wants, some kind of allocation of our limited resources is required. If all our wants cannot be satisfied, some mechanism must be employed to determine which are to be satisfied first, and in what measure. A problem of choice is always present. That is to say, we must *economize;* this is the essence of economics.

It should be noted that the necessity for economizing applies at three very important levels: that of the individual consumer, the business firm, and the whole economy. "Flash" Sigurdsson, the varsity tailback, will find that, in spite of his generous athletic scholarship, there is a constant temptation for him to spend more than his monthly income. His wants exceed his ability to pay. The large volume of consumer loans outstanding at any given moment indicates that many families are trying to satisfy more wants than full payment out of current income will allow. Business firms, too, are frequent borrowers of capital funds; their resources are also limited, and they must economize. Even mammoth corporations like General Motors may find that if they use funds to carry on one project, they will have to curtail expenditures somewhere else. And as impressive as the performance of the entire American economy has been since World War II, it is clear that we do not have an unlimited capacity to produce. The production of more of one thing requires the production of less of something else whenever our resources are fully employed. This limitation on our over-all capacity to produce is particularly apparent in time of war. In order to get more war materials, it becomes necessary to produce less of civilian goods—in order to have more guns, we must do with less butter. The scarcity of resources implies the necessity for economizing; this is true in peace as well as in war, and it holds for a wealthy nation as well as for an underdeveloped country.

If the economy is to satisfy consumers' highest-ranking wants, somehow those goods which they want and are able and willing to pay for must be produced. Out of the hundreds of thousands of goods which our resources—our men, machines, and materials—might be used to produce, it is important that the particular commodities which will satisfy those wants to which we have given top priority be produced in adequate quantities. It would be uneconomic to produce too many books at the expense of producing too few paper dolls. What, then, determines which and how much of the countless products that might be produced actually will be produced? Which of the many combinations of factors of production which might be employed in the production of a given product actually will be so employed? Who is to receive the products which are produced? These are the central problems of economics.

The determination of what is to be produced and how it is to be produced is a problem of almost infinite complexity. Consider briefly a quite different and much simpler problem, the operation of a production assembly line in a modern automobile factory. Here there is no question as to what is to be produced, but the purely technological problem of how the thousands of parts are to be assembled into a product which will provide satisfaction to its owner is almost overwhelming. When one visits the automobile plant, he observes a maze of overhead wires which feed electric power to portable motorized tools; bodies of a variety of colors and types float through the air, timed to arrive at the right spot at just the right moment; skeleton cars in various degrees of completion creep along the final assembly line, which is fed by tributary and subassembly lines; and the necessary number and kinds of parts, tools, and workers are stationed along the assembly line just where they are needed. One pauses in admiration for the wit of man when he realizes that the lack of even a small bolt would be sufficient cause to bring the entire complex machinery to a halt until the shortage was eliminated. Such stoppages cannot be permitted to occur.

It is clear that behind such industrial operations there must be a centralized planning agency. Detailed blueprints must have been worked out well in advance, and everything must follow a carefully considered time schedule, with each part of the organization performing its specialized function in strict coordination with the activities of all other parts. Our ability to devise and execute such plans has made possible the minute division of labor which characterizes contemporary large-scale production and which has contributed to the constantly improving standard of living that our people enjoy today.

But, it should be noted, no matter how carefully and accurately the executives, engineers, and economists of the automobile industry plan their operations, they are dependent upon their suppliers —perhaps several thousands of them—for raw materials, parts, and tools. The production of the steel which the automobile industry uses, for example, represents a scarcely less complex industrial process than the fabrication of the automobiles themselves. This means more careful planning, and not only must the several processes in steel production be coordinated with each other, but, in addition, the plans of the steel industry must intermesh with those of the automobile industry—and all other industries for which steel is a raw material. The resources of the economy must furthermore be marshaled in such a way that food, clothing, shelter, and countless other goods and services will be produced for the workers in the steel, automobile, and other industries. These resources must be used to produce goods of the appropriate kind and in sufficient amount; if we produce more lambchop frills than we can use and less penicillin than we need, we are guilty of waste. And if, as has frequently happened in the past, we do not use some of our resources at all, our economic sin is compounded. This is under any circumstances undesirable, and in time of national emergency it may be critical.

The Organizing Principle

What, then, is the organizing principle by which a private-enterprise economy determines what is to be produced and in what amounts? How does a capitalistic society determine with which resources and in what combinations a given commodity is to be produced? And, since some wants cannot be satisfied, what determines in our economy whose wants will be left unsatisfied or only partially satisfied?

The answers to these questions indicate the prime economic difference between a private-enterprise economy such as ours and a totalitarian economy such as that of Soviet Russia. The Russian communists have attempted to solve the problem of what is to be produced, how it is to be produced, and for whom it is to be produced by setting up a central planning agency with power to regiment the economy's resources in any way which it chooses in order to produce the goods it decides need to be produced. If the central commissariat decides that the production of heavy industrial equipment is more important in the years just ahead than increasing consumer living standards, for example, steps will be taken to allocate productive resources to those industries with the result that less is produced for immediate consumption. Everything operates on the basis of the master plan, and the wishes of the individual as consumer and producer are subservient to those of the state.

A private-enterprise system has no central commissariat or commission or bureau or brain trust set up to tell each worker what job he must work at and to determine what goods are to be produced and how the national product is to be divided among consumers. What then prevents our producing more automobiles than we are able to produce tires and gasoline for if there is no over-all production plan? If planning is so essential for each individual firm, how can the whole economy work without a master plan? There clearly must be some organizing force to prevent complete confusion and chaos, but if there is no deliberative body with power to allocate resources among various competing uses, what is the organizing principle in a private-enterprise economy?

The answer is that a private-enterprise economy uses the impersonal forces of the market to determine the allocation of its resources. Market forces are reflected in price changes, and prices determine what is to be produced, how it is to be produced, and for whom it is to be produced. Let us contrast the workings of the Russian communistic economy with that of the American capitalistic economy when both are confronted with the same type of problem. Suppose that the Russian planners have miscalculated with the result that they have produced more mushrooms than they had intended but fewer artichokes. It will be necessary for them to increase the ration of mushrooms to consumers and to reduce the ration of artichokes. That is to say, they will encourage the consumption of what is abundant and discourage the consumption of what is in short supply. As they revise their estimates for the coming year, they will plan to increase the production of what is in short supply (artichokes) and decrease the output of what is relatively abundant (mushrooms). The function of the central planning board may be put in these terms: to encourage the *consumption* of what is in oversupply and to discourage the consumption of what is in undersupply; to encourage the *production* of what is in undersupply and to discourage the production of what is in oversupply.

Suppose, now, that in the United States the mushroom crop is larger than had been anticipated, whereas the artichoke crop is below expectations. The oversupply of mushrooms would be reflected in the market by a decline in price. This would have two effects: (1) The consumption of mushrooms, because of their low price, would be increased. (2) The production of mushrooms, because of lower profits to producers, would be decreased. The undersupply of artichokes would cause artichoke prices to rise and would have the opposite effects: (1) The consumption of artichokes would be decreased. (2) The production of artichokes would be increased. The function of prices in a capitalistic economy is identical with the function of the planning commissariat in a communistic economy[1] and may be put in these terms: to encourage the consumption of what is in oversupply and to discourage the consumption of what is in undersupply; to encourage the production of what is in undersupply and to discourage the production of what is in oversupply.

The important role of profits in the allocation of resources in a private-enterprise economy should be noted. The price of a commodity in undersupply tends to increase. A rise in price increases the spread between the producing firms' revenues and costs. This added profit serves as a magnet, drawing other resources into this line of production. In this way the relative undersupply of a good tends automatically to be corrected. Conversely, if a product is in oversupply, the fall in its price reduces profits and may cause losses. These losses will drive resources away from the production of the good in oversupply. Because of the central importance of

---

[1] Even the Russians have found it necessary to make use of prices in rationing goods to consumers. To this extent the Russian system is a departure from pure communism. And, more recently, both the planning and control of the various industrial sectors have been substantially decentralized.

profits and losses in guiding firms into and out of various lines of production, the free-enterprise system has sometimes been described as the "profit system," although the term "profit-and-loss system" would be more descriptive.

If profits and losses were not present to direct firms into different lines of economic activity, some central directing body would be required. But as long as the price mechanism is free to operate and to utilize the profit-and-loss guide, a private-enterprise economy is able automatically to channel its available resources into those areas of production which are indicated to be desirable by the consuming public. The determination of which goods and services are to be produced is really made in the final analysis by the consumer himself. Every dollar spent for a good constitutes a vote for the production of that commodity, and the number of votes cast determines what will be produced. These dollar votes set up the consumer ranking of wants. The wants which will be satisfied are those which are most intense in a pecuniary sense, and they may be different from the most intense physical wants of the people. But the important thing is that the fundamental decisions which run the economy are made by millions of individual consumers shopping in the nation's market places. This has been referred to as the "principle of consumer sovereignty," and it is the organizing principle which in a private-enterprise economy renders a governmental planning agency unnecessary.

Allocation of Resources by the Price System

It may be helpful to think of a private-enterprise system as a great web of economic interrelationships. Each filament hangs from at least two points. The worker depends on the employer for a job and income, but the latter depends on him for productive services. The household depends on the retailer as its source of food, but the store owner depends equally on the householder's purchases for his own income. The city depends on the country as its source of agricultural products, but the farmer relies equally on the city for his tractors, clothing, and processed foods. And the student depends on the teacher as a purveyor of knowledge, but the teacher cannot teach without students.

The whole complex of private enterprise hangs together well despite the absence of central planning. In *The Wealth of Nations,* the first of the "great books" in economics, Adam Smith, writing about the time of the American Revolution, observed that each in-

dividual follows his own self-interest, mindless of the good of society; in doing so, however, he also promotes the social welfare by
placing his labor and property in those slots where they will be
most productive.[1]

More specifically, how are resources allocated through the market mechanism? Consider a stretch of unused oceanside land
along Miami Beach. Zoning regulations would not permit the
erection of a paper mill on the beach, but—more important for
the present discussion—neither would the laws of economics. The
owner of the land will readily see that the opportunity for a maximum rental income (or selling price) lies in awaiting an attractive
offer from someone who wishes to erect a hotel on the site. The
hotel builder will be able to outbid all other potential users of
the property because the land will be productive of more income
to him than to the owner of any other sort of enterprise. It is
important to see also that this is as it should be from a social point
of view. The land will be put to the use in which it can contribute most to consumer satisfaction. Some may object that only
the wealthy consumer will derive any satisfaction from this use of
the land. Their quarrel is with the distribution of income and
wealth among the American people, however, and not with the
efficiency of the market mechanism in allocating the land to its
most productive use.

To illustrate the principle of allocation further, consider the
case of a corporation president who has come up through the
ranks. He may be a better bookkeeper than his best accountant,
a better shipping clerk than anyone in the company, and a better
engineer than he can hire. Yet his most productive activity—the
one which will add most to the corporation's (and his own) income
—is the making of top-level decisions. He will refrain from spending his time on the accounts, on the shipping platform, and on the
engineering drawings, delegating these responsibilities completely
to others.

Similarly, regions find it advantageous to specialize in production which brings the maximum income, neglecting other opportunities which they might exploit quite efficiently. Sugar beets, for
example, could be grown more efficiently in a purely technical
sense in the corn belt than in Michigan or Colorado; yet they are
not grown in quantities in such states as Iowa and Illinois. The
reason is that although sugar-beet output per acre would be greater

[1] Adam Smith, *The Wealth of Nations* (New York: Modern Library, Inc.,
1937), p. 423.

in Illinois than in Colorado, Illinois finds corn production even
more profitable. In this case Michigan and Colorado may be said
to have a "comparative advantage" in the production of sugar
beets, while Illinois and Iowa have a comparative advantage in
corn production. The bookkeeper, clerk, and engineer similarly
can keep their jobs because they have a *comparative* advantage in
these pursuits over their capable boss, who cannot do their work
and at the same time tend to his executive duties in which he has
a comparative advantage.

To generalize, specialization by an economic unit, whether it is
as small as the individual worker or a plot of land or as large as
an entire nation, is based on the desires of owners of resources
to earn the largest possible incomes. This means that each unit
of each resource must be devoted to the employment which that
unit can *most efficiently* perform in view of product and resource
prices because such action will bring in maximum personal income.

It is important that the beginning student grasp the essential
nature of the allocative process as it works in a private-enterprise
economy; it is also important, however, to avoid coming away with
a wholly unsophisticated faith in the perfection of the process
as it actually operates in the world in which we live. Much space
will be devoted in subsequent chapters to an examination of these
deviations. For the present it is sufficient to note that in fact there
is substantial monopoly power in the hands of many businessmen
and labor-union leaders, that legislation affecting economic matters
is always shaped in part by lobbyists and others representing interested groups (farmers, manufacturers, labor unions, bankers,
physicians, etc.), that during certain periods not all available productive resources may be utilized, and that national emergencies
may require special interference by the Federal government with
the normal economic process. And, as was mentioned earlier, the
proper allocation of resources is a separate problem from that of
the desirable distribution of income and wealth.

The Flow of Money, Goods, and Services

Viewed broadly, a private-enterprise system is one in which individuals sell the productive services of their labor and property
to enterprises in exchange for money income and in which enterprises sell goods to individuals in exchange for the money thus
earned. This two-way traffic is continual, but its volume is, of
course, greater in years of full employment and high national

FIGURE 1.1. THE WHEEL OF INCOME

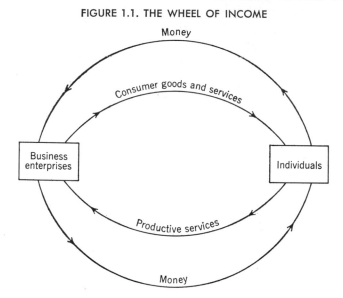

income than in years of depression. The circularity of the economic process can best be shown by a simple diagram.

The upper half of Figure 1.1 depicts the flow of money from individuals to business enterprises in exchange for consumer goods and services. From the point of view of individuals this flow represents the cost of living; from the point of view of the business enterprises it represents business receipts. The lower half of the figure shows the flow of money from enterprises to families in exchange for the productive services of labor and property. From the point of view of the business enterprises this flow represents the cost of production; from the point of view of the individuals it represents personal income. This figure is meant to provide only a very general picture. Actually many people work for Federal, state, and local governments instead of private firms. Enterprises make purchases from one another as well as from individuals, and families save a portion of the money income which they receive and spend only a part of it. And many of the products of enterprises are not goods for immediate consumption but consist of durable items such as houses, factories, ships, and machines which yield their services over an extended period of time. The Wheel of Income, nevertheless, provides a useful simplified picture of the flow of money and goods between individuals and business enterprises and merits careful study. We will return to it when we embark upon a study of national income.

2

CONSUMER DEMAND

Everyone has heard that prices are set by "the law of supply and demand," and, because economists concern themselves to such a degree with the study of prices, it has been suggested by the more cynical that if one could teach a parrot to answer "supply and demand" to any question, the parrot would have been transformed into an economist. Since, as we saw in Chapter 1, prices play such an important part in the allocation of both final products and productive factors, and since the complexities of the private-enterprise system are welded into a relatively efficient operating machine through the workings of the price system, it is not surprising that the study of price formation should occupy a considerable part of the study of economics.

Even if the supply-and-demand answer of the parrot were true, however, it would not be worth much. Any answer that can be stretched to fit all situations is entirely too general to be of significant value. Upon closer examination it will be seen that "supply" and "demand" must be taken very broadly if the answer is to be true at all. If these are merely used as convenient terms to indicate separate categories of forces determining price, the parrot might be correct, but his statement would be relatively useless. In a more precise sense, supply and demand do not always determine price. It is the purpose of this chapter to discuss more fully the specific meaning which the economist attaches to "demand."

The Nature of Consumer Demand

Demand implies, in the first place, a desire for a good or service. No demand exists for those things which possess no utility, *i.e.*, capacity to render satisfaction. But demand implies in addition to this an ability and a willingness to pay for the good or service. If one of these elements—desire, ability to pay, willingness to pay— is lacking, it may be said that "potential" demand exists. Such institutions as advertising, salesmanship, and installment credit are designed to convert potential into "effective" demand.

Many things other than price affect the desire, ability, and willingness to purchase a good or service. The major determinants of an individual's ability to buy are, quite obviously, his wealth and income. The latter includes not only current income but also expected income. Further, the prices of closely related goods and services have a great deal to do with one's willingness to purchase a particular commodity. The price of pork is a major factor in shaping a consumer's decision about buying beef at current prices. Estimates of future price trends also affect consumer behavior. If potential buyers of color TV sets anticipate a substantial decrease in prices, they may postpone purchases longer than they otherwise would.

THE LAW OF DEMAND

But the current price of the good or service itself must be of primary importance in determining the amount that will be bought. In order to isolate the relation between the price and the amount of the good that a consumer will be willing to purchase during any given period, we must assume that all other things affecting demand remain unchanged. It is clear that, other things being equal, the higher the price of a commodity, the fewer units of it will be demanded by any given consumer. That is to say, there is an inverse relation between price and quantity demanded: the higher the price, the smaller the quantity demanded; the lower the price, the greater the quantity demanded. If the price is sufficiently high, consumers will try to find a substitute for the commodity. The substitute will be a second choice, but if the price differential between the first and second choice is sufficiently great, consumers will purchase the second choice. One may assume, for example, that if the price of butter and margarine were the same or nearly so most consumers would buy butter, but if butter is priced at 80 cents and margarine at 20 cents per pound, many who prefer butter will switch entirely or in part to margarine.

The inverse relationship between price and quantity demanded may be called the fundamental law of demand. The nature of this relationship may be represented in either of two ways: (1) arithmetically, by the use of a "demand schedule," or (2) geometrically, by the use of a "demand curve." There may be a few exceptions to the fundamental law, but its application is so nearly universal that they may be disregarded. Table 2.1 represents a hypothetical consumer's demand schedule for milk.

Table 2.1. Mr. A's Demand for Milk

Price per quart, cents	Quantity demanded, quarts per week
35	4
30	6
25	7
20	8
15	9
10	11

The demand schedule is read as follows: *If* the price of milk is 35 cents per quart, Mr. A will demand 4 quarts per week; *if* the price is 30 cents, the quantity demanded will be 6; *if* the price is 25 cents, the quantity demanded will be 7; and so on. This is not to suggest that Mr. A has actually gone to the trouble of determining what quantities of milk he would buy at all prices between 10 cents and 35 cents per quart. If the price is, in fact, in the neighborhood of 25 cents, it is only necessary for him to determine what he will buy at the current price. But if in the morning the milkman leaves a note saying that after the first of the month the price will be 30 cents a quart, Mr. A. will have to determine whether or not he will reduce his milk consumption. To determine the number of quarts which he would buy at 10 cents a quart would be a purely academic question and one not likely to be of interest to Mr. A. We may assume, however, that for Mr. A and for every other milk consumer in the market there is a demand schedule which indicates for all prices the quantities of milk which would be demanded.

FIGURE 2.1. MR. A'S DEMAND FOR MILK

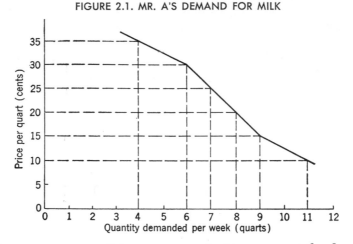

For many purposes it is more convenient to represent the demand for milk as a graph rather than as a schedule. Figure 2.1 represents graphically Mr. A's demand for milk and is referred to as a demand curve. The various quantities that would be demanded at the several prices indicated in Mr. A's demand schedule have been plotted, with price per quart indicated on the vertical, or *y*, axis and the quantity demanded measured on the horizontal, or *x*, axis. A line has been drawn to join the several points plotted on the assumption that if the price were, for example, between 20 and 25 cents, the quantity demanded would be between 8 and 7 quarts per week. The demand curve is read in the same way as the demand schedule: *If* the price of milk is 35 cents per quart, Mr. A will demand 4 quarts per week; *if* the price is 25 cents, the quantity demanded will be 7; and so on.

It is important to note that a consumer's demand curve describes the situation as of a particular moment of time. The arrival of a baby in Mr. A's household might cause him to increase the quantity of milk he would take at any price; in that event his demand curve would shift to the right. This is one of those factors other than price which influence willingness to purchase. If, on the other hand, Mr. A happened to hear a persuasive medical lecture on cholesterol, his demand curve would shift to the left—that is, at any price he would be willing to buy fewer quarts of milk than before. For some commodities the demand curve may shift forward and backward with considerable rapidity. A consumer's demand curve, accordingly, represents a sort of instantaneous photograph; it describes a situation as of a given time.

FIGURE 2.2. MR. A'S DEMAND FOR MILK IN-
CREASES—When a Baby Arrives

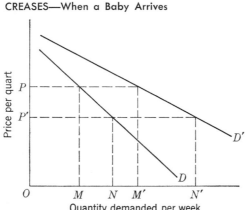

Quantity demanded per week

The nature of the shifting of demand curves is illustrated in Figure 2.2. *D* represents the original demand curve. At price *OP* the quantity demanded would be *OM;* at a price of *OP′* the quantity demanded would be *ON.* Suppose now that for some reason the demand increases, and the consumer's new demand is represented by the curve *D′.* At price *OP* the consumer would now take *OM′* units, and at price *OP′* he would take *ON′.* At any price on the new curve *D′* the consumer would demand more units than he would have taken at that price when his demand was represented by curve *D.*

It is not accurate to speak of an "increase in demand" unless at any price more units will be demanded than before, that is, unless the demand curve has shifted upward and to the right. Suppose that the price is originally at *OP* and the quantity demanded is *OM.* Now, if the price falls to *OP′,* the quantity demanded will be *ON.* This does not represent an increase in demand; demand is still represented by curve *D.* The quantity demanded has increased, but the demand has remained unchanged. Demand does not change unless the curve shifts. A change from *D′* to *D*—that is, a shift to the left—would, of course, represent a decrease in demand.

A change in any one or several of the underlying forces other than price affecting a consumer's desire, willingness, or ability to pay is said to change *demand.* A change in price causes a change in *quantity demanded.* It is necessary to make this distinction quite clear in order that the influence of price may be analyzed separately from that of such determinants of demand as taste and income.

MARKET DEMAND

Market demand is simply the summation of the individual demands of the consumers who comprise the market, and the market demand schedule or market demand curve may be determined by adding together the schedules or curves of all the individuals in the market. We may illustrate the nature of market demand by assuming that the market consists of five consumers of milk such as Mr. A. (If there were 5,000 or 5,000,000 the principle would be the same.) If the price is 20 cents per quart, we have seen that Mr. A would demand 8 quarts per week. Suppose that at this price Mr. B would take 15 quarts, Mr. C 6 quarts, Mr. D 20 quarts, and Mr. E 3 quarts. The market demand for milk at a price of 20 cents would then be $8 + 15 + 6 + 20 + 3$, or a total of 52 quarts per week. Similarly, the quantity demanded at all other prices could be determined, and a market schedule or a market demand curve could be determined.

We have seen that, other things remaining the same, almost without exception a greater quantity of a commodity will be demanded at a lower than at a higher price. Consumer demand curves, and consequently market demand curves, slope downward from left to right. The demand curve may be a straight line, it may be concave or convex, or it may look like descending stairsteps; but regardless of its particular shape, it must have a negative slope over most of its range. The fundamental law of demand tells us this, but it tells us nothing concerning the degree of responsiveness of quantity demanded to price changes. We must take notice of the im-

FIGURE 2.3. MILK AND BEER DIFFER—In Buyer's Response to Price Change

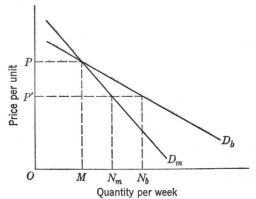

portant fact that the same drop in price for two commodities may cause the quantity demanded of one to increase much more than that of the other. This is illustrated in Figure 2.3. The curve D_m may be assumed to represent the market demand for milk and the curve D_b to represent the market demand for beer. The curves are drawn so that they intersect at price OP. At that price the quantity demanded is the same for each commodity; if the price of milk is OP, the market will take OM units of milk, and if the price of beer is OP, the market will take OM units of beer. Now suppose that the price of each commodity falls to OP'. Since the price has fallen, the quantity of each demanded will increase. But the market will increase its purchases of milk only from OM to ON_m, whereas its purchases of beer will increase from OM to ON_b. The figure indicates that the demand for beer is more responsive to a change in price than is the demand for milk.

Elasticity of Demand

We were able to compare the demands for milk and beer in Figure 2.3 only because these two commodities are measured in similar units and may be sold at roughly comparable prices. But suppose that one desired to compare the demands for oranges and baby carriages, or even to compare the demands for dozens of oranges and crates of oranges. No such simple comparison would be possible. In this case, if comparisons are to be made, it is necessary to introduce the idea of *relative* rather than absolute responsiveness of demand to a price change. This concept, known as "elasticity of demand," was developed by the famous English economist, Alfred Marshall, writing about 1890.[1] Marshall's innovation consisted in concentrating attention on the *percentage* change in amount demanded in relation to the *percentage* change in price which causes the response. He termed the ratio of these two percentages the elasticity of demand.

If a very small change in price, say 1 per cent, calls forth an equal percentage change in quantity demanded, the elasticity of demand between those prices is said to be unity, or 1. If a very small change in price causes an even smaller percentage change in quantity demanded, the elasticity of demand between those prices is less than 1. If a very small change in price results in a greater percentage change in quantity demanded, the elasticity of demand

[1] Alfred Marshall, *Principles of Economics* (London: Macmillan & Co., Ltd., 1938), 8th ed., pp. 103–104.

between those prices is said to be greater than 1. A somewhat crude but very useful rule of thumb for determining the elasticity of demand may be derived from Table 2.2.

Table 2.2. Demand and Total Expenditure Schedule

Price	Quantity demanded	Total expenditure
$10	0	$ 0
9	1	9
8	2	16
7	3	21
6	4	24
5	5	25
4	6	24
3	7	21
2	8	16
1	9	9
0	10	0

This table consists of a demand schedule with a total expenditure column added. If the price is $10 per unit, the table indicates that no units will be demanded, and, accordingly, consumer expenditure on the commodity at that price will be zero. If the price is $9, one unit will be bought, and total consumer expenditure will be $9, and so on.

It will be observed that as the price falls total expenditure increases for a time, reaches a maximum, and then decreases. Why does this happen? Since the total expenditure column is the product of two terms, price and quantity demanded, and since each time we reduce one term we increase the other by an equal amount, why does the product not remain constant? It will be noted that the sum of price and quantity demanded does remain constant at 10.

The explanation for the behavior of the total expenditure column is to be found in the fact that, percentagewise, the subtraction of one unit from price is quite a different thing from the addition of one unit to the quantity demanded. Consider the drop in price from $9 to $8. The decrease in price of $1 represents a relatively small percentage change—a little over 11 per cent. But the corresponding change in quantity demanded from one to two represents a 100 per cent increase. That is to say, a relatively small percentage change in price has resulted in a very large percentage change in quantity demanded, and the demand between prices $9 and $8, therefore, has an elasticity greater than 1.

Consider now the effect of a drop in price from $2 to $1. This

FIGURE 2.4. CONSUMERS SPEND MOST—Where
Elasticity is Unitary

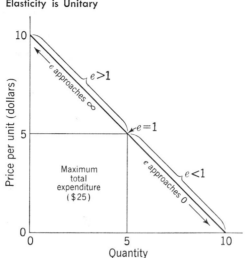

50 per cent reduction in price has resulted in a much less than 50 per cent increase in quantity demanded, and between these two prices, accordingly, the demand has an elasticity of less than 1. One may generalize by saying that as long as total expenditure increases as prices decrease, elasticity of demand is greater than 1; if total expenditure decreases as price decreases, elasticity of demand is less than 1; and if total expenditure remains constant as price changes, elasticity of demand is equal to 1.

This relationship of elasticity to total expenditure is illustrated graphically in Figure 2.4. Total expenditure may be represented by the area of a rectangle drawn within the triangle limited by the demand curve and the price and quantity axes, since total expenditure is price multiplied by the quantity taken. If the demand curve is a straight line it will have an elasticity of 1 at its mid-point, an elasticity of greater than 1 in its upper half, and an elasticity of less than one in its lower half.[1] Elasticity continually falls as price is lowered. In spite of the fact that the actual shape of a demand curve may not be linear (*i.e.*, a straight line), this conclusion holds good in a great many cases; for most commodities the elasticity of demand will probably be greater at higher than at lower prices.

[1] It can easily be seen from the figure that at high prices a tall and narrow rectangle represents total expenditure and that as price is lowered the area of this rectangle increases. The largest possible rectangle is one whose sides cut each side of the triangle in half. At prices below this the rectangle becomes low and wide but is reduced in area.

Let us consider the famous mineral-spring illustration used by Cournot, a French mathematician and economist, in 1838. An owner of a spring which costs nothing to operate is concerned with the appropriate price to be placed on the mineral water, which is wanted for its healing powers. He wants to set the price which will provide the greatest possible total revenue; he will, then, try to establish the price where the elasticity of demand is unitary. He will neither try to charge the highest possible price nor to sell the greatest possible quantity, since either of these policies would result in a lower total revenue for him.[1]

By saying that the demand for a commodity is elastic we are also saying that there are other commodities which are good substitutes for this one. For example, the demand for one particular brand of gasoline is probably highly elastic since other brands are close substitutes. If the price of X gasoline rises and the prices of other brands remain constant, consumers will promptly shift their purchases from X gasoline to other brands—there will be a high degree of responsiveness of demand to a change in price. On the other hand, the demand for gasoline of all makes taken together is probably inelastic; a general rise in gasoline prices will likely have only a limited effect on gasoline consumption since there is no satisfactory substitute as a motor fuel.

APPLICATIONS OF THE ELASTICITY CONCEPT

The concept of elasticity is extremely useful in analyzing many problems faced in real-world situations. In spite of the paucity of data concerning the actual forms of the demand function, and thus of accurate measures of elasticity, price decisions must be made by business firms, government agencies, and other organizations. For example, a large Florida marketing cooperative has substantial

---

[1] Elasticity at a particular price (as opposed to elasticity between two prices) can be measured precisely by use of the following formula:

$$e = \frac{dq/q}{dp/p}$$

where e represents elasticity, dq an infinitesimally small change in quantity demanded, q the quantity demanded at the original price, dp an infinitesimally small change in price, and p the original price. By using this formula (which is actually a definition of elasticity in mathematical symbols) we can determine not only whether elasticity is greater than, less than, or equal to 1, but we can say, for example, that elasticity is 1.1 or 0.8 or 10.2. Since the demand curve is negatively inclined (*i.e.*, it slopes downward from left to right), the elasticity of demand will be represented by a negative number, *e.g.*, $e = -2.3$. In practice, however, the algebraic sign is ignored; an elasticity of -5 is considered to be greater than one of -4. See Marshall, *op. cit.*, pp. 839–840.

power to regulate the quantity of oranges shipped out of the state each season. A knowledge of the elasticity of demand for oranges is essential for wise policy decisions on the part of this agency. If the cooperative wants to maximize the income of citrus growers in a bumper-crop year, it should attempt to impose restrictions on the shipment of oranges which would move the price of oranges to the point where the elasticity of demand is unitary, i.e., where total expenditure by consumers on oranges is maximized. If under existing regulations the elasticity of demand is greater than 1 at the established market price, the shipping regulations should be relaxed.

Public commissions charged with the responsibility for determining the appropriateness of rates for such enterprises as railroads and public utilities often must take into consideration the elasticity of demand for the product. This has been especially true of the Interstate Commerce Commission in its decisions regarding freight rates. Because of the overbuilding of railroads during the nineteenth century and the rapid development of competitive carriers such as trucks and pipelines, the American railroads have often been in a difficult position. In order to obtain more operating revenue, railroad management has frequently sought ICC approval for either general rate increases or boosts in particular rates. On such occasions the Commission must weigh all available evidence in order to determine whether a rate increase will actually increase or decrease railroad revenues—that is to say, the Commission must determine whether the demand for railroad services is, in fact, elastic or inelastic. If the ICC should order a rate increase and the revenues of the railroads then should fall off, neither the interests of the carriers nor of the public would be served.

Following World War II most of the nations of the world were confronted by what was termed a "dollar shortage"; they needed more dollars to buy goods from the United States. England devalued the pound sterling from about $4.02 to $2.80 in an effort to gain more dollars. This meant that an American could buy a British good for $2.80 that formerly cost $4.02. Since the price in dollars was reduced, it was expected that Americans would buy more British goods. But would they buy enough more to make up for the loss in revenue on each unit sold? Would the total dollar expenditure by Americans—which, of course, was the dollar receipts of the British—be greater at the lower dollar price of British goods than at the higher? In deciding to devalue the pound the British needed to estimate the elasticity of American demand for British goods.

Demand schedules and demand curves have so far been discussed as if they could be statistically estimated. The fact is that difficult problems are encountered in any attempt to compute from real data the demand schedule for a given commodity during a particular period of time. Demand schedules for such commodities do exist, but it is often almost impossible to sift out the data necessary for deriving them. The major difficulty to be somehow surmounted is that the underlying determinants of demand seldom remain constant. And the demand curve can only be derived easily when such things as income, tastes, prices of other commodities, etc., do remain unchanged. Statistical procedures may be used to remove the effects of certain changes from the computations, but these are frequently unreliable. Attempts are, nevertheless, being constantly made to compute actual demand curves. The nature of demand affects the policy decisions of business firms and government officials, and the more information they have available the more probable it is that the proper decisions will be reached.

For our purposes, however, the demand schedules and curves may be considered as analytical tools to be used in the building up of the body of economic analysis. We know that such schedules exist, and we will proceed to use them in spite of the difficulties that might be encountered if we were called upon to construct them from statistical data.

3

SUPPLY OF CONSUMER GOODS

It was pointed out in Chapter 1 that man's wants are infinite or insatiable whereas the means of satisfaction are limited. Chapter 2 discussed the relation between the quantity of goods demanded and price, since "demand" in this more specific sense, rather than "wants" in a broader sense, is the prime guiding force in a private-enterprise economy. Next it is necessary that we examine the concept of "supply" because this gives more specific content to the basic fact of the limitation of resources.

Motivation of Supply

Sellers, like buyers, are assumed to be attempting to satisfy their own wants as fully as their resources will permit. This means that suppliers of goods will wish to sell at the highest prices that are possible. In this way sellers maximize their own incomes and place themselves in the best position possible for making their own purchases.

The study of supply involves an additional complication not encountered in demand analysis since the quantity of a good supplied in a given period depends not only on price but also upon the possibility of storing the good until a later time and upon the possibility of further production. More specifically, we noted in the preceding chapter that the amount of a good which buyers are willing and able to purchase *in a given time* period depends on its price. In the case of supply, it is useful to consider not just one time period but several. These are designated: (1) the "very short run" or "market" period; (2) the "short run"; and (3) the "long run." This classification of supply periods is rather arbitrary but it has been found to be useful in understanding different types of economic problems. The nature of supply in these three periods will be separately considered.

The Very Short Run

One of the basic questions upon which economic analysis throws some light is that of how market prices are determined, assuming that there are many buyers and sellers of a particular commodity. How, for example, is the daily price of fresh eggs determined in a given market? This is an example of a "very short run" problem.

Looking in this chapter only at the supply side, it is not difficult to see that there exists at any moment in any region an inventory of eggs which has been built up through the efforts of many farmers, suppliers, and chickens. The owners of these fresh eggs must dispose of their stock within a short time although they have some leeway in withholding part of their inventory from sale on any particular day if they believe this will be profitable. Cold storage firms and egg processors will, of course, be able to reserve eggs from ultimate sale for a much longer time, but this need not concern us immediately since from the point of view of the commodity being used as an example (fresh eggs) they are buyers rather than sellers.

The willingness of egg owners to supply eggs in a given market can be reflected numerically by a supply schedule. This is the counterpart of the demand schedule described in Chapter 2. There is a positive relation between price and amount supplied since a higher price makes it advantageous to sell more of the commodity immediately rather than to withhold inventory for later sale.

In Table 3.1 it is assumed that the total inventory which sellers in a particular market are holding is 1,000 dozen. At a price of 75 cents per dozen or more they will be willing to sell all of these eggs immediately. At lower prices they will reserve part of the supply, hoping to find better market conditions in the near future. At

Table 3.1. Very Short-run Supply of Eggs

Price per dozen, cents	Quantity supplied, dozen
35	0
40	400
45	550
50	650
55	740
60	820
65	890
70	950
75	1,000
80	1,000
85	1,000

the low price of 40 cents per dozen a total of 600 dozen would be withheld from the market.

It is important to understand that the supply schedule alone does not tell us what the price of eggs will actually be. Demand and supply must be considered simultaneously before price determination can be described. What this supply schedule shows is the attitude of sellers with regard to selling eggs. Behind this subjective attitude of sellers is, of course, the objective matter of the actual inventory which has been accumulated for sale. It is not difficult to see that the supply schedule in the very short run also depends a great deal on sellers' expectations of market conditions in the near future. If Easter Sunday is near, sellers are apt to hold out for better prices than otherwise. Availability and cost of storage space and the need for cash also influence sellers' ability and desire to hold existing stocks off the market. If storage space is costly, egg owners will be more ready to get rid of their stocks. If they are in need of cash they will also be in a poorer position to hold out for a relatively high price.

The supply schedule of Table 3.1 can readily be translated into the supply curve of Figure 3.1. It can be seen that the supply curve turns vertical at a price of 75 cents per dozen. Even at a better price, suppliers could not offer more than 1,000 dozen for sale if this constitutes their whole inventory. At prices below 75 cents per dozen part of the inventory will be reserved for future sale, the amount reserved, for example, being 110 dozen at a price of 65 cents. At a price of 35 cents or lower none will be offered for immediate sale; that is, the entire inventory will be reserved for future sale.

In translating the supply schedule of Table 3.1 into the supply curve of Figure 3.1 a somewhat troublesome problem of units arises.

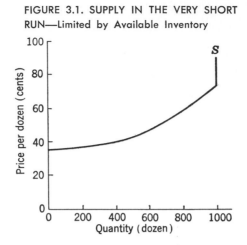

FIGURE 3.1. SUPPLY IN THE VERY SHORT
RUN—Limited by Available Inventory

Any table can list only discrete changes in a variable, whereas the assumption implicitly made in connecting the plotted points on a chart is that quantities and prices *in between* the discrete numbers are possible. Thus we cannot tell from Table 3.1 whether any eggs would be supplied at a price of 38 cents per dozen, but in drawing the supply curve it is tacitly assumed that there would be some amount supplied at this price, *i.e.*, 240 dozen. This type of problem helps explain why charts are usually handier to use than tables in economic analysis.

In the very short-run problem just examined an absolute limit governs the amount which can be supplied to the market because, for analytical purposes, it is assumed that no additional production is possible. This is not because of any lack of resources to produce the commodity in question but because so short a period is being considered that no production can occur. In other cases the absolute limit on amount supplied is due to the nonavailability of resources to produce additional units of a particular good. Only a certain number of original van Gogh paintings exist, for example; and, although resources must be expended on simply preserving them, the number cannot be augmented. For such a commodity the supply curve also is vertical, at least in the price ranges above those at which owners will refuse to sell. This example makes it clear that the designation "very short run" is a somewhat arbitrary one. It is most appropriate for reproducible goods, but may apply to non-reproducible commodities if the amount supplied cannot be increased even over a longer period.

FIGURE 3.2. SUPPLY OF PERISHABLE GOOD
—In Very Short Run

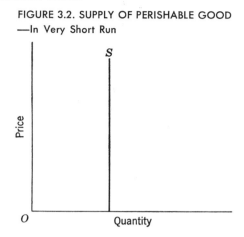

PERISHABLE GOODS

The nonvertical portion of the supply curve in Figure 3.1 is traceable to the possibility of holding fresh eggs off the market for a short time. The entire supply curve consequently becomes a vertical line in the case of highly perishable commodities. An appropriate example might be strawberries in a city retail market on Saturday when it is clear that they will no longer be fit for sale on Monday. Even here sellers may hold out for fairly high prices in the morning and afternoon, but by evening they will probably be willing to sell their remaining stock for whatever it will bring. So far as the evening sales, at least, are concerned, the supply curve will look like that of Figure 3.2, the vertical line being drawn at the quantity corresponding to the stock still on hand. The vertical supply curve reflects a condition in which the sellers are at the mercy of buyers in the sense that they will take anything they can get for the strawberries. They hope to get a high price, of course, but will take a very low price or even give the berries away, if necessary. It will be noted that no actual numbers are used in this chart, since it is only meant to be representative of a type of economic situation. Nevertheless, the origin of the axes, designated as *O*, does represent both a price and a quantity of zero.

Another example of the fixed-supply case may be found in the type of situation in which the suppliers receive nonmonetary gratification from an activity and yet desire to sell their services for whatever they will bring. Two sandlot baseball teams may pass the hat among spectators in order to collect some money to defray expenses or possibly even make a profit. Yet they may be so anxious to play that they will meet all the costs themselves if necessary. The commodity (one ball game per week, for example) will be supplied at any price, yielding a vertical supply curve.

Services which must be furnished during a specified period of time according to terms of a contract or other law also illustrate the fixed-supply case. For example, the Interstate Commerce Commission, acting under legislatively granted powers, requires railroads to furnish passenger service between designated points regardless of how many passengers decide to use the service. If the run proves to be too unprofitable the railroad company is likely to apply for the right to discontinue the service, but even if the application is approved, it cannot do so until a designated date. As a consequence, the supply of this transportation service is fixed for a period of time and can be represented by a vertical supply curve. The possibility of reservation of supply is shut off by law.[1]

PERIODICALLY PRODUCED GOODS

An interesting and important example of very short-run supply is found in the case of periodically harvested grains. Between harvests, there is a fixed supply available in the country (assuming no imports or exports). The rate of consumption of this fixed supply must be so regulated that the grain will neither be used up too rapidly nor too slowly. It is another of the marvels of a free price system that this sort of rationing over time is accomplished without the use of a regulatory authority.

Suppose this year's rye harvest is being consumed so rapidly that the nation is in danger of running out of rye bread before the next rye crop is harvested. Owners of the existing stock of rye will decrease the amounts which they offer for sale (say in December) in view of the apparent profitability of deferring the sale of a greater amount until a later date. This causes a "decrease in supply" compared with a previous period, and such a decrease is reflected in a shift of the supply curve upward and to the left, as in Figure 3.3. Actually, speculation and a well-organized "futures" market in rye will enter into the rationing of the crop over time, but

---

[1] The rate (price) which can be charged for passenger travel is also regulated by law. However, since the amount of revenue received from the provision of a legally required amount of passenger train service depends on the number of customers, the "price per trip" can conceivably fall as low as zero (when no passengers ride). This causes the supply curve to be vertical so long as only the legal minimum of service is furnished.

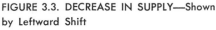

FIGURE 3.3. DECREASE IN SUPPLY—Shown by Leftward Shift

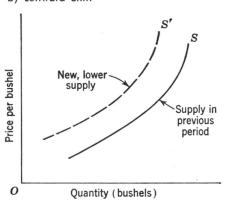

this subject will be deferred until a later chapter since it involves demand as well as supply.

The Short Run

The very short-run supply situations discussed so far have arisen from a fixity of supply owing to: an assumed lack of time for new production to occur (eggs); the nonavailability of resources for further production (van Gogh); nonmonetary gratification in the act of supply itself (ball game); legal requirement that a certain amount of service be rendered (railroad passenger service); or periodic production (rye). For most commodities, the supply can be greatly increased, given enough time to channel the necessary additional resources into production. (It should be remembered, however, that increasing the output of one good requires that resources be withdrawn from the production of other goods—unless enough new labor and capital can be drawn into the economic system.)

The "short run" is defined as a period long enough to change the rate of use of existing plant (factories, machines, farms, etc.) but not long enough to change the amount of plant in a given use. If the latter can be changed the analysis is said to be "long run." It is assumed that in the short run labor can be hired or laid off, raw-material flows can be augmented or diminished, and such inputs as electric power can be altered in amount. For example, the rate of output of color TV sets can be altered in the short run, but new factories cannot be established. Thus, more variance is possible in the rate of supply in the short run than in the very short run, but less than in the long run.

For the short run the supply curve for a particular good may look like SRS in Figure 3.4. If managers of existing plants wish to do so they can reduce the rate of output to zero. Or they can turn out any rate of output they wish up to the limit of their plant capacity. The amount they will wish to produce depends on the price they expect to get for their TV sets or other product. The SRS curve slopes upward from left to right, because at higher prices it will be profitable to produce at a greater rate than at lower prices. Cost of production is a factor here, but this somewhat complex consideration will be deferred to Book Two.

The Long Run

Long-run supply (LRS) is also shown on Figure 3.4. If, for example, people lost all interest in color TV, output could be brought down to zero and the resources devoted entirely to other products. On the other hand, if color TV becomes extremely popular, a yearly output of millions of sets could be secured by allocating enough labor and capital to this field. The latter possibility causes the long-run supply curve to extend much farther to the right than the short-run supply curve. For purposes of analysis it is assumed that no new invention or change in available resources occurs even in the long run. That is, both the short-run and long-run supply curves are based on the assumption of the continuation of existing technology, total supply of resources, and resource prices. Actually, there may be marvelous new cost-cutting inventions or upward revisions in

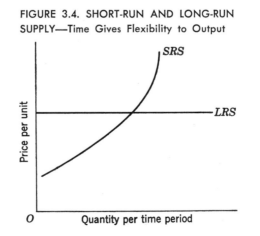

FIGURE 3.4. SHORT-RUN AND LONG-RUN SUPPLY—Time Gives Flexibility to Output

labor prices, but such possibilities do not enter into the basic supply analysis. Detailed consideration of the nature of the long-run supply curve also involves study of cost of production.

Summary View of Supply

"Supply," like "demand," is a relationship between price and quantity. Whereas the amount demanded increases as price goes down, the amount supplied usually increases as price goes up. Also, the supply curve, like the demand curve, reflects alternative opportunities rather than a series of events. In Table 3.1, for example, we say, "if the price of eggs were 55 cents per dozen sellers would supply 740 dozen, and if the price were 60 cents a dozen sellers would supply 820 dozen." The supply schedule does not tell what price will actually be. This depends on the interaction of demand and supply.

For purposes of analyzing different types of problems, economists distinguish between the "very short run," the "short run," and the "long run." These periods are rather arbitrary but are nonetheless useful. They do not refer to definite periods of calendar time but rather are based on the sort of economic events which can affect supply (such as the creation or reduction of plant capacity). In the steel industry the long run may cover a period of years required for building new steel mills, whereas in the residential construction field new capacity can quickly be set up merely by bringing machinery and tools from other fields (*e.g.*, commercial construction). In calendar time the latter long run is much shorter than the former long run.

The possibility of augmenting or diminishing supply depends greatly on the time period under examination, increasing as the time period increases. In the long run tremendous increases in the rate of production of a given commodity (*e.g.*, guided missiles) can be attained by the diversion of resources from other uses. In the short run the range of possible production is much more limited. In the very short run production cannot take place at all.

4

COMPETITIVE PRICE

In the two preceding chapters we have introduced the two fundamental relationships in economics, the demand relationship and
the supply relationship. The first traces the functional dependence
of quantity demanded, for any one good or for any group of goods,
on price. The amount of any good or service taken off the market during any given period of time by a single consumer, or by all
consumers taken together, will depend upon the price at which
the good or service may be purchased. In general, consumers will
purchase more at lower prices than at higher prices, provided that
the many other things that might possibly affect consumer choices
remain unchanged. The demand relationship between price and
quantity demanded is an *inverse* one; price and quantity demanded
normally move in opposing directions. The supply relationship,
on the other hand, traces the functional dependence of quantity
supplied on price. The amount of any good or service which producers or suppliers place on the market is affected by the price at
which the good or service may be marketed or sold. In general,
producers or suppliers will supply more at higher prices than they
will at lower prices, provided that the many other things which

affect their decisions remain unchanged. The supply relationship between price and quantity is a *direct* one; price and quantity supplied normally move in the same direction.

Each of these relationships allows a unique function of price to be examined. Let us first look at the demand relationship.

If other things remain unchanged, the higher the price the lower the quantity demanded. Price affects the quantity demanded, and in so doing, it serves the function of *rationing* scarce goods and services among the many possible demanders. Price is essentially the institutional device which the economy employs to parcel out the available goods and services, which are scarce, among the many possible consumers, whose wants are virtually unlimited. Prices are, in brief, the *rationing devices* of the free-enterprise economy.

There would, of course, be no rationing function to perform if goods were so plentiful that economizing in their usage became unnecessary. But then we should not be studying economics at all. Economic goods are scarce; that is, there is less of each commodity available in total than people would want to consume if there were no restraints imposed. We are not interested in studying the behavior of people in using free goods.

The Rationing Function of Price

The manner in which prices ration economic goods is not difficult to understand. If goods are in short supply at prevailing prices and sellers find their shelves becoming empty and reordering difficult, they may, for a time, post signs: "One to a Customer," "First Come, First Served." Before long these sellers will see that it is more satisfactory—and more profitable—to increase selling prices. At the higher prices the quantities consumers are willing to buy will diminish. Some buyers may take as much as before, but most of them will reduce their rate of purchases, and others will drop out of the market altogether. The limited supply will, in this rather simple way, be rationed among consumers. Those who are the most willing and able to pay will get the commodity. Those who are unwilling or unable to pay the higher prices will be eliminated. Goods are rationed to those whose dollar demand is strongest, and not necessarily to those whose real or physical needs are greatest, if the latter could, in fact, be measured.

Similarly, if store managers note that the turnover of goods is slow and that shelves are becoming filled with unsold merchandise, they will find it necessary to lower prices in order to stimulate con-

sumption. Close-out sales, end-of-the-month sales, bargain base-
ments, high trade-in allowances, and special price reductions are
all outward indications of prices serving their proper and normal
function in rationing the available supply among potential demanders. Quite independently of the historical cost of producing goods,
if the supply becomes too great at the established prices, this will
generate price reductions.

Even a society whose food supply consisted exclusively of manna
from heaven and which carried on no food production at all would
find it necessary to utilize prices if the manna were not sufficient to
provide everyone with all he wanted. If no one produced food,
and manna fell to the earth each Wednesday morning at ten o'clock
but in a quantity not quite sufficient to keep everyone fully satisfied for the week, prices would be employed to prevent the waste
of manna.

THE FIXED-SUPPLY CASE

In order to isolate the rationing function of price, let us consider
a commodity in absolutely fixed supply; we may suppose that
there is just so much of the commodity available and that there is
no way, at least in the short run, to increase the amount which
consumers may buy. In such an event, price changes must result
from each change in demand. If the demand should increase—that
is, if the demand curve should shift to the right—the price would
rise; if the demand should decrease, the price would fall. This is
essentially the manna-from-heaven case, and for certain problems
in the real world supplies of goods can be best considered as relatively fixed and demand forces to be the primary determinants of
price. This is especially true if the period under consideration is
very short, because, as we have already seen, supply can change
significantly only over rather long time periods.

The case of the commodity in fixed supply is represented graphically in Figure 4.1. Quantity demanded and quantity supplied are
measured along the x axis, and price is measured along the y axis.
D represents the demand curve for the commodity in question.
Since it slopes downward from left to right, it indicates that the
higher the price, the less will be demanded. For example, at price
OP_c, the quantity demanded would be ON units, but at a higher
price such as OP_p, only OL units would be taken. The curve S
represents the supply curve. Since it is assumed in this case that
the supply is fixed, the curve is drawn as a vertical line; OM

FIGURE 4.1. THE FIXED-SUPPLY CASE—Price Is
Determined by Demand

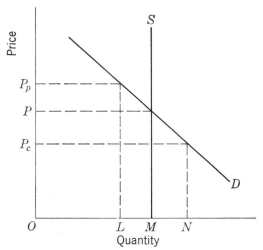

units are available to consumers at any price. If the price is OP_c,
the quantity supplied is OM; if the price is OP_p, the quantity supplied is still OM.

If we take the demand and supply curves as given in Figure 4.1,
the market price will be OP, and the quantity bought and sold will,
of course, be OM. That the intersection of the supply and demand
curves determines the equilibrium price can be demonstrated as
follows. If the price were higher than OP, such as OP_p, the quantity demanded at that price, OL, would be less than the quantity
supplied, OM. If the price remained at OP_p, the difference between OM and OL, which is LM, would be wasted. But since suppliers of the commodity are willing, if necessary, to accept a lower
price than OP_p, and since, if they are to get rid of their entire stock,
they must sell at a lower price, the price cannot remain at that
level or at any price above OP. Similarly, if the price is less than OP,
for example, OP_c, the quantity which consumers want to buy will
be greater than the total amount available; specifically at price
OP_c the quantity demanded will be ON, which exceeds the amount
available by MN units. Since sellers in the fixed-supply case
wish to realize as high a price as will permit them to dispose of
their entire stock, they will raise the price until the quantity demanded just equals the quantity supplied, which, in this case,
means a price of OP. This is called an "equilibrium price," because

FIGURE 4.2. DEMAND INCREASES WITH
FIXED SUPPLY—The Same Amount Is Sold
at a Higher Price

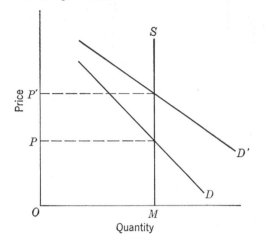

if the price is set at *OP*, it will tend to remain there unless either
the demand or the supply curve shifts. At equilibrium, the quantity
demanded will just equal the quantity supplied.

Suppose now that for some reason, for example an increase in
the income of the community, demand increases. This is represented in Figure 4.2 by a shift of the demand curve to the right.
On curve *D'* the quantity demanded at any price is greater than on
curve *D* at the same price, and if demand shifts from *D* to *D'* it is
proper to say that demand has increased. When demand is *D*, equilibrium price is *OP*. When demand is *D'*, price is *OP'*. In both
cases the quantity exchanged is *OM*. The cause of the increase in
price from *OP* to *OP'* is the increase in demand from *D* to *D'*. This
is the meaning of the statement made earlier that, in the case of
absolutely fixed supply, demand is the determinant of price.

The fixed-supply case corresponds reasonably closely with a
number of real world situations. For example, two letters written
by Edgar Allan Poe have recently been placed on the market at a
price of $5,000. It is obvious here that price can only serve one
function, that of rationing a limited supply among potential demanders. It is of little current concern to Poe whether his letters
command a price of one cent or thousands of dollars. The function
of price in this case is solely that of rationing. If the dealer offering
the letters at $5,000 succeeds in marketing them at that price, this
indicates that the market has successfully rationed the available

supply of Poe letters in a manner which has created little stir and commotion. To illustrate this rationing function of price in somewhat more detail let us suppose that the dealer offers the Poe letters for $1,000. This would immediately generate a rush on orders, and the dealer would find many more demanders than his supply warrants. He would, if he held his price at this low figure, find it necessary to use some other means of rationing. He would have to decide somewhat arbitrarily which of the many demanders should get the Poe letters.

The problem of wartime rent control in this country, and continued rent controls in several of the European countries, also fits the fixed-supply case reasonably well. For any given short period, the total supply of housing units may be considered as being relatively stable. We may assume that the curve S in Figure 4.1 represents the supply of residential units of a given type in Paris. If the demand for housing of this type is represented by D, the equilibrium price (rental) would be OP. If rent controls are present, however, and if they are at all effective, rents are not allowed to be so high as OP. Let us assume that the maximum rental payment for a unit of this type is OP_c. It may be readily seen that price no longer serves its rationing function fully or adequately. The number of residential units demanded at the ceiling price (OP_c) exceeds the number of units supplied, MN units being demanded in excess of those supplied. As a result we should expect to find that other, nonprice, schemes for rationing the available supply would be developed. And this prediction (and here is a good example of the sort of scientific predictions which the study of elementary economics should enable you to make) is shown to be true from a cursory look at the situation where rent controls remain effective. In Paris, apartments are extremely difficult to secure. Various priorities and waiting lists are established. Huge bonus payments (nominally illegal) accompany the acquisition of rental units. And the story is even told that native Parisians seeking apartments scan carefully the hospital lists to locate the seriously ill in order to be able to secure their housing accommodations after their possible death. The effect of the government enforcement of rent controls is to alter the distribution of scarce housing units among the people. If price were to be allowed to assume its full rationing function and rise to the market-clearing or equilibrium level, some people would have to give up currently used space because they could no longer afford it. They would find it necessary to double up with friends or relatives, or to move into smaller or less attractive quarters. Under rent controls the available housing is distributed among potential demanders in a more or less accidental manner, and there is always an apparent "shortage" in the sense that many potential demanders would be willing to pay the price but cannot find accommodations. We may say that with rent controls, housing is both scarce and short. With free market pricing, housing is scarce (as is any economic good) but there is no shortage.

These examples have been introduced here to illustrate the rationing function of price in isolation from the supply-motivation function. They should have shown that, quite independently of any possible effects on supply, prices are necessary if serious rationing problems are to be avoided.

The Production-motivating Function of Price

In addition to the rationing function, prices also serve the extremely important function of calling forth, or motivating, supply or production. The relationship between supply and price has been discussed at some length in the preceding chapter. It was noted that as the time period under consideration lengthens, the effects of price on calling forth supply become more pronounced. This function of price tends to overwhelm the rationing function in significance as the time period under consideration becomes very long.

THE FIXED-DEMAND CASE

In the preceding main section we illustrated the rationing function of price through the use of the fixed-supply example. We may reverse this procedure here and illustrate the production or supply-motivating function of price through using a fixed-demand case. Real-world illustrations are more difficult to find here, and we shall have to let our imagination roam a bit more freely. It is difficult to think of a commodity or service for which the quantity demanded is fixed regardless of price. Individuals will, almost without exception, demand smaller quantities at higher than at lower prices. If, in fact, there were such an imaginary commodity characterized by fixed demand, a sufficiently high price would cause individuals to purchase nothing else.

For many commodities, however, the quantity demanded is relatively independent of price over the normal price ranges, and we need not be concerned at this point about the reactions of consumers to abnormally high or abnormally low prices.

FIGURE 4.3. THE FIXED-DEMAND CASE—
Price Is Determined by Supply

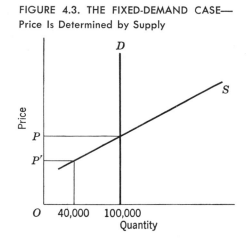

If we consider the government as a demander we may find several reasonably realistic examples. Let us suppose that the Department of Defense decides that 100,000 more men are needed for the armed services. It will attempt to get 100,000 men, and the price or wage at which this number of men will volunteer for duty is essentially irrelevant to the government's decision. The demand curve for soldiers is vertical at the desired number of men. This is shown in Figure 4.3. Price can serve no rationing function in this case since quantity demanded remains unchanged regardless of price.

There will, of course, exist some supply relationship. This is translated into geometrical terms as S in Figure 4.3. Let us now assume that the government decides to utilize the price mechanism in getting the desired number of men. The supply curve S indicates the price (wage or salary) which will be necessary to bring 100,000 men into the armed services. If a price (wage) of *OP* is set, exactly 100,000 men will be attracted to join. This price is set solely by the shape of the supply curve, and the demand relationship has no influence over price. Price serves in this case to motivate or to bring forth an adequate supply; it does not have a rationing function to perform.

To illustrate still further this supply-motivating function of price, let us assume more realistically that the government decides not to utilize the price mechanism fully. Assume that it decides to pay only a stipulated wage or salary, and that this amount is well below that salary required to bring forth the desired number of men. Obviously, the government is not going to get the needed number of men by this device. In terms of Figure 4.3, we may assume

that the salary is set at *OP'* (say $100 per month). But this salary
will only attract 40,000 men into the armed forces, whereas 100,000
are "needed." Such a procedure is precisely the policy which has
been traditionally followed by our government (and most other
governments since the eighteenth century) in recruiting its army.
Some supply-motivating device additional or supplementary to
price (wage or salary) must be introduced. The first and obvious
device is persuasion through the medium of posters—"Uncle Sam
Needs You," "Aid in Your Country's Defense"—singing radio and
TV commercials about army life, etc. Persuasion of this sort is rarely
effective, however, unless the price is close to the equilibrium one.
If the price remains substantially below that required to bring forth
the needed amount, more severe devices must be introduced. In
our particular example, the supplementary device becomes con-
scription or the draft. Through this device the required number of
men is attained by direct coercion. Price is replaced in its supply-
motivating role.

This example of the securing of adequate men for service in the
armed forces is a useful one in illustrating the supply-motivating
function of price, but it is also useful in that the problem posed is
currently being debated in national councils. Serious proposals have
been advanced recently to replace the draft with a system of incentive payments which will attract sufficient men both to enter the
armed services and to remain once they have entered. The advantages of using the price mechanism to attract adequate men to the
armed forces have become more important in this age of highly advanced technology. Given our traditionally democratic institutions,
men cannot be drafted for service for periods long enough to warrant training them in highly technical skills. The draft as a supply-
motivating device loses much of its earlier attractiveness.

Competitive Price Formation

We have examined the two basic functions of price in each of two
extreme situations. In the first, we assumed supply to be fixed so that
price served only to ration this supply among potential demanders.
In our second case, we assumed that the quantity demanded was
unaffected by price, so that the sole function of price became that
of bringing forth an adequate supply. In most situations existing in
the real world, price serves both these functions and serves them
simultaneously. Price is necessary to ration an available supply
among demanders and to bring forth supply to meet demand. And it

is adjusting to these two functions that price is formed in competitive markets. As Alfred Marshall suggested, price is determined by both demand and supply, with these two forces acting as separate blades of scissors.

As in so many cases, the actual process of price formation may be best illustrated by assuming for a moment that price is not used. Let us suppose that an authoritarian government decides that its citizens should have one million pairs of shoes during the next year. It does not want to use price in any way. It is clear that at a zero demand price many more than the million pairs will be demanded. Some rationing scheme (tickets, cards, priorities) must be used to distribute the shoes among the citizens. But no shoes will be produced at the zero supply price. So the government will also have to introduce a supply-motivating scheme. It will have to draft or conscript enough labor, plant, and equipment to secure the production of the one million pairs of shoes.

How would the free market solve this problem? First, there would be no government decision concerning the number of shoes produced. This decision would be the result and not the antecedent of the price-making process. A certain initial price for shoes would prevail. At this price some shoes would be produced. If this quantity were not sufficient to meet all demands at that price, the price would rise. This, in turn, would cause an additional quantity to be supplied and reduce the amount demanded. Finally, after a process of adjustment in both quantity demanded and quantity supplied, some price would be established at which these two are equal. Quantity demanded would just equal quantity supplied. This is shown graphically by the intersection of the demand curve and the supply curve.

It is useful to examine in somewhat more detail the characteristics of this final position or market price. There are no unsatisfied demanders or unsatisfied suppliers. No one who would like to buy, and who is willing to pay the price, finds that he is unable to buy. No one who would like to sell, and who is willing to accept the price, finds that he is unable to sell. "Clearing the market" is the term for this state. The market for the commodity in question is "cleared" in the sense that no surpluses or shortages exist.

It may also be noted that the market-established price generates the maximum of trade in the commodity. At any higher price, more of the commodity will be offered by sellers, but less will be taken by buyers. The total amount traded will be less than at the market price. Similarly, at any price below the market price, more will be demanded by buyers but less will be supplied by sellers. Therefore, fewer total units will be traded than at the equilibrium or market price.

Shifts in Demand and Supply

It is appropriate now to consider in somewhat greater detail the effects on price of shifts in demand or supply. The demand for a given commodity may increase, for example, if the income of the community increases, if the prices of other commodities increase and the given commodity is substituted for them, or if there is a change in tastes which makes the commodity more desirable to consumers. If the supply curve is upsloping and does not shift, and if the demand increases, *i.e.*, if the demand curve shifts to the right, both the price and the quantity exchanged will increase. If in Figure 4.4 we assume that the original demand is *D*, price will be *OP*, and the quantity exchanged will be *OM*. If now for some reason demand increases from *D* to *D'*, the price will rise from *OP* to *OP'*, and the quantity bought and sold will increase from *OM* to *OM'*. Conversely, if we assume that the original demand curve was *D'* and shifts to *D*, that is, if the demand decreases, the price will fall from *OP'* to *OP*, and the quantity exchanged will decrease from *OM'* to *OM*.

If now we assume that the supply increases with no change in demand, because of a bumper-crop yield, for example, or a new and cheaper method of production, price will fall and the quantity ex-

FIGURE 4.4. AN INCREASE IN DEMAND—Increases Price and Quantity Exchanged

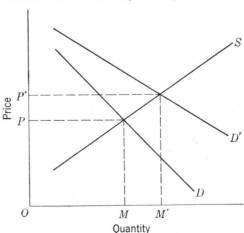

FIGURE 4.5. AN INCREASE IN SUPPLY—
Decreases Price, Increases Sales

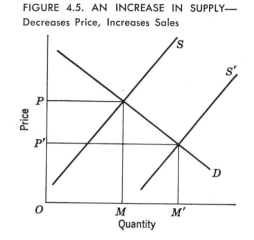

changed will increase. This is illustrated in Figure 4.5. If the original demand and supply are indicated by curves *D* and *S*, the original price will be *OP*, and the quantity exchanged will be *OM*. As a result of the increase in supply to *S'*, price will fall to *OP'*, and the amount bought and sold will increase to *OM'*.

The Meaning of Equilibrium Price

The concept of equilibrium price should never be taken for more than it actually is. It is not a real price in a real market. It represents that price which would tend to be established in a particular market during a given time period provided that everything affecting the supply and demand schedules remain unchanged. The fact is that the underlying forces of demand and supply do not remain fixed, particularly as the time period under consideration increases in length. The concept of an equilibrium price is, nevertheless, extremely useful for purposes of economic analysis. It makes for a much clearer understanding of the forces which do determine real prices than would otherwise be possible.

In this context it is not difficult to appreciate the virtual impossibility of predicting accurately the level of the actual price of a particular commodity at a specific time. The prognosticator not only would need to know the actual shapes of the demand and supply curves but would also have to predict how much and when these functions would shift relative to each other. So many of these underlying forces are so dependent on unpredictable factors, such as the personal whims of consumers, business executives, and government officials, that accurate prediction is impossible. But businessmen, public officials, and consumers must make some predictions, and the study of economics can help by providing a mechanism by which the various price-determining factors can be sorted out, classified, and separately analyzed. The economist cannot accurately forecast the price of beef in Kansas City on next July 1, but he can say that the price will be high enough to prevent an apparent shortage and low enough to prevent an apparent surplus if markets are free. No one will want beef and be willing and able to pay the market price for it and be unable to find it. No butcher will be unable to sell his beef at the going price. The recognition of the simple fact that prices in free markets tend to be established at levels which will clear the market should go far toward separating the sense from the nonsense in much popular discussion of economic matters.

The Virtues of Competition and the Evils of Monopoly

Implicit in the discussion of price formation by demand and supply has been the assumption that there exists effective competition in the markets considered. It is now necessary to examine briefly the meaning of competition. By a competitive market we shall mean that there are many buyers and many sellers. In the ideal sense, there should be a sufficient number of buyers and sellers so that no single unit possesses any control over price. We shall, however, leave off such complex refinements at this stage of our analysis and think of competition in a market as signifying many buyers and many sellers.

Why is market competition of this sort desirable or beneficial? The answer stems from the characteristics of the demand and the supply functions. If, for example, there should be only one seller of a commodity, this seller would be confronted with the whole market demand curve for the product. He could see that an arbitrary restriction upon supply would enable him to charge a higher price for the commodity. On the other hand, if there should be only one buyer, he would be confronted with the whole market supply curve. He would see that by an arbitrary restriction of demand the commodity could be purchased more cheaply. In either case, such reductions of supply or demand with a view toward increasing an individual profit position would be contrary to the workings of the market system.

A competitively determined market price mirrors the payment

FIGURE 4.6. RESTRICTION OF SUPPLY OR
DEMAND—Drives Wedge between Demand
Value and Supply Value

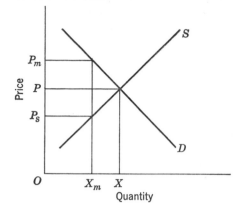

from buyers to sellers which reflects both buyers' and sellers' evaluation of the product. An arbitrary, or monopolistic, restriction of supply with a view toward increasing price above this competitive level may establish a price above that which is necessary to bring forth supply. If this happens, the functioning of the entire price system in allocating economic resources among alternative uses breaks down.

This point may be readily illustrated by means of a simple demand and supply graph, which is shown in Figure 4.6. *OP* represents the price which would be established if the market were fully competitive on both the demand and the supply sides. Now suppose that a single firm gains control of the entire supply. This firm decides that it can increase profits by restricting supply to OX_m, with the resultant price being OP_m. At this newly established monopoly equilibrium, buyers would be paying a price OP_m; but the minimum price necessary to get OX_m resources into this particular market is shown by OP_s. The monopolizing of this particular market on the seller's side has resulted in the undue restriction of the supply of this particular product relative to other products and services in the economy.

Monopoly on the buyer's side may also be readily illustrated, although this is a much less normal occurrence in the real world. Suppose that the total amount purchased were to be concentrated in the hands of a single individual or firm. This single purchasing unit would realize that it could lower its buying price if the amount demanded were to be reduced. By arbitrarily reducing its demand to

OX_m, the price which the buyer must pay could be reduced to OP_s. And, the buyer might be in a considerably improved profit position as a result of such a change. In this way, it is easy to see that either monopoly on the selling side or monopoly on the buying side (sometimes called "monopsony") acts to reduce the amount of the product which will be exchanged and to create a "wedge" or "spread" between the actual *demand value* of the product to buyers and the *supply value* of the product to sellers. And the *supply value* of the product reflects *costs*, or, in other terms, the demand value of the resources in other uses. Only in fully competitive markets are *demand values* equal to *supply values,* and therefore, only in such markets do prices reflect accurately consumer evaluations of products and services relative to each other. Only in competitive markets does the price system serve properly its resource allocating function.

5

GOVERNMENT RESTRICTION
OF COMPETITION

Competition is vital to the operation of a private-enterprise system. To the extent that it is absent in a particular market the consumer interest is not served; the economic system becomes less "efficient" in satisfying wants. It is not surprising, consequently, that the Federal government is active in the antitrust field (as will be described in Chapter 7). It is, however, paradoxical and disturbing that the same Federal government is simultaneously engaged in actions which curb rather than promote competitive pricing. State and local governments, especially, appear to exert more effort in the direction of encouraging monopoly than in maintaining competition, and it is probably true that the monopoly problem in the United States would not be a serious one if all government-supported monopoly were eliminated. Economic analysis can frequently be helpful in determining the effects of government interference with competition. This chapter considers certain government policies which have the effect of discouraging competition and which are, accordingly, suspect from an economic point of view.

Fair Trade

An especially clear example of action by both state and Federal governments to discourage competition is found in the so-called "fair-trade" laws. These laws permit manufacturers of a large variety of drugstore merchandise, books, liquor, jewelry, cigars, electrical appliances, sporting goods, and many other items to specify either the minimum or the exact price at which their products may be sold by retailers. Many retailers do not wish to be bound by resale-price-fixing agreements with manufacturers and will not sign such contracts. The state laws, however, usually contain "nonsigner clauses" which make the price agreements binding on all retailers if any retailer makes such a contract for a particular product.

Most commodities of a nature suitable to fair trading move in interstate commerce. Price-fixing agreements between manufacturers and retailers, accordingly, would normally subject the participants to prosecution under the Sherman Antitrust Law. In order to avoid this legal pitfall, the National Association of Druggists and other groups prevailed on Congress to include in the Miller-Tydings Act of 1937 a proviso which exempted resale-price agreements made under state laws from prosecution under the Federal antitrust law.

In spite of reverses met in the courts of a few states, the fair-trade philosophy rode high until 1951 when the United States Supreme Court decided (in the Schwegmann case) that retailers who did not sign the price agreements could not be forced to adhere to the resale prices set in contracts made by others. A period of much more competitive retail trade, marked by drastic price cuts in many fair-traded items, followed this decision.

The fair-trade forces quickly devised a new proposal, and they secured speedy passage and Presidential approval of the McGuire Act in 1952. This law, an amendment to the Federal Trade Commission Act, declares that nothing in the antitrust laws shall render it unlawful to require sellers—signers and nonsigners alike—to adhere to price-fixing agreements regarding trade-marked items where such agreements are legalized in intrastate commerce by state laws. Under this Act a private contract between a single seller and a manufacturer again became binding on all sellers.

The real Achilles' heel of fair trade has turned out to be the state courts rather than the United States Supreme Court. In recent years many states have declared their fair-trade laws to be unconstitutional, the center of legal attack being the "nonsigner clause."

Other state courts have held their acts to be unenforceable. At the high tide of retail price fixing there were 45 state fair-trade laws, but some two-thirds of these were subsequently rendered inoperative.

Some manufacturers have been staunch supporters of the fair-trade principle; others have taken advantage of the situation by introducing new varieties and brands which are fair traded at lower prices than existing commodities or are not fair traded at all; still others have attempted to "work both sides of the street" by selling well-known brands at established prices through dealers, and at the same time permitting "discount houses" to cut their retail prices as desired in order to gain volume sales. This practice has brought many complaints from dealers and other traditional outlets. The retail jewelers, for example, complained to the Federal Trade Commission that they were being used as a "show case stimulus to the business of discount houses" which disregarded the fair-trade prices to which the jewelry shops adhered.

Proponents of fair trade claim that these laws are needed to protect small business from price cutting by the large stores. If a particular album of phonograph records, for example, is fair traded at $6.75 by the manufacturer, no small music-store owner need worry about price competition from a department store or chain food store. In addition, many manufacturers who have obtained wide public acceptance for their products through extensive advertising feel that they have a right to prevent the "cheapening" of their brand name by price cutters. Their complaint is really against the practice of using "loss leaders" (sales on which little or no profit is made as a lure to bring customers into a store). Although there is some validity to this complaint, in the long run a manufacturer may be helped since the volume of sales will be stimulated by loss-leader prices and since a certain advertising value attaches to the very existence of larger quantities of a branded item in consumers' hands.

The American public has a sentimental attachment to small business and, consequently, a tendency to support government policies which purport to aid such firms. This feeling is grounded mainly on a fear of large business monopolies. It is inconsistent, however, to favor monopolistic pricing via the fair-trade laws as an aid to small business. Efficiency is secured by competition in all segments of the economy, and there is no reason why a particular segment, such as retailing, should be excepted. The presumption is that retailers should compete among one another on a price basis just as should firms at any other levels. If a firm cannot continue to exist in such an environment it must be relatively inefficient in some respect (location, size, etc.). Social economy is not fostered by the government's "bailing out" inefficient companies. If, for example, a drugstore is unable to sell toothpaste as cheaply as a chain food store can, it should not expect to be able to handle this commodity in large volume. The buying public should secure the full price advantage made possible by the most efficient system of production and distribution, proper location, and good management.

In the long run, even the individual retailing firms may not gain from resale-price agreements. New firms are usually able to enter the field without difficulty, and they are likely to do so because of the apparent profits to be gained from the high retail markups. In addition, established firms retailing non-fair-traded items are likely to add fair-traded goods. This explains in part the relatively recent tendency of chain food stores to add kitchen utensils, drugstore items, and phonograph records to their line of wares.

It also seems probable that most gains by manufacturers from resale-price-maintenance contracts are merely temporary. New manufacturing firms producing closely competing and non-fair-traded items tend to be attracted by the actual or apparent profits. The fair-trading manufacturers themselves frequently sell a similar product at a lower price under a different label or, as mentioned earlier, sell the same product through discount outlets.

To the extent that fair-trade prices can be effectively maintained, they have the effect of "cartelizing" a segment of the retailing trade. The essence of a cartel is that prices are set by centralized authority rather than by competition. The best-known cartel arrangements have existed for such internationally traded commodities as matches, magnesium, sulfur, and coffee, but they are also common in intrastate commerce in such fields as barbering, dry cleaning, and undertaking. In general, cartel arrangements in interstate commerce are illegal, but in so far as the fair-trade laws permit manufacturers to specify minimum retail prices, cartel pricing is legal. Whereas privately organized cartels are always subject to breakdown owing to the withdrawal of some of the cooperating firms, cartelization by fair trade has the backing of the police power of the state. Price cutters are subject to fines. The recent weakening of the fair-trade movement is an encouraging manifestation of the power of competition and constitutional government to overcome unwise legislative action on economic matters.

The Sales-below-cost Laws

The same desire to curb price competition that has motivated the fair-trade laws underlies laws prohibiting "sales-below-cost" in certain segments of the economy. Early in 1956 there were 47 sales-below-cost laws which had been enacted by 35 states.[1] Some of these laws apply to all products while others apply to one or a few industries. The laws are known as "unfair-sales acts" and "unfair-practices acts." The former apply to retailers and wholesalers; the latter apply also to manufacturers. Like the fair-trade laws, these acts have been the subject of numerous tests in court and frequently have been found unconstitutional. As of late 1955 only 6 states—Arkansas, California, Kentucky, Montana, Washington, and Wyoming—had unfair-practices acts in force.[2] However, unfair-sales acts of broad or specific coverage were common. For example, 16 states had unfair-sales acts for cigarettes.[3]

Most of the sales-below-cost laws provide for a cost survey by the appropriate trade association to establish a cost below which prices are not allowed to go. Thus the "cost" which provides a floor under prices is usually not that of the individual seller but is rather some "standard" cost determined by a survey. Since it is to the sellers' advantage to overstate cost in such circumstances, an upward bias is inevitable. The trade association or other interested groups which conduct the surveys, furthermore, have an incentive to establish uniform markups sufficiently high to cover the costs of the less efficient firms.

In general, sellers have more freedom under the sales-below-cost laws than under the fair-trade laws. Under a variety of enumerated special circumstances, sellers are permitted to cut price below the standard cost. Closing-out sales, sales of damaged goods, and sales of perishable and seasonal items are usually exempted.

One of the justifications inevitably set forth by supporters of sales-below-cost prohibition is that in the absence of such legislation retailers will use particular items of widespread consumption (*e.g.*, cigarettes) as loss leaders in order to attract customers who will buy

[1] Jay D. Cook, Jr., "Cost Concepts and Problems under State Unfair Sales and Practices Acts" (Ph.D. dissertation, microfilmed, Ohio State University, 1956), p. 16. Much of the information in this section is taken from this comprehensive study.

[2] *Ibid.*, p. 40.

[3] *Ibid.*, p. 32.

other goods on which markups are adequate or excessive. Although this argument has some merit, the loss to society due to the curtailment of competitive pricing by sales-below-cost prohibitions appears to make such laws clearly undesirable.

If prices and costs are to perform their proper function of weeding out firms or products which are unneeded from a demand viewpoint or inefficient from a cost standpoint, it is necessary that there be no legal restrictions on prices. At any time goods may sell above, at, or below cost per unit depending on the demand and supply situation in the industry. If price is persistently above unit cost it provides a signal to other enterprisers that here is a suitable field to enter. Labor and capital move into such activities and away from those where costs cannot be met. In this way the "invisible hand" described by the first great economist, Adam Smith, in 1776 operates without central direction to allocate resources in accordance to consumers' wants and the dictates of engineering and economic efficiency. It is clear that legal rigging of prices to keep them above some standard cost interferes with the ability of a private-enterprise system to function effectively. While lack of demand might still cause a movement of resources as some firms abandon a product, consumers are not given the opportunity to buy at lower prices from the more efficient firms.

Farm Programs

Probably the most publicized government activities to support prices are found in the field of agriculture where the "parity-price program" and the "soil bank" are at present in effect. There is, perhaps, somewhat more justification for governmental interference on behalf of producers in agriculture than in most segments of the economy since fluctuations in farm prices and incomes tend to be especially severe. This can be explained by the highly competitive nature of agriculture due to the large number of independent firms. Farm output tends to remain high in years of depressed aggregate demand and prices must fall sharply in a competitive market, due to relatively inelastic demand. This results in lower farm incomes. On the other hand there is little unemployment in the farming sector during depressions. The farm groups argue that if the government is to take action to relieve unemployment by public works or other means in the sectors where depressions are characterized by reduced production and employment, it should also take action to keep the prices of farm products from falling so low during such

FIGURE 5.1. SUPPLY INCREASING FASTER THAN
DEMAND—Leads to Falling Agricultural Prices

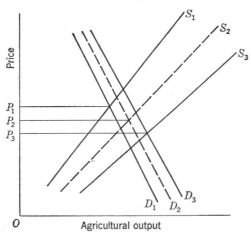

periods. That is, they argue that "employment" with inadequate
income is not unlike unemployment. This has provided much of the
rationale for the government's program of supporting farm prices.

Federal agricultural policy is aimed not only at relieving low
farm prices when economic activity is depressed but is also supposed to counteract low prices of a more chronic sort due to relative
oversupply of farms and farmers. Even in prosperous years farm
prices tend to be low compared with nonfarm prices. Chronic over-
production of many farm commodities arises because improved
technology in agriculture has been increasing output more rapidly
than the demand for agricultural products has increased. As a result,
agriculture is a declining segment of the economy in terms of employment.

Figure 5.1 illustrates this problem. Demand for farm products has
increased over time from D_1 to D_2 to D_3, but this increase in demand is more than offset by the increase in supply from S_1 to S_2
to S_3. As a result, farm prices tend to fall from P_1 to P_2 to P_3, if free
market forces prevail. This chart is, of course, only broadly illustrative of a historical situation. It does not hold true for all products,
but is roughly appropriate for such important commodities as wheat,
corn, cotton, and tobacco.

In most segments of the American economy falling prices and declining incomes motivate labor and capital to move to "greener
pastures." And actually farm employment has declined in both a
relative and an absolute sense. Early in the history of America

about nine out of ten persons working were on farms, whereas today only about one worker in ten is in agriculture.[1] The rate of migration away from the farm has not been sufficiently rapid, however, to prevent downward pressure on farm prices. In addition, the per capita consumption of "fattening" foods such as bread has declined, limiting the rate of growth in aggregate demand for wheat, and cotton consumption per capita has been diminished by the invention of new textile fibers.

Parity Prices

Study of the remarkable mechanism of free markets has led many economists to look with great distrust at efforts to boost the income of particular economic groups by means of deliberate government support of prices of the goods or services sold by such groups. If relief is deemed necessary it should be in such a form as to minimize its impact on the allocation of resources dictated by consumers' choices. Yet the Federal program of parity prices is a glaring example of relief via interference with prices, Also it is a strange sort of relief program in that most of the relief goes to those who appear to need it least—that is, to the large, well-equipped, productive farms which have a great deal to sell.

The support levels below which farm prices are to be prevented from falling are determined by an elaborate formula which compares the prices of products which farmers sell with the prices they must pay for goods which they buy. The ratio of farm prices to the prices farmers pay is related to the corresponding ratio prevailing during the base period, 1910 to 1914. (For some products a later pre-World War II period is used.) The basic idea is that if a bushel of wheat exchanged for one blue work shirt of a defined quality in the base period, a bushel of wheat should still exchange for one blue work shirt today if the wheat farmer is to maintain his economic status within our society.

One of the difficulties with the parity concept is that the buying pattern of the farmer changes with the times; the typical farm family today spends a significant part of its budget on goods which were unknown in 1910. Besides, the rate of technological improvement in agriculture may have been quite different from that of the goods farmers buy. If, for example, improvement in methods of producing wheat have outrun improvement in the methods of producing

[1] *Report of the Secretary of Agriculture, 1956* (Washington: U.S. Government Printing Office, 1957).

blue work shirts, an appropriate exchange ratio might be 1½ bushels of wheat for one shirt. The attempt to maintain "parity" at one to one runs counter to the way the economy is supposed to operate.

Actually, farm prices are usually not supported at full parity as calculated by the Department of Agriculture but at some percentage of parity. A great deal of discussion, lobbying, and playing of politics goes on each year before this percentage is arrived at for each commodity. For the past several years much interest has centered on "flexible price supports" which permit the Secretary of Agriculture to use discretion in fixing the exact level of price support. In other words, supply and demand are given more consideration, yet are not allowed to do the whole job.

Flexible price supports became partially effective with the 1955 harvest and were utilized more fully in 1956. They ranged from 75 to 90 per cent of parity.[1] Prices may be supported in several ways. The Commodity Credit Corporation may make direct purchases by entering the market for the particular commodity. For storable commodities, the more common practice is the making of "nonrecourse" loans to farmers. These are loans secured by the expected crop, but in the event that the price of the commodity turns out to be so low that the value of the crop is less than the amount of the loan, it is understood that the farmer may simply default on the loan and the government will take title to the crop in full payment of the loan. The farmer will, of course, sell the crop and repay the loan if the market value of the crop is greater than the amount borrowed.

In either case, the total effect is to establish a floor under the prices of agricultural products (although it is possible for prices to fall somewhat below support levels). The Commodity Credit Corporation, a Federal corporation, acquires inventories of storable products in the process. As of June 30, 1956, the CCC held over $2.5 billion worth of wheat, and about one and one quarter billion dollars' worth each of upland cotton and corn. Stocks of some two dozen other commodities, including butter, cheese, and peanuts, were also in government storage. The magnitude of this program can be judged by the fact that as of the same date the CCC held almost $6 billion in inventories, valued at cost, and in addition had outstanding almost $2.3 billion in loans. The government regularly incurs large "losses" by selling inventories below cost or giving them away in foreign aid or for other purposes.

The parity-price program provides us with an excellent and important example of an analytical use of the demand-supply analysis

[1] *Ibid.*

FIGURE 5.2. PRICE SUPPORT—Brings Surplus Problem

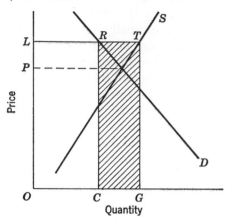

of the preceding chapters. In Figure 5.2 the curve D represents the total private demand for a particular agricultural commodity; S represents the short-run supply curve for the industry, namely, the amount which farmers will wish to supply at different possible prices. If there were no interference with the market, the price would tend to be established at the competitive equilibrium level OP. This is the free market price. Assume, however, that the support price is OL. At this price, private buyers will demand only the quantity OC, whereas farmers will desire to put an amount OG on the market. The government will have to buy the quantity CG in order to make its support price effective. Total expenditure by government is represented by the shaded area $CRTG$; total expenditure by private buyers is $OLRC$, giving sellers of the commodity a total income of $OLTG$. It is likely that private consumers will pay more for the smaller amount which they buy than under the free market price. (Whether this will be true depends on the elasticity of the demand curve over the relevant range.) It is certain, however, that farmers' total income will be boosted by the price-support program as long as the government is willing and able to buy up the surplus. Except under unusual conditions the government will not be able to dispose of its inventory at a price as high as OL, and the CCC will incur losses. In addition, taxpayers must pay the storage cost and often meet a further expense of deterioration of the stored good. The latter can be a serious problem for perishable commodities such as butter.

The Soil Bank

Proponents of legislation in the economic field usually coin a name which is likely to have popular appeal. Examples are the "fair-trade" laws, the "parity-price" program, and the "soil bank." The latter term is pleasing since everyone likes to have money in the bank. Actually, the soil-bank program provides for taking land out of production, that is, putting it to a poorer use than would be dictated by normal economic ends. Most people have a feeling that any sort of "conservation" is a good thing; and the soil-bank program is advertised as a step to "reduce surpluses, improve income, and strengthen conservation."[1] The question is seldom asked: "Why spend public money to conserve farm land when its very chronic oversupply is responsible for the farm problem?"

Under the "acreage-reserve" part of the soil-bank program, farmers who reduce their planted acreage of such basic crops as wheat, cotton, corn, tobacco, peanuts, and rice below the established allotments are given payments for such land. Land put "into the bank" is usually limited in amount by law, and grazing as well as the raising of crops is not permitted.

Under the longer-range portion of the soil-bank program, conservation is given particular emphasis. Farmers promise to plant trees or grass on their crop land for periods of 3 to 10 years. Annual "rent" and also 80 per cent of the cost of the young trees which are planted is paid by the government. Many "city-slickers" have taken advantage of this program to buy run-down farms and plant them with trees. Often this would be the most economical use of the land anyway, but the conservation program makes it particularly attractive. In numerous cases farmers upon retiring at 65 have placed entire farms in the soil bank, thereby drawing both social security and soil-bank checks, while still engaging in a nonstrenuous type of agriculture, *i.e.*, tree farming.

The basic objective of the soil-bank program—which is only the current version of a series of acreage-reduction schemes that have been in effect since the depression years of the 1930's—is to reduce the size of the surpluses the government must buy to support prices. In terms of Figure 5.3, the basic purpose of the soil-bank program is to decrease short-run supply, that is, to shift the supply curve to

[1] *Report of the Secretary of Agriculture, 1956* (Washington: U.S. Government Printing Office, 1957), p. 2.

FIGURE 5.3. SOIL BANK—Supposed to Cut
Surpluses

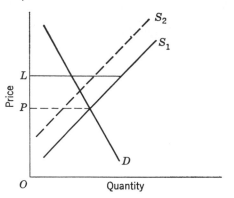

the left. If S_1 represents the supply which farmers would market in
the absence of the soil bank, the hope is that this can be cut back
to a position such as S_2 by means of the withdrawal of acreage. If
this reduction of supply were actually accomplished, the amount
and cost of the surplus to the government would be reduced, and
it is possible that the payment for the surplus plus payments under
the soil bank would be smaller than payment for the surplus alone
in the absence of the acreage restriction.

In practice, however, it is difficult to reduce surpluses significantly by means of the soil-bank device. Farmers tend to place the
poorest land in the reserve, plant rows closer together, and fertilize
more heavily. For example, yearly cotton yields averaged 300
pounds per acre between 1946 and 1955 but jumped to 435
pounds per acre in 1956.[1] Clearly, farmers *like* to grow things and it
is extremely difficult to stop them from doing so.

Each session of Congress and most meetings of national farm
groups bring forth a bewildering array of proposals for modification
of the farm program. In addition to controversy over the correct
per cent and period, there is often discussion of a system of *income*,
rather than price, parity. Some authorities advocate a policy of permitting farm prices to reach competitive levels and then making
direct subsidy payments to farmers to the extent that prices fall below
parity levels. Limitations on the amount of soil-bank payments have
been established at $3,000 for the 1958 crop, but this has kept the
large farms out of the soil bank, and in this way made its operation
less effective. Whether this limit should be on a per farm or per

[1] "Soil Bank Blues," *Wall Street Journal*, November 4, 1957.

farmer basis is a moot point. In the former case a farm might be split into many smaller units for purposes of soil-bank participation.

The details of the farm program change each year, but the entire situation demonstrates forcibly the arbitrary nature of the solutions which emerge when the free price system is abandoned. Endless formulas, loopholes, flaws, political moves, and administrative problems show up. Little is done to solve the basic problem. In fact the malallocation of resources is perpetuated, since marginal farmers are encouraged to remain in farming rather than to leave their farms. To the extent that this is a proper field of government activity at all, it appears that some way must be found to move the more marginal farmers into profitable nonagricultural occupations. No other program is consistent with the basic principles which underlie the proper operation of a private-enterprise system.

Marketing Agreements and Orders

Closely related to the Federal price-support program are "marketing agreements" and "marketing orders" covering a number of commodities, often perishable in nature, which do not receive direct support through loans and purchases. Marketing agreements are based on the Agricultural Marketing Agreement Act of 1937, which permits the Secretary of Agriculture to enter into contracts with handlers of any agricultural commodity and exempts such agreements from the antitrust laws. Marketing agreements are of most importance for milk, but have also been made for such commodities as cauliflower, citrus fruit, grapes, pears, plums, peaches, potatoes, and peas.

Under the terms of marketing agreements, processors or other handlers agree to pay farmers no less than designated minimum prices. In other cases, farm prices are indirectly supported by means of controlling supply through a "control board" established under the terms of an agreement or by direct (involuntary) order of the Department of Agriculture. Marketing agreements require approval of handlers of not less than 50 per cent of the commodity and of at least two-thirds of the growers. Like the fair-trade laws, however, agreements are binding on nonsigners as well as on signers.

Marketing agreements eliminate sharp price fluctuations, price uncertainty, and price pressure on farmers, which are frequent sources of complaint in the absence of such agreements. As in the case of direct price support, however, the benefits of the scheme seem to be heavily outweighed by its demerits. Marketing agreements were introduced during the depression of the 1930's as a relief measure, but they were continued through periods of farm prosperity. Like direct price supports, they give most relief to the wealthiest farmers. Quantities which cannot be sold at the minimum prices are diverted to inferior uses. For example, surplus-milk production is often diverted to the production of ice cream, which in part accounts for the relatively low prices at which this product is frequently retailed. Fluid milk itself, a basic food of infants and the aged, is kept artificially high in price.

An especially unfortunate aspect of Federal support of milk prices is that it also tends to encourage similar support at the state level. That is, the likelihood of Federal control causes many states to set up milk boards or commissions in order to keep control within their own boundaries. Such boards are active in most states in fixing minimum prices for milk at both the farm and retail levels. Efforts at elimination of state control often founder owing to fear of substitution of Federal control. In this case, if the state does not "get" the consumer, the Federal government probably will.

Where abundant pasture is available and feeds are cheap, the farmers themselves are apt to be disappointed with the results of minimum milk prices. Like resale-price maintenance and prohibition of sale below cost, minimum-price agreements tend to attract additional producers. The result may be that, despite higher prices received per unit, the typical farmer may enjoy only ordinary returns for his labor and capital, since new sellers will encroach on his sales volume. He cannot cut price in order to move unsold supplies, except for secondary uses. Once the excess capacity has been attracted, it is extremely difficult to remove minimum prices or discontinue supply limitations, since the short-run effect of such action would be precipitation of price warfare and the elimination of weaker competitors. Farmers are likely to vote against removal of marketing agreements for this reason. Consequently, the main hope for consumer relief lies with legislative bodies, which have shown few signs of willingness to risk the displeasure of agricultural interests.

Building Codes

Space limitation permits only brief mention of one of several other important ways in which government action serves to interfere with free market determination of prices. Most of these, like the fair-trade laws and the agricultural program, tend to serve politically influential seller interests at the expense of consumers. Building codes as they exist in many communities are an outstanding example. They exemplify a familiar pattern in which certain restrictions are actually needed in order to ensure safety and other legitimate ends, but where many additional and unnecessary restrictions are imposed to benefit sellers by curbing competition. The restrictions contained in the building codes are imposed by local governmental bodies, and they are usually supported by labor unions, contractors, and established material suppliers. Sometimes the restrictions are embodied in union agreements with employers instead of being legislated explicitly in the form of building codes. Licensing provisions for particular occupations frequently also contribute to the web of monopolistic restrictions in the construction industry.

For example, the use of "ready-mix" concrete (which is mixed in the truck on the way to the job) has been prohibited in some instances. Lathers have at times secured a prohibition of the use of factory-cut lathing, while in other cases the installation of doors which are not glazed on the job has been forbidden.[1] The width of the paintbrush has been limited in some cases, and in others the use of paint-spraying equipment has been banned. In a well-known instance it was necessary for a contractor to employ an electrician for a full day so that he could plug in an electric pump in the morning and unplug it in the afternoon. The last hour of "work" was paid at the overtime rate because the standard day for electricians was shorter than for other workers.[2]

All such restrictions and make-work provisions tend to increase costs and thus restrict supply. This is accomplished not only by preventing established firms from reaching least-cost input combinations but also by preventing entry of new firms producing close substitute products. The building codes have in one instance proved to be a major obstacle to the development of an entirely new industry —the prefabricated production of residential homes.

The effects on resource allocation are clear. The supply price of housing tends to be increased; this causes a reduction in the quantity of housing units demanded. As a result, fewer resources are devoted to housing than the principle of consumer sovereignty would dictate. Total real income is reduced through artificial restrictions

---

[1] Stephen P. Sobotka, "Union Influence on Wages: The Construction Industry," *Journal of Political Economy*, Vol. 61, p. 131 (April, 1953).

[2] Miles L. Colean and Robinson Newcomb, *Stabilizing Construction: The Record and Potential* (New York: McGraw-Hill Book Company, Inc., 1952), p. 121.

and limitations on cost-reducing methods of production. Real income is diverted from consumers to sellers of construction services and materials.

Summary

In this chapter we have discussed in some detail a few of the many governmental programs which tend to interfere with, rather than promote, the workings of the competitive market mechanism. A complete list would indeed be lengthy, and it would include many regulations which appear necessary and desirable for non-economic reasons. Among these are sanitary regulations, quarantine rules, licensing requirements, fire regulations, etc., all of which may involve economic effects which are detrimental to the consumer and beneficial to producer groups. The economic effects need not be decisive in determining the appropriateness of such public policies, but they should at least be taken fully into account. The discussion of this chapter should reveal the usefulness of economic analysis in understanding more fully the total impact of many governmental policies.

6

MONOPOLISTIC PRICING
OF PRODUCTS

Although competition is the organizing principle of a private-enterprise economy, everyone who has anything to sell prefers to be a monopolist. Paradoxically, the most vocal supporters of the private-enterprise system are often among the worst offenders in this respect. The reason for the universal desire to monopolize is not difficult to understand. Competition from other sellers always tends to hold down the price which can be secured for a given commodity or service, thus reducing the profitableness of the sale that could otherwise be enjoyed by a single seller (monopolist). Ordinarily, we think in terms of sellers of physical items of merchandise—food, clothing, shoes, cars, etc. We should not, however, overlook those who sell services (*e.g.*, TV repairmen, lawyers, doctors, and landlords). Further, everyone who works for someone else is a seller of labor services, while such institutions as banks, building and loan associations, and finance companies are in business to sell credit to borrowers. All of these sellers prefer to have substantial monopoly power, and frequently they take all possible steps to secure this advantage.

This should immediately make clear an important role of government in an economic system organized on a private-enterprise
basis. The central government, with the aid of state and local governments, should act as a referee in the great game of business to
try to keep the players within the rules, that is, competitive. This is
the basic idea behind the antitrust laws, which have had a measure
of success in breaking up some large monopolies and in inhibiting
the growth of others. Other Federal and state laws, however, have
frequently had the opposite effect—that of *promoting* monopoly—
as was described in some detail in Chapter 5. The existence of
monopoly-promoting laws frequently is based on success in the
political arena on the part of groups which reflect the universal desire for monopoly power mentioned above.

Strength of Competitive Forces

Fortunately for the health of our economic system, competition
has great force despite the constant efforts of sellers to move in the
direction of monopoly. Every seller has competition from others
who are selling more or less similar products or services. For example, a single power company generally has an exclusive franchise to
sell electricity in a given locality. Although possessing a great deal
of monopoly power (which has led to the regulation of rates by
publicly appointed commissions), even the power company has
competition from sellers of gas, coal, and oil, which may be substituted for electricity in cooking and heating. Less directly, electricity must compete with all other commodities for the consumer's
dollar. Since each family's income, like resources in general, is
limited in amount, all goods upon which income is spent are rivals
to a degree.

Strictly speaking, each seller of a product or service which is
different in any way from the product or service of other sellers
is a monopolist. Thus Esso gasoline is not precisely the same commodity as Texaco, Shell, Sinclair, or Amoco gasoline, so the seller of
each brand can properly be designated a "monopolist." Yet there
is strong competition for sales among the makers and distributors of
these and many additional brands of motor fuel. Thousands of
other commodities are sold under brand names, such as magazines,
chocolate bars, aspirin, breakfast foods, and life-insurance policies.
Some economists call this type of situation "monopolistic competition"—the competition among many producers of quite similar
products each of which is differentiated from others at least in name.

This terminology, while usefully suggestive of the interplay of both monopolistic and competitive forces in our economy, is not really necessary. The term "monopoly" is sufficient, since there is a difference in degree, but not in kind, between the competition faced by a power company and the competition among sellers of different brands of gasoline, tooth paste, or cosmetics. Substitutes may be quite remote or very close, but there are always some substitutes, and hence there is always some degree of competition. At the same time there is usually some degree of monopoly power, and the consequences of such power are examined in the present chapter.

Economics of the Monopolistic Firm

The basic difference between a firm which is a member of a perfectly competitive industry and a monopolistic firm is that only the monopolist has some control over the price which he can charge. While the supply put on the market by an entire competitive *industry* helps determine price, the individual firm cannot do so but must sell at the prevailing market price. A monopolistic firm, however, is by definition the only seller of a particular commodity and, consequently, it can set price within certain limits.

Usually it is possible for a monopolist to adjust his rate of output of a commodity quickly in order to place it on the market at a rate which will be the most profitable to himself. This requires a careful consideration not only of the revenue which can be secured by selling different quantities per time period (*e.g.*, different amounts of telephone service per month) but also of the production cost to the company of different quantities.

MONOPOLY PRICE WHEN COSTS CAN BE DISREGARDED

Under some circumstances, cost may be entirely or virtually disregarded. The problem confronting the monopolist is then simply one of estimating the demand for his commodity carefully and selecting a price which will bring in the greatest total revenue. If, for example, there has been an unusually large plum crop, a strong association in existence to maximize growers' incomes might choose to market only a portion of the crop.

Geometrically speaking, if *D* in Figure 6.1 represents the demand for plums and *OS* the quantity which has been grown, a monopolistic marketing group would place only *OA* on the market. (The rectangle *OPRA* is the largest which can be inscribed under the demand curve. Since its area represents total income to the growers,

FIGURE 6.1. MONOPOLISTIC RESTRICTION
—Raises Price to Consumers

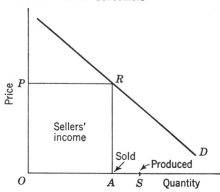

the most profitable price is *OP* and the best amount to sell is *OA*.)
From the growers' point of view sales should be restricted in order
to maintain price, though from a social viewpoint it would be better if all that is grown were sold.

The general situation depicted in Figure 6.1 is representative of
that which exists for coffee beans. Countries which grow this popular commodity regularly attempt by mutual agreement to regulate
the quantity shipped to the United States and other consuming
nations. The amount of coffee which must be kept out of export
channels (*e.g.*, by burning) depends on the size of the crop. Conceivably the total crop might be so small that no restriction whatever would be needed. If the quantity harvested were *OA* or any
smaller amount, no restriction on marketing would be required.
Monopolistic restriction of the number of acres planted in coffee
trees is also likely to take place as a means of holding down coffee harvests. The similarities between monopolistic international
coffee controls and our own farm policies is evident.

A similar situation may exist for a monopolist who has invested
his money in any sort of land or equipment and who has acquired at
least a temporary overcapacity from the point of view of maximizing
the immediate return on his investment. For example, the owner of a
parking lot may have had an eye to future expansion of traffic when
he bought his lot and, consequently, have one which is currently
oversized. Rational pricing policy on his part does not call for setting
a price low enough to fill the parking lot. Rather, he should attempt
to gauge demand and to set price in such a way as to bring in
maximum income. In terms of Figure 6.1, he may have room to
park *OS* cars, but his self-interest should lead him to price *OP*

at which only *OA* cars will be parked. This assumes a single price for all cars. Actually, the existence of unused space might lead the lot owner to give some cars a lower rate—that is, to discriminate in their favor—in order to obtain more income. A suitable device for such discrimination might be the leasing of space on a weekly or monthly basis at a lower rate per hour.

Similarly, the existence of a partially filled college football stadium on a fair day is not proof of an erroneous estimate of demand or of an improper pricing policy if the educational institution is attempting to make profits. If, however, the objective is to permit as many people as possible to enjoy viewing the game, a lower price is appropriate; that is, a price should be established which will equate the number of seats sold to the number available. Unfortunately, the businessman's viewpoint of the desirability of maximizing profits is often carried over into fields where it is inappropriate, and college athletic events are apt to be a case in point.

In the same manner, the existence of unrented apartments or offices in a large building, unsold seats in a passenger train, or unused barber chairs is not necessarily a reflection of improper pricing policy from a private, monopolistic point of view. This type of situation was called the "fixed-supply" case in Chapter 3. If the fixed supply exceeds the amount which can be sold at maximum income, the seller in possession of monopoly power is likely not to sell the entire amount on hand. The social loss due to monopoly is especially clear in this case since society is deprived of the use of already produced goods.

THE TOTAL REVENUE CURVE

In the situations just described the firm with monopoly power does not need to consider cost of production since it has already made commitments (*e.g.,* investments) which insure that a more-than-ample supply will be available. The managerial problem of maximizing income then involves selection of the best price and quantity to be marketed. This may occur either through setting the price and selling whatever amount the market will take or else by determining the quantity to be marketed and letting price be determined by the strength of demand. The former procedure would probably be followed by an industrial firm, whereas a marketing cooperative would be likely to follow the second procedure.

A useful geometrical device for viewing the profit-maximizing procedure in either event consists of a "total revenue curve." This shows the total income which the monopolistic seller would obtain per

FIGURE 6.2. TOTAL REVENUE CURVE—For
Monopolistic Seller

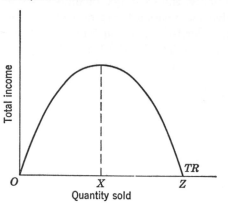

time period by selling various quantities. The height of the curve
corresponding to each quantity is derived by the multiplication of
that quantity by the price at which the monopolistic seller could
dispose of that amount.

Total revenue, as shown in Figure 6.2, increases at first as more
is sold, reaches a maximum if *OX* is sold, then declines, conceivably
reaching zero if so much (*OZ*) were put on the market that it would
have to be *given* away. Quantity *OX* in Figure 6.2 corresponds
with quantity *OA* in Figure 6.1. Consequently, the same observations are pertinent, namely, that the monopolist seeking to maximize
profit will sell his entire stock of a good if he has available *OX* or
less, but will limit his sales to *OX* if he has on hand more than this
amount and if circumstances permit such a limitation.

TOTAL REVENUE AND TOTAL COST

If total cost goes up as more is produced, and if output can be
adjusted to the desired rate, the monopolistic firm should always
stop short of the output which brings in maximum revenue. This is
illustrated in Figure 6.3, which shows total revenue and total
cost. Obviously, the firm should attempt to turn out and sell the
amount *OB* where total revenue minus total cost is at a maximum.

The total cost curve needs some explanation. It will be noted
that it starts not at the origin but at the height *OF*. This is because
certain costs go on even if the plant is shut down. For example, the
company will incur some depreciation of buildings and equipment,
fire insurance premiums will still have to be met, interest on borrowed funds will continue, land rent must be paid, and salaries will

FIGURE 6.3. MAXIMUM PROFIT TO MO-
NOPOLIST—Where Revenue-Cost Spread Is
Largest

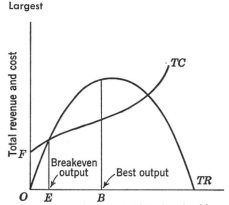

continue to be paid to at least a portion of the personnel. Total cost becomes greater the larger the rate of output because of the need to hire more labor and use more materials, fuel, and other variable inputs. At first total cost typically rises at a decreasing rate (reflected by the downward concavity of the *TC* curve), because better proportions between fixed capital (land, machines, etc.) and variable factors (*e.g.*, labor) are attained and each additional unit turned out adds less to total cost than did the one before it. After a certain point the curve becomes concave upward, that is, increases at an increasing rate as poorer proportions of fixed and variable factors are required for a higher rate of output. The famous law of diminishing returns (which will be explained in more detail in a later chapter) is at work here.

The type of diagram shown in Figure 6.3 is often called a "break-even chart" and is used frequently by businessmen. It is so named because it clearly shows the minimum output at which the firm can just cover all of its costs, *i.e.*, at output *OE*. This type of chart is probably more useful as a planning device than in connection with actual operation of the firm. Before investing in an enterprise a businessman must ordinarily be convinced that the demand-cost situation which will be met will make it possible at least to break even, or better, of course, to make a profit. "Breaking even" is a more favorable situation than it appears at first glance since "cost," as defined in economics, includes a normal interest return on invested capital as well as appropriate payments to all other resources employed.

FIGURE 6.4. FIRM SHOULD OPERATE—If It
Meets Variable Costs

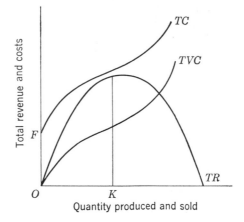

It is necessary to guard against a logical error when the use of a break-even chart for operating purposes is considered. If commitments which have *already been made* result in the inevitable occurrence of some fixed costs, it is not rational to shut down an operation merely because it is impossible to break even on total costs. Instead, the firm should keep operating if it can cover total *variable* costs and make anything to apply against fixed costs. The saying "half a loaf is better than none" is suggestive of rational action, since it is better to obtain revenue to meet part of the fixed costs than none at all.

The monopolistic firm's break-even chart in Figure 6.3 can be modified to reflect the above point by adding a total variable cost curve. Curve *TVC* in Figure 6.4 shows total outlays for such controllable costs as labor, materials, fuel, and power at different possible rates of production. Figure 6.4 also differs from Figure 6.3 in that the total revenue curve is so low that the company cannot possibly meet total costs unless there is a change for the better. It is, nevertheless, better to remain in operation, producing at the output *OK* where the excess of income over total variable cost is at a maximum and where the deficiency of income under total cost is at a minimum. The owners of the firm would not be happy about the situation since a less-than-normal return would be earned on the capital invested in the firm and perhaps a less-than-normal return would be secured by management if work were provided on a nonsalaried basis. If the situation promises to remain this bad, capital will not be reinvested in the enterprise. But the important point is that if capital is already "sunk" in this venture, it is important to continue to operate in order to recoup part of it for investment elsewhere. An alternative would be to sell the firm (for example, for stockholders to dispose of their common stocks), but this would not help because stock prices would reflect the low level of earnings on the firm's fixed assets.

Monopoly and Profits

Figure 6.4 constitutes a diagrammatic warning that monopoly power does not automatically ensure profits, although abnormal profits are always the motivation for attempts to secure a monopolistic market position. Many patented items are never produced because businessmen feel demand-cost conditions would not permit profitable production. Even if original demand-cost conditions are satisfactory, profits made by early firms may be reduced or wiped out by the appearance of other enterprises which sell close substitutes. Businesses which require little capital and experience tend to be overcrowded and chronically unprofitable, for example, filling stations, gift shops, concrete-block plants, and small grocery stores. Ease of entry is vital to the existence of pure competition, but the entry of new firms producing close substitutes is often effective also in reducing the profits of firms which have gained monopoly power by selling differentiated products. Where entry is extremely difficult owing to the large investment needed, profits tend to be more dependable as long as national income is high. The monopoly power which firms in such industries possess is sometimes defended by economists as socially desirable to the extent that the attraction of abnormal profits is required to induce the large investment necessary for entry into the field. If entry of new firms is impossible because of protection in the form of an exclusive patent or franchise, a monopolist may be able to secure substantial profits over a period of many years.

Profits thus serve the same function in monopolistic industries as in competitive ones. They attract new firms, and the subsequent entry of new firms tends to eliminate abnormal profits. The major difference between monopoly and competition in this respect is the rate at which new firms can take away the abnormal or excessive profits of existing firms.

SELLING COSTS

The typical firm does not merely accept demand as it is but attempts to influence it by means of advertising. These efforts may be passive, as when a grocer paints his store front red and puts up a sign bearing his name, or extremely active, as when a large firm broadcasts a "commercial" on television or buys a huge electric display on Broadway.

In terms of the analysis of this chapter, the purpose of advertising is to shift the demand curve for a firm's product upward and to the right, or alternatively, to raise the total revenue curve so that any quantity will bring in a greater income due to the better price which it will command. The success or failure of the advertising depends on whether it raises total revenue more than total cost. In practice this may be very difficult to judge, and much advertising is probably carried on more in fear of unfortunate repercussions on demand if advertising is curtailed than because of positive knowledge of its benefits.

The social effects of advertising are widely debated. On the one hand, it is claimed that heavy advertising is often needed to create the large market required for low-cost production. Also, it is clear that certain kinds of advertising, such as want ads and grocery store ads, add to consumer information and consequently are socially useful. On the other hand, much advertising either tells the consumer nothing about the product or tends actually to mislead him, and heavy expenditures of scarce resources are made in the attempt to lure customers from one firm to another where products are actually very similar. Free radio and TV programs are an interesting by-product of advertising in the United States. To the extent that the alternative is government-controlled broadcasts, the contribution of advertising in this sphere seems to be a valuable one. To the extent that the alternative is pay TV, with the price system performing its usual function in our economy, the social gain from free TV is less clear.

EFFICIENCY AND EMULATION

Even a firm with great monopoly power, for example, one which turns out an unusual and popular product under patent protection, has an incentive to be efficient in order to increase profits. The compulsion toward efficiency tends, however, to be less powerful than under highly competitive conditions where the inefficient will be weeded out.

In so far as new firms, attracted by monopoly profits, are able to produce close substitute products, a profitable monopoly position tends to be eroded over time. If the monopoly power is derived by virtue of building the first filling station at a busy highway intersection, other stations will probably locate at the same corner or close by if the first station seems to be unusually profitable. Similarly, the first TV station to cover a suitable population area may be quite profitable, and this will almost inevitably cause others to apply for channels. In this case the right to use a TV channel is a valuable public property which we give away instead of selling to the highest bidder. Not only are public revenues lost in the process but officials in charge of granting or denying applications for channels are frequently plied with favors. The same situation exists because the Federal government gives away desirable air routes instead of selling them to the highest qualified bidder.

To the extent that monopoly power derives from certain unique properties of a good or service, others will strive to imitate or improve on that quality and, if successful, will reduce the advantage of the first seller. An important function of advertising from the firm's point of view is to preserve the illusion of uniqueness even after it no longer exists.

Even in the provision of services there is a marked tendency both to attempt to establish unique characteristics and for rivals to attempt to duplicate. For example, the successful antics of one rock-and-roll singer are adopted by others who would also like to become rich. The highly successful textbook is likely to be imitated in some respects; in response the successful author and his publisher attempt to thwart the rivals by seeking fascinating new facets in each revision.

THE ROADS TO MONOPOLY

From a social point of view the most dangerous monopolies are those where substantial duplication by other sellers is very difficult or impossible and where important commodities are involved. It was pointed out in Chapter 5 that the police power of the state is often successfully mobilized by those seeking to maintain a monopolistic advantage. The patent system has often provided for the exclusion of competition to a greater extent than seems appropriate as a spur to invention. Affiliations of industrial and financial firms, which often employ one or more directors in common, can sometimes be employed to deprive would-be rivals of the financing necessary to enter a field. Out-of-date tables pertaining to risk in a field of insurance where loss experience has declined tend to bring about monopolistic premium rates, the tables providing a measure of protection to the firms against rate competition.

Another route to monopoly is through the merger of firms in the same general line of business. A great wave of mergers followed the financial panic of 1897 in this country. Such companies as U.S. Steel, Standard Oil, and American Tobacco attained tremendous size and monopoly power. An allied monopolistic movement of the nineteenth century was built on a form of organization known as a "trust." This form of affiliation is looser than the merger; cooperating companies maintain their indentities but delegate to a "trustee" the power to determine certain important policy matters for the group. Since the trustee controls all the corporations, he will see that none of them is hurt unduly by competition within the group. The antitrust laws, as originally passed by Congress, were directed particularly against this form of monopoly.

The most common origin of monopoly power—but usually power of a less dangerous sort—is that already mentioned, *i.e.*, the differentiation of products by means of brand names. Most consumers' goods except for the frequent exclusion of fresh vegetables, fruits, sea food, and meats, are sold under brand names, and sellers miss few opportunities—skywriting, subway ads, subliminal solicitation—to impress their trade-marks on the public mind. Brand names are of less importance for industrial goods such as metals, building materials, pipe, and machine tools because of the greater expertness of the professional buyers employed by wholesalers and manufacturers. In selling brand-name goods to householders the aim is usually to reduce competition by creating the impression that substitutes are not "just as good." Usually there are some physical differences in products sold by different firms, but even where commodities are identical, as in the case of different brands of aspirin or cornstarch, sellers attempt to differentiate their wares by means of distinctive packages and highly publicized trade-marks.

The Social Impact of Monopoly

From a social point of view monopoly, with few exceptions, is objectionable. A given sum spent on a monopolistically produced good gives the consumer command over a smaller "bundle" of productive services than if the sum had been spent on a competitively produced good. There is a strong tendency for price to be driven down to actual unit cost of production in a highly competitive market, whereas to the extent that monopoly power is present, price can continue to be marked up well above average cost. Monopoly profits mean that the consumer is really paying more than the product is "worth" in a broad sense, the consumers' loss being the monopolist's gain. The basic guiding principle of consumer sovereignty loses part of its force, being partially replaced by "producer sovereignty."

Selling costs (especially advertising) are often excessive when monopoly power is being sought by means of differentiation.[1] Most advertisements (and high-pressure salesmanship) give little actual information about the product or its price, being designed merely to keep the product in the public mind. The problem is intangible, and the authors do not volunteer to attempt to measure its importance. Yet it appears to be true that a substantial waste of resources is involved in the heavy advertising by which Americans are so steadily bombarded. Also, the basic principle of consumer sovereignty is to some extent compromised when wants are molded by advertising instead of being taken as they are.

Stated more generally, monopoly is objectionable because it distorts the utilization of our resources in such a way as to reduce the national real income, and it acts in such a way as to distribute income in a way which most people consider to be less satisfactory than would occur under pure competition.

The only important exception to this generalization is that in some industries in order to operate efficiently a single firm must be so large in relation to the market that monopoly is both inevitable and desirable from the social point of view. In the case of such public utilities as streetcar, electric, and telephone companies it is desirable to permit either private or public monopoly and, at least in the event of private ownership, to regulate rates through publicly appointed commissions. This special case will be explored more fully in Book Two.

---

[1] It should be clearly understood that this sort of observation does not necessarily constitute a condemnation of advertising as engaged in by the individual firm (which may have to advertise in order even to survive.) It is, instead, a social view of the wastefulness of many selling activities which might conceivably be curtailed by a revision of our tax laws, for example.

7

GOVERNMENT ANTITRUST POLICY

The unfortunate social effects of monopoly have long been widely recognized. Nevertheless, the legislative problem of what measures are appropriate as a check on monopolistic tendencies and the administrative problem of determining when sufficient violation of the law has occurred to require prosecution have never been solved to the satisfaction of social scientists. A knowledge of economics can shed a good deal of light on the nature of the monopoly problem and its possible solutions, but does not give definitive answers to many of the questions involved.

As long as we limit ourselves to broad generalizations, it is appropriate to observe that monopoly should be restrained; competition is the norm from the point of view of being conducive to the greatest satisfaction of human wants. But in the real world it is clear that the ideal cannot be fully realized. Every seller who has identified his product with a trade-mark or brand name enjoys a degree of monopoly, and every entertainer attempts to develop a "style" which will differentiate his product from others. Monopoly elements of this sort are not obviously to be discouraged, although many observers do feel that too much labor and capital are steadily poured out in a partially self-canceling and largely noninformative selling effort. The real question which society faces is to determine how much and what kinds of monopoly should be tolerated. There is a strong presumption in favor of eliminating government activity where it is not clearly needed, or where its cost will not clearly outweigh its probable benefits. By the same token, many government activities clearly yield a social profit, and antimonopoly action is especially likely to do so.

The Sherman Act: Our Main Antimonopoly Law

A summary examination of the history and present status of the government's attempts to regulate business monopoly reveals the scope and extent of the difficulties in this area. It has often been stated that monopoly in economics must mean one thing, and monopoly in law another. If government is to take legal action against monopolies some precise definition of monopoly needs to be incorporated in the legal framework. Since, however, this has proved to be a difficult task, the basic antimonopoly law in this country goes to the other extreme and makes the definition as general as possible. The Sherman Antitrust Act, which was passed in 1890 and which remains today the core of governmental action against business monopoly, declares: "Every contract, combination in the form of trust or otherwise, or conspiracy, in restraint of trade or commerce among the several states or with foreign nations, is hereby declared to be illegal."

If "restraint of trade" is interpreted in the strict economic sense as the power to restrict supply in order to increase price, almost every industry is monopolistic and almost every firm is subject to prosecution. It is readily understandable why this literal economic interpretation has never been placed on the Sherman Act. The way was left open for the courts to determine the legal meaning of the term "restraint of trade." In 1911 the law was used to prosecute successfully two of the outstanding monopoly combinations in the country, Standard Oil and American Tobacco. In handing down the decisions in these cases, however, the Court enunciated the so-called "rule of reason" as applied to antimonopoly action. In effect, the Supreme Court rewrote the Sherman Act by stating that not all restraints of trade were illegal, but only those which were "unreasonable."

The implication of these cases seemed to be that the test of "reasonableness" was whether there was deliberate action on the part of firms to freeze out all competitors by fair means or foul. As a result, firms were encouraged to restrict their monopolistic practices after 1911 to those of the more gentlemanly types. They were encouraged to allow a few small competitors to exist as long as they remained relatively unimportant. This trend was reaffirmed in the 1920's with the decisions in the U.S. Steel and the International Harvester cases. In these cases the Supreme Court was faced with the question of determining how large a concern needs to be in order to constitute an effective monopoly. Taking an extremely conservative view, the Court held that the existence of apparently undisturbed competitors was sufficient to demonstrate the absence of unreasonable restraint of trade. The Court stated in the U.S. Steel case that "the law does not make mere size an offense."

NEW VIEW REGARDING SIZE?

In recent years there has apparently developed a judicial view that mere size may, after all, be an antitrust offense. In the Alcoa case, which was won by the government after 13 years of litigation, the size of the Aluminum Company of America *was* considered to be basic to the exercise of monopoly power. Unlike the Standard Oil Company and the American Tobacco Company some four decades earlier, Alcoa was not broken into smaller units. Instead, some competition was injected into the industry when the surplus government-owned aluminum capacity (which was created during World War II in order to prevent a potentially disastrous shortage of this metal for military aircraft) was sold to private buyers. The Reynolds Metals Company and the Kaiser Aluminum and Chemical Company purchased these facilities.

A difficulty involved in assessing the importance of size as an impediment to competition is that both absolute size and size relative to the market served enter into the consideration. If there is only one department store in a small city which is well-isolated from others, that store is large relative to its market area although in absolute terms it will not compare with Macy's in New York or Marshall Field and Company in Chicago. The store in question may still be too small to carry the variety of goods which customers would like to have available. Even if the store were considered by the courts to be engaged in interstate, rather than intrastate, commerce, the social welfare would be unlikely to be promoted by antitrust action even if price markups were excessive. If the department store were dissolved into two competing units, each would be of less satisfactory size than the one which previously existed.

If, on the other hand, a firm is large both relative to its market area and in an absolute sense, and if it engages in interstate commerce, its activities may be looked at with more skepticism by the antitrust authorities. Actions which would attract little notice on the part of a small firm may become questionable when engaged in by a large one.[1] This stems from the fact that the effects of such actions are of greater magnitude when carried out by a large firm which is apt to have widespread economic and political power.

WHAT IS A COMMODITY?

One of the many problems faced by the antitrust authorities stems from the practical difficulty of defining "industry" or "product." It is difficult to show conclusively that a particular company has dangerous monopoly power with respect to a commodity when it is hard to say what the commodity is. Would a firm possessing the exclusive right to the production and sale of pearl buttons be considered a monopoly so dangerous as to warrant government prosecution? The answer depends upon whether or not we wish to define "pearl buttons" as a separate commodity category. Or would it be preferable to define "buttons" as the commodity, and say that we should consider the whole button industry? But even here, would a firm possessing effective control over the production and marketing of buttons of all types be a dangerous monopoly from a public-policy point of view? Perhaps not, unless it also controlled the market for zippers. Should the commodity grouping be widened to "fasteners," or something of the sort?

A second major task facing the government, or its advisers, in dealing with this subcategory is the determination of what constitutes sufficient control over the market for a commodity to warrant government intervention. If a single firm possesses exclusive control over the sale of a particular good or service, and the technical characteristics of the industry are such that concentrated control is not necessary, most students would agree that governmental action to curb the monopoly is appropriate. But if government action were limited to this type of situation, there would be little or no government action. What if a single firm controls 90 per cent the market, with the remaining 10 per cent being made up of several small firms? Or what would be the answer if this percentage were 80, 70, 60, or 50? Again, in answering this ques-

[1] This point is made by J. B. Dirlam and I. M. Stelzer in "The DuPont–General Motors Decision: In the Antitrust Grain," *Columbia Law Review,* January, 1958, p. 26.

tion, economic analysis can give no definitive answer. The higher the degree of concentration the greater will be the power of the large concern to raise price and restrict production, but it is usually not clear how much concentration is socially tolerable. Also, it is possible that even when great monopoly power is present such power will actually be used with restraint—though it may be dangerous to rely on this.

In recent years the Federal Trade Commission has been active in publishing "concentration ratios" for American industry. These ratios show the percentage of national output accounted for by the four largest firms in each industry. Extremely high ratios exist, for example, in primary aluminum, automobiles, small arms ammunition, telephone and telegraph equipment, and electric lamps. On the other hand the ratios are very low in such fields as printing, baking, brick and concrete block manufacturing, and metal fabrication.

Although, statistics on concentration are useful, they do not in themselves measure monopoly power and hence are not a direct guide to antitrust action. One of their defects is that they are compiled on a national basis, whereas many firms sell only on a regional or local basis. Concentration of economic power for such firms would not show up in the ratios. In another respect the ratios are too restricted in their area of coverage rather than being too broad. This is true when a significant amount of the commodity is imported. The automobile industry is an example of one in which this would be of some importance.

It is also evident that the degree of measured concentration depends a great deal on how broadly or narrowly the "industry" is defined. This is the same type of problem mentioned in connection with zippers, buttons, and fasteners. Thus the statisticians and antitrust officials really face the same sort of problem, namely, what commodities are actually close substitutes for one another and how many firms actually sell goods which are from an economic point of view, essentially the same thing? In any case, it appears that the current popularity of concentration measurement is related to the recent view that, after all, large size may be an antitrust offense or at least make suspect certain actions which would not cause concern if carried out by smaller companies.

INTENT TO MONOPOLIZE NO LONGER NECESSARY?

The above-mentioned new emphasis on size in relation to market seems to mean that *intent* to monopolize no longer need be proved by the antitrust officials in cases falling under the Sherman Act.[1] Instead, the evidence of market domination may be circumstantial in nature and need not involve "predatory" practices. The *ability* to monopolize or strong indirect evidence of collusive action may be enough. For example, in the 1946 American Tobacco decision there was a judicial finding of conspiracy among three tobacco companies to fix prices even though there was no direct evidence of collusive price fixing. The main evidence was circumstantial, hinging on the manner in which prices charged by the companies moved together. Prices of relatively standardized commodities can easily move in similar patterns without explicit agreement each time a change is made if a practice of "price leadership" is followed. Under this practice there is an implicit or explicit "agreement to agree"; when the leader alters price the others automatically match the change. As a consequence of the 1946 tobacco decision the whole practice of price leadership is now a more hazardous one for American industry.

The United Shoe Machinery case of 1953 seems also to reflect this new antitrust mood. This company, along with the Aluminum Company of America, had long been used by economics professors as an example of a firm with much monopoly power. The United Shoe Machinery Corporation produced 75 to 95 per cent of the shoe machinery manufactured in the country and followed the practice of leasing rather than selling the machinery to shoe manufacturers, thus preventing the growth of competition from secondhand shoe machinery. (In the automobile industry the secondhand market offers competition—of a sort—to new car sales.) In the decision reached in this case, the corporation was not found to be guilty of predatory practices, but was found instead to have followed normally aggressive business procedures. Nevertheless, the extent of market domination was deemed to be excessive, and United Shoe Machinery was ordered to offer its machinery for sale on terms that would not substantially favor leasing, and was not permitted leases in excess of five years. In addition to creating a secondhand market for shoe machinery, this court order promoted the growth of independent repair services, since previously the company had tied in repairs with its rental contracts.[2]

[1] It is not possible to make positive statements in this field because judicial opinion can change somewhat from case to case, especially when important changes in membership occur in the Supreme Court and other important courts. Yet broad shifts in interpretation of the law are significant.

[2] "The Supreme Court, 1953 Term," *Harvard Law Review,* Vol. 68, p. 142 (1954–1955).

A relatively recent example of the rare phenomen of dissolution under the Sherman Act, and one which rivals in magnitude the breaking up of U.S. Steel and American Tobacco in 1911, was the 1952 court action in the case of the Big Five motion-picture producers. Major producers of movies were forced to sell their affiliated theaters. It was decreed that about 1,300 theaters be operated by newly formed theater companies and that over 1,200 theaters be sold to independent exhibitors.[1] This act of dissolution may be viewed as legally enforced "disintegration." The industry was formerly "vertically" integrated, that is, one stage in the production of a commodity (exhibited movies) was controlled by firms at a different stage in the total process, and this type of control was deemed to bring about undue restraint of interstate commerce.

Some Victories over Basing-point Pricing

Since World War II the government has gained important victories over "basing-point" pricing in interstate commerce. The most famous historical example of this pricing scheme was the "Pittsburgh-plus" system used by the steel industry for many years prior to 1924. Under this system, all steel mills in the United States[2] calculated their delivered prices *as if* the steel were all produced in Pittsburgh and delivered by rail. Actually, much steel was produced elsewhere, and a good deal was shipped by water rather than by rail. Nevertheless, steel manufactured in Chicago and shipped by water to Milwaukee was priced as if it had come by rail from Pittsburgh.

The steel industry changed to a "multiple-basing-point system" in 1924 after the Federal Trade Commission ordered it to "cease and desist" from the Pittsburgh-plus practice. Under the revised system several locations in addition to Pittsburgh were designated as basing points. The delivered price in any locality was then calculated by taking the mill price at the *nearest* basing point and adding rail freight from that point to the destination. Although this was an improvement over the economically outrageous "Pittsburgh-plus" system, it still caused many buyers to pay "phantom

[1] Vernon A. Mund, *Government and Business* (New York: Harper & Bros., 1955), 2d ed., p. 237.

[2] Except for a few deviations, especially pertaining to Detroit and Birmingham mills.

freight"—that is, to pay for freight not actually involved in the delivery of steel. This occurred whenever steel was bought from a steel mill which was closer than the nearest basing point. Or it could occur even if the nearest basing point was actually the closest of all mills. In the example used earlier, if Chicago were the nearest basing point to Milwaukee, there would still be phantom freight if the price included railroad transportation from Chicago whereas water shipment actually occurred.

The only system which avoids phantom freight charges is an f.o.b. mill system where actual freight is added to the actual mill price. This system has been used by the steel industry since a 1948 Supreme Court decision which upheld a Federal Trade Commission order to the portland cement industry to "cease and desist" from its multiple-basing-point system. The cement industry, of course, also gave up its basing-point system. Other important industries, such as the corn refining, automobile, gasoline, copper, zinc, and flooring industries, have also made use of basing-point pricing. Most of the important systems have been abandoned, but basing-point pricing is still in effect for some products. Nevertheless, this field is one in which the antitrust authorities can be considered to have won important victories for society.

Mergers vs. the Clayton Act

The Sherman Antitrust Act of 1890 was strengthened in several ways by the Clayton Act of 1914, which had as its main purpose the plugging of certain loopholes which had shown up during the intervening quarter century. Such practices as price discrimination, interlocking directorates, intercompany stockholding, tying contracts, and exclusive-dealer arrangements were declared to be illegal if they lessened competition substantially or created a monopoly.

Congress in 1914 also passed the Federal Trade Commission Act as part of President Wilson's antimonopoly program. This law created the Federal Trade Commission to administer the antitrust program. Many businessmen favored the establishment of the FTC in order to clarify what could, and what could not, be done without violating the law. As has already been noted, however, clear and unchanging rules are hard to enunciate in this tricky field.

Among the more important and spectacular matters with which the Federal Trade Commission is concerned are mergers and acquisitions of companies. These are illegal under the antitrust laws when they tend to create a monopoly or to lessen competition substantially. A great difficulty, however, is that the Commission can institute proceedings against a merger only *after* it has been carried out; it does not have the power to stop even a clearly undesirable merger from occurring. FTC officials feel that this power is needed to make possible effective action against improper mergers. The FTC position appears to be justifiable in that it is very difficult to undo a corporate package once it has been securely tied.

As a consequence of our weak antimerger legislation, we have had several great waves of mergers and acquisitions even since 1914. About 800 mergers occurred in 1920 and, after a dip, the number rose to about 1,200 in 1929. The severe depression of the 1930's reduced activity along this line, but since termination of World War II the number has been climbing again.[1] Large dairy companies have been especially active in acquiring other firms in the same line of business. Coupled with Federal and state controls which so often make price competition in this area illegal, the merger movement in the dairy industry appears dangerous from a social point of view.

INTERCOMPANY STOCKHOLDING: DUPONT AND GENERAL MOTORS

Among the specific prohibitions of the Clayton Act is that of intercompany stockholding where the effect is to create a monopoly or significantly to lessen competition. An interesting victory for the Federal government occurred in this area in 1957 in the DuPont–General Motors case.[2] The government's case was based on the heavy ownership of General Motors stock by the DuPont company and the tying effect of this intercompany stockholding on the auto manufacturing firm's purchases of materials.

At the time of the trial the DuPont firm owned 23 per cent of the outstanding GM stock, but the percentage had been as high as 36 in the early 1930's. In addition, members of the DuPont family had substantial holdings in the same stock. Shortly after World War I, Pierre DuPont was chairman of the board of General Motors, but in recent decades there had apparently been considerable independence on the part of GM directors. It was, however, decided by the Supreme Court that sufficient evidence existed of strong influence on the buying policy of the colossus of the

[1] Federal Trade Commission, *Report on Corporate Mergers and Acquisitions* (Washington: U.S. Government Printing Office, May, 1955).

[2] Information about this case has been taken from J. B. Dirlam and I. M. Stelzer, *op. cit.*

automobile industry by the giant chemical company—especially with regard to body paint and fabrics—so that the intercompany stockholding should be eliminated. This is another example in which definition of the commodity in question is important in shaping opinion as to the state of competition. "Automobile finishes" were considered to be distinct from paint in general. Otherwise General Motors' purchases would have appeared to constitute an unimportant part of DuPont's paint output.

An Appraisal

In recent years our antitrust program has been increasingly effective. Some noteworthy successes have been attained, expecially with regard to basing-point pricing, price leadership, patent monopoly, intercompany stockholding, and sheer size in relation to markets. This is not to say that society can rest on its antitrust oars, since any accomplishments constitute only a small fraction of what needs to be done in the constant battle against unduly restrictive monopoly. Frequently many years of costly legal battle are involved in a single antitrust action. On the other side of the ledger, however, is the fact that the very existence of the antitrust laws, together with costliness of antitrust defense, undoubtedly prevents businessmen from engaging in many privately gainful, but socially objectionable, activities which they could otherwise enter with impunity.

8

DEMAND FOR LABOR SERVICES

In Chapter 1, the wheel of income was employed to provide a broad, general, and simplified view of interdependence in the economy. This wheel of income is reproduced in Figure 8.1. The private-enterprise economy is essentially a two-market system. The first market consists of activities of private individuals or families as purchasers and business enterprises (firms) as sellers. This is sometimes called the market for final products and services, and it is shown as the upper half of the income wheel. The preceding chapters have been almost exclusively devoted to an analysis of the forces determining the prices of these products and services, which represent outputs of business units and inputs to private households. In order for the income wheel to be brought to full circle, there remains the important task of analyzing the forces which determine the prices of services for which the roles of buyers and sellers are reversed. The lower half of the income wheel depicts the second market, one in which private individuals are the sellers and business firms are the purchasers. For the most part, private individuals sell services to business firms, by far the most important of which are labor services in their various forms.

FIGURE 8.1. THE WHEEL OF INCOME

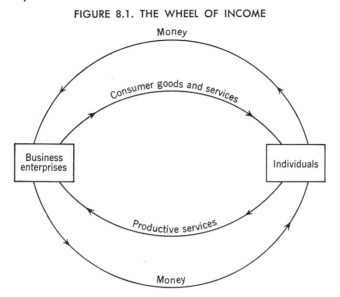

Labor services are not the only services sold by individuals, however; the services of capital goods of various types—land, buildings, machinery, etc.—are also sold. Individuals may, of course, either sell the services of a capital good to a firm, as is done when a building is leased annually, or sell the capital good directly, as is done when the building is purchased outright by the firm. Even in the latter case, the amount which the firm is willing to pay for the building will be based on its estimate of the value of the services which the building will render in the future.

The major distinction between labor and the other types of productive factors, which may all be grouped together and called "capital," is that the outright purchase alternative does not exist in the case of labor. A firm can only hire labor services; it cannot purchase a laborer outright. It could do this only if slavery were legal.[1]

The services or resources sold by individuals to firms constitute inputs to the firms and outputs of private households. This wheel-of-income approach is oversimplified, however, and account must be taken of the fact that not all inputs of firms are purchased

---

[1] There are some exceptions in which laborers are actually purchased in an economic sense. The example that conveniently comes to mind is that of professional baseball players. Under the famous and much debated reserve clause, players' contracts are freely purchased and sold among the various clubs. Even here, however, the athlete cannot be forced to play (although failure to do so may end his baseball career).

from private individuals. Significant portions of the total inputs of firms are at the same time outputs of other firms. The products which are not outputs of the household sector but which do serve as inputs of firms may be called "intermediate" products. The behavior of firms selling this type of product is not essentially different from that of firms supplying products and services directly to final consumers. The behavior of firms purchasing intermediate products is no different from that of firms purchasing productive inputs from private individuals. Hence, there is no need for separate discussion of the determination of intermediate-product prices.

While not all inputs of firms are outputs of private individuals, neither are all outputs of private individuals inputs for firms. Many individuals, for example, medical doctors, lawyers, dentists, and baby sitters, sell productive services directly to other private individuals. The demand for such services is in all respects similar to the demand for final consumer goods sold by firms. The supply of these services sold directly is of the same nature as that of labor services sold to firms. For our purposes, therefore, we can analyze the input market *as if* all inputs to firms were outputs of individuals, and *as if* all outputs of individuals were inputs to firms.

It will be found that the prices of inputs are determined by the forces of demand and supply, just as are the prices of outputs. The reversed roles of the demanders and suppliers, however, create some fundamental differences in the analysis and make a special examination of input markets necessary. This analysis of input or productive-service prices has sometimes been called "distribution theory," since in a free-enterprise economy the forces which determine the prices of productive services at the same time determine the distribution of income. Again a glance at the wheel of income is useful in showing that the payments made by firms to the owners of productive services are the personal incomes of the owners of these inputs. The income that any individual can earn in a free-enterprise economy is determined by the *amount* of productive services (inputs) which he has to sell to firms and by the *prices* at which he can sell these services. As a matter of fact, by far the most important price to almost any individual is the price at which he can sell his productive capacity, and, for most individuals, this means his labor services. This single price outweighs in significance to him any price which he pays as a buyer in any final-product market.

The prices for input units may be determined by the interplay of competition among firms for inputs on the buying side and by competition among individual sellers of inputs on the selling side. To the extent that we have concerned ourselves in previous chapters with the firm's attempt to maximize profits, we find that we have already analyzed to some degree the firm's behavior in buying inputs. As a matter of fact, the behavior of a firm can always be analyzed in two separate ways. The first is by concentrating on output units, the second by concentrating on input units.

In one sense, the output decisions of firms may be considered as primary and the input decisions as derivative, for consumers' choices in final-product markets determine which outputs will yield profits and which losses. Consumers' choices guide the firms in their decisions concerning what is to be produced. This is the working out of the principle of consumers' sovereignty discussed in Chapter 1. Firms' demand for input units is derived from their decisions concerning what to produce, how to produce, and how much to produce. The demand for productive services may, therefore, be called a *derived* demand, since it stems from the final consumers' demand for the product which that input will help to produce. There exists a demand for coal miners because there is a demand for coal; as the demand for coal increases, so does the demand for miners. A demand for shoemaking machinery exists because of the demand for shoes. If everyone suddenly started going barefoot, the demand for shoemaking machinery would vanish. When beaver hats went out of style, the demand for beaver hunters was reduced, and the total income of those engaged in beaver hunting was depressed.

In analyzing the pricing of inputs or productive services, we shall find that a distinction must be made between the competitive and the monopoly cases, just as in the pricing of final products. This chapter and the next will discuss the formation of prices for input units when the buying and selling sides of the market are both fully competitive. This requires that there be sufficient numbers of both buyers and sellers for no one to exert control over the price. Firms, as buyers, must accept market-determined supply prices; individuals, as sellers, must accept market-determined demand prices.

Before firms' demand for inputs can be thoroughly examined, the nature of the production process itself must be recalled. All firms perform the task of transforming input units into output units. In accomplishing this transformation they attempt to secure a profit. The process of transformation involves the combining of several types of input in varying amounts in such a way as to produce one or several types of outputs. A laundry combines water, soap, starch, machines, labor, buildings, paper, and a bundle of dirty clothes and transforms them into a nicely starched bundle of clean clothes. A delivery concern combines labor, trucks, gasoline, oil, street surface, and packages in downtown locations and transforms these into packages on your doorstep.

Almost without exception, the individual firm is faced with alternative ways of combining inputs to produce the same output. The problem of choice is present, since one input unit may be substituted for another. The firm is faced with two basic decisions: (1) how to combine input units to produce any output at the lowest possible cost and (2) how much output to produce. The answers to both of those questions will clearly depend, in part, upon the prices of the various productive services which serve as inputs to firms.

The Demand for Labor

THE LAW OF DIMINISHING RETURNS

Just as we did in discussing costs of production, we shall find it helpful to take certain inputs as fixed. Let us suppose that a firm has made certain currently irrevocable decisions concerning how much of all types of inputs to employ except one. We shall call these "fixed factors," and the payment for them represents "fixed costs." The one input which may be varied we shall call the "variable factor." It should be emphasized that this may be any of the various types of input. For the sake of convenience, we shall call it "labor" and call the fixed input "capital." If the fixed capital is in the form of land, our assumption could imply that we have a given amount of land, say 10 acres, and we may cultivate the plot of land with 1, 2, 3, 10, 100, or n workers. The proportions between land and labor are variable. As we add successive units of the variable factor to the fixed factor, the total output, or product, will perhaps increase at an increasing rate for a while, but soon it will start increasing at a decreasing rate and will ultimately reach a maximum. This may be stated differently as follows: The *additional* product resulting from the use of additional units of the variable factor may for a time increase, but soon the additional product resulting from the use of an additional unit of the variable factor will begin to diminish and will become successively smaller as more units are added. This principle is called the law of variable proportions or the law of diminishing returns. It is a physical law, not an economic one, although it is extremely important for economic analysis. Although no fully satisfactory proof of the law has been devised, it appears to be universally true. Partially satisfactory proofs have been provided, based both on empirical evidence and on deductive logic. It has been observed, for example, that food concentrates may be used to increase the output of milk from a dairy cow, but after a point the additional output resulting from additional units of concentrate diminishes.

Once having stated the law of variable proportions, or diminishing returns, we need to make use of it in deriving a firm's demand curve for units of a given type of input. Perhaps the best approach will be to take as an example a wheat farmer of classical Greece, where the monetary unit was wheat. Given a plot of land fixed in size, how many units of the variable factor, labor, would this Grecian farmer desire to purchase at all possible prices? Suppose the production function (the relation of output to input) were that shown in Table 8.1.

Table 8.1. Production Function of a Grecian Farm

Number of laborers applied to a given amount of land	Total product per year, bushels	Marginal product, bushels
0	0	
1	700	700
2	1,050	350
3	1,250	200
4	1,350	100
5	1,400	50

If the wheat farmer were a competitive purchaser of labor, as is assumed in this chapter, he would have no control over the wage rate. Labor would be available to him at a given wage, and he could hire as much or as little as he desired. It can easily be seen from the production function of Table 8.1 that if the wage rate were more than 350 bushels per year, but below 700, only one worker would be employed. The addition of a second worker adds only 350 bushels to total product, and, unless this amount were greater than the wage, it would not pay to hire a second man. At any wage less than 350 but more than 200, two workers would be hired, and so on. These results may be found most di-

FIGURE 8.2. THE DEMAND FOR LABOR—Is
Based on Its Marginal Productivity

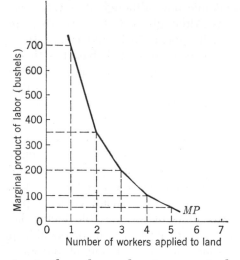

rectly by referring to the column showing marginal product. Similar to all marginal concepts in economics, the marginal product is defined as the addition to the total product as an additional unit of variable factor is added. The marginal product schedule becomes the farmer's demand schedule for labor. This is illustrated geometrically in Figure 8.2.

The demand curve for the variable input factor is found to slope down to the right, just as did the demand curve for a final product. The inverse relation between quantity demanded and price still holds. There is a fundamental difference, however, between this and the downsloping demand curve for a consumer's good. There the downslope was based on a consumer's desire for the good, which diminished in intensity as more of the good was purchased. Here the downslope is based upon a much less subjective phenomenon—the objective physical law of declining marginal produce, or diminishing returns.

THE MARGINAL REVENUE PRODUCT

The wheat farmer of classical Greece was employed in our example because wheat, the output produced, was also money in the civilization. To make the example more realistic and up to date, but unfortunately somewhat more complex, we must introduce money into the picture. A modern wheat farmer does not pay wages in wheat money; rather he sells his wheat for a money return and purchases the labor which he employs for a money wage. The curve of declining marginal physical product derived by adding more units of the variable factor to the fixed factor no longer constitutes a demand curve. The additional physical output of successive workers must be translated into money terms. If the wheat farmer is also selling in competition, as is usually the case, he can sell any amount of wheat at a given price per bushel. If the production function were identical with that of the Grecian farmer, and the market price of wheat were $2 per bushel, the demand schedule for labor could then be derived by combining the marginal physical product and the price. This is shown in Table 8.2.

Table 8.2. Derivation of Marginal Revenue Product

Number of laborers applied to a given amount of land	Total product per year, bushels	Marginal product, bushels	Marginal revenue, price	Marginal revenue product
1	700	700	$2	$1,400
2	1,050	350	2	700
3	1,250	200	2	400
4	1,350	100	2	200
5	1,400	50	2	100

If the farmer employs one worker, his total revenue is $1,400. The addition of a second worker would add 350 bushels to total product; this 350 bushels could be sold at $2 per bushel. Therefore, the addition of the second worker would add $700 to the farmer's revenue. At any wage above $700 it will not pay to hire the second man; at any wage below $700 it will pay to hire him.

In this case, the demand curve is derived from both the law of diminishing returns and the price of the product. The multiplication of marginal physical product by marginal revenue per unit (which is the same as price per unit, since output is sold competitively) gives "marginal revenue product." It represents the addition to the farmer's revenue resulting from the addition of an input unit.

The marginal revenue product curve derived from the schedule in Table 8.2 is shown in Figure 8.3. Although this curve is based on a combination of both the marginal physical product of the input and the price of the output, its downslope is due solely to the law of diminishing returns, just as before. This is because the price at which the output may be sold remains fixed, since we

FIGURE 8.3. THE MARGINAL REVENUE
PRODUCT CURVE

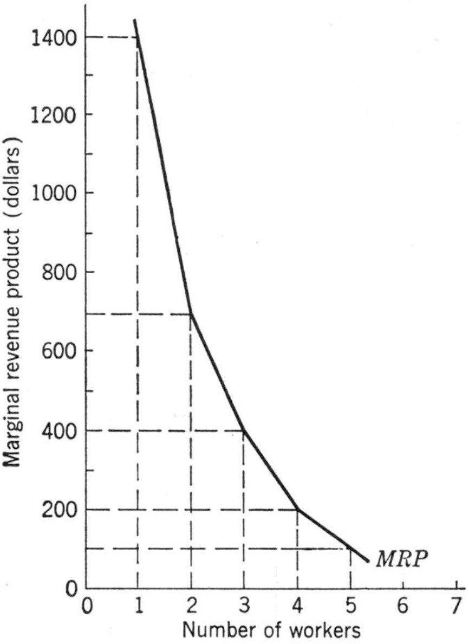

assumed that the wheat farmer was selling his product in a competitive market.

If, however, the firm purchasing inputs should be a monopolist on the output side, the corresponding marginal revenue product curve would have a downward slope for an additional reason. Suppose, for example, that the wheat grown by this farmer has certain unique curative properties. Not only would the law of diminishing returns be operative, but, in addition, the demand price at which output could be sold would decline as more output units were put on the market. This may be illustrated in Table 8.3. The production function is identical with that in the two earlier

Table 8.3. Marginal Revenue Product for a Monopolist

Number of laborers applied to a given amount of land	Total product per year, bushels	Marginal product, bushels	Price per bushel	Total revenue	Marginal revenue product
1	700	700	$4.00	$2,800	$2,800
2	1,050	350	3.50	3,675	875
3	1,250	200	3.20	4,000	325
4	1,350	100	3.00	4,050	50
5	1,400	50	2.75	3,850	−200

schedules. But now instead of being able to sell as much wheat as he desires at a fixed market price per bushel, the farmer finds that the more he wishes to sell the lower the price he must accept. He can market the first 700 bushels for $4 per bushel but must lower the price to $3.50 in order to sell 1,050 bushels, to $3.20 to sell 1,250 bushels, to $3 to sell 1,350 bushels, and to $2.75 to sell 1,400 bushels.

The marginal revenue product has the same meaning as before. It is the addition to total revenue which results from employing an additional input unit. It constitutes the demand curve for the variable factor, as in the earlier example. Algebraically, however, it is no longer equal to the marginal physical product multiplied by the price of output. From a glance at the schedule in Table 8.3, it is apparent that the marginal physical product resulting from the addition of the second man multiplied by the price at which the output produced by two men could be sold would be $350 \times \$3.50$, or $1,225. This figure is sometimes referred to as the value of the marginal product. But the employment of the second worker would not increase the monopolistic firm's total revenue by $1,225, but by only $875. This is because, for the extra 350 units to be sold, a price 50 cents lower per unit must be accepted on the first 700 units. So the actual addition to total revenue is
$$(350 \times \$3.50) - (700 \times \$0.50) = \$875$$

Input Analysis for the Firm

A firm which seeks to maximize profits and which is buying inputs competitively will purchase input units up to the point where the added income due to hiring another input unit is equal to the price of the input. The equilibrium position in terms of the purchase of input is, therefore, represented by the equality of the marginal revenue product and the price of the input. This may be shown geometrically in Figure 8.4, where D represents the marginal revenue product curve of the variable input to the firm. If the input price is OP_1 regardless of the number of units hired (as is the case when input is bought competitively), OX units of input will be employed. If less than OX units were employed, the addition to revenue caused by adding another input unit would exceed the cost of employing that unit. If employment were expanded beyond OX, the addition to revenue would be less than the cost of employing the additional unit. Consequently, the proper input is OX.

The curve D may also be used to show how the firm's employ-

FIGURE 8.4. FIRM USES FEWER INPUT UNITS—
When Input Price Increases

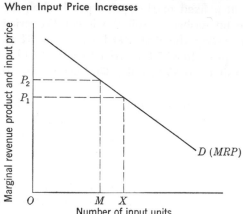

ment of input units will vary as input price varies. If this price
increases from OP_1 to OP_2, the firm's employment of this particular
type of input will drop to OM. The marginal revenue product
curve is the short-run demand curve of the firm for the productive
factor which is considered as variable. Employment will fall to
OM at price OP_2 only if the other factors of production *remain
fixed.* There are no fixed factors of production in the long run.
Given sufficient time to make all adjustments, the firm may be
motivated by the input price increase to shift both the scale and
the method of its operations.

This point may be illustrated by a simple example. Suppose the
firm depicted in Figure 8.4 is a large 10-cent store. When renting
the building and purchasing the inventory stock, the firm's management was required to make a rough prediction about the average
level of wages which the firm would have to pay its prospective
employees—clerks, janitors, etc. Let us assume that the prediction was made that the average wage rate for clerks would be
that shown by OP_1. The size of the inventory stock, the number of
departments, the number of items to be stocked, the opening and
closing hours, and numerous other variables were originally set
on the assumption that clerks' wages would remain at OP_1. The
firm considered itself to have attained the "least-cost combination"
of inputs for its expected market situation. Now let us suppose
that these wage rates go up to that represented by OP_2. This
may have happened for several reasons; for example, a missile
plant may have been constructed in a nearby town, increasing all
wage rates in the surrounding territory. With the increase in clerks'

wages to OP_2, employment will be reduced from OX to OM within a reasonably short period of time after the wage increase. Clerks who are retained may be required to take care of a larger average number of sales counters. The goldfish clerk may now also have to sell parakeets and parasols.

Since the number of departments, capital equipment, etc., were all originally determined on the assumption that the wage rate OP_1 would remain unchanged, new plans will be made now that the wage rate has risen. Until it makes the necessary adjustments, the firm will not have reestablished the least-cost combination of inputs. First, labor-saving devices may be introduced. Self-service may be allowed to replace some clerks through installation of machines which vend soft drinks, for example. Second, the scale of operations may be varied; some departments may be dropped altogether, and those which continue to be operated may include fewer items of merchandise. Opening hours may be moved from 8 to 9 A.M., and the store may be open only one night rather than two nights a week. Given sufficient time for the management to shop around, it may even be that a smaller building will be rented. After all these adjustments are made, it appears most likely that the employment of clerks will be reduced even more than it was in the short run. Given time for full long-run adjustment, employment will probably fall below OM in Figure 8.4. The firm's demand curve for this type of labor is likely to be more elastic in the long run than in the short run. This conclusion applies generally to all input factors; the demand curve is more elastic in the long run than in the short run.

A change in the price of the variable input is not, of course, the only thing that would cause a firm to modify its employment of the other factors of production. The price of any of these other factors may change, and this would encourage the firm to purchase more or less of such factors. And this, in turn, would independently change the demand curve for the factor initially considered as variable.

Let us make this point clearer by reference to our 10-cent-store case. Let us assume that the firm is operating initially as before with OX clerks employed and that the wage rate is OP_1. Figure 8.5 shows this situation. Now let us suppose that the firm has a chance to rent a larger, air-conditioned building on a more centrally located street in the town for the same monthly payments now being made for the building currently occupied. After the move to the new quarters is complete, the marginal revenue productivity

FIGURE 8.5. DEMAND FOR LABOR INCREASES
—With Increase in Capital

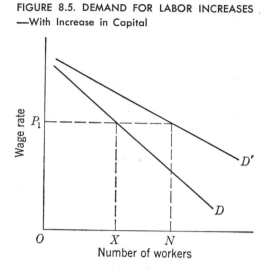

of clerks shifts upward. The new demand curve is shown by D' in Figure 8.5. If the wage rate for clerks remains at OP_1, employment will be increased from OX to ON. The increase in the value of the cooperating factors, in this case represented by a larger and better building and a more efficient location, has served to increase the demand for labor.

Market Demand for Productive Services

We have shown how the individual firm's demand curve for an input factor is derived. This is all that is required as a basis for the next step, that of deriving the market demand curve. In the case of consumer goods, we found that the market demand curve for any product was derived by the addition of the demand curves of all individual consumers. The same process is necessary for productive services. The preceding analysis has been concerned with the demand curve of an individual firm in a competitive buying position. To arrive at the total market demand curve for any given input factor it is necessary to add up the demand curves, *i.e.*, marginal revenue product curves, of all individual firms purchasing the input.[1]

[1] A logical difficulty arises, however, when this is attempted. For in deriving the marginal revenue product curve for an individual firm that sells its output in competition, the price of output is held constant. But if all firms in a competitive industry expand by hiring more units of the variable factor, then industry output expands, and the price of the output falls. While the price of output

The position of the market demand curve for a productive service depends on the total amount of cooperating factors present, just as does the demand curve for the individual firm. The greater the amount of cooperating resources in the economy, the higher will be the demand curve for a productive factor. This is the same as saying that the "productivity" of the factor is higher, the greater the amount of other factors present. The simple recognition of this fact goes a long way toward explaining the differential rates of return in separate geographical areas. For example, the productivity of labor (taking the whole labor force in this simple case) is higher in the so-called "developed" countries than in the so-called "undeveloped" countries primarily because the average amount of capital equipment per worker is much greater in the former. One primary explanation for the continually increasing productivity of the American labor force is found in the continued additions to the country's capital stock, *i.e.*, in net capital formation.

---

would not fall as a result of one firm's expansion, it will fall as the whole industry expands. It suffices here to point up this difficulty; little more could be added by a more extensive discussion. If there are monopoly output sellers among the competitive input purchasers, there arises no difficulty in adding their marginal revenue product curves. This is because the variations in output price as input changes are already taken into account in the marginal revenue product curves.

9

COMPETITIVE DETERMINATION
OF WAGE RATES

The prices of productive services, like other prices, are determined by the interactions of the forces of demand and supply. In Chapter 8, we discussed the demand side when purchasers are in competition for inputs. Account must now be taken of the supply side of the picture in the situation where the suppliers of productive services sell competitively. In dealing with the demand side, we were concerned with the behavior of firms which, we may assume, seek to maximize profits. On the supply side, however, we must examine the behavior of individuals, and here it often is not clear just what they are trying to maximize. Since labor services are by all odds the most important input supplied to firms by individuals, we shall first consider the behavior of individuals in putting labor services on the market.

Supply of Labor Services in the Short Run

Once we know the market demand schedule or curve for labor services of a given type, we need to derive a functional relation-

FIGURE 9.1. SUPPLY CURVE FOR LABOR SERV-
ICES—May Be Vertical for an Individual

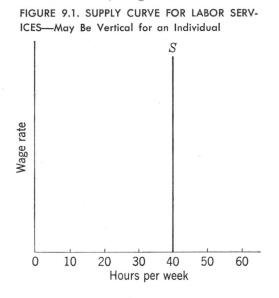

ship between quantity supplied and price, *i.e.*, a supply schedule
or curve, if we are to determine the price of this service. However,
no clearly defined relationship of this sort exists. In the first place,
custom, tradition, and legal and institutional restrictions largely
set the number of hours of work for most individuals. Even if desires to work more or less were present, these could not be readily
fulfilled. A relatively small proportion of the total labor force is
able to change substantially the number of hours worked in response to an increase in the wage rate. If there is no possibility
of response, the supply curve of labor services for an individual
is represented by a vertical line at the traditional number of hours,
say a 40-hour week. This is illustrated in Figure 9.1.

In the second place, even if individuals are free to vary the
amount of work done in response to changes of the wage rate,
and everyone does possess such freedom in some degree through
his power of determining how often he will be absent, "sick,"
etc., it is not clear just what the nature of the response will be.
An increase in the hourly wage rate enables an individual to
earn the same income with fewer hours of work, and, if he enjoys
leisure (or dislikes work), he may well decide to work less as a
result of a wage increase. On the other hand, each hour's leisure
will cost him more in terms of sacrificed income. Leisure will be
more expensive than before the wage increase, so the worker who
wants to secure the advantages of higher income may work more.

The direction of the response will vary from worker to worker, and it will depend in each case on the individual worker's subjective evaluation of leisure and money income. For many individuals who do possess considerable freedom to work as few or as many hours as they please, the wage rate they are able to earn will have little or no influence on their decision. This is especially true of those people who work in the more agreeable jobs, those who "live to work" rather than "work to live." This group includes many of the professional classes.

One rather peculiar type of response is perhaps worthy of mention here. There is some evidence to indicate that, for some groups, more labor services will be offered at higher wage rates than in the low wage ranges, but once the wage rate rises above a certain level, further increases will cause less rather than more work to be offered.

Since no universally applicable relationship exists between the amount of labor services supplied and the wage rate, the best representation of a short-run supply curve is probably the vertical line which we have used in the fixed-supply case. For most problems which economic analysis is called on to answer, this extremely rough approximation is sufficient. As of a given moment, there is a relatively fixed number of workers in the total labor force. The approximation becomes more acceptable and useful when particular occupational and geographical segments of the labor force are studied. There is a fixed number of plumbers in a particular town at any given date, for example, and the quantity of plumbing services supplied does not change greatly in a short time period, even should wage rates change.

If the assumption of fixed supply is accepted, the short-run determinant of the price of labor (the wage rate) is the demand for labor (marginal revenue productivity). The equilibrium wage rate for any kind of labor is established at the point where the total market demand curve for that type of labor intersects the supply curve. This is shown graphically in Figure 9.2.

OW represents the equilibrium wage rate which will tend to be established in the market when there are OX workers of this occupational category. That is, OW represents the equilibrium wage rate provided that the market for this type of labor service is competitive on both the buying and selling sides. It is the equilibrium wage rate, because this is the only rate which will cause all the workers to be employed and at the same time allow business firms to be purchasing as much of this type of labor as they desire at

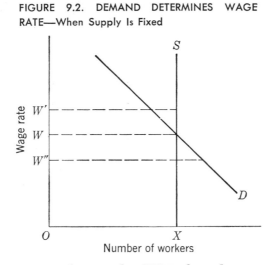

FIGURE 9.2. DEMAND DETERMINES WAGE RATE—When Supply Is Fixed

the going wage. In other words, *OW* is the only wage rate which clears the market, or makes the quantity demanded equal to the quantity supplied. It may be seen that at any wage rate above *OW*, say *OW′*, the amount of labor demanded by the market would be less than the amount offered. Therefore, those workers who would remain unemployed would offer to work for less than *OW′*, and wages would fall. On the other hand, if the wage rate were below *OW*, say *OW″*, there would be more workers demanded than would be available. Business firms would find it advantageous under these circumstances to increase wage rates, and as a result the wage rate would tend to increase to *OW*.

If the supply of labor of the type depicted increased, this would be represented by a shifting to the right of the fixed-supply curve, and if conditions of demand did not also change, this would cause a reduction in the equilibrium wage rate. Conversely, if supply were reduced without a change in demand, the equilibrium wage rate would go up.

The Long-run Supply of Labor

Although the assumption of a fixed supply is perhaps most appropriate for short-run analysis, whether applied to the whole labor force or only to a particular segment, this assumption is clearly not appropriate when longer period considerations are taken into account. The size of the labor force, as well as the occupational and geographical groupings within that force, is continually changing. We must now examine the relationship between the long-run changes in the size of the labor force and the level of wages and salaries.

THE CLASSICAL THEORY

The classical economists of the early nineteenth century developed a famous theory concerning the long-run supply of labor. They reasoned in the following way: If the wage rate for common labor should rise much beyond the level which allows laborers barely to subsist, there would be a tremendous increase in the number of children, and in the long run the size of the labor force would be increased enough to bring wages down to subsistence levels again. On the other hand, if wages should fall temporarily below the level required for the common laborer to live and support his family, famine and pestilence would be widespread, and the number of laborers would be reduced sufficiently to bring wages again to the subsistence level. This is the familiar theory of population promulgated by Thomas Malthus. It is graphically depicted in Figure 9.3.

The Malthusian theory of the long-run supply of labor has been fairly well discredited by this time, at least as applied to the world of Western civilization although it may still be substantially correct for certain other areas of the world. There are occasional references to the doctrine, and some neo-Malthusians still are found, but, for the most part, the direct dependence of the total

FIGURE 9.3. LONG-RUN SUPPLY OF LABOR
—As Viewed by the Classical Economists

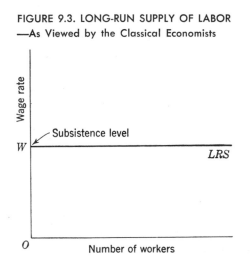

supply of labor upon the level of wages has been refuted, both empirically and deductively. Economists in recent years have generally left the theory of population to the sociologists, because of the fact that non-economic forces are more important in determining the rate of increase in population than those factors which are purely economic in nature. Economic forces, however, are still important and should not be overlooked, although the relationships are sometimes remote and difficult to trace. A recent example to indicate that economic forces still loom large in affecting the rate of change in population is the temporary decline in the rate of population increase in the 1930's, which must be largely attributed to the great depression. The sharp increase in the United States birth rate during and after World War II is probably traceable in part to the favorable employment opportunities and prospects.

LONG-RUN SUPPLY FOR SINGLE OCCUPATIONS

Although little can be said about the relationship between the long-run rate of increase in total population, and thus the size of the over-all labor force, and the level of wages, this is not true for different occupational categories. There are distinct relationships between the size of a particular segment of the labor force and the wage or salary rate in that occupation relative to other occupations. For example, if the wages of bricklayers increase relative to those of plasterers, there will not be much shifting between the two occupations in the short run. But given a sufficient time period, the increased wages of the bricklayers will (in the absence of restrictions) attract more apprentices to that trade relative to the other, and the supply offered will increase. Thus, the supply curve for bricklayers in the long run may be represented as being relatively flat in the neighborhood of the wage rate offered for jobs requiring similar degrees of skill and of about the same nature. This will be true, of course, only if workers may freely enter and leave occupational groups. Figure 9.4 represents this sort of supply curve.

If the wage for bricklayers fell below *OW*, there would be no workers willing to work in this business if a long enough time were considered. Of course, there would be workers willing to work for less than *OW* for a considerable period—those who had been trained in this occupation, especially if they had worked in it for a long time. But as new workers offered themselves for employ-

FIGURE 9.4. LONG-RUN SUPPLY OF BRICK-
LAYERS—Depends on Wages in Alternative
Occupations

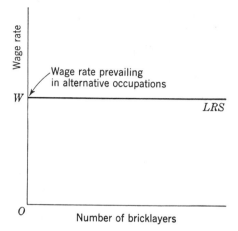

ment, none would become bricklayers, and ultimately no one
would be willing to work for less than the wage *OW*, since he
could earn more in similar work elsewhere.

A decrease in the demand for bricklayers, due perhaps to the increased utilization of concrete block, would have the effect in the
short run of reducing bricklayers' wage rates. But in the long run,
as bricklayers shifted to other occupations and no new apprentices
entered the trade, the wage rate would rise again to a level comparable to that of other generally similar occupations such as pipe
fitters, plasterers, and carpenters. Both the short- and long-run
adjustments may be illustrated in Figure 9.5.

Suppose *OW* is the wage rate, *OX* the initial number of workers,
and D_1 the market demand curve for bricklayers. A reduction in
demand, represented by the leftward shift of demand to D_2, then
occurs. Since the supply in the short run is fixed at *OX*, the wage
will have to fall to *OW'* if all the workers are to remain employed.
But if other occupational groups have not been affected by the
same forces which caused this change in demand, the supply
curve for bricklayers will shift to the left as workers leave the occupation and as new workers fail to replace those who retire.
As the short-run supply curve shifts to the left, the equilibrium
wage rate will tend to increase and will continue to do so until it
is again approximately *OW*. The new final equilibrium will be
reached when the number of bricklayers is represented by *OX'*
and the wage rate is *OW*, which is equivalent to that earned in

FIGURE 9.5. SHORT-RUN AND LONG-RUN
ADJUSTMENTS IN WAGE RATES

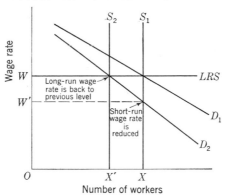

similar occupations. The long-run supply curve is represented by
a horizontal line at the original wage—the line *LRS* in Figure
9.5. Just as we observed in analyzing price formation in competitive product markets (Chapter 4), we find that demand is the
primary determinant of price in the short run and supply is the
primary determinant in the long run.

OCCUPATIONAL DIFFERENCES IN WAGES

If all types of jobs were alike in terms of the agreeableness or
disagreeableness of the work, and if all workers were freely able
to choose among all possible occupational categories, the only wage
differences among occupations would be short-run ones arising
from shifts in demand. Wage differences would all tend to be
eliminated under these conditions by the shifting of workers and
the entry of new workers into the jobs offering the highest rewards.
Obviously, however, neither of these two conditions is approxi-
mated in the real world. Some types of employment are clearly
more desirable than others. Each type carries with it some nonpecuniary attributes, all of which may be summed up in terms
of agreeableness or disagreeableness. Some men prefer farming
because they like the open air and the freedom from supervision
which it offers. Others may prefer a more routine job; they can
put in their eight hours and forget about it. Few men choose to
become racing-car drivers, because of the personal dangers involved. In some jobs, the length of the earning period is longer,
making those jobs more attractive than others. All these factors
operate to make for permanent differences in wage or salary rates
among occupational groups.

Even if the second condition, that workers can freely choose among all occupational categories, were fulfilled, permanent differences among occupational groups would tend to arise. Under these circumstances, the jobs which people generally deemed to be the most agreeable would be the lowest paid; jobs which people deemed to be least desirable would be the highest paid. If, for example, the wages of schoolteachers and garbage collectors were equal, and if all garbage collectors could become schoolteachers, which is the condition assumed, then all (or at least a substantial proportion of) garbage collectors would become schoolteachers. School boards would find that they could lower teachers' salaries, since the supply had increased, and garbage companies or sanitary commissions would find it necessary to increase the wages of garbage collectors, since the supply had decreased. Under these conditions, schoolteachers would permanently receive lower wages than garbage collectors because people prefer schoolteaching as an occupation to garbage collecting. This type of permanent difference is called an "equalizing difference" in wages. It is a difference in money income or wages which is necessary to equalize the total advantages (pecuniary plus nonpecuniary) to be gained in each of the various occupations. Although this is a far-fetched example, it goes a long way toward explaining the relatively low salaries of schoolteachers. Such salaries are not low primarily because of the fact that schoolteachers in most states are unorganized or that they are employed by a public agency. They are low primarily because schoolteaching is a relatively desirable profession, because entry into the occupation is relatively easy, and because enough people are willing to accept salaries lower than those paid in comparable occupations.

But, of course, the second condition assumed in our example above is not present either. Not all workers are free to choose among all occupational categories. Garbage collectors cannot often become schoolteachers even if they desire to, because they do not have the educational training to enter that profession. The long-run adjustments in supply, therefore, can take place only within occupational groupings in which shifting is possible. For example, in spite of the short earning period, professional baseball playing is considered a highly desirable occupation by most young men. If all men at the age of eighteen could become professional baseball players if they desired, there would probably be so many entering the business that wages would be notoriously low (as they are in the Class D leagues). But the fact is that only

a small proportion of men are able to become top-notch professional baseball players; only this group could enter the profession if they tried. This becomes a "noncompeting" group in the
sense that those outside the group cannot compete with those in
the group in spite of differentials between the total advantages
of this occupation over those of other occupations which might
otherwise make long-run supply shifts come about.

The relative importance of differences in natural abilities and
differences in acquired or environmental characteristics has long
been a much debated question. Plato argued that the division
of labor was mainly attributable to differences in the natural abilities of men. Adam Smith, on the other hand, remarked that the
difference between the "philosopher and a common street porter
. . . seems to arise not so much from nature as from habit, custom,
and education."[1] We do not need, however, to resolve this debate
here. Whether because of differences in natural ability or because
of environmental differences, men cannot freely enter all occupations. Those occupational groups for which the supply is limited
relative to the demand will tend to receive higher wage rates than
will those occupations which are open to almost anyone. The fact
that garbage collectors' wages are not high despite the disagreeableness of garbage collecting can be explained by the fact that
almost any able-bodied worker can become a garbage collector.
There are no educational qualifications necessary and no particular skill is required.

A century ago, the average wage rates of white-collar or clerical
workers were considerably higher than those of manual workers.
This was true in spite of the fact that for most people white-collar
work was more desirable. But educational requirements prevented
more than a small fraction of the total labor force from competing
for white-collar jobs, whereas there were few literacy requirements
for manual work. The advent of public education, however, has
served to break down the restrictive barrier between these two
major occupational groups. A larger and larger fraction of the
labor force has been able to enter the clerical group, with the
result that white-collar wage rates have continually fallen relative to those of manual workers. The breakdown of the educational
barriers formerly separating the groups has allowed the "equalizing" differences to begin to work themselves out. Manual workers
now in many instances receive higher wages than white-collar

[1] Adam Smith, *The Wealth of Nations* (New York: Modern Library, Inc.,
1937), p. 15.

workers. This differential is sometimes fallaciously attributed wholly to the fact that more of the manual workers are organized. This argument overlooks the fact that white-collar work is considered to be more agreeable by many people who are willing, accordingly, to accept lower wages in order to do that type of work.[1]

A fundamental goal of a free society must be that of equalizing opportunity among individuals. One of the major means by which this goal is achieved is by making it possible for individuals to enter the occupations of their choice. If competition prevails in labor markets and if public action to equalize opportunity continues, differences other than the equalizing differences will tend to be gradually reduced. They will not be entirely eliminated, because of the special physical or mental qualifications required in some occupations. As we shall see later, however, the major deterrent to interoccupational adjustments in long-run supply lies in monopoly restrictions on entry imposed by certain occupational groups in an effort to protect their income positions.

GEOGRAPHICAL ADJUSTMENTS IN LONG-RUN SUPPLY OF LABOR

Another important type of adjustment which takes place in the labor force is geographical, and much of what has been pointed out in regard to occupational groups applies geographically as well. If the demand for a particular type of labor increases in a certain area but does not change elsewhere, there will be a migration of labor to the high-wage area. This migration will continue until wage rates are roughly equalized for similar types of jobs. This, of course, is one of the major explanations of the continuing migration of workers from the South to the North. Workers realize that they can earn higher rates of pay in Northern industrial communities than they can on Southern farms. As they migrate North, the average wage rates there are lowered below what they would have been in the absence of migration. As the workers leave the South, Southern wage rates tend to increase above what they otherwise would have been. Thus, the migration tends to promote a long-run equalization of wage rates for similar jobs among geographical regions. This type of long-run adjustment may be illustrated in the diagrams of Figure 9.6.

In Figure 9.6, D_n represents the demand for labor in the North, and S_n the supply of labor initially available in that area. The aver-

---

[1] For a general discussion of interoccupational differences in wages see Milton Friedman and Simon Kuznets, *Income from Independent Professional Practice* (New York: National Bureau of Economic Research, Inc., 1945).

FIGURE 9.6. NORTH-SOUTH WAGE DIFFERENTIAL—Is Reduced by Northward Migration

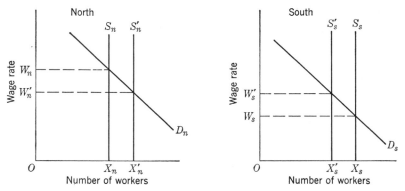

age Northern wage rate is OW_n. On the right-hand side, D_s, S_s, and OW_s represent the demand, supply, and average wage rate in the South. As long as OW_n is substantially greater than OW_s, workers will continue to migrate from the Southern region to the North. This will tend to shift the supply curve for Northern labor to the right, shown by S_n', and the supply curve of Southern labor to the left, shown by S_s'. This migration will tend to lower Northern wage rates and increase Southern wage rates, bringing the two more nearly into an equality with one another. Of course, it should never be overlooked that in analyzing problems of this nature we are still employing our helpmate, *ceteris paribus.* Here we have had to assume that the demand curves for labor in the two regions remained unchanged. Actually the demand (productivity) curve of labor is continually shifting upward in both regions because of increased capital investment and improved technology. With this recognized, it is highly likely that Northern wage rates in general are never actually reduced by in-migration of Southern workers. They continue to increase, but they increase at a slower rate than they would were the South made a separate country and immigration prohibited.

Money wage rates for similar jobs may never be fully equalized in all geographical areas even in the same economy and even if all the adjustments are allowed to take place. Equalizing differences may be present in this sense, also. If Southern workers, on the average, prefer the smell of the sweet magnolias to the hustle and bustle of urban Northern life, they may well decide that life in the South is more agreeable. There will be a nonpecuniary advantage to work in the South. Thus, wage rates in the North might be permanently higher for similar jobs, the difference being necessary to make Northern jobs equally attractive on all counts with Southern jobs. There is no clear evidence, however, that this sort of equalizing difference does explain any or all of the present differences in wage rates in the two areas. The differences which do exist may be more readily explained by the fact that the long-run resource adjustments have not been carried out.

10

LABOR MONOPOLY

We have seen that the effect of monopoly in output markets is to increase profits to the seller and raise prices and reduce the quantity of goods available to the consumer as compared with the situation which would obtain in a competitive market. Sellers, although they may pay lip service to competition, constantly try to differentiate their products in order to give them some power to set prices. Sellers of inputs, or productive services, like sellers of outputs, prefer a monopolistic position to a competitive one. The selling side of the productive-service markets is, as a matter of fact, probably more saturated with monopoly elements than any other sector of the economy at the present time. It is important, accordingly, that the effects of this type of monopoly control be examined. This consists, for the most part, of a consideration of monopoly in the selling of the most important type of input, which is, of course, labor.

Monopoly in the Sale of Productive Services

Monopoly is defined here as before: it is the power of a seller or sellers to influence the selling price. Viewed in this fashion, it is clear that few single sellers of labor services are in a position to act as monopolists in the sale of their services. This position could be attained only in those instances in which a person possesses some extremely unusual and valuable ability or skill. There is, for example, only one Perry Como, and, in the minds of his admirers, there are no close substitutes. In the sale of his services Perry is able to act as a monopolistic seller; he has the power of influencing the price which he can secure for his services.[1]

Usually, an individual offering his labor services independently is forced to accept a given wage, determined either by the market, if the market consists of many buyers, or by the single buyer, if the market is monopsonistically[2] controlled. This lack of control by the individual seller of labor services over his wage (which determines his income position in society) provides an important part of the historical explanation for the growth of labor organizations. The individual worker was felt to be helpless before the impersonal forces of the market, particularly before monopsonistic buyers. The consumer, of course, is also helpless before the impersonal forces of the product market, particularly before monopolistic sellers of output, but this has not provided a rationale for consumer associations to any degree comparable to labor unions. The explanation for these different reactions to similar situations probably lies in the feeling that the consumer is faced with alternative choices in buying, but in many cases the individual worker is faced with virtually no choice at all. In addition, it is difficult to organize consumers because they frequently have directly opposite interests in their roles as producers and consumers; the automobile worker as a buyer would like to see the price of cars kept low, but he is more interested in high wages, and that may not be possible unless automobile prices are high.

In order to combat the "inequality in bargaining power," as the helplessness of the individual worker in dealing with his employer has been called, labor organizations have been established among large groups of workers. With the development of labor unions the

[1] An impression of the profitability of monopoly of this sort may be gained from a report by Hal Humphrey from Hollywood. The fees charged for guest performances for the 1957–1958 TV season are reputed to be $50,000 for a single appearance for Elvis Presley or three for $100,000; $40,000 for Frank Sinatra; and $25,000 each for Marlene Dietrich and Sammy Davis. *The News and Observer,* Raleigh, N.C., August 30, 1957, p. 11.

[2] The word *monopsonist* comes from the Greek words for "single" and "buyer." A monopsonist is a monopolist on the buying side of the market, *e.g.,* the owner of a cotton mill who hires all the spinners and loom-fixers employed in a town.

services of whole groups of workers are sold by a central organization to which all of the employees belong. The union negotiates with the employer concerning the wage rate, hours of work, and other conditions of employment. The individual worker surrenders his price (wage) negotiation power to the union.

It must be recognized from the outset that labor organizations are essentially monopolistic in their economic nature. One of the primary functions of labor organizations, and the main economic function, is to exert some control over wage rates.[1] If this power exists, such organizations must be classified as monopolistic sellers in input markets. A significant difference exists, however, between such institutional sellers of labor services and monopolistic sellers of final products. The sellers of output may be assumed to attempt to maximize profits or net revenue. For labor unions no such simple motivating force may be assumed. In the first place, profit, in the sense applicable to a firm, cannot be calculated for a union since the cost to the individual workers of producing labor services is essentially subjective. The real cost of providing labor services, is, of course, the alternatives sacrificed. These may comprise leisure hours, cultural pursuits, further training, etc. Viewed in this way it is clear that the real cost of laboring varies from worker to worker. The revenue of the union in terms of the total wage bill might be estimated, but profit in the sense of total revenue minus total cost cannot be the magnitude which the labor union seeks to maximize.

POSSIBLE GOALS OF LABOR UNIONS

A possible goal of a labor union might be to maximize the total wage bill. In this case the labor organizations would attempt to set a wage rate at the point where the elasticity of demand for labor is unitary. This is similar to the mineral-spring case discussed in Chapter 2. This wage rate is indicated by OW in Figure 10.1, where D represents the demand for labor. The union would attempt to establish the wage rate OW, and OX would represent the number of workers employed at that rate. The total wage bill will be maximized at this rate. If, however, the number of union members happens to be greater than the number which employers are willing to hire at this income-maximizing wage, the union is not likely to follow this policy rigorously. It still might be the desirable policy for all the workers if those who remained employed at this wage could

[1] It should be emphasized that we are neglecting the non-economic aspects of labor organization. This is not to deny or even to assess the relative importance of the non-economic functions of labor unions.

FIGURE 10.1. POSSIBLE GOALS OF UNION WAGE POLICY

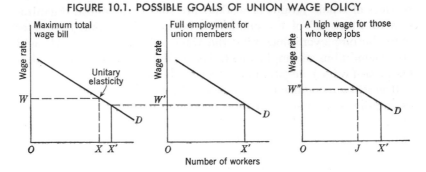

Number of workers

be convinced that they should contribute toward the support of the unemployed members. For example, with reference to the left-hand diagram of Figure 10.1, if the total union membership is represented by OX', the enforcement of a wage of OW would cause XX' members of the union to remain unemployed. But the total wage bill would be greater at wage OW than at the wage at which all the members could find employment. The maximum income per worker could therefore be attained by enforcing the wage rate of OW for OX workers and then collecting sufficient dues from the OX workers to subsidize the XX' unemployed members. But the accomplishment of this feat might require considerably more internal discipline than most unions can muster.

A second, and more probable, goal of labor unions is to secure the highest wage rate consistent with full employment for almost all the union members. Referring to Figure 10.1, middle diagram, suppose that there are OX' workers of a particular type, say, plasterers. If all these workers belong to the union and the union attempts to avoid unemployment among its members, it will try to get a wage rate of OW'. This rate will be the same as would exist in the short run in the absence of unionization. To the extent that the union has been able to restrict membership, however, the wage rate OW' will be above the long-run wage which would result under pure competition. This explains why many unions are anxious to hold down their membership by such means as the closed shop, long apprenticeship, high initiation fees, and similar restrictions.

A third possible goal of union activity is to secure a high wage rate for workers who remain employed, without much consideration either to possible unemployment among union members or to the effect on the total wage bill. This appears to be a common policy in some of the large industrial unions. Under this policy the wage rate may be established at a rate higher than OW, say OW''

of the right-hand diagram, even if there are OX' union members. It is frequently difficult for union leaders to estimate the employment effects of any particular wage increase which the union is striving to secure. The union is then likely to take a chance that employment will be nearly as large at the higher rate as at the lower; union leaders frequently seem to assume that the demand for labor is highly inelastic. An additional reason for the adoption of this wage policy is found in the fact that unions are typically controlled by older members who because of seniority rights would be less likely to be laid off if a considerable volume of unemployment did result from the higher wages.

EFFECTS OF LABOR MONOPOLY

The over-all effects of labor monopoly are much the same as those of output monopoly. The allocation of resources could be improved by a shifting of resources from the unorganized sectors of the economy to the organized sectors of the labor market. Labor monopoly, by restricting the inputs employed in the organized plants and industries, restricts the outputs of firms hiring union labor and increases prices of final products. A redistribution of income is probably effected in favor of unionized workers as compared with the nonunion labor force.

We have been assuming in our analysis that the demand for labor remains roughly constant while supply forces are allowed to shift; demand is among the "other things" assumed to remain the same. If, however, demand does shift, the same general conclusions are forthcoming. The fact that unions were able during the war and postwar periods to increase wages significantly without large-scale cutbacks in employment is largely explained by the continuing upward shift of demand for final products. With an increase in demand for firms' outputs, induced by inflation, firms seek to expand their inputs. If all or most union members are already working, the union will be able to get higher wages and keep most of its workers employed. It is likely to consider this policy preferable to one which would retain the old wage rate and allow new workers to join the union or nonworkers to come on the job. Workers on the inside looking out are not likely to be greatly concerned about the plight of workers on the outside looking in.

Government Policy toward Labor Monopolies

Those who favor strong unions and those who oppose them frequently resort to arguments which are characterized more by passion than by consistency. Foes of the unions, for example, sometimes charge that unions have not, in fact, raised wages, and they point out that in many organized industries wages have not risen as fast as nonunion wages have. These same people, however, are likely to argue that unions are responsible for the wage-price spiral; unions have, they insist, raised wages faster than productivity has increased. Clearly, either unions are responsible for wage increases or they are not; we cannot have it either way depending upon which best serves our immediate purpose. Union leaders, on the other hand, insist that prices go up first and wages must be increased so that workers can maintain their standards of living; high wages, they argue, are not inflationary. But during periods of depression those in the labor movement persistently contend that wages must be increased in order to increase the workers' purchasing power and thus restore prosperity. We can hardly accept the argument that the demands of unions are inflationary when we need a little inflation but not inflationary when inflation is already a threat. Determining suitable public policy in the area of labor monopoly is extremely difficult because we approach the consideration of these problems with preconceived prejudices and sympathies, and the economist's kit of tools, helpful as it is, leaves a number of important questions unanswered.

Partly as a result of the encouragement given to organized labor by the National Labor Relations Act (Wagner Act), which was passed in 1935, the membership of labor unions in the United States increased from less than 4 million in 1935 to over 15 million in 1950. Although less than one-fourth of the total labor force is affiliated with the union movement, 80 per cent or more of workers in such industries as the following work under union agreements: coal mining, construction, railroads, men's and women's clothing, portland cement, aircraft, automobiles, and meat packing. As a result of the increasing strength of organized labor following the enactment of the Wagner Act together with the great loss of man-hours resulting from strikes (during the years from 1945 to 1947 there was an average of over 4,000 strikes per year with an annual loss of more than 62 million man-hours of labor), there was considerable public resentment against labor unions. This led to the passage of the Labor-Management Relations Act (Taft-Hartley Act) in 1947, which attempted to "amend" the Wagner Act by defining certain "unfair labor practices" which unions were forbidden to engage in.

The underlying philosophy of both the Wagner Act and the Taft-

Hartley Act seems to be that it is the function of government to maintain some degree of equality in bargaining power between workers and employers. But as union membership increased, it began to appear to many Americans that the pendulum had swung too far and that, at least in certain basic industries, organized labor now had an unfair advantage in its negotiations with management. Most of the labor legislation enacted by state governments during this period was designed to restrict union activities rather than to foster collective bargaining. Among these laws were the "right-to-work" statutes, which hold that laborers are entitled to engage in lawful work anywhere and under any conditions they choose, and employers are entitled to hire anyone they choose regardless of whether the laborer is a dues-paying union member. The Federal government's "equalizing" function now took the form of setting up a number of forbidden practices on the part of unions which were labeled "unfair" in the Taft-Hartley Act. Among these was the prohibition of the "closed shop," *i.e.*, employment cannot be restricted to union members. (Workers may, however, be forced to join the union within 30 days if a "union shop" has been voted by the employees.) The policy to which we are committed seems to require that the government make a dispassionate determination in the most passionate of all areas of economic conflict as to which side is the weaker, and by strengthening the weak side and penalizing the strong to maintain as great a degree of equality of bargaining strength as possible.

From a moral or ethical point of view, this program has much to commend it. If one side has the right to combine to improve its position, it may be argued that the other side has a similar right. But the economic argument for labor monopoly to bargain with an employers' monopoly is less secure. There may, indeed, be a strong presumption in favor of the view that the wage rate resulting from bilateral monopoly will more nearly approach the competitive level than a wage set by a monopsonist who hires labor in a nonunion market. But this cannot be demonstrated by economic analysis. There is no way of knowing when the opposing forces have been equalized and one monopoly has just neutralized the other.[1] The alternative policies seem to be (1) to attempt to solve the problem of monopoly by creating still more monopoly or (2) to attempt to solve the monopoly problem by eliminating monopoly. One difficulty with the first solution is that it might lead to stalemates,

---

[1] See Fritz Machlup, *The Political Economy of Monopoly* (Baltimore: Johns Hopkins Press, 1952), p. 376.

and if the conflict were resolved by the government's tipping the scales one way or the other, it would incur the ill will of the side which lost, throwing the economic problem into the political arena. Labor, for example, hailed the Wagner Act as its "Magna Charta" but condemned the Taft-Hartley Act as a "stab in the back." The second solution also appears to be impracticable. The dissolution of monopoly, or even the reduction of monopoly power, is difficult. It is extremely unlikely that the reduction of the monopoly power of labor and management could progress at the same rate, but the curtailment of labor monopoly without a corresponding reduction of employers' monopoly power would undoubtedly have significant political repercussions which might make the entire effort unworkable.

The power struggle between big business and big labor is frequently a bitter one. Sometimes, however, there appears to be more of a conspiracy between the two than a struggle, the conspiracy being directed against the consumers. Particularly when national income is rising, employers in oligopolistic industries appear often to accede willingly to union demands for higher wages in order to be able to justify price increases. The existence of high corporate taxes has the effect of reinforcing this tendency. In other cases, there is outright collusion between employers and unions to limit the entry of new firms into a field. This occurs quite frequently in the construction industry, where workers may refuse to work for contractors who are not association members or may be willing to install only materials produced or handled by certain companies.

What generalizations may be made concerning the gains and losses to the economy resulting from the imposition of higher wage rates by labor-union activity? If unions are formed in industries where firms buy labor competitively, higher wages on balance are likely to be injurious. Some laborers gain, but the gain is at the expense of others who are unemployed or whose wages are lowered, at the expense of reduced profits to management, and at the expense of higher prices for consumers. The allocation of resources is distorted, and the real income of society is reduced. If, on the other hand, unions are formed in industries in which firms enjoy monopsony profits which have been gained by paying labor less than the value of its marginal product, labor may gain by appropriating a portion of these profits with no loss to the economy as a whole. How often is this latter case met in reality? This question cannot be definitely answered, but these observations are pertinent:

1. If firms are enjoying monopsony profits, the situation would be

helped by making easier the entry of new firms into the labor market. Unless there are restrictions on such entry, monopsony profits cannot be maintained indefinitely. The entry of new firms would increase the demand for labor, causing wage rates to rise. But the existence of labor unions is likely to retard rather than to encourage the entry of new firms into local areas having an over-supply of labor.

2. If laborers in certain firms are receiving less than the competitive wage rate, an increase in the mobility of labor would improve the situation. Labor unions, unfortunately, by making labor less rather than more mobile, tend to worsen the situation.

3. Even if some firms in an industry enjoy monopsony profits at the expense of labor, it seems unlikely that all firms in a given industry will be in such a sheltered position, and if wages are increased by union activity for the industry as a whole, some firms may be forced out of business, and, while employment in the firms which survive may be greater than before, employment in the industry as a whole may be reduced.

We may conclude that labor organizations do improve the lot of some workers, but, if the gains to unionized labor do not come from increased productivity, they must come at the expense of other elements of the economy. Economic analysis is unable to determine in these cases whether the gain to one group more than offsets the loss to others. About all that can be said with confidence is that, if the alternative to labor unions were perfectly competitive markets for labor as well as for final products, the alternative would unquestionably be preferable.

INDUSTRY-WIDE BARGAINING

We turn our attention finally to a consideration of the effects of industry-wide bargaining. Nationwide strikes have caused considerable public resentment toward labor in recent years, since a work stoppage in steel, coal, automobiles, or rubber has a paralyzing effect on the entire economy, and this is particularly critical in time of national emergency. Whereas a local strike is usually a source of inconvenience and irritation to the local community, an industry-wide strike may jeopardize the security of the entire nation. The ability of a union to declare a strike on a very broad front increases its power, and proposals to outlaw such strikes are made from time to time.

It is more difficult to generalize about the economic effects of industry-wide bargaining than about the effects of wage increases granted to a small local union, because higher wages for an entire industry not only affect costs of production but may have a significant effect on incomes of workers, who represent a substantial fraction of the entire economy. Three preliminary observations may, however, be made:

1. If the workers in a basic industry such as steel obtain a wage increase, that is likely to set the pattern for wages in other industries, and the effect of the wage increase in steel is likely to be much greater than it would have been had only steelworkers been involved.

2. Industry-wide agreements sometimes contain an "escalator" clause, which ties the wage rate to the cost of living; if the living-cost index goes up a prescribed amount, the workers are automatically entitled to a wage boost which will maintain their standard of living. Even when such a clause is not included in the wage agreement, much of the effort of unions is directed toward maintaining or raising their members' living standards. Particularly in times of emergency, when resources are being diverted to the production of military goods, prices rise because of the relative shortage of consumers' goods. Since fewer goods are available, price is performing its proper rationing function; since fewer goods are available, living standards on the average must fall. If organized labor is able, however, to maintain its standard of living by virtue of wage contracts tied to the price level, the full reduction in consumption will have to be borne by those whose money incomes do not keep pace with the rise in prices. This represents, of course, a reallocation of income from nonunion members and consumers who do not depend on labor income (*e.g.*, retired persons) to organized labor.

3. A third fundamental objection to industry-wide bargaining is that it imposes uniform wage rates throughout areas where conditions may not be uniform. Because of labor immobility it is quite likely that within a given industry there may be areas of labor undersupply and other areas where labor is in oversupply. Under competitive conditions a differential in wage rates would result, but if wages must be uniform throughout the industry by virtue of a contractual agreement, some workers in labor-surplus areas will have to seek employment in other industries where they are less productive.

Let us analyze the effects of an industry-wide wage increase in a basic industry on the volume of employment during a period of business recovery. Since the marginal revenue product curve for labor in each firm slopes down from left to right, the immediate effect of a higher wage rate will be a reduction of employment in each firm. This is likely in the short run to retard the rate of recovery for the economy as a whole since the immediate objective is to increase the volume of employment. Whether the longer-run effects of the wage increases will be stimulating or depressing turns on the elasticity of demand for labor. If the market demand for labor is highly inelastic—*i.e.,* if the firms employ nearly as many workers at the higher wage as at the lower rate—the total wage payment will be greater after the increase in wages than before. This means a greater income for labor, and this will be reflected by an increased demand for goods by laborers and, indirectly, an increased demand for labor, which may more than offset the reduction in employment resulting from the wage increase. It should be noted, however, that in so far as labor income has increased at the expense of income recipients in other sectors of the economy, total demand will have increased only if laborers spend a larger part of their additional income than other groups of the economy do.

If, however, the demand for labor is quite elastic, an increase in wages will be accompanied by a reduction in labor income as well as a reduction in employment. Those unemployed as result of the increase in wages will seek work in other industries, and the increased supply of labor in those areas will cause wages to fall. When the demand for labor is highly elastic, accordingly, it is clear that wage increases will serve as a check on industrial recovery, reducing labor's income in the industries that raise wages and further depressing wage rates in other areas.

Whether the demand for labor is in fact elastic or inelastic depends upon the expectations of management, and these are affected by many factors. When business is expanding and future prospects appear to be good, the business community is likely to be optimistic. In this atmosphere a wage increase may seem to be a relatively small deterrent to profits, and the number of workers employed at the higher wage may be virtually as great as at the lower level. Businessmen may, in fact, assume that higher labor incomes will result in greater consumer demand and that this will have a generally stimulating effect on business activity. By the same token, when the business outlook is unfavorable and expectations are poor, an increase in wages or even a refusal by the union to take a wage cut may intensify the prevailing spirit of pessimism and cause the rate of unemployment to be accelerated.

Summary

The effects of industry-wide bargaining on the volume of employment may be summarized as follows: From the point of view of the firm, an increase in wages represents an increase in costs, and this tends to cause the firm to reduce output and employment; from the point of view of labor, an increase in the wage rate may mean either an increase in total labor income or a decrease in income, depending on the elasticity of demand for labor. If the demand for labor is highly elastic, it is clear that the volume of employment will be reduced, since both the cost factor and the income factor work in that direction; if, on the other hand, the demand for labor is highly inelastic, the income factor may make for an increased demand for labor, and this may balance or offset the adverse cost factor. It may be noted in conclusion that since the income effect may work toward an increase in employment only when the demand for labor is inelastic and the elasticity of demand depends on many and varied factors, and since organized labor represents only about one-fourth of the total labor force, arguments for higher wages based on "purchasing-power" effects should be viewed with considerable skepticism. Even when demands by unions for higher wages do result in an increase in employment, these gains are likely to be more than offset by the unhappy effects of the higher wages on the allocation of income between union members and the rest of the economy. If higher wages are achieved without a corresponding increase in labor's productivity, such gains as organized labor may enjoy are obtained at the expense of someone else. Whether the new allocation of national income imposed by the demands of organized labor is better or worse than the old allocation depends on welfare considerations which lie outside the limits of economic analysis. But much policy has been made in the field of labor economics without reference to the contributions which economic analysis can make, and this threatens to jeopardize the position of labor and do injury to the economy as a whole.

11

RENT, CAPITAL, AND INTEREST

The inputs of firms consist not only of the labor services of persons whom they employ but also of the services of material goods which they either buy or hire. To the extent that inputs consist of materials which are used up within a short period of time (*e.g.*, flour in the production of bread), the material is usually purchased outright by the using firm. When the required input consists instead of the services of a durable good, it is necessary for the firm either to buy the capital good or to rent it. In the latter case, title remains with the owner, but the services of the good belong for a specified period to the renter. Examples are numerous—the renting of office space by a lawyer, the renting of punch-card machines by a government agency, or the renting of vacant property by the operator of a parking lot. Rental prices for the services of particular capital goods are determined by the forces of supply and demand in much the same way as is the price of labor inputs.

The Concept of Economic Rent

So far we have used the terms "rent" and "rental" to denote the price paid for the use of a capital good. These terms should be

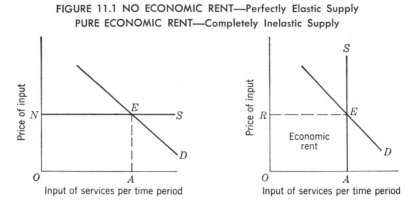

FIGURE 11.1 NO ECONOMIC RENT—Perfectly Elastic Supply
PURE ECONOMIC RENT—Completely Inelastic Supply

distinguished from "economic rent," which, in economic analysis, has been given a different definition. To the economist, economic rent is the income received by any sort of productive factor *over and above what it could earn in the next best use.* The rental income received by the owner of a capital good is likely to consist of economic rent to a considerable degree, since capital goods are often highly specialized to a particular use. In the short run, most capital goods are specialized as to use. In considering the concept of economic rent, we are, therefore, concerned with specialization over a period sufficiently long to allow resources to be shifted from one use to another. For example, sandy soil in an area may be permanently suitable only for growing pine trees. The entire earnings of the owner of such land are economic rent, because the land has only one use. On the other hand, a fertile plot of land near a large city could command a high rental but might yield little or no economic rent to its owner because of its adaptability to a large number of agricultural and commercial uses, the best of which may be virtually no better than the next best. The two situations, which are limiting cases, are represented on the two sides of Figure 11.1.

In each case the demand is the marginal revenue product of that type of productive service in its best employment. On the left side of the diagram, the supply of the input to the particular use pictured is drawn as perfectly elastic. This shows that the owner of the input will make none available to this use at any price below that which it could secure in another use; this other use, it is assumed, would hire the entire input at a price per unit of ON. (The principle is similar to that of the adjustment of labor among comparable occupations, which was discussed in Chapter 9.) As a consequence, the factor of production (*e.g.*, the well-located and fertile plot of land) receives no economic rent. Its income is determined entirely by the competition among alternative uses rather than by any one best use.

On the right side of Figure 11.1, the supply of input services is shown as perfectly *inelastic* to the particular use. This indicates that the factor has no alternative employment. Its income is determined entirely by the demand in the particular industry to which it is suited; this income is called "pure economic rent." The sandy-soil example illustrates this case. Its rental or sales value is determined entirely by the demand for pine lumber and turpentine.

ECONOMIC RENT AS PART OF RETURN

Many types of skilled labor and capital goods are better adapted to one particular use than to any other but are capable of doing two or more jobs. In this event, the remuneration received is a combination of economic rent and competitively determined income. Tool-and-die makers, for example, are highly specialized to that activity. If demand for their services in that line falls off, they will suffer a sharp cut in wages. If we assume that their only alternative employment is as unskilled labor, the income received in tool-and-die making over and above that which could be earned in common labor would be called economic rent. This sort of situation is pictured in Figure 11.2.

The wage rate which could be earned in an alternative occupa-

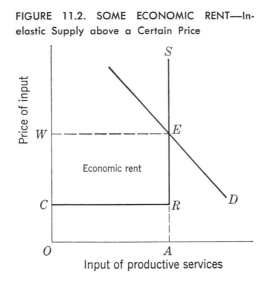

FIGURE 11.2. SOME ECONOMIC RENT—Inelastic Supply above a Certain Price

tion is assumed to be *OC*. It is further assumed that all the *OA* skilled workers (*e.g.*, tool-and-die makers) could secure employment in this alternative occupation. This means that they will not be willing to accept less than *OC* in the employment being considered but will, of course, accept as much more as they can get. Supply becomes perfectly inelastic above wage rate *OC* at the input *OA*. The actual wage rate obtained will be *OW*, and total income to these workers will be *OWEA*, of which *CWER* is economic rent. In this example, we have assumed that there are no "equalizing differences" which would cause workers to consider any factors other than relative money wage rates in choosing between occupations.

Similarly, most capital goods are not completely specialized to one use. A truck, for example, can usually be employed to haul any of a large variety of commodities; a building constructed to house a hardware store and a dentist's suite of offices may be shifted, if necessary, to use by a grocery store and a physician. An ordinary plot of land may be used to produce several different crops, or, alternatively, rented out for use as a fairground. In all of these cases, the supply of the capital good to any particular use is made less than perfectly inelastic by its alternative use possibilities. This is true despite the fixity in the total existing quantity of such goods on hand at any time. Like the tool-and-die makers, such semi-specialized capital goods receive income which is in part economic rent.

The moral to be drawn from the theory of economic rent is quite clear. Any worker or capital good which is highly specialized to a single occupation is in a vulnerable position. As long as demand is strong in that particular industry, the worker or capital good will receive a favorable return for its services. If the demand in that industry falls off, however, this will occasion a sharp cut in remuneration, since satisfactory alternative employments are not available. On the other hand, a capital good which is adaptable to several uses, without any changes in form or with only minor modification, receives little of its income in the form of economic rent, and the owner will be in a stronger position in the event of a downward shift in the demand for its services. It is usually desirable for a worker to have more than one skill. (It is seldom wise to attempt to become a Jack-of-all-trades, however, since this may involve mastery of none.) In the case of a college student, premature professional specialization may leave him with few alternative occupational possibilities and therefore highly dependent on the demand for his special training.

LONG-RUN ADJUSTMENTS IN ECONOMIC RENT

We have mentioned the vulnerability of the recipient of economic rent to a decline in demand for his specialized services. If, on the other hand, the demand for such services increases, the economic rent will increase sharply because of the short-run inelasticity of supply. Suppose, for example, that there is an increase in the demand for air-conditioned office buildings in a particular city. The rental price (and the economic rent) on those buildings which are already air-conditioned will increase. Some adjustments in supply may be forthcoming in the form of conversion of suitable non-air-conditioned buildings into air-conditioned ones, but after this has occurred rentals will probably still be very favorable to those who were wise enough, or fortunate enough, to invest in this field. Rentals may be much greater than the amount necessary to pay all operating expenses, including depreciation and a normal return on the capital invested in construction.

These extra profits will normally attract new investment in the construction of air-conditioned buildings, but the acquiring of new building sites and accomplishment of the construction are likely to occupy several years. (Expansion of the air-conditioning industry itself may occasion delay.) During this period, above-normal profits will continue to accrue to the owners of buildings already air-conditioned. Eventually, however, the construction of new air-conditioned office buildings will bring rentals down to a level where only ordinary returns are made on investment in that field. "Windfall" profits, which were due to the luck or wisdom of early investors in the field, will disappear.

If, on the other hand, the demand for some specialized capital good declines, causing earnings to be less than normal, a reverse sort of adjustment will take place. Suppose the demand for hotel accommodations in a city declines because of the erection of new motels. New hotels will not be built, and existing ones are likely to be undermaintained. Hotel owners will gradually withdraw part of their capital from this use. They may reinvest the funds so withdrawn in completely different capital goods—for example, in oil fields. In a long-run sense, capital is not specialized in form and consequently does not receive economic rent. Instead, it earns a competitively determined return.

Similarly, an individual who has specialized training and experience in a particular occupation may be able to retrain himself for another type of work if a change in vocation appears desirable.

The working life of an individual is not sufficiently long to permit very many complete switches of occupation, however. An education which is broad enough to permit relatively speedy retraining is apt to provide a safer background than is a highly specialized education.

The Capitalization Principle

We have discussed the payments for the services of capital goods. What is the relationship between the value of these services and the value of capital goods themselves? It is not correct to say simply that the value of a capital asset is the aggregate income which it can bring to its owner over its useful life. It is necessary to *discount* all returns which will be received in the future in order to find their value today.

The process of discounting is just the opposite of computing compound interest. A sum kept in a savings account will be increased periodically by the amount of interest earned, calculated at the rate announced by the bank, and if the interest is left on deposit the owner of the account receives further interest on this interest. In discounting, however, we start with a future payment or a schedule of future payments and calculate the capital sum which will yield this income at a given rate of interest.

Suppose that, under the terms of a will, Joe Jones will receive $1,000 payable on his twenty-first birthday, which will occur in exactly two years. What is this future income worth today? (The question might be a practical one, since it would probably be possible for Jones to sell his claim to the $1,000 to someone who would look upon the transaction as a suitable investment.) The value of $1,000 to be received in two years would be found by "discounting" this sum at a suitable rate of interest. If 5 per cent were an appropriate interest rate, the present value C would be found from the formula $C = \dfrac{\$1,000}{(1 + 0.05)^2}$. This capital value works out to be $907.03. This is equivalent to saying that if one invests $907.03 currently at an interest rate of 5 per cent compounded annually, its value would grow to $1,000 in two years' time. Similarly, the present value of the future payment of $1,000 which will not be secured until six years from today would be found by dividing by one-plus-the-interest rate raised to the sixth power.

In the above example, only one payment is due the beneficiary of the will. Suppose instead that the payments will continue to be

received for an indefinitely long period into the future, as is likely
to be the case with urban land, for example, which may be rented
out for a very long period for use as a building site or other purpose.
The capitalization formula then simplifies to the following: $C = I/r$,
where C is capital value, I is annual income, and r is the annual interest rate. This, then, is the formula for finding the capital value of
a perpetual income; simply divide the expected annual income by
an appropriate rate of interest. Suppose, for example, it is believed
that an urban lot will bring a net rental (after property taxes and
upkeep) of $1,000 a year for as long into the future as one can see.
At an interest rate of 5 per cent it is worth $20,000. This is the
obverse side of the process which indicates that an asset worth
$20,000 will provide an annual income of $1,000 if the return is 5
per cent.

In the case of a capital good which depreciates with use (*e.g.,* a
power shovel), the capitalization formula $C = I/r$ may still be used
if I is defined as anticipated yearly income after allowance for depreciation. Or I may be thought of as the annual quasi-rent minus
depreciation. When proper allowance is made each year for
depreciation, the annual net income can be considered to be a
perpetual income. It is made perpetual through the ability to purchase a new capital good whenever the old ones wears out.

The discussion of the capitalization formula immediately raises
the problem: What interest rate should be used in capitalizing any
particular asset? Actually, this presents a difficult problem in any
real case of capitalization. The individual making the calculation
must select an interest rate which appears to represent the rate of
return being received on newly produced capital goods of the
same general sort. This interest rate will be higher in more risky employments than in those where the chance of failing to collect the
interest or of losing the principal is small. An interest rate of 25
per cent might be appropriate, for example, in finding the capital
value of an American-owned oil well in a Central American repub-
lic with an unstable government. On the other hand, a low interest
rate (perhaps 4 per cent) might be appropriate in figuring the
value of land rented on a 99-year lease to a well-established utility
company in this country. Since the capitalized value of an asset
varies inversely with the rate of interest, the high interest rate used
would serve to keep down the estimated value of the oil well, while
the low interest rate used would enhance the calculated value of
the land leased to the utility company.

When buyers and sellers of capital assets argue about an appropriate sales price, they may be considered really to be bargaining with respect to what the annual income from the asset will be and as to what constitutes an appropriate interest rate on such an investment. The seller tries to make the expected annual income appear as large as he can and the appropriate interest rate as low as possible. The shrewd prospective buyer will point to a probable low income from the good and to the uncertainty of the return as justifying a low selling price.

The Rate of Interest

We have just seen how the interest rate enters into the evaluation of capital goods through the capitalization process. There remains the question as to how the interest rate itself is determined. This is one of the more perplexing problems in economics.

THE PRODUCTIVITY OF CAPITAL

Interest is based on the productivity of capital goods, or, speaking more broadly, of "capital"—which is the aggregate of all goods (including land) in existence at any time. The productivity of capital makes it worth while for firms generally to pay the owners of capital goods rentals which will not only cover depreciation of these assets but also provide a further return. Competition among firms for capital makes the payment of such an interest return not only worth while but necessary. Not all capital-goods owners, however, receive such a net return over their cost of production; rentals may be sufficient only to cover depreciation or may fail even to do that. But to the extent that resources are properly allocated, the current output of capital goods will consist of items which can actually earn a return over their lifetime above cost of production. This is true whether the new capital goods are replacements for existing ones or additions to the total stock of capital.

A useful way of viewing the determination of the rate of interest, in the long run under pure competition, is the following:

Interest rate $= X$ dollars per year net income (above depreciation) $\div$ cost of producing a capital good yielding X dollars per year net income

This formula is not quite correct,[1] but it is sufficiently close to be instructive. It shows that under competition the interest rate de-

[1] The inexactness of the formula results from the fact that interest is involved in the cost of production of any capital good; hence the interest rate

pends on the net productivity of new capital goods and on their cost of production. Thus if $50 per year net income can be secured by producing a capital good which costs $1,000 (or $50,000 secured by producing a good which costs $1 million), the rate of return is 5 per cent. The interest rate tends to be equal for all capital goods in the same risk category, since otherwise resources will be shifted from the production of items yielding smaller returns to those yielding more net income.

The rate of interest obtained by new buyers of *old* capital goods tends to be equated to the interest rate yielded by *new* capital goods through adjustment in the selling prices of old capital goods in accord with the capitalization principle. This must be so because no one with funds to invest will rationally buy an old capital good (*e.g.*, a ten-year-old apartment building) unless he can get it at a price which will yield him at least as high a rate of interest on his investment as he could secure from a new asset of a similar nature (*e.g.*, a new apartment building). Similarly, the owner of an old capital good will not normally have to sell it for a price so low that it will yield a new buyer a higher rate of return than he could secure by buying a new capital good, since prospective investors are in competition with one another.

Thus new buyers of both new and old capital goods of any given sort tend to receive the same rate of interest on their investments when there is competition on both the buying and selling sides. For example, when the United States Treasury early in 1953 began selling a new issue of long-term bonds yielding $3\frac{1}{4}$ per cent, the price of already existing long-term bonds immediately fell because of the higher rate on the new issues. Old owners of old capital goods may, however, receive much higher or much lower returns on amounts which they have invested, since their returns are affected strongly by shifts in the demand for the specialized services of their capital goods.

Interest as the Price of Borrowed Money

The rate of interest may also be thought of as the price of the use of money. Whenever a loan is made, some sort of I O U passes from borrower to lender as evidence of the loan, and the I O U specifies

---

actually appears on both sides of the equation. This has been pointed out by Professor Frank H. Knight. A more correct (but formidable) formulation has been given by him in several articles, including "Capital, Time and the Interest Rate," *Economica* N.S. I (1934), pp. 257–286.

the rate of interest to be paid as well as conditions of repayment of the principal. The I O U's may take many forms: for example, a businessman's note given to his bank, a bankbook given to a depositor (who has loaned the use of his savings to the bank), a corporation bond which shows that the holder has loaned money to the company, or a government bond which evidences borrowing on the part of a public agency.

While the interest rate can be considered to be the price paid for the use of someone's money, it is more basic to consider it the return on capital, as has been done in the present chapter. Money is completely unspecialized purchasing power made available to borrowers who then generally use it to buy materials, equipment, or other assets of a more or less specialized nature. It is rational to borrow money and invest it in capital goods if the net rate of return from the use of such equipment promises to exceed the rate which will have to be paid to the money lender. Corporations whose managers are wise enough (or lucky enough) to float large bond issues when interest rates in the money market are low are in an advantageous position in that it becomes more likely that they will be able to invest the proceeds at a relatively profitable interest rate.

Whether one is considering interest as the net return on investment in capital goods or as the payment to holders of I O U's, it should be recognized that the return varies greatly according to the risk of loss of principal and interest. Pure interest is received only on capital goods or I O U's of great safety (such as on a plot of land rented on a 99-year lease to a large utility company, on a government-insured savings account, or on a short-term United States government bond).[1] All less safe capital goods and I O U's frequently earn a return above pure interest which is a premium for the greater risk involved.

THE INTEREST RATE RATIONS INVESTIBLE FUNDS

The interest rate under competitive conditions can clearly be said to perform a rationing function with respect to investible funds. In order to be able to afford to pay interest on a loan and ultimately

[1] The risk in holding a bond which will mature (repay the principal) at a more distant date is greater than the risk in holding a bond of near-term maturity, because the market value of the former will drop sharply if there is a general rise in interest rates. Not even United States government bonds are completely safe with respect to the principal sum unless one holds the bond until the maturity date, or unless one buys savings bonds which carry a definite redemption schedule.

to repay the principal, a firm must put the borrowed funds to good use. This tends to exclude the less productive employments and thus to ration new savings to firms better able to use them. Other possible users of new capital will have demands which will not be effective at all except at interest rates below the going rate. These uses will receive none of the new capital, and this is as it should be, since the prospective productivity of capital is too low in such fields to justify the use of new capital there.

The rationing, or allocation, function of the interest rate is so important that even a completely communistic society, in which individuals receive no interest income, must account for interest or suffer the consequences in terms of lower production efficiency. Entries for interest must be made on the books of a completely planned economy in order to secure a reasonably correct allocation of scarce capital among the various industries. If one industry uses ten times as much capital as another but both use the same amount of labor, the total cost of production is much greater in the first industry; this would not be evident if interest were disregarded. The planning authorities could not make any proper comparison of utility of output and cost of input if they failed to account for interest. Their inherently difficult job of planning would become virtually an impossible one.

The "production-motivation" function of the interest rate in a private-enterprise economy is less clear than the capital-rationing function. Capital in any economy is built up through the allocation of a sufficient quantity of resources to uses other than current consumption. Under conditions of full employment of resources, an increase in the production of capital goods is brought about by an increase in saving and investment which causes input units to be transferred out of consumption-goods production and into capital-goods production. Increased saving decreases the demand for consumption goods; increased investment increases the demand for capital goods.[1] Under conditions of less than full employment, it may be possible to increase the output of capital goods without reducing the output of other goods by putting idle resources to work.

[1] Backward economies, such as those of some Asiatic nations, generally have such large populations in relation to resources and technological knowledge that they find it necessary to devote practically all their resources to the production of food and other nondurable goods. Consequently, they are able to accumulate little capital without outside help. They are poor because they have limited capital, and they are unable to accumulate capital because they are poor.

The production-motivation function of the interest rate is traceable in part to its effect on the rate of saving. This effect is not clear. Some (probably most) families and firms pay little or no attention to interest rates when they make their decisions regarding saving. Some who calculate more closely find the prospect of higher interest rates an incentive to increase their savings. Others who are aiming at accumulating a certain sum by a particular date find that they need to save less if interest rates are higher, since interest will do more for them in reaching their goal. This inverse relationship between saving and the interest rate is especially important with respect to savings which are placed in endowment and annuity policies sold by insurance companies. The lower the interest rate which insurance companies can earn on such savings, the higher the premiums they will charge on the contracts. Consequently, a large number of families find it necessary to save more as interest rates go down. On balance, the volume of new savings in any time period appears not to be affected greatly by the rate of interest. For this reason, and for others to be developed in later chapters, the effect of the interest rate on capital accumulation is not so clear as its capital-rationing function.

Part 2

ELEMENTS OF INCOME THEORY

12

MEASUREMENT OF NATIONAL INCOME

From time to time the American economy seems to be struck with a case of general paralysis. For reasons which are never clear to the man in the street and sometimes appear to mystify the experts, factories close down; prices and wages fall; a significant fraction of the working population is unemployed; many who have jobs work only part time; some people, particularly professional workers such as teachers, preachers, and physicians, work full time but may be able to collect only a part of their wages; morale everywhere is low. The situation would be less deplorable if only the wicked suffered, but, in fact, those who have been thrifty may find their savings wiped out through drastic declines in security and property values, those who have attained skills may discover that there is no demand for their special abilities, and the virtuous may have to wait until they get to heaven to reap their rewards. Even a college diploma will not guarantee a person steady employment; during the depression of the 1930's the abbreviation Ph.D. was sometimes held to stand for posthole digger, and some college graduates were unable to find employment even as unskilled manual laborers.

If the economy were highly competitive in all ways, widespread and protracted unemployment of economic resources would be improbable. An oversupply of goods or labor would be followed by a decline in prices or wages, markets would be cleared, and unemployment would probably be short-lived. The fact that extensive and prolonged periods of depression have occurred in the contemporary economy indicates that there are powerful forces at work which need to be scrutinized with great care. This is indicated also by the recession of 1958 in which, during the early months at least, increasing unemployment and continued inflation went hand in hand.

On the other hand, there are times, such as in the years immediately following World War II, when there seems to be almost too much prosperity. Virtually everyone who wants to work is employed and factories are humming, but prices also are moving rapidly upward. Families find that the dollar is continually shrinking in value, and the weekly wage needed to maintain living standards must be constantly increased. Persons living on fixed incomes of moderate size are extremely hard put to make ends meet and many are likely to yearn for a sharp break in prices such as occurred in the 1930's.

The term "business cycle" is frequently used to refer to fluctuations in the level of business activity, and, although this phrase probably implies a regularity in the timing and magnitude of periods of prosperity and depression which the facts do not bear out, it does quite properly suggest something of a seeming inevitability of fluctuations in the level of business activity. Some instability may be necessary: this is a debatable point, but certainly the extreme instability of the past need not and should not be allowed to continue in the future. Widespread and protracted unemployment of the sort experienced during the great depression of the 1930's is tragic in its effects and a monument to our lack of understanding a quarter century ago of the basic factors which determine general business activity. And as already suggested, the opposite problem of inflation is also a serious one.

Stimulated by the world-wide depression of the 1930's, many economists have in recent years turned their attention to a study of aggregates of economic data in an effort to understand the causes of such economic catastrophes. Rather than concerning themselves with data relative to individual firms or industries, these economists have investigated the nature of such aggregates as the national income, total savings, and total investment. This newer, broader branch of economics is often called "macroeconomics," the economics of large units, as contrasted with "microeconomics," the economics of small units, such as firms and industries. The pioneer work in macroeconomics was John Maynard Keynes's *The General Theory of Employment, Interest, and Money,* published in 1936. Few books of our time have been more influential than this one, and it is with the concepts developed by Keynes and others that we shall be concerned in the chapters on national income.

The present chapter does not attempt to explain how over-all income is determined, but instead describes the principal statistical measures which have grown out of the aggregative approach to income. Some knowledge of these measures and their purposes can usefully be combined with the theory of income determination to be developed later.

Two Views of National Income

There are two distinct ways of viewing national income: (1) as the summation of the net value of final goods and services produced during a period; and (2) as the summation of wages, salaries, interest, rent, and business incomes received during a period. The first method amounts to an evaluation of all final outputs of the economy at prevailing prices. The second method must, logically, give the same answer as the first, since the selling value of output must be equal to cost of production plus profits.

In calculating national income by the first method, it is necessary that only final goods and services (those which are not resold) be counted. A great deal of duplication would be involved, for example, if the value of portland cement were counted when it was sold by the producer, again when sold by a distributor, again when sold by a transit-mix concrete company, and again when sold by a builder to a new home buyer, incorporated in a basement floor. Instead, it is necessary that only the value of the basement floor be counted, since this includes the original value of the cement, the value added in transportation and distribution, the value added by the concrete mixer, and the value added by the builder. Actually, the value of the floor would not be reported separately but would be picked up statistically as part of the value of new residential construction. (Even here the statistician would have to make some "educated guesses" since data in the field of construction are poor.)

In calculating national income, the statisticians of the U.S. Department of Commerce are guided in part by what is practicable rather than by what should theoretically be included. Conceptually,

the national income should include such items as the value of
housewives' services; lawnmowing and maintenance services of all
sorts provided by male members of American families; baby-sitting
services, whether paid for or furnished gratis by grandparents;
and vegetables, fruits, and flowers raised in the home garden and
orchard.[1] Since such items cannot be estimated closely in dollars,
however, they are omitted, leaving the national income rather
substantially understated. This omission probably makes little real
difference except when there is an important change in the magnitude of such uncounted income. For example, during World War II
millions of women switched from housework, where their services
are not counted, to factory work, where their wages and product do
count as national income. It has frequently been asserted that civilian consumption was higher throughout World War II than just
prior to the war despite the huge volume of munitions output which
we attained. This conclusion has been derived directly from the
published national-income data but should be viewed skeptically
for the reason just given. In a broad sense, leisure is also a type of income as long as it is not available in an excessive amount because of
involuntary unemployment. During the war a six-day week was
common, leaving many people with less leisure time than they
would have chosen had they been able to work only as long as they
preferred additional income to additional leisure. This further reduces the wartime significance of the national-income estimates as a
measure of national "psychic" income.

Another important respect in which there is a compromise between
theory and feasibility is in the treatment of durable consumers' goods.
If a new automobile will last ten years, for example, only about one-
tenth of its original cost (less ultimate scrap value) should be
counted as income each year. Actually, the entire value of new cars
is counted as national income in the year in which they are produced.
In the case of owner-occupied homes, however, the error which
would be involved in leaving out the yearly value of housing services
consumed would be so great that an estimate of their value is actually
made and included in national income.

The above discussion should not cause one to regard the national-
income estimates as worthless, but rather it should serve as a warning
that due caution must be exercised in their interpretation. Any substantial movement in the national-income figures from year to year
undoubtedly reflects important changes. On the other hand, a varia-

---

[1] The Department of Commerce income estimates include an imputed value
for home-produced food for farm families but not for urban families.

tion of small magnitude, *e.g.*, a one-billion-dollar decline, should not be taken too seriously, since the error probably contained in the estimates plus variations in the unmeasured items is likely to be of greater magnitude.

National-income Concepts

The Department of Commerce compiles data corresponding to five different concepts of national income.[1] Like rubbing alcohol, all should be used with caution, for the reasons which have just been set forth. While all five are national-income measurements in a broad sense, the term "National Income" also refers to a particular one of the measurements. National Income in the particular sense and Gross National Product are the most widely publicized measurements. The latter (GNP) is somewhat easier to understand. It is the total output of final goods and services during the year, measured at their market values. The statistical job would be harder, but GNP could also be found by measuring the total outputs of all firms and deducting inputs bought from other firms. This would amount to a summation of the *value added* by each firm to the materials and semiprocessed goods which it processed, the value additions resulting from the application of labor, capital, and managerial skill.

Not all of the goods and services produced in any one year represent "income." Some goods and services must be produced to replace the capital used up during the year if the total stock of capital is not to be reduced. Therefore, in order to arrive at a figure for National Income, "capital consumption allowances" must be deducted from Gross National Product. This really amounts to deducting the value of the capital which is "used up" in producing the total income and which, therefore, must be replaced if future income is to continue to be produced.[2]

National-income Data

Department of Commerce estimates of Gross National Product and National Income for selected years are shown in Table 12.1. We have included 1929 because it was a year of great prosperity, which,

[1] These are designated Gross National Product, Net National Product, National Income, Personal Income, and Disposable Income.

[2] United States government statisticians also make other deductions, but these are of little importance to the student's elementary understanding of the national-income concept.

Table 12.1. Gross National Product and National Income
(In billions of dollars)

	1929	1932	1939	1953	1954	1955	1956	1957	1958 (est.)
GNP	$103.8	$58.3	$91.3	$363.2	$361.2	$391.7	$414.7	$434.4	$430.0
NI	87.4	41.7	72.5	302.1	299.0	324.1	343.6	358.0	355.0

however, ended on a sorrowful note after the most violent stock-market crash in our history; 1932 is shown because it was the worst year of the most severe depression which the nation has experienced; 1939 is included because it was the last year prior to World War II in which United States munitions production was of negligible proportions; and 1953 through 1958 are included to show the recent trend.

The severity of the decline of business activity from 1929 to 1932 and the hesitant pace of recovery during the next seven years are shown by both statistical series. The much higher level of income since World War II is easily seen in the table. Data for 1954 show clearly that there was a minor "recession" in business that year. The 1958 figures show a decline in economic activity compared with 1957.

Real Income

The figures of Table 12.1, however, overstate the fluctuations in real gross product and real income, that is, in the physical volume of goods and services turned out. Prices changed radically over the period covered by Table 12.1, falling sharply from 1929 to 1932 and (except for some rather short-lived setbacks) rising over the next two and a half decades. Because part of the decline in GNP and NI from 1929 to 1932 is accounted for by the drop in prices which occurred, real gross output and real income did not fall so sharply as their dollar measures. Similarly, the real gain after 1932 was less spectacular than it appears, since a sizable part of the recorded rise was due to price inflation.

In order to eliminate the influence of changing prices on such dollar measurements, statisticians "deflate" the data by dividing by appropriate index numbers of prices. As an illustration of the statistical process of deflation (which must not be confused with the other meaning of the term, namely, a general decline in prices), suppose a vendor sells $1,000 worth of $1 neckties in a given year. For the next year he decides to charge $2 a tie instead of $1, and sells $4,000 worth during the year. What has happened to the physical volume of his sales? Obviously, his "real" sales have doubled. Arithmetically, this is determined by dividing $1,000 by $1 and $4,000 by $2 in order to get physical sales of 1,000 and 2,000 ties, respectively, in the two years.

When the dollar aggregates pertain to a number of commodities rather than to just one, it is not so simple to find the correct divisors. Conceptually, one should divide by average prices which have been computed by giving to each commodity the same weight (importance) in the average as it has in the dollar aggregate. In practice, such average prices (which are called index numbers when expressed in a percentage relationship to a base period) are only an approximation to the average which is really appropriate. Despite these shortcomings, deflated income aggregates give us a much more correct picture of real economic changes than do the unadjusted dollar data in a period of violent price changes such as have characterized the past three decades.

Table 12.2 shows Gross National Product adjusted to dollars of

Table 12.2. GNP Measured in 1939 Dollars
(In billions of dollars)

1929	1932	1939	1953	1954	1955	1956	1957
$ 85.9	$61.9	$ 91.3	$176.5	$174.2	$186.7	$192.0	$194.8

Price index numbers (1939 = 100)

120.8	94.2	100.0	205.8	207.4	209.8	216.0	223.0

Source: Department of Commerce.

1939 purchasing power—that is, deflated by an appropriate price index which uses 1939 as a base. Even though the purpose of national-income accounting is to measure fluctuations in the real volume of final goods and services produced, it is necessary to use dollars in order to add together the thousands of diverse commodities and services which are measured physically in a large number of different units (pounds, tons, gallons, etc.). It is consequently necessary to settle on a dollar of unchanging purchasing power so that the standard of measurement will not change at the same time that the thing being measured is varying.

The "deflated" GNP data of Table 12.2 have been derived by dividing the GNP of Table 12.1 by the price index numbers for the corresponding years. This permits a better measure of the "real" growth in the economy's output since deflation removes the effect of price changes. That is, the adjusted GNP figures in Table 12.2 may be considered to show what GNP *would have been* if 1939 prices had prevailed every year. (In 1939 the actual and deflated GNP are, of course, the same since 1939 prices *did* prevail in 1939.)

The price index numbers are in themselves shocking, since they show clearly the extent of inflation since 1939. For example, the 1957 index, 223.0, shows that there was a 123 per cent rise in the prices of goods in general in the 18-year span between 1939 and 1957. Among other things this illustrates the danger involved in holding a large part of one's personal assets in cash, bonds, annuities, or other claims to a fixed number of dollars. An individual who kept $10,000 in such a form over this period would be unlikely to have in this fund as much purchasing power today as he had 18 years ago even if he allowed interest to accumulate during the period. That is, inflation would have robbed him of all his interest and part of the real value of his principal.

From 1939 to 1957 the increase in GNP in actual dollars was a very impressive 376 per cent. Removal of the influence of price inflation has a great effect: measured in 1939 dollars the increase in GNP over the same 18-year period is 113 per cent. This is still an impressive figure since it reflects a more than doubling of the aggregate volume of goods and services produced by the American economy.

Still another adjustment is needed, however, in order to secure the fairest picture of the extent of the gain. This adjustment is for United States population, which increased from about 130 million in 1939 to about 171 million in 1957. This adjustment is made by dividing the deflated GNP data of Table 12.2 by the United States population of the corresponding year. This gives a measurement of *real income per capita*. After this adjustment the increase between 1939 and 1957 is 62 per cent. Even this figure cannot be said to represent the percentage gain in the volume of consumers' goods available per person, since capital goods (*e.g.*, machinery) are included in GNP. The process of deflation for price-level changes and population changes at least provides a warning as to the care which must be used in drawing conclusions from national-income statistics. It serves to warn us that although productivity is rising impressively, the basic problem of scarcity has by no means been overcome. Talk of an "economy of abundance" is extremely misleading, representing wishful thinking or the overoptimistic pronouncements of the economically unsophisticated.

GNP Components

Both Gross National Product and National Income can usefully be broken down into major components, and this is a regular part of the Department of Commerce reporting activity. GNP is the summation of market values of final goods and services produced, and it is of interest to see what groups purchased this output and in what amounts. The disposition of the 1957 output is shown in Table 12.3, figures being expressed in dollars of that year.

Table 12.3. Major Components of GNP—1957
(In billions of dollars)

Personal Consumption Expenditures	$280.4
Gross Private Domestic Investment	64.4
Net Foreign Investment	3.2
Government Purchases of Goods and Services	86.4
Total	$434.4

The largest figure, Personal Consumption Expenditures, shows purchases made by individuals and nonprofit institutions for consumption purposes. This includes food, clothing, haircuts, permanent waves, and all sorts of other nondurables, plus durable goods such as automobiles, boats, and furniture. Residential buildings purchased are, however, excluded and placed instead in the second category—Gross Private Domestic Investment.

Some consumers' goods are secured without the expenditure of money, and the national-income statisticians include allowances for such goods in the Personal Consumption Expenditures figures. Food, housing, clothing, and fuel received directly by some workers as part of their pay are included here. Similarly, the value of housing services derived from owner-occupied homes is estimated and included, as is the value of food and fuel which are both produced and consumed on farms. As suggested earlier in this chapter, it would be logical to include the value of household services furnished by members of families and perhaps even the value of leisure time, but Federal officials have not considered it wise to do so.

The second row in Table 12.3, Gross Private Investment, shows the aggregate purchase of new residential buildings, industrial plants, new machinery, and other durable producers' goods such as power lines and pipelines. Some of these purchases merely serve to replace worn-out buildings and equipment, but it should be remembered from the earlier discussion that no distinction is made between replacement and other items in the computation of GNP. Finally, any net build-up of farm and nonfarm business inventories is counted here. Such build-ups can usefully be thought of as a temporary purchase by farmers and other businessmen of their own goods. The temporary inventory accumulations may be either voluntary or involuntary; that is, enterprisers may feel it desirable to carry larger stocks or may end up with larger stocks than they wish because of inability to sell as much as they expected. (This point is of considerable importance in the theory of income determination examined in the next two chapters.)

The third item, Net Foreign Investment, is somewhat more difficult to understand. Roughly, it may be thought of as the excess of our exports over our imports. Actually, the figure is obtained by computing gross dollar receipts by United States residents and subtracting gross dollar payments made to foreigners. Many transactions in addition to merchandise imports and exports give rise to international payments. These will be studied in a later chapter. For present purposes it is enough to see that our net foreign balance (exports minus imports) is summarized in the term Net Foreign Investment.

It will be noted in Table 12.3 that Net Foreign Investment in 1957 is $3.2 billion. This indicates that the United States exported more than it imported in 1957. The actual excess of exports over imports was greater than this figure indicates, however, since amounts bought by the Federal government and distributed as economic aid and military assistance to foreign nations are included instead in row 4.

The $86.4 billion of government purchases includes compensation paid to civil and military employees, since presumably their output is commensurate with their pay. It also includes purchases by the government from domestic businesses and from abroad. Interest on government debt is not included, but this decision is rather an arbitrary one. To the extent that the Federal debt, for example, represents borrowing for purposes of investment in capital goods (factories, power systems, national parks, public housing, etc.) interest on the debt should be counted in GNP and National Income. To the extent, however, that the debt was incurred for such purposes as meeting payrolls during the war and producing munitions which were destroyed by the war, it is perhaps inappropriate to count interest on public debt as part of the national product and income; it becomes, instead, a "transfer payment," *i.e.*, a transfer of money between persons and institutions which is not associated with current production. All transfer payments (relief to the needy, gifts, inherit-ances, etc.) are excluded from National Income.

Other difficult problems of classification are connected with gov-ernment activity. For example, payments to soldiers' dependents are counted in soldiers' compensation, and hence in National Income, but benefits under the GI bills are excluded as being a further reward for past, rather than current, services. Also, work-relief payments, which were large during the depression of the 1930's, should be in-cluded or excluded depending on whether the work or the relief was predominant. Here the quality of the planning which goes into work-relief projects is of prime importance.

National-income Components

It is useful also to get an impression of the division of National In-come among broadly defined groups of recipients and types of re-muneration. Such a breakdown of the 1957 data is given in Table 12.4.

Table 12.4. Distribution of the 1957 National Income
(In billions of dollars)

Wages, salaries, and supplements	$254.4
Corporate earnings	39.6
Earnings of unincorporated business	28.7
Farm income	12.1
Rental income	10.4
Net interest	12.8
Total	$358.0

It will be noted that employees' compensation in the form of wages, salaries, and supplements—the latter term also comprehending such items as employer contributions to social security and private pension plans—amounted to about two-thirds of the total national income. Profits of corporations—a favorable topic of the labor-union leaders in recent years—amounted to a sizable chunk, 11 per cent. It should be recognized, however, that corporations are not ultimate recipients in the same sense as are the receivers of the other listed shares. Part of the profits which remain after taxes are paid out as dividends to stockholders to be spent as they wish (after income taxes), and part of corporation earnings are reinvested by the company officials.

The income shown for noncorporate business includes earnings by professional people such as doctors, lawyers, and public ac-countants in business for themselves. If they worked for others, their salaries would go instead into the first category. Similarly, a portion of farm income is really compensation for labor services contributed by the farm families which would be added in with wages, salaries, and supplements except for the fact that the farmer is in business for himself.

Rental income includes not only explicit money earnings received by those who rent out real property but, it will be remembered, also the estimated rental value of owner-occupied homes, minus depreciation, maintenance, and similar costs. Royalties received on patents and copyrights and from the ownership of such natural resources as oil wells and iron mines are included here.

Interest income, as stated earlier, excludes all interest on government debt. In addition to cash interest received by individuals on nongovernmental bonds and other I O U's, this item includes very substantial earnings received by insurance companies on policyholders' funds but not paid out currently to policyholders.

Other Measures

The present chapter has emphasized Gross National Product and National Income. As was indicated, however, three other measures are also regularly computed. Many of the differences among the five measures are, perhaps, of more interest to those who are responsible for compiling the data than to the typical consumer. If the data are actually put to an analytical use, rather than merely being followed casually in order to see how well the economy is doing, it is important to select the particular national-income measure which, theoretically, is most pertinent to the problem at hand.

For example, the retail jeweler who is concerned with the effect of over-all economic activity on his own business could best follow the fluctuations in Personal Income or Disposable Income. The latter figure shows income available after payment of Federal, state, and local taxes; consequently it should most nearly represent the amount which private consumers have available for purchasing goods and services. A firm selling farm machinery would be likely to pay particular attention to the farm income portion of National Income. The income measure must be carefully adapted to the use to which it is put.

The size of the national income is of vital importance to the nation, and national-income theory, to be developed in subsequent chapters, consequently constitutes an important part of modern economics. It should be kept in mind, however, that aggregative data inevitably conceal important information regarding the constituent elements. This is true even when a broad breakdown is attempted, as in Table 12.4. Many Americans live in poverty even when national income is high and many groups, such as retired persons and clerical workers, may face declining standards of living even when national income is increasing. Much of what may be termed "political economy" is an outgrowth of a great tug of war between different organized groups in the nation, each trying to get a larger share of the economy's output. Some measures of their relative success will be included in a later chapter dealing with the distribution of income.

13

NATIONAL-INCOME DETERMINATION

The national-income data compiled by the Department of Commerce provide us with a reasonably accurate measure of the level of economic activity, and fluctuations in national income reflect movements in employment, production, and prices. This chapter will discuss the forces which determine fluctuations in national income. We know that serious fluctuations have occurred in the past and may recur in the future. What caused the tragic depression in the 1930's and inflation in the 1940's and 1950's? What caused the recessions of 1949 and 1953? And how was it possible to have both inflation and recession in 1957?

First of all, a distinction must be made between national real income and national money income. As we have indicated, goods and services produced in the economy can be "added up" only in money terms. But an increase in money income may not represent an increase in the amount of real goods and services produced; such an increase may reflect merely an increase in the level of prices. We are interested in both money income and real income. When real income is below that which our available resources might produce, the

156

economy is not operating as it should. And when money income is too high relative to real income, inflation is likely to be present.

In order to discuss the causes of fluctuations in real income, we must first discuss the causes of fluctuations in national money income. After this step is taken, we may show how shifts in national money income may or may not be accompanied by changes in national real income.

The Income Equations

In the preceding chapter we showed that it is possible to measure national income in two separate ways. First, we may measure Gross National Product in terms of the total receipts by individuals during a particular period. To get this figure we add up wages, salaries, rental payments received, dividends, etc. Secondly, we may measure Gross National Product in terms of the total value of goods and services produced during a particular period. Taking care to avoid double counting, we should get this by adding up the total value of all final goods and services produced during a particular period. From each of these measures for Gross National Product we must deduct an item which represents replacement of capital equipment which is used up or worn out during the period studied. Quite obviously that portion of the national product which is necessary to maintain the capital stock of the country is not "income" in any meaningful sense.

Let us now examine each of these two measures of national income more closely. For simplicity in discussion, let us use some symbols. We shall call national money income Y. Looking first at the income as measured by receipts, we know that individuals can do only one of two things with this income, if we forget momentarily the ever-present necessity of paying taxes. Tax payments aside, the individual must either spend this income or save it. If we label consumption spending as C and saving as S, we get the first basic income equation:

$$Y = C + S \qquad (1)$$

(We shall add T for tax payments and we shall also add expenditure for foreign goods later, but for the time being let us forget about these.)

Let us now look at income as measured by the value of goods and services produced. These goods are of two different sorts. First, there are those goods destined for direct consumption. We can call the value of these goods C, and this is obviously the same C which appears in Equation (1). The amount which individuals spend in purchasing consumption goods is clearly equal to the value of consumption goods sold to individuals, measured in retail or final values. Goods and services purchased for direct consumption are not, however, the only kind of goods produced. A significant share of total production takes the form of goods which are used to produce other goods. These are called capital goods—buildings, machinery, equipment, etc. Goods of this type are not directly purchased by consumers, but by business units. We may call the expenditure on these goods "investment" and use the label I to refer to the total value of such expenditure. Since all goods must fall into one of these two categories, we can now set up the second basic income equation.

$$Y = C + I \tag{2}$$

It is important to recognize that the "investment" discussed here represents expenditure on or the value of capital goods. Care should be taken lest this usage become confused with the meaning of "investment" in ordinary conversation. In the latter the term generally is taken to refer to the expenditure on any earning asset, be it a common stock, a bond, or physical capital. But in the national-income theory, which we shall outline in this and the following chapters, "investment" refers only to the purchase of capital goods.

National income is equal to national income. This seemingly nonsensical statement suggests that the left-hand sides of the two equations above must be equal. That is, if we have successfully and correctly carried out the measurement, the Y in Equation (1) must be the same Y as that of Equation (2). This simple fact allows us to proceed further, and to state that the right-hand sides of the equations must also be equal. In algebraic terms, this suggests that,

$$C + S = C + I \tag{3}$$

The expenditure on consumption goods, the C on the left-hand side, is obviously equal to the value of consumption goods, the C on the right-hand side of Equation (3). This allows us to cancel out the two, leaving

$$S = I \tag{4}$$

This states that saving must be equal to investment expenditure.

The algebra through which we have reached our conclusion is not difficult. But the logic of this equality must be more carefully examined.

The Equality of Saving and Investment

Why must the amount of income saved be identical with the amount of net investment expenditure? This is one of the central points in the modern theory of income determination, and it is essential that the answer be made quite clear. The act of saving (which is the converse of the act of spending) is carried out by both individuals and business units. Saving by families takes the form of putting aside a portion of income received for use in a rainy day, for old age, for vacations, to meet certain unexpected contingencies, to finance college education for children, etc. Saving by business firms takes the form of retaining some part of profits earned rather than paying them all out to owners. The actual process of saving may assume different guises. Irrationally cautious people may bury a few dollars in a fruit jar in the back yard and add to this hoard each month. Others may rent strongboxes; others may sew money up in the mattress. But more frequently saving by individuals means increasing bank deposits, demand and time, increasing share purchases in building and loan associations, increasing life-insurance purchases, increasing purchases of stocks and bonds.

The act of investment is evidently quite different. Investment is the purchase of capital goods (machinery, buildings, equipment, durable goods, etc.). It is largely, but not wholly, undertaken by business firms. Since the act of saving and the act of investment appear to be quite distinct, there would seem initially to be no reason why the two magnitudes must be equal in total, during any time period, even in the extremely simplified analysis of this chapter.

What is there that associates the total amount of saving with the total amount of investment? Some of the saving is directly carried out with a view toward investment. Much of business saving is planned with the direct purpose of expanding the purchase of capital equipment. For this portion of the two magnitudes, the saving decision and the investment decision are almost identical. But for that portion of saving undertaken by individuals, why should investment expenditure arise to offset this?

The banking system, which will be examined in subsequent chapters, does provide a mechanism through which private savings may be channeled into actual investment. If individuals save and increase their bank deposits, a greater amount of loanable funds becomes available to banks—funds which may be loaned to business firms seeking to purchase capital goods, that is, to invest. But the banking system does not operate to keep the two magnitudes, total saving and total investment, in exact equality or even moving toward equality. Economists of a few decades ago did place a great deal of faith in the banking system in this respect. Their reasoning was as follows: If savings became greater than the amount of investment expenditure undertaken, banks would find themselves unable to lend all of the money which they desire to lend. The supply of loanable funds would then exceed the demand for them at the established rate of interest. This divergence between quantity demanded and quantity supplied would force the rate of interest down. With the lower rate of interest, more funds would be borrowed for investment purposes and less saving would be attempted. The interest rate would move upward and downward in this way until total savings and total investment were brought into equality. This chain of reasoning is not entirely wrong, but the forces making for adjustment are not strong. Investment expenditures may, to some extent, be financed out of bank credit, but the amount of bank credit outstanding at any given moment of time depends only remotely on the supply of savings. In addition the response of investment and saving to changes in the rate of interest may not be strong and may not even be predictable as to direction.

The Definitional Identity between Saving and Investment

If the interest rate does not serve the function of keeping saving and investment equal, we must search for some other variable. We may approach this task by first determining why saving and investment must be equal in any one period of time. This will turn out to be a definitional equality.

If consumption spending plus investment spending is not sufficient to purchase all of the goods produced in the economy during a particular period, there will be some unsold goods. Some business firms will be disappointed in their selling plans. Inventories will be accumulated. Let us suppose that a specific firm finds itself unable to sell a radio which it has priced at $50. At the end of the period considered this firm has one more radio on its shelves than it had intended to have. It follows that this firm has $50 less income from goods sold than it had hoped for. In one sense, therefore, we can say that this firm has "invested" in radios to the amount of $50. It has "purchased from itself" the additional radio which is added to its inventories. If each firm which has accumulated inventories can be thought of as doing this, quite clearly total saving and total investment expenditure are identical. This is so because every unit of real goods produced must be purchased for consumption purposes, purchased for investment purposes, or not purchased at all, in which case it would represent an addition to inventories.

Now let us examine the opposite case. Suppose the single firm considered was able to sell one more radio than it had planned to sell during the period. This would cause inventories to be $50 below the desirable level. The firm has, therefore, "invested" $50 less than intended. In this way, we make an adjustment so that total saving and total investment are equal by definition. This adjustment factor represented by the build-up or run-down of inventories explains the equality in the Equation (4) shown above.

Income Fluctuations Equate Saving and Investment

By definition, in any particular period of time saving and investment must be equal. Income itself is the variable which shifts so as to keep the two magnitudes equal. Obviously, the owner of the business firm in our example would not continue to plan on stocking radios which add to his inventories. He will begin to take steps to reduce his planned purchases. He will order fewer sets from his distributor, who will, in turn, find it necessary to cut back on his rate of purchases from the manufacturer, who will, in turn, then reduce output. We find that fluctuations in inventories which are generated by the difference between spending plans of individuals as consumers and selling plans of individuals as producers cause the planned rates of output to shift. And it is this shift in real output, real income, which serves to bring money saving and investment into equality. For this reason the saving-investment equality is extremely important.

We may first define a position of equilibrium in national income. Equilibrium in national money income is attained when the rate of income is such that it will be maintained with no tendency to move upward or downward in a reasonably short period of time. This equilibrium will be characterized by an equality of saving and investment in the nondefinitional sense. That is to say, business firms will not find inventories accumulating unduly nor will they find their inventories being depleted too rapidly. Nothing in the situation will be of such a nature as to encourage firms to expand or to contract their current rates of output and sales. Similarly, consumers will be able to buy all that they desire at current prices, and nothing in the situation will cause them to want to buy more or less during the next spending period. All of the goods which are produced but not purchased directly by consumers are being purchased for investment purposes.

Let us assume that such an income equilibrium is actually attained. This is a useful device because it provides us with a starting point from which we can analyze changes. Now we shall assume that a change in plans occurs. Let us suppose that individuals now decide to save a greater share and to spend a smaller share of their income than before. It should be clear, of course, that particular individuals may save more without this action resulting in more total saving, since, if other individuals save less, the total may remain unchanged. We are dealing here with aggregates, however, and we are, therefore, concerned only with changes in total saving. Our assumption is simply that people decide to increase their aggregate net saving (decrease aggregate spending). Let us employ our customary helpmate, *ceteris paribus*. In this case, the principal other thing that must remain unchanged is the amount of investment expenditure that business firms plan to undertake. Firms continue to base production and sales plans on the previously established equilibrium rate of spending.

PLANNED SAVING AND PLANNED INVESTMENT

Any divergence between the savings plans of individuals and firms and the investment plans of firms and individuals means that someone is going to be disappointed. In other words, someone is going to find himself unable to carry out his previous plans, as in the case of our radio firm example above. In this particular model, as people begin saving more, that is, putting a greater portion of their income into bank deposits, government bonds, etc., their expenditure on consumption goods and services must be correspondingly reduced. Firms will experience a reduced consumer expenditure on goods and services. Difficulties in moving goods will appear; store shelves and warehouses will fill up. Firms will not be able to sell at established prices all of the goods and services which have been produced. For it must be kept in mind that, under our assumptions, production was based on the expectation that sales would continue at the previously established equilibrium rate. Therefore, inventories will accumulate as a result of the decline in consumer purchasing. This net addition to inventories will represent "investment" under the meaning employed here, and total savings and total investment, owing to this adjustment factor, will remain identical. But this sort of "investment" is different from the more normal expenditure for capital goods. This net increase in inventories was neither anticipated nor planned. Business firms had expected to be able to sell more goods and services than they find themselves able to sell. They are left holding the bag, so to speak, full of extra and unsold goods. They are disappointed because their plans have not been carried out. They have really been forced to "invest" more than they intended.

One thing is certain. Business firms will not continue to expect the previously established and higher rate of sales. They will rather quickly revise their selling plans downward as a result of the inventory build-up. They will reduce their planned investment. This takes the form of reduced orders for both inventories and capital goods. Rates of output will be reduced for many commodities, and, with this, the amount of employment. Layoffs and unemployment will appear. The initial reduction in consumption expenditure (the increase in saving) will, therefore, create unemployment through its effects on the plans of business firms. Money incomes and real incomes are both reduced as a result of the attempts of firms to adjust to the situation with which they are faced.

The above analysis is a useful one in that it does allow some important short-run predictions to be made. But it has left out one important factor which the careful reader may have noted. With the reduction in consumer demand the retailer may be able to sell the same quantity of goods as before *if he will reduce selling prices*. Clearly firms will be under pressure to reduce selling prices as well as to reduce output. But many firms will prefer to reduce sales rather than prices. This stems from two causes. First, many producers have at least some degree of monopoly power, that is, some control over the prices which they may charge. They realize that a reduction in sales will allow them to maintain prices at the earlier levels even in the face of reduced aggregate demand. Other firms may be in oligopolistic industries in which price-cutting may lead to price wars. Second, even if the firms were willing to cut prices drastically in order to remove unsold goods in the face of a decreased consumer demand, they would be able to do so permanently only in those instances where prices are considerably higher than average variable costs. If variable costs are to be lowered, prices paid by firms for productive services employed must be reduced. The most important of productive inputs is, of course, labor. Therefore, a general money-wage reduction is required. But money-wage reductions are likely to be exceedingly difficult to secure, especially in industries where labor is highly organized. For these two reasons, prices and costs are often extremely slow in adjusting to downward movements in demand. Where this is true the primary adjustment which firms make to shifts in demand must be in terms of output. We have many examples of this. In the recession of 1957 industrial production shifted downward, largely as a result of a slowdown in business expenditure on capital goods, but the price level moved upward. The rigidity which is inherent in the price and wage structure requires that adjustments to demand shifts take the form of changes in rates of output.

How long will the adjustment process continue? How much will output or real income be reduced? Quite clearly firms will continue to reduce output so long as inventories are accumulating, and output will be stabilized only when plans and realizations again become synchronized, that is, until planned investment is again equal to planned savings. A new equilibrium level of income for which this would be true is approached in the following way. As employment and/or rates of pay are reduced, total money payments to owners of productive services are reduced. In other words, personal income receipts are lowered. Out of the lower incomes, individuals will be able to save less than before. This reduction in money income flow is the primary mechanism which serves to bring planned saving into equality with planned investment. National income will fall, in this example, until people's ability to save is reduced enough to conform to the new, and reduced, investment plans of firms. The initial attempt made by individuals to increase total savings may actually result in their saving less because the changed pattern of spending generates a reduction in income. This possible reduction in total savings as a result of an attempt of people to save more has been called by many writers "the paradox of thrift."

OTHER TYPES OF ADJUSTMENT

In this example we have traced the effects of an attempt by consumers to increase aggregate savings. This is only one of the several changes in behavior which might affect the level of income. Similar models may be used to trace the effects of other changes. It should not be difficult to see that the opposing case in which consumers try to increase spending will lead to opposing conclusions. An increase in planned consumer spending, which is the same as a reduction in planned savings, will deplete business inventories, making investment less than was intended. Or, should inventories not be sufficiently large, not all of the planned purchases may be carried out, and this will require some unplanned savings. The newly increased demand for consumer goods will cause firms to place additional orders with manufacturers. As output is expanded, income payments rise. At the higher money income, savings will be greater. The national money income will move upward until planned saving and planned investment are again in equality.

Similar effects to those in these first two examples will be produced by a change downward or upward in the spending attempts of business firms. If firms attempt to reduce investment spending as a result of a shift in expectations, this will cause national money income to be reduced. If, on the other hand, firms try to expand investment expenditure, national money income will go up. Changes upward or downward in the level of investment have been considered by some economists to be a major determinant of the level of national money income. This is because they have assumed consumer spending and saving habits to be more stable over time than the investment plans of business firms. If this proposition is, in fact, true (and recent experience as well as recently derived empirical data cast some doubt on its validity) investment spending becomes the key to fluctuations in national money income.

An upward movement in money income generated by any increase in spending, whether by consumers or firms, may or may not be accompanied by similar movements in real income and, thus, employment. In the case of an upward shift, the effects on real income and employment depend upon the characteristics of the initial position. If unemployment is present, increased spending will tend to call for the additional production and employment. But if the economy is running at reasonably full prosperity, with most productive resources employed, the primary effect of an increased rate of spending will be an increase in prices, that is, inflation. Consequently, an increase in national money income is not desirable at all times. Such an increase is desirable only if it is accompanied by an increase in real income. It is undesirable if accompanied merely by inflation.

A downward movement in money income, generated by any decrease in spending, will probably cause some reduction in real income and employment, especially in the short run. There is no necessity that real income and employment be reduced provided that prices of both final products and of productive services, including wages, can move downward in rapid adjustment to the reduction in aggregate demand. But the modern economy contains sufficient institutional rigidities to cause such adjustments to be difficult at best, and also to cause the adjustment process to be slow.

This chapter has summarized the forces which determine fluctuations in national income in a very simple model. Several important things have been left out, including the effects of government action. These will be brought into the analysis at a later stage. But before this step is taken, the next chapter will analyze the income-determining forces of the simplified model more carefully.

14

NATIONAL-INCOME ANALYSIS

The preceding chapter showed, in a very general way, that fluctuations in national income (both in money and in real terms) may be caused by changes in the spending-saving plans of individuals and business firms. In this chapter, a somewhat more rigorous and detailed formulation of the analysis will be presented. The analysis will include a discussion of some of the underlying forces which affect spending-saving plans of families and firms.

The Determinants of Consumption Expenditure

One of the major innovations made by Lord Keynes when he developed the basic framework of the modern theory of income determination was the introduction of the "consumption function." This function defines the relationship between the amount of consumption spending (and saving) and the level of income. An essential element of the Keynesian approach is the importance of current income receipts in determining consumption spending.

From an examination of data on consumption spending and income receipts, a reasonably close relationship seems to be present.

FIGURE 14.1. CONSUMPTION FUNCTION
FOR A FAMILY

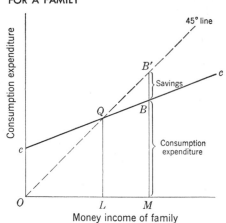

Some of the characteristics of this relationship (function) seem intuitively obvious. For most families, and, therefore, for the whole economy, the amount of spending increases as the level of income increases. In more formal terms, the consumption function, whether for an individual family or for the entire economy, must have a positive slope. Additional and more restrictive properties were placed on this relationship from a study of the data. The data showed that the higher the income level the smaller the proportion of income that was spent, or, to say the same thing conversely, a larger proportion of income is saved at higher income levels than at lower income levels. Again to state this in more formal terms, this property suggests that the positive slope of the consumption function must be less than unity.

The relationship between consumption expenditure and current income for a single family is illustrated geometrically in Figure 14.1. The money income currently received by an individual family is represented on the *x* axis, consumption expenditure on the *y* axis. The line *cc* represents the consumption function. If money income is *OM*, *MB* is the amount of consumption expenditure which will be undertaken. The fact that consumption spending increases as income increases requires that the line *cc* slope upward to the right.

The *ratio* of consumption expenditure to income may also be shown in Figure 14.1. If consumption expenditure were the only means of using money income so that all of one's income were always spent for consumption goods, then the line *cc* would lie along a line drawn at a 45-degree angle from the origin. At any point on

FIGURE 14.2. SAVING FUNCTION FOR A
SINGLE FAMILY

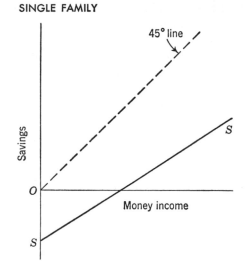

this 45-degree line the ordinate is equal to the abscissa, that is, the distance above the *x* axis is always just equal to the distance to the right from the *y* axis. If the entire income *OM* were spent, consumption expenditure would be *MB'* instead of *MB; OM* is exactly equal to *MB'*. By comparing the actual amount of income expended for consumption goods and services with the maximum amount which could have been spent if all the income received were used in this way, that is, by comparing *MB* with *MB'*, the ratio of consumption spending to income may be derived.

The difference between the amount of consumption expenditure and the total money income received represents savings. Therefore, savings can also be seen in relation to money income in Figure 14.1. At income *OM*, savings are represented by *BB'*. At any income, savings are represented graphically by the distance between the line *cc* (the consumption function) and the 45-degree line.

The relationship between savings and current income receipts can be represented directly. This is illustrated in Figure 14.2. Instead of measuring consumption expenditure along the vertical axis, we now measure saving. The line *ss* represents the savings function.

It may be noted that Figures 14.1 and 14.2 are so drawn that at an income level shown by *OL* all the income received is spent for consumption goods and services (*OL = LQ*). *OL* represents, of course, a very low income level, and it is realistic to assume that at very low incomes families must spend all they can get and are unable to save anything. At incomes lower than *OL*, the figures are drawn so as to show that the expenditure on consumption goods and services is actually more than money income received; the line *cc* lies above the 45-degree line. The line *ss* in Figure 14.2 lies below the horizontal axis. This implies that, at extremely low incomes, families must beg, borrow, or steal in order to survive. If incomes are extremely low for only a short period, a family can live on previous savings, or borrow, until a higher level of income is again attained. Over a longer period of time, previous savings would be wiped out, and the family would no longer be able to borrow. But with modern welfare institutions operating, these families would qualify for relief, community-chest assistance, etc. At incomes lower than *OL*, negative savings may be said to be present. Not only is all the money income which is received in exchange for productive work spent, but more is spent.

Figures 14.1 and 14.2 represent the consumption-income relationship and the saving-income relationship for an individual family. Aggregate relationships for the whole economy are required for extending the analysis. The aggregate functions may be derived conceptually by adding the schedules for all individuals.

Investment Expenditure and Income

Investment spending must also be examined in more detail than it was in the last chapter. Probably, the decisions of business executives to purchase additional inventories or new equipment, to construct new buildings or repair old ones, etc., are not so closely tied to current or recent income levels as are the decisions of consumers. Instead, investment decisions are primarily dependent on the state of business expectations. If the business community expects consumer spending to be high and the economy generally to be prosperous, firms will normally decide to invest substantial sums in replacing and modernizing plant facilities and in expansion. If, on the other hand, there is a general expectation that a recession is on its way, little investment will be undertaken. Investment spending probably depends more on the way in which income is expected to change than on the level of income at any time.

Nevertheless, there is probably a direct relationship between the level of income and the amount of investment spending which will be scheduled, since the expectations concerning future incomes depend in part on the size of current income. Investment plans of businessmen are closely related to business profits. If substantial profits have been received during a period, it seems probable that business-men will expect such profits to continue to be received in the future. And it is during periods of high incomes that aggregate profits are highest. In this somewhat indirect way, periods of high income are as-sociated with high investment expenditure. High profits not only provide the incentive for new investment but also provide the funds for such expenditures to the extent that earnings are "plowed back." On the other hand, if profits are not being made, as is the case for most firms during depressed periods of low income, firms' managers tend to be pessimistic. Few of them will foresee prosperity, and firms generally are likely to contract investment expenditure.

In addition to the relationship between the level of national income and the volume of investment expenditures due to businessmen's ex-pectations, a second factor may operate to tie investment spending directly to income changes. As income increases, consumption spend-ing also increases. This increase in the demand for consumption goods will tend to cause firms to demand more capital equipment which goes into the manufacture of such goods unless excess capacity is initially present. This derived demand for capital goods may affect the capital-goods industries more significantly than it does the con-sumption-goods industries.

This may be shown by a simple example. Suppose that the daily rate of sales of Coca-Cola in a small Southern town is 2,500 cases. Suppose further that it takes 10 bottling machines to produce 2,500 cases, or 1 for each 250 cases. Suppose further that the average length of life of a bottling machine is ten years, and, on the average, 1 unit is replaced each year. Then the normal annual production of these units of equipment for sale in this town is 1 per year.

Now suppose that consumers increase the quantity purchased by 20 per cent because of an over-all increase in income. This means that 3,000 cases instead of 2,500 will be demanded. To produce this amount, 12 instead of 10 units of capital equipment will be required. So 2 additional bottling machines must be produced to supplement the initial 10, plus the 1 which is produced to meet the normal re-placement requirement. If this situation is representative of the econ-omy as a whole, the capital-equipment industry must expand by 200 per cent as a result of an increase in final product demand of 20 per cent.

This is, of course, an extremely abstract and oversimplified ex-ample. If consumer-goods industries possess excess capacity, there may be no increase in the demand for capital equipment. Further-more, capital equipment need not remain in a fixed ratio to final

FIGURE 14.3. AGGREGATE INVESTMENT FUNC-
TION

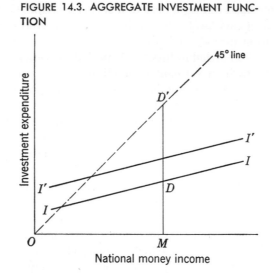

National money income

output. In spite of these necessary weaknesses, the acceleration principle, as it is called, is useful in indicating the manner in which
an increase in consumer spending may generate subsequent demand for investment and in showing why fluctuations may be more
violent in capital-goods than in consumer-goods industries.

THE INVESTMENT FUNCTION

The investment function may be shown geometrically in Figure
14.3. In this case, this relationship can better be considered initially
to be in aggregate terms, that is, we are relating total net investment expenditure by all firms to total income of the economy. National money income is measured along the x axis and total net investment expenditure along the y axis. The line II represents the investment function. Any point on II shows the amount of investment
spending which business firms will be planning to undertake at that
level of income. Thus, if national money income were OM, investment spending undertaken would be MD. By drawing in the
45-degree line as before, the ratio of investment expenditure to income may be seen. Since MD' is equal to OM, this ratio at income
OM is MD to MD'.

The Determination of National Money Income

The way in which national money income is determined in this
simplified model may now be indicated. By combining the savings

function and the investment function, money income may be determined. This is possible because, as we have shown in the preceding chapter, total investment expenditure must be equal to total savings. This is illustrated in Figure 14.4. The line SS represents the aggregate savings function for the whole economy; this is derived by adding up or aggregating the saving relationships for the individual units in the economy. The line II is the aggregate investment function.

National money income is determined where aggregate investment is equal to total savings, that is, at X. This is the only level of income at which planned savings will be equal to planned investment. In order to understand this process of income determination more fully, let us again assume initially that national money income is equilibrium at OX. Now assume that, for some reason (perhaps as a result of the favorable outcome of a national election), the business community becomes more optimistic about future prospects for the economy. This will cause business firms to expand, or attempt to expand, investment spending. The investment function in Figure 14.4 shifts upward from II to I'I'. Initially, firms will not be able to expand aggregate investment as they wish. Inventories will be depleted by the amount KK'. This depletion of inventories and the existence of unfilled orders will cause manufacturers to expand output and employment, provided that unemployed resources exist initially. In this case money income goes up from OX to OX' through a real expansion in production. If, on the other hand, substantially full employment was present before the change in investment plans, the money income increase from OX to OX' takes the form of price increases. The upward movement in money income will (in either case) continue until all spending plans are satisfied. As money income increases, a greater amount of money savings becomes possible.

The analysis used here can be applied to any of the possible changes in spending or savings plans of individuals or firms. If planned investment should be reduced, a fall in income would result. If planned savings increases, income will also fall. On the other hand, if planned savings decreases, income will go up.

The analysis of this and the preceding chapter should indicate that there appears to be nothing which tends to cause the equilibrium level of national money income to approximate that which is most desirable. The equilibrium level might well be one of inflationary magnitude, or it might be one low enough to generate a significant degree of deflation and unemployment. All the theory does is to define that level of national money income which will tend to be established in an economy in which the government is truly neutral, or conceptually nonexistent. The only factors determining this equilibrium-level income in such a model economy are the plans of consumers concerning spending and saving of the income received and the plans of business firms concerning investment.

SOME COMPLICATIONS ARE INTRODUCED

In our discussion above, we have omitted several important factors which serve to influence the determination of national money income. We must now add these to the picture.

The Government in the Economy

The major income-determining factor to be introduced is the activity of the government, which exerts an increasingly important influence on the flow of income in the modern economy. Total spending is not composed of consumption and private investment alone; to these must be added government expenditure on goods and services. In terms of the total spendings equation defining national income [Equation (2) in Chapter 13], we must now add a third item, G, to represent government expenditure.

$$Y = C + I + G \qquad (5)$$

The G in Equation (5) does not include everything that the government spends, since a large part of public outlay goes to finance *transfer payments* such as social-security benefits, interest on the national debt, and veterans' benefits. These payments are not made in exchange for real goods and services which are currently produced. They are, in a genuine sense, *negative taxes*. The G used in the income Equation (5) includes only public expenditure on real goods and services such as Jupiter missiles, hydrogen bombs, highways, and government bookkeeping.

The government also reduces potential spending and saving by the imposition of taxes. In other words, consumption spending and saving no longer exhaust the total means of disposing of income which is received. The receipts version of the income equation must also include an additional item. Income may be spent, saved, or paid in taxes. Equation (1) of Chapter 13 becomes

$$Y = C + S + T \qquad (6)$$

The transfer payments which are not included in G of Equation (5) are included in T as negative items. A man who pays an annual tax of $1,000 but who receives $1,000 in social-security benefits would not affect the aggregate value of the T of Equation (6). Some difficulties in the analysis arise when business taxes are taken into account. These taxes are paid directly by firms and do not, therefore, reduce the stream of money-income payments made to individuals. For our purposes, however, we may make the simplifying assumption that the amount collected in business taxes would be paid out in dividends if the taxes were to be removed.

The total amount of taxes collected by government (on balance) need not match precisely the expenditures made by government of real goods and services. Once this is recognized, no longer can it be said that equality between planned savings and planned investment is the required condition for maintaining stability in national income. From Equations (5) and (6) we get,

$$I + G = S + T \qquad (7)$$

We see that planned savings plus planned net tax collections must equal planned investment expenditure plus planned government expenditure. If, for example, G should exceed T, then S must exceed I. If the government budgets for a deficit of, say, $5 billion, planned private savings must exceed planned private investment if national money income is to be kept on an even keel. On the other hand, if the government intends to collect more in taxes (a purely hypothetical speculation?) than it intends to spend, planned private investment must exceed planned private savings if income is not to fall. Only if the budget is balanced, and at a stable level, will the

FIGURE 14.5. NATIONAL INCOME MAY
BE AFFECTED—By Taxes and Government
Spending

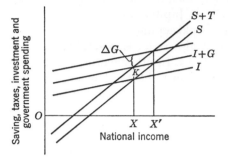

equality of planned savings and planned private investment ensure income stability.

The modified analysis may be demonstrated quite readily in Figure 14.5, which is developed from Figure 14.4. The intersection of the $S + T$ function and the $I + G$ function now determines income instead of the intersection of the saving function and the investment function. As we have drawn Figure 14.5, income will be established at OX. It is noted that the effects of government activity are neutral in this case. The intersection of the S function and the I function lies along the line drawn from X to K.

The Foreign-trade Balance

A second important influence on the level of national income, which has, to this point, been neglected, is the foreign-trade balance. So far, in our analysis we have assumed that the economy is closed and no foreign trade takes place. In the real world, foreign trade does take place, and this factor must be taken into account in the analysis. Foreign purchases made in this country constitute another form of expenditure on goods and services domestically produced. In terms of the income equations developed earlier, the income-expenditure equation becomes,

$$Y = C + I + G + E \qquad (8)$$

where E represents "exports."

On the earnings or receipts side an adjustment must also be made. Income earned in this country but expended for foreign-produced goods and services constitutes a net drainage or leakage from the domestic-payments stream. There are now four ways of disposing of income: consumption spending, savings, paying taxes, and purchasing foreign goods and services (importing). The relevant income equation becomes,

$$Y = C + S + T + F \qquad (9)$$

where F represents "imports."

Care must be taken, of course, in defining "imports" and "exports" in the above equations, but these difficulties need not concern us at this point. It can readily be seen that foreign trade can exert an expansionary or a contractionary influence upon the level of national income, depending upon the sign and size of the "net foreign balance." This term may be defined as exports minus imports, or in symbols, $E - F$. If exports exceed imports in value, the net foreign balance is positive. This means that international transactions exert an upward influence in national income, adding to the stream of total spending. If imports exceed exports, foreign trade exerts a depressing influence on the level of national money income. This may be highly desirable when domestic inflation is threatened, but it may be undesirable if unemployment is present.

The two items, imports and exports, correctly defined, may be expected to remain roughly in balance unless one country is investing in other countries. Foreign countries can buy in the United States only if they are selling something to us or borrowing from us or receiving handouts from us; otherwise they do not possess the dollar exchange with which to purchase American goods. A long-term difference between the export and the import items must involve some creation of the wherewithal with which the deficit country may purchase. A leading reason why the United States was able, in the nineteenth century, to import more in dollar value than she exported was that British business firms were investing capital in the construction of American railroads. Since World War I, our exports have been greater than our imports because we have been lending or giving large sums to foreign governments. We are "investing" abroad.

The foreign-trade factor could readily be incorporated in the geometrical analysis of Figure 14.5, but the student can easily visualize the effects on total income of changes in imports and exports.

The Multiplier

Concentration upon spending as the major determinant of national income and recognition of the circular flow of income in the economy have provided the basis for the development of the "multiplier" concept. Recalling the income wheel discussed in Chapter 1, it is clear that a large part of the income received by individuals returns directly to the income stream as expenditure on consumer goods and services. This suggests that the addition of one new dollar of spending anywhere in the income flow process will generate "multiplying" effects on income as the circular flow continues during succeeding spendings periods.

If individuals may be presumed to spend a rather fixed proportion of additional income received, a degree of arithmetical precision is given to the income multiplier. Suppose, for example, that people spend, on the average, $8, and save $2, out of each additional $10 of income which they receive.[1] Now suppose that, without anything else changing, some business firm expands investment spending by $1. If new savings of $1 are to arise to match this additional investment, income will have to expand by $5. The new investment dollar will have to generate a fivefold increase in income; the value of the multiplier must be 5.

This concept may be clarified by a more detailed look at the multiplying process in the simplified example. The firm purchases an additional dollar's worth of machinery. The sellers of the machinery receive an additional dollar in revenue which is paid out in wages, dividends, or other forms of income payment. Since we have assumed that people spend $\frac{4}{5}$ of any additional income, those who receive the dollar will spend 80 cents and save 20 cents. The 80 cents is spent for consumer goods and once again it becomes income to private families. Out of this 80 cents, when it is received as income, 64 cents will be spent, and 16 cents will be saved. This process will continue, with the effects becoming less and less pronounced in each income period, until income has expanded by the full $5. The multiplying effects of the additional dollar added to the spending stream will finally vanish when the full amount has "leaked" out of spending into savings, either personal or business. At this point, the effects of the initial increment in investment will have subsided, and national income will again be generated at a rate equal to that prevailing prior to the injection of the additional dollar. Table 14.1 illustrates the multiplier process.

Only if the $1 increment in investment continues over successive

[1] The ratio between the additional amount of consumption expenditure and the additional income is technically defined as the *marginal propensity to consume*. Algebraically, it is defined as $\Delta C/\Delta Y$. Geometrically, it is the slope of the consumption function. This should be distinguished from the *average propensity to consume*, which is C/Y.

spending periods can income in *any one* period be expected to rise by the full value indicated from the multiplier. If a dollar increment is added in *each* successive period, eventually a point will be reached when the additional spending is made up of (1) the incremental dollar currently being added, (2) the 80 cents second-round effects of the $1 increment in the immediately preceding period, (3) the 64 cents third-round effects of the $1 increment made two periods back, etc. In this way the secondary effects of the increment to investment in each period may be concentrated in

Table 14.1. Multiplier Effects of $1 Increment in Investment
(Marginal propensity to consume equals ⅘)

Spending period	(ΔY) Income	(ΔC) Consumer expenditure	(ΔS) Savings
1	$1.00	$0.80	$0.20
2	0.80	0.64	0.16
3	0.64	0.512	0.138
4	0.512	0.4096	0.1024
5	0.4096	0.32768	0.08192
6	0.32768	0.262144	0.065536
.	. . . .	. . . .	. . . .
Total	$5.00	$4.00	$1.00

one period, and income of the period will be greater by the full amount of $5 in our simple example.

It should be emphasized that the multiplier can work negatively as well as positively. A reduction in spending, with other things remaining unchanged, will generate some multiple contraction in income.

This multiplier concept should not be taken to represent too much. It really says little more than was said in Chapter 13, that is, a change in investment will tend to generate an increase or decrease in income. The arithmetical exactitude of the value of the multiplier depends solely on the presumed stability in the marginal propensity to consume. Recent empirical findings have suggested that this propensity is much less stable than was previously thought to be the case. The multiplier concept remains useful, however, if not taken too strictly, because it does tend to focus attention on the cumulative effects of initial changes in spending.

The concept should not be limited to investment alone, since it applies equally well to any change in spending. The additional spending of a dollar on consumption goods would likewise have generated a fivefold increase in income in the example above. The concept is especially useful in indicating the cumulative effects of changes in the economic variables which are subject to control by government. A change in the government's expenditure without any increase in taxes will serve to increase income by some multiple of the change in the government deficit, provided that private investment plans are not directly affected by the deficit financing.

The effects of a change in the size of the government deficit may be shown in Figure 14.5. An expansion in the rate of government spending which is maintained without an increase in taxes, and with no other offsetting effects, would shift the $I + G$ function upward by the amount ΔG, where ΔG represents the increment in government spending. The increment in national money income XX' is seen to be greater than the increase in government spending. The ratio between the increase in income (XX') and the initial increase in government spending (ΔG) is the multiplier. It may be seen that the value of this ratio depends on the slope of the savings and investment function. The greater the slope of the saving function, that is, the greater the proportion of an increment in income that will be saved, the smaller will be the multiplier effects of a government deficit. If the government decides to cut down its spending without changing the tax rate, a negative multiplier effect will be introduced, and a cumulative reduction in income will set in.

An Evaluation of the Theory

National money income at any one time has been shown to be determined by the decisions of consumers to spend and save; the decisions of businessmen to purchase investment goods; the decisions of legislative bodies and government officials concerning the size and balance of the government budget; and the decisions of both natives and foreigners relating to purchases of home-produced and foreign-produced goods and services. The first question to be asked in any evaluation of this theory is: Is it useful in helping to understand the causes of and to predict changes in income? The ability to predict is the basic test of any theory, and it is especially important here. If undesirable fluctuations are to be prevented, it is essential that movements of the important determining variables be predicted in advance with reasonable accuracy. For this requirement to be fulfilled, the economic variables must not be subject to unexpected and random changes. The most important of these variables in magnitude is consumer spending. *If* the relationship of consumer spending to income remained relatively stable over time, an estimation of income payments would make possible a rough prediction of consumer expenditure. The government item is relatively predictable and controllable. And, for this country, year-to-year changes in the foreign-trade item are not appreciably large. This leaves investment expenditure as the variable most subject to erratic fluctuations, and therefore this variable is held by some to be the major determinant of changes in the level of income. Fluctuations up and down in money income are held to be largely the result of waves of optimism and pessimism pervading the business atmosphere. National money income is considered to be a direct function of investment expenditure.

The "if" mentioned in the preceding paragraph proves, however, to be a big one. Between 1929 and 1940 there was a steady correlation between consumption spending and income. But this relationship was greatly disturbed during and after World War II. As a matter of fact, a group of Washington economists made a serious error in predicting a significant depression in late 1945 and early 1946 largely because they were using the consumption-income function of the 1929 to 1940 period as the basis of their predictions. But consumption spending proved to be greater in 1946 than this earlier relationship would have indicated. As a result, inflation rather than depression became the actual postwar problem. Since this time, economists have become much more cautious concerning their ability to predict with any degree of accuracy the swings in income by the use of statistics based on the theoretical analysis presented above. Although it is admitted that income is a major factor determining the amount of consumption spending, it is now recognized that other important variables affecting such spending are also present which are not explicitly accounted for in the analysis. These may include past income, expected income, the price level, and the real value and liquidity of assets owned. The consumption function shifted upward in 1946 from its 1940 position mainly because people had accumulated large cash and government-bond holdings during the war period and had also built up unsatisfied desires for goods which had been unavailable for several years.

The most recent studies indicate that the type of income received is very important in determining the responsiveness of consumption spending. If an individual considers an addition to his income to be *permanent*, he may expand spending to a considerable extent. On the other hand, if the individual thinks that a particular addition to his income is temporary or accidental, that is, a windfall gain, he may save most of it. For example, the man who receives a $1,000 increase in his annual salary may expand his consumption to a much greater extent than the man who receives a $1,000 inheritance or veteran's bonus. As actually measured, incomes are made up of both permanent and transitory components. Improvements in the usefulness of this income-spending approach in making actual predictions probably depend upon the development of some means of separating these permanent and transitory aspects of incomes.[1]

The distinction between permanant and temporary increases in income may also be important for public policy. For example, a temporary tax cut in early 1958 as an antirecession measure was opposed on the grounds that consumers would not increase spending sufficiently precisely because they would consider the tax-induced increase in personal income to be temporary.

[1] The discussion of this paragraph is based on the work of Milton Friedman, *A Theory of the Consumption Function* (Princeton, N.J.: Princeton University Press, 1957).

15

MONEY AND THE PRICE LEVEL

A major weakness in the theory of income as it was discussed in the preceding chapters is its failure to include monetary factors as important determinants of the fluctuations in national money income. While concentrating on spending decisions of firms, individuals, and government, it largely neglects the monetary system and the monetary policy of the government. This neglect must now be remedied, for the theory is incomplete as it now stands. Monetary factors may act to influence the level of money income in several ways, and since movements in real income are likely to accompany shifts in money income, it follows that monetary factors can also influence real income.

Monetary Policy and Decisions to Spend

The theory of income determination does not completely leave out of account monetary influences. A more appropriate statement would be to the effect that the theory assumes (without making the assumption explicit) that a particular type of monetary system is in existence and that a certain kind of monetary policy is being followed. It assumes a monetary system and a monetary policy which will allow decisions to spend to be carried out without difficulty. For example, when we traced through the effects of a change in investment expenditures on income, it was assumed that business firms would have no difficulty in securing the additional funds required. This is a reasonably realistic assumption in the modern economy: an expansion in investment expenditure may be carried out by increased borrowing from the banking system. But the monetary and banking system in its present form is only one of many conceivable systems which could be utilized. The particular monetary system which does exist in our economy and some of the alternative monetary policies will be discussed more fully in later chapters. It will be sufficient here to show briefly how a change in monetary policy might influence income.

Suppose that national real income is at such a high level that further increases in national money income would lead only to inflation and hence would be undesirable. The analysis of the preceding chapters has shown how a further increase in money income might be prevented by a reduction in government spending or an increase in taxation. But monetary policy can also be effective in accomplishing this objective. Suppose that businessmen (perhaps expecting even more inflation in the future) plan to invest considerably more in subsequent time periods than they are now investing. Anticipating the expanded investment, the government might inaugurate a restrictive monetary policy through its control of the banking system. This would probably take the form of making the borrowing of funds more difficult, for example, by increasing the rate of interest to be charged on bank loans. The way in which the government could curtail borrowing will be explained in some detail in later chapters.

Investment decisions depend to some degree upon the rate of interest. If a project under consideration is expected to yield a return substantially above the rate at which money can be borrowed, sound business practice would indicate that the money should be borrowed and the project undertaken. Consequently, while many potential projects might prove profitable at interest rates of 2 or 3 per cent, these same projects might well prove unprofitable at 5 or 6 per cent rates. Investment expenditure is related to the level of interest rates in an inverse fashion. If other things are the same, a higher rate of interest will reduce the amount of investment expenditure and thus lower national income.

Not only does the level of interest rates affect spendings decisions of firms; individual families are also affected. Especially important is the influence of the rate of interest on expenditure for residential construction. If money can be borrowed on long-term mortgages for 4 per cent (as was possible for a few years after World War II under the GI home-loan guarantee), the monthly costs of owning a home will be significantly lower than if the money could be borrowed for no less than 6 per cent.

The influence of monetary policy on spendings decisions of firms and individuals is not limited to the effects generated by direct operations on the interest rate. The supply of money can be varied, and this may affect the rate of interest, a large supply tending to make people more willing to give up money, thus lowering the interest rate. The money supply may also have a direct influence on spendings decisions. In addition, as was mentioned earlier, the amount of consumption expenditure depends partly on the real value of assets held by consumers, especially the total purchasing power of their money and government bonds. Monetary policy designed to increase the cash holdings of individuals may, therefore, have a tendency to increase consumption spending and thus to raise income.

The Theory of the Price Level

Since monetary and price-level factors, both of which are important in influencing economic fluctuations, are partially left out of account in the theory of income, for many purposes an alternative theory may yield more productive results. The alternative theory concentrates directly on the money supply and people's desires to hold money and tries to explain economic fluctuations in terms of the general level of prices rather than in terms of income.

The monetary approach begins with a fundamental equation which ties together the important variables affecting the general level of prices. If P represents the general level of prices, T the total volume of transactions carried out during the period under study, M the quantity of money, and V the velocity of circulation of money, *i.e.*, the rate at which money turns over, the equation takes the form $MV = PT$.[1] This is sometimes called the "equation of exchange." From one point of view, the equation states the obvious

---

[1] Serious problems are involved in the precise definition of the form of the variables in the equation. Properly, each variable must be in terms of an index number of the composite magnitude represented, and each index number must be related to the same base. See Clark Warburton, "Elementary Algebra and the Equation of Exchange," *American Economic Review*, Vol. 43, pp. 358–361 (June, 1953).

fact that the amount expended during any period MV equals the value of the goods and services sold PT. The fact that the equation may be a truism does not prevent its being extremely useful.

The equation serves to place the important monetary variables in a precise relationship to each other. In so doing, it allows a logical chain of reasoning on monetary matters to be followed. A glance at the equation shows that an increase in the quantity of money M must be accompanied by either a decrease in velocity V, an increase in the general level of prices P, or an increase in the volume of transactions T. That is, if the supply of money increases, people may either hold it for longer periods on the average, thus decreasing velocity, or they may spend more. If they spend more, the money demand for goods and services is increased. If the supply of goods and services remains unchanged, the increase in money demand will cause prices to be bid up, increasing the price level P. If the increased spending is accompanied by an increase in the volume of goods and services T, as would perhaps be the case in times when resources were unemployed, the price level need not be increased. The equation thus shows that an increase or a decrease in the quantity of money may be counterbalanced by changes in either one or all of the other variables.

If national output is high and resources are fully employed, it is not likely that the physical volume of transactions can be increased a great deal.[1] In addition, it is probable that people will not, in such situations, substantially change their habits concerning the average length of the period for which a unit of money is held; *i.e.,* velocity will not change substantially. In these circumstances, an increase in the quantity of money (and/or money substitutes such as government bonds) will probably exert a primary effect on the level of prices, serving to generate inflation.

On the other hand, if there is significant unemployment and business generally is in a depressed state, an increase in the quantity of money may exert its primary effect on increasing the volume of transactions with little or no effect on prices. If the increased quantity of money induces more spending, the demand for goods and services will increase. This increased demand need not cause prices

[1] A qualification must be introduced here. Since T represents an index of the total volume of transactions, it includes financial as well as real output transactions. The inclusion of financial transactions creates difficulties in the use of the equation, since an increase in T could come about without an increase in real output, for example, in a stock-market boom. These difficulties may be substantially eliminated in a more rigorous version of the equation, but this cannot be elaborated here.

to rise, however, if it generates an increase in supply to match the increase in demand. The increased spending will thus serve largely to increase production and employment. However, if expectations are extremely pessimistic, there is the possibility that an increase in the quantity of money may not generate an increase in total spending; the right-hand side of the equation will not be affected at all if velocity declines sufficiently to offset the increase in M. In this case, an increase in the quantity of money would serve merely to increase the cash balances of those groups holding money for longer periods. People, on the average, would simply turn over their money more slowly. Although a decline in velocity might offset an increase in the money supply to some degree, it seems highly unrealistic to assume that it will ever fully do so. An increase in the quantity of money will, therefore, normally generate some increase in spending, thus increasing either the general level of prices or the volume of goods and services produced, or both. A decrease in the quantity of money (or money substitutes) would have effects in the opposite direction from those traced above, serving to decrease the level of prices or the volume of real output unless offset by an increase in the velocity of circulation of the reduced money stock.

The emphasis on the quantity of money as the causal variable in the equation of exchange stems from the fact that it is the one most susceptible to control by the government. Independent shifts in any of the variables may also cause changes in any or all of the others, including the quantity of money. If the average wage earner suddenly decides to hold a larger cash sum in his pocket than he did before, for example, the velocity of the existing money supply will be reduced. This change might cause the banking system to expand the money supply in an offsetting fashion, but if not, a reduction in spending would ensue. Or, in the converse case, if a law were passed requiring that all wage earners be paid daily instead of weekly, the velocity of circulation would be increased. With more frequent pay periods, the typical family would keep the average income dollar on hand for a shorter period of time. Fewer dollars would do the same amount of work in exchanging goods and services. Unless a reduction in the quantity of money accompanied the changed length of pay period, an increase in spending, and consequently an increase in the price level or in the volume of transactions, would result.

Just as with the model used in the theory of income discussed in the preceding chapters, the real usefulness of the equation of exchange depends on its ability to facilitate prediction. This ability depends on whether or not the proper variables have been included and whether or not these variables can be measured and their changes predicted. The equation does bring together important variables. Some of these are, however, extremely difficult to compute statistically, and such a computation would be required for prediction. The equation of exchange has been employed for prediction purposes in the so-called "quantity theory of money." The proponents of this theory generally assume that the velocity of circulation is approximately constant over short time periods. They further assume that the volume of transactions remains unchanged (an assumption which is approximately valid only when the economy is operating at full capacity). With these restrictions placed upon it, the equation of exchange then indicates that an increase or decrease in the quantity of money will exert a direct influence on the level of prices. This version of the "quantity theory" has been properly criticized for neglecting possible shifts in velocity and changes in the volume of transactions.

Comparison of the Income Theory and the Equation of Exchange

The velocity of circulation occupies a position in the monetary theory of economic fluctuations which is similar to that occupied by the consumption-income relationship in the income theory. If velocity does not remain relatively stable over short-run periods, *i.e.*, if people's habits concerning cash holdings do not remain approximately stable over time, changes in total spending cannot be predicted from changes in the quantity of money. Similarly, if the consumption-income relationship is not stable but is subject to erratic fluctuations, changes in money income cannot be predicted directly from changes in the volume of investment expenditure. The appropriateness of these two different theoretical approaches to economic fluctuations depends in part on the relative degree of stability in these two variables, *i.e.*, velocity of circulation and the propensity to consume.

The choice between using the income theory and the monetary theory of economic fluctuations also depends on the purposes which are to be accomplished. The income theory concludes that the decisions of people to spend or save, the decisions of businessmen to invest or not to invest, and the decisions of government budget makers are the active determinants of national money income and thus of the level of real income and prices. This conclusion implies the corollary assumption that the monetary variables (the quantity and velocity of money) are passive, that is, that the monetary system is of such a nature that it adjusts automatically to changes in the spendings decisions. As the following chapters discussing the monetary system will make clear, this assumption is a relatively realistic one in the economy today. This may be shown by a single example.

Suppose that a wave of confidence causes businessmen to expand their investment plans. To finance the added investment, additional funds will be required. These funds may come from expanded bank loans, security sales, or reductions in the cash reserves of firms. In the first case, the money supply (which includes currency and bank deposits) is increased. The increase in M would indicate by way of the equation of exchange that either the price level or the volume of transactions or both would increase. The monetary approach therefore arrives at precisely the same conclusion as the income approach, *i.e.*, that national money income would increase if investment increased. In this example, however, the income approach is the more descriptive, because the initiating force is the decision made by businessmen to increase investment. The increase in the money supply was secondary to this decision and was effected by the additional demand for bank loans.

For other than purely explanatory purposes, the monetary approach frequently proves to be more useful. In the example just considered, the added investment expenditure is able to exert an effect on money income only because the supply of money is adjustable. And while the investment decisions are made by private individuals and, therefore, are not directly controllable by government in a free economy, the regulation of the quantity of money has traditionally been accepted as an appropriate governmental function. The monetary approach becomes superior in that it concentrates on the one variable which may be directly controlled, the money supply. The velocity of circulation cannot, of course, be so readily controlled. Decisions to transfer funds from active to inactive accounts, and vice versa, are decisions made by private individuals. But such shifts may be offset by opposite shifts in the quantity of money.

From the comparison of the two approaches, it should be evident that they are alternative and complementary to each other. The theory of income is incomplete unless the influence on total spending exerted by the supply of money and the price level is taken into account. The theory of the price level is incomplete unless shifts in velocity brought about by changes in saving-spending decisions are included.

The Inflationary Process

It is necessary to discuss more carefully than we have done heretofore the meanings of the terms "inflation" and "deflation." When the general price level is increasing, inflation is said to be occurring. It should be emphasized that the movements in the general or "average" level of prices should be distinguished from movements in individual prices. During inflation, not all individual prices need be increasing, and among those which are increasing the rate of increase need not be uniform. Any individual price is set by the particular supply-and-demand forces affecting that product or service. Some prices may be remaining stable or even declining, while the total economy is experiencing inflation. For example, the prices of automobile tires remained roughly stable during the inflation accompanying and following World War II. This came about because supply increased as rapidly as demand in this particular industry. Inflation is taking place whenever enough prices of important commodities and services are increasing to cause a general index of prices to rise.

Another way of stating the same thing is in terms of the value or purchasing power of money. Inflation is occurring when the purchasing power of the monetary unit is falling. The general price level and the value of money are really two sides of the same coin.

Inflation occurs when an increase in the total money demand for goods and services, total spending, is not offset by an increase in the total supply of goods and services. The increase in total spending may come from any of several sources—investment spending, consumption spending, or government spending. It may be accompanied by an increase in the quantity of money or by an increase in the velocity of circulation or both. The increase in money demand will not affect all goods and services alike, and this fact points up one of the major evils of inflation. Some prices tend to rise faster than others. It is likely that final product prices will be the first general category affected. There may be considerable time lags between the increases in final product prices and increases in the prices of productive services. This time lag may be shortened, however, if sellers of productive services anticipate the increases in product prices, as some labor unions have done, and exert pressure for wage increases in advance.

Let us trace through in very simple terms the effects of an increase in money demand for consumers' goods. Firms will find inventories dwindling and will be quick to realize that they can increase selling prices. The increase in prices will serve to increase business profits in several ways. First of all, inventories may have been purchased at preinflation prices. A profit is secured by merely holding inventory. But this type of profit has sometimes been called "paper profit," because when firms find it necessary to replace inventory they will increase the demand for goods at the wholesale level. Wholesale prices will go up, and the pure inventory profits will vanish. A second source of profits is found in the type of contracts used in purchasing inputs of productive services. Many inputs are purchased on the basis of long-term contractual arrangements. For example, having agreed to pay for labor services at a certain wage rate for a year, the firm is assured of constancy of labor input prices during the contract period even though output prices may increase. Prices of such inputs as utility services are likely to move upward slowly because of regulation by government agencies. A third source of inflationary profit is associated with the capital investment which has been made in fixed plant and equipment. If the capital goods were purchased during a preinflation period, depreciation charges are fixed over the length of the life of these assets and do not go up as output prices rise. When replacement becomes necessary, however, the depreciation reserve may not be sufficient to replace fully the fixed capital used up. In this sense, the high profits reported by business firms during periods of inflation reflect in part the failure of the accountants to deduct "true" depreciation charges from gross profits.

While final product prices and profits tend to increase before the prices of productive services or inputs increase, among the various inputs there is a great difference in the rates at which prices rise. In recent years, escalator clauses have been included in some wage contracts. These clauses are designed to tie the rate of wages directly to the cost-of-living price index. But whether or not escalator clauses are used, most strongly organized labor groups are able to keep wage rates roughly in line with upward movements in product prices. Many farmers have been able to secure government guarantees against both inflation and deflation through the device of "parity prices."

Other groups are not so fortunate, and upon them really rests the incidence of the inflationary process. Inflation is extremely harmful to the class of so-called white-collar workers. This group is largely unorganized and is unable to exert political and economic pressure in its own behalf. Wages and salaries paid to this group tend to move slowly during inflation, lagging far behind the upward movement in product prices (the cost of living) and in wage rates for strongly organized groups. But the most severely hit of all groups during inflation is that composed of individuals and families living on relatively fixed incomes. This group includes those living on pensions, beneficiaries of annuity contracts, recipients of bond interest, social-security beneficiaries, etc. For this group, an increase in the general level of prices is equivalent in result to the imposition of a tax which cannot be shifted to anyone else. In one sense, the best way of looking at the redistributive effects of inflation is through a comparison of its results with a tax and expenditure scheme which would have the same effects. A tax levied on all people with relatively fixed incomes, with the proceeds of the tax to be paid out to all people with more flexible incomes (stockholders, organized wage earners), would produce redistributive effects precisely equivalent to inflation.

In addition to these harmful redistributive effects, general inflation contains other evils. There are welfare effects in that additional resources are used up merely by the incentive to reduce cash balances below their most convenient levels.[1] If an individual expects prices to keep on rising, he will change his spending pattern and make every effort to transform his assets so as to take advantage of the expected price increases. Cash will be a highly undesirable form of asset in such cases; individuals will try to convert cash assets into real property, such as land, buildings, automobiles, or into equity shares, such as common stock. This very attempt to convert cash into other assets (increasing velocity of circulation) will drive up the price level, and the expectation of rising prices will be fulfilled. If inflation continues long enough or rapidly enough to convince the general public that the upward movement in prices is permanent and will continue without reversal, explosive inflation is apt to ensue. This is an example of a situation in which people's thinking that something will happen and acting accordingly will itself ensure that the expected will happen.

[1] See Martin J. Bailey, "The Welfare Cost of Inflationary Finance," *Journal of Political Economy*, Vol. 64, pp. 93–111 (April, 1956).

It should be recognized that the stability that is present in the general level of prices stems always in part from the continued faith of the people in stability. There always exists in the public mind some vague sort of idea concerning "the value of the dollar," usually based on the average purchasing power of money over several years. The mere existence of this idea serves to keep people from losing faith in the monetary system and letting inflation become explosive. If this faith is lost, however, prices skyrocket and economic chaos is the almost inevitable result.

A type of inflation slightly different from that just discussed has come to be recognized in recent years; this is "repressed" inflation. It usually comes about when the money supply expands but this expansion is not allowed to exert the usual effect on prices because of direct controls imposed on prices by the government. In this case, the excess purchasing power will result in added expenditure on goods and services not subject to control, in the appearance of black markets, in expanded security purchases, and in the accumulation of cash balances creating a source of inflationary spending once the controls are removed.

The Deflationary Process

"Deflation" is said to be occurring when the general price level is falling. The deflationary process, however, is not symmetrical to the inflationary process, as we have indicated. With a net reduction in total spending, downward pressure is exerted on prices, but many prices do not move downward as readily as they move upward. This difference may be attributed to several causes.

First of all, the character of markets is important here. In the case of upward shifts in money demand, prices will tend to be increased regardless of the type of market. In the case of downward shifts in demand, however, the markets which are monopolistic must be distinguished from those which are competitive. If all markets were fully competitive, prices would be set by the impersonal forces of demand and supply, and they would move downward as easily as upward in response to demand shifts. In the real world, however, few markets are fully competitive. Sellers generally do possess some control over price and, therefore, may not immediately respond to a reduction in demand with price reductions. Many will prefer to adjust output rather than price. There will be some price reductions, but, in general, prices are likely to be slow in moving downward. Firms in industries which are oligopolistic will be fearful of setting off price-cutting wars by initiating price reductions.

Another reason for the failure of output prices to move downward readily is the stickiness of input prices to firms. If a firm is to reduce output prices substantially, it must be able to reduce variable costs. This requires a reduction in input prices. But sellers of inputs, notably labor, may choose to accept unemployment and layoffs rather than take wage cuts.

The longer the deflationary process continues the more probable it is that significant price reductions will extend to all markets. And there are other steps which amount to almost the same thing as price reductions. Services are expanded and merchandise is frequently improved in quality.

The redistributive effects of deflation are similar to those of inflation, except, of course, in the opposite direction, but they are not likely to be so significant because of the stickiness in prices. Those in the fixed-income group stand to gain at the expense of other groups in society. This remains true, however, only so long as they can retain their source of income. The white-collar workers may gain in relative income position. But the threat of unemployment is constantly present during such periods, so any gains made are precarious ones. As a matter of fact, there are few groups who actually gain during a period of deflation and depression. It is also important to note that those who might gain are not powerful politically. This is another way in which deflation is not symmetrical with inflation. Many groups which are politically powerful feel that they have a vested interest in inflation and, therefore, seem likely to support governmental policies which are designed to encourage it. But after the great deflation-depression of the 1930's, there will be little support in the foreseeable future for policies aimed actively at promoting deflation or allowing deflation to continue once it has started.

The deflationary process affects expectations as does the inflationary process, but, again, in the reverse direction. If people once get the idea that prices are going to continue to fall, their own actions will ensure that prices will fall. With the expectation of falling prices, cash will become desirable as an asset form. Real property and equity shares will become undesirable and will fall in price. Under such circumstances, little may be gained from a policy aimed merely at increasing the money supply. The increase may be absorbed in additions to inactive cash balances and may affect total spending, and, therefore, prices and incomes, little if at all.

16

BANKS AND THE MONEY SUPPLY

An economist has been described as a man who knows all about money and does not have any of it. Like most epigrams, this one states only a partial truth. The fact is, of course, that the economist does not know all about money. It might be more accurate to say that an economist knows that what most people believe about money is not true.

One of the popular misconceptions is the belief that money is valuable because it is "backed up" by something of value. It is pointed out, for example, that one can take a dollar bill to the bank and get in exchange a silver dollar, and the silver, it is supposed, has some kind of intrinsic value. While it is true that the silver in a silver dollar is worth more than the paper in a paper dollar, it would be a mistake to assume that the value of the paper dollar results from the silver with which it is backed up, and this for two reasons.

In the first place, much of the value which the silver dollar possesses derives from the fact that silver is used as money; if silver were to be demonetized, much of the demand for silver would disappear, and silver would lose a considerable fraction of its worth. It can scarcely be argued that paper money is valuable because it is redeemable in silver, and silver, in turn, is valuable because it is used as money.

A second point to be made in this connection is that a silver dollar contains considerably less than a dollar's worth of silver, the exact value of the silver in the dollar fluctuating with each change in the market price of silver. If one wished to buy silver, he would do better to buy it on the silver market than to get it at the bank. And what may be more disturbing is that there is even less silver in ten dimes, four quarters, or two half dollars than there is in a silver dollar. Since ten dimes do, in fact, exchange for a silver dollar, we must conclude that the value of neither the dimes nor the dollars is determined by the value of the silver which they contain. A paper dollar and a silver dollar are not fundamentally different; the silver dollar simply uses a somewhat more expensive raw material than the paper dollar uses. But both are "token" money; both are valued far beyond the worth of the materials used in their manufacture.

Since January 31, 1934, the U.S. dollar has been defined as $15\frac{5}{21}$ grains of gold $\frac{9}{10}$ fine, which is equivalent to $35 per fine ounce. If the dollar is by definition $\frac{1}{35}$ of an ounce of gold, then $\frac{1}{35}$ of an ounce of gold must be worth $1, and the price of gold will not fluctuate below that price as long as the legal definition of a dollar remains unchanged. If one could take a $5 bill to the bank and get in exchange for it a $5 gold piece containing $\frac{5}{35}$ of an ounce of gold, he could get $5 worth of gold for his paper money. Prior to 1934 one could redeem his paper money in this way and receive in exchange for paper money its face value in terms of gold. But since that time gold coins have not been permitted to circulate. If one cannot get gold in exchange for paper money, it is clear that paper money is not valuable because it is secured by gold.

As a final confusing element it may be observed that the Federal Reserve Banks are required to hold reserves against Federal Reserve notes (our most important kind of paper money) consisting of 25 per cent in gold certificates and the remainder in acceptable securities of the United States government and business firms. That is to say, our most important type of currency is backed up mainly by I O U's of businessmen and government—promissory notes and government bonds; our money is backed up by debt! The relative importance of the several kinds of money in circulation in the United States is indicated in Table 16.1.

Since silver certificates are backed up by silver dollars which do not contain a dollar's worth of silver, and since gold certificates do not circulate anyway and are backed up by gold which is not permitted to circulate, and since Federal Reserve notes are backed up by gold certificates and instruments of debt, what does determine the value of money?

By the value of money is meant essentially the same thing as is meant by the value of anything else; *i.e.*, the quantity of other

Table 16.1. Kinds of Money in Circulation in the United States, June 30, 1957
(In millions of dollars)

	Amount	Per cent of total
Gold certificates......................................	$ 33	0.02
Credit money issued by the government:		
Token coins.....................................	1,642	1.13
Silver certificates...............................	2,163	1.48
U.S. notes.......................................	321	0.22
Credit money issued by the Federal Reserve Banks:		
Federal Reserve notes............................	26,329	18.00
Federal Reserve bank notes.......................	133	0.09
Credit money issued by other banks:		
National bank notes..............................	62	0.04
Demand deposits.................................	115,561	79.02
Total..	$146,247	100.00

Source: *Federal Reserve Bulletin.* The figures show amounts outside the Treasury and the Federal Reserve Banks. Federal Reserve bank notes and national bank notes are being retired from circulation. The $33 million worth of gold certificates represents the amount which has been lost, destroyed, or sent abroad; gold certificates do not actually circulate.

things which it will command in exchange. If a given amount of money will exchange for a considerable quantity of other goods, money may be said to have a relatively high value; if the quantity of other things which can be obtained with a given amount of money decreases, the value of money is said to be decreasing. That is to say, if the price level is high, the value of money is low; if prices are low, the value of money is high. What the value of money is at any particular time is the resultant of the several complex forces which were described in the preceding chapter. Among these factors is the quantity of money. If there is an oversupply of money in relation to the work it has to do, whether the currency is backed up dollar-for-dollar with gold coins which are

allowed to circulate freely or whether the money supply consists
of unredeemable paper, prices will be high; *i.e.*, the value of money
will be low.

Sources of the Money Supply

In the United States at the present time only about 3 per cent
of the money supply is issued by the United States Treasury; about
18 per cent is issued by the Federal Reserve Banks, and the remainder—almost 80 per cent—is issued by private banks. *Demand
deposits held in local banks represent the bulk of our money supply.* If the total quantity of money becomes too great or too small,
the perils of inflation or deflation become real. As we observed
earlier, the quantity of money is important because it is the one
variable affecting the level of prices and incomes which is most
easily controlled by government. It is, indeed, a major function of
the Federal Reserve System to control the supply of money in
such a way that neither too much nor too little is in circulation.[1]
This suggests several questions which need to be answered. What
actually determines the amount of money in existence? What is
meant by demand deposits, and why are they included as a part
of the money supply? How does the central bank influence the
amount of demand deposits held by local banks? These questions
will be considered in this and following chapters.

The American commercial-banking system consists of two sets
of banks: the local banks ("state" or "national" banks) and the
Federal Reserve Banks. All national banks are "members" of the
Federal Reserve System, and state banks which qualify may join
the System. The local banks are commercial banks; *i.e.*, their primary function is to accept deposits of individuals and firms and
to make loans for relatively short periods, usually thirty to ninety
days. There are twelve Federal Reserve Banks located throughout
the country. These are "banker's banks," and they deal primarily
with the member banks, the United States Treasury, and foreign

---

[1] *Cf.* "Statement before the Subcommittee on General Control and Debt
Management of the Joint Committee on the Economic Report, 82nd Congress," by Malcolm Bryan, President, Federal Reserve Bank of Atlanta, Mar.
19, 1952, p. 6: "The Federal Reserve System, as a central banking organization, has only one fundamental power, the power to create and extinguish bank
reserves, either through its own investment account or by lending to commercial banks, and thus to influence the supply of money. All other powers are
merely incidental or facilitating."

governments. All member banks are required to buy stock in the Federal Reserve Bank of their district and to maintain a deposit there. The member bank's deposit in the Federal Reserve Bank serves two important functions: (1) it assists in the "clearing" of checks drawn on one bank and deposited in another, and (2) it serves as a "reserve" which the member bank must maintain against its own demand deposits. Both of these functions will be explained in the discussion which follows.

The Formation of a Commercial Bank

We shall illustrate the operation of the commercial-banking system by supposing that we organize a local bank and by observing the changes that take place in its balance sheet as it engages in various transactions. The balance sheet is the statement of the bank's assets, liabilities, and net worth listed by major categories. The principal liability consists of deposits, which the bank owes to its depositors.

Suppose that we are able to interest local investors in organizing a new bank in our town. We form a corporation and issue 4,000 shares of capital stock with a par value of $100, thus acquiring $400,000 in cash.[1] At this early point in the bank's history, the balance sheet will look like this:

ABC NATIONAL BANK
Balance Sheet No. 1

Assets		Liabilities	
Cash	$400,000	Capital stock	$400,000
Total	$400,000	Total	$400,000

The next step is to find a place to do business. Since we want people to have confidence in the security of their deposits, we want to buy an impressive building, perhaps one with a marble front. Suppose that we purchase such a building which costs a total of $382,000; in addition, we purchase $12,000 of stock in the Federal Reserve Bank, since all member banks are required to do so in the amount of 3 per cent of their own capitalization. The balance sheet now takes on the following form:

[1] National banks actually sell their stock above par, which gives rise to "paid in surplus." To simplify the balance sheets, this has been neglected here.

ABC NATIONAL BANK

Balance Sheet No. 2

Assets		Liabilities	
Cash......................	$ 6,000	Capital stock..............	$400,000
Land and building..........	382,000		
Federal Reserve stock.......	12,000		
Total...................	$400,000	Total..................	$400,000

Our bank is now ready to begin business. We announce a grand opening day and invite everyone in to see our fine new facilities. We decorate the bank with flowers sent to us by well-wishers; we put on our company manners and behave like fraternity men during rush week. We proudly show off our new vaults, pointing out the thickness of the walls and the extreme care we have taken to make the building burglar-proof. We take special pride in our drive-in window where customers may make deposits and cash checks without leaving their cars. During the course of the day we persuade a number of people that this is the bank with which they should do business; by the end of the day we find that a total of $100,000 in cash has been deposited with us. For simplicity, let us assume that these are all "demand deposits" subject to withdrawal by check; our savings department is not yet ready to do business. The $6,000 cash which we had before the opening will probably suffice as "till money." Consequently, we shall deposit the entire $100,000 in new cash in the Federal Reserve Bank. These actions are reflected in the third balance sheet.

ABC NATIONAL BANK

Balance Sheet No. 3

Assets		Liabilities	
Cash......................	$ 6,000	Capital stock..............	$400,000
Deposits in Federal Reserve...	100,000	Demand deposits..........	100,000
Land and building..........	382,000		
Federal Reserve stock.......	12,000		
Total...................	$500,000	Total..................	$500,000

If the legal reserve requirement is 20 per cent, our bank must maintain a deposit in the Federal Reserve Bank equal to at least 20 per cent of our demand deposits. The required legal reserve against our present deposits would be $20,000.[1] Since at the moment we actually have a deposit in the Federal Reserve Bank of $100,000, we have *excess reserves* of $80,000. This is shown in Step 1 of Exhibit 1 on page 202. Only that part of the balance sheet necessary for an understanding of the process of deposit creation is shown in Exhibit 1.

The Deposit Multiplier

As shown in Step 2 of Exhibit 1, our bank can safely lend $80,000—the amount of its excess reserves. The borrowers will probably take the proceeds in the form of checking accounts at the ABC bank.[2] But they are unlikely to leave these sums in the bank long, since they have borrowed and are paying interest in order to be able to make purchases, for example, of merchandise with which to replenish stocks. (We are assuming that the original $100,000 in deposits will remain in the bank somewhat longer, since it is made up in part of funds placed in the bank for safekeeping or to be held as a reserve for contingencies.)

Step 3 assumes that all the checks drawn against the loan-created demand deposits in the ABC Bank are deposited in other commercial banks. This would cause our bank to lose $80,000 in reserves at the Federal Reserve Bank, since checks in that amount

[1] The pattern of legal reserve percentages in effect on July 1, 1958, is given in the table below:

Bank	Net demand deposits			Time deposits		
	Legal minimum	Legal maximum	Actual	Legal minimum	Legal maximum	Actual
Central Reserve City....	13	26	18	3	6	5
Reserve City..........	10	20	16½	3	6	5
Country..............	7	14	11	3	6	5

Source: *Federal Reserve Bulletin.*

[2] For the sake of simplicity, we shall ignore the amount of interest collected by the bank. If interest is charged at the annual rate of 4 per cent and the loans are made for 90 days, the interest or "discount" on loans of $80,000 would be $800. Normally the discount is applied at the time the loan is made, and the Loans and Discount account would be $80,000, demand deposits would be increased by $79,200, and the $800 would be placed in Interest Collected but Not Earned, a liability account. At the end of the 90 days, the interest collected would go into the Undivided Profits account. It will be noted that this device makes it possible for the bank to advertise a 4 per cent interest rate while actually charging somewhat more, since borrowers do not actually secure use of the full $80,000.

Exhibit 1

Expansion of Money Supply by Banking System
(Assuming uniform 20 per cent reserve requirement)

Step 1. ABC National Bank has $80,000 in excess reserves

ABC NATIONAL BANK	
Federal Reserve account.....$100,000	Deposits..................$100,000

Step 2. And can safely lend this amount, building up borrowers' deposit accounts

ABC NATIONAL BANK	
Federal Reserve account.....$100,000	Deposits..................$180,000
Loans.................... 80,000	

Step 3. The newly created deposits are likely to be quickly checked out. In clearing process ABC's reserves may be reduced to minimum

ABC NATIONAL BANK	
Federal Reserve account.....$ 20,000	Deposits..................$100,000
Loans.................... 80,000	

Step 4. But checks on ABC Bank are deposited in various banks which, in the clearing process, secure larger Federal Reserve accounts

STAGE II BANKS	
Federal Reserve accounts....$ 80,000	Deposits..................$ 80,000

Step 5. Having excess reserves of $64,000, these banks can safely lend that amount

STAGE II BANKS	
Federal Reserve accounts....$ 80,000	Deposits..................$144,000
Loans.................... 64,000	

Step 6. As newly created deposits are checked out, reserves are reduced to legal minimum

STAGE II BANKS	
Federal Reserve accounts....$ 16,000	Deposits..................$ 80,000
Loans.................... 64,000	

Step 7. But banks in which checks are deposited can, in turn, extend credit and create deposits

STAGE III BANKS	
Federal Reserve accounts....$ 64,000	Deposits..................$115,200
Loans.................... 51,200	($64,000 + $51,200)

And so on, until a theoretical maximum of $500,000 in deposits can exist in the system because of the $100,000 in cash originally deposited in the ABC National Bank. (The $500,000 in deposits includes this original deposit.) Loans will total $400,000, since all but the first deposit have been created through bank loans.

would be charged to the ABC Bank's Federal Reserve account in the clearing process. The amount would be credited to reserve accounts of banks in which the checks were deposited. As shown in Step 4, these "Stage II" banks now have new deposits and new reserves of $80,000, of which $64,000 are excess reserves by virtue of our assumed 20 per cent legal reserve requirement.

New loans can safely be made in the amount of these excess reserves. Thus deposits in Stage II banks can be increased by $64,000 to $144,000. As the newly created deposits are checked out, reserve accounts are lowered to the legal minimum of $16,000, but Stage III banks now have excess reserves, permitting them to lend $51,200, as shown in the last partial balance sheet of Exhibit 1.

Eventually a theoretical maximum of $400,000 in new loans and new deposits can be created by the system. Counting the $100,000 originally deposited in the ABC National Bank, there would exist $500,000 in deposits, which would be based on the original $100,000 cash deposit. The $100,000 will all have become required reserves, the ownership of which will have been spread among a large number of banks as shown in the third column of Table 16.2. The table also summarizes the new deposits and loans which would appear at each of the stages in the expansion. It should be noted that the deposits which remain after newly created deposits are checked away are the ones which are counted at each stage in this table.

Table 16.2. Deposit Expansion by Commercial Banks

	New deposits	New loans (80%)	Reserves kept (20%)
ABC Bank.............	$100,000	$ 80,000	$ 20,000
Stage II banks..........	80,000	64,000	16,000
Stage III banks.........	64,000	51,200	12,800
Stage IV banks.........	51,200	40,960	10,240
Stage V banks..........	40,960	32,768	8,192
Stage VI banks.........	32,768	26,214	6,554
Stage VII banks........	26,214	20,971	5,243
....	....	....	....
....	....	....	....
Other banks...........	104,858	83,887	20,971
All banks..............	$500,000	$400,000	$100,000

The assumptions upon which the foregoing bank-credit expansion process was based were kept somewhat unrealistic in order to simplify the illustration. No additional cash was assumed to be required for till money by the bank despite the build-up of deposits. Actually there would probably be some increase in this use of cash, so that less than $100,000 of the new cash would find its way into the Federal Reserve Banks to serve as new reserves. It was also assumed that all checks drawn were deposited in banks *other* than those against which they were drawn. Actually, some checks are redeposited in the same bank. If officials of the ABC Bank, for example, had been willing to take a chance that this would happen, they could have expanded loans by somewhat more than $80,000. Had they done so, however, the expansion possible in Stage II would have been less than that shown. The ultimate result would have been the same—a theoretical maximum of $500,000 in deposits throughout the system because of the $100,000 in new cash made available by depositors to any one bank or any combination of banks.

Contractions of the Money Supply

The multiple expansion of deposits by the banking system based on the acquisition of new reserves can (and frequently does) work also in reverse. A *loss* of reserves can force multiple *contraction* in loans and demand deposits and hence in the nation's money supply.

Using the same simplifying assumptions as before, suppose that $10,000 in cash is withdrawn from the ABC National Bank and is held outside the banking system. Assume that the position of the bank prior to this withdrawal was as follows (with respect to key accounts):

ABC NATIONAL BANK

Federal Reserve account......$20,000	Deposits..................$100,000
Loans...................... 80,000	

In order to secure the $10,000 cash which depositors demand, the ABC Bank will withdraw that amount from its Federal Reserve account. Its position will then be as follows:

ABC NATIONAL BANK

Federal Reserve account......$10,000	Deposits...................$90,000
Loans...................... 80,000	

The ratio of reserves to deposits is now below the required 20 per cent—a condition which must quickly be rectified. Our bank will be obliged to tighten up on credit in order to secure a net repayment of loans so as to obtain the funds needed to build up the reserve account. Since deposits are now $90,000, the reserve account must be brought up to $18,000 (20 per cent of $90,000). Loans outstanding must be reduced by $8,000 to raise the bank's Federal Reserve account by this amount. For simplicity, we are assuming that all checks paid to the ABC Bank in retirement of loans are drawn against other banks. Our bank would then have a favorable clearing balance of $8,000 at the Federal Reserve Bank; this would build its reserve account up to the required $18,000, the key accounts appearing as follows:

ABC NATIONAL BANK

Federal Reserve account......$18,000	Deposits...................$90,000
Loans...................... 72,000	

Since other banks would lose $8,000 in reserves owing to unfavorable clearing balances, they, in turn, would be forced to reduce loans under the assumption that they had no excess reserves. They would be forced to reduce loans by $6,400; their deposits would be down by $8,000. The induced contraction of loans in the next stage would be $5,120, and the deposits in this stage would fall by $6,400. The end result of the process would be a maximum theoretical contraction of $50,000 in demand deposits and $40,000 in bank loans as a result of the $10,000 loss of cash to the banking system. In this way a fractional-reserve banking system tends to be subject to sharp contractions as well as expansions of deposits and loans. The nation's money supply may be subjected to large fluctuations resulting from attempts made by the public to change the form of their asset holdings from demand deposits to cash or from cash to deposits.

Summary

The models of deposit expansion and contraction which have been used in this chapter have been artificially simplified in order to bring some of the essential elements into bold relief. The fundamental fact is that most of our money supply is not issued directly by the United States Treasury but is created (and destroyed) by the commercial banks. Actually, the Federal government, through operations of the Treasury and Federal Reserve System, has a good deal of control over the money supply (as will be explained in the next chapter). The fact remains, however, that under our banking system the money supply is governed to a substantial extent by the actions of bankers and private borrowers. When waves of optimism or pessimism affect their actions, the fractional-reserve system permits sharp increases or decreases in the money supply to occur.

Under conditions of full employment an increase in the supply of money will probably not be offset by a reduction in velocity or an increase in transactions and will consequently exert an inflationary effect. A sharp contraction in the money supply, on the other hand, is likely to cause a general fall in prices. Thus the commercial-banking system, operating on a particularly vulnerable fractional-reserve basis, exerts a powerful influence on our economic well-being. This has led to a measure of central regulation of the banking business which will be described in the next chapter.

17

THE FEDERAL RESERVE SYSTEM

Some notice was taken of the Federal Reserve System in the last chapter, but its role there may have appeared to be only a passive one of holding legal reserves for member commercial banks and acting as a clearinghouse for checks. Actually, the System has the important positive power of influencing the lending operations and consequently the money-creating capacity of commercial banks throughout the nation. In large measure this control power is exercised by means of actions which increase or decrease the reserve accounts of member banks in the Federal Reserve Banks.

The principal controls utilized by the Federal Reserve System are summarized in the following listing. Each will be discussed in some detail:

1. Adjustments in rediscount rates
2. Changes in legal reserve requirements of member banks
3. Open-market operations
4. Moral suasion
5. Selective credit controls

Adjustments in Rediscount Rates

When an individual borrows from a commercial bank, the latter frequently "discounts" the loan by the amount of interest charged, turning over to the borrower only the remainder of the capital sum. The bank may, in turn, "rediscount" the businessman's note at the Federal Reserve Bank in its district, that is, borrow and leave the note as collateral. This action adds to the reserve account of the borrowing bank, thus increasing its ability to make further loans. Since the commercial bank's discount rate generally exceeds the Federal Reserve's rediscount rate, the operation is profitable to the former as long as the demand for loans by businessmen is sufficiently brisk.

Instead of rediscounting commercial paper (businessmen's notes), a commercial bank may borrow from the Federal Reserve Bank on its own note. In either case, the Federal Reserve credit extension builds up the commercial bank's reserve, permitting the bank to make additional loans of approximately the amount of its borrowing and making possible a much greater expansion of deposits by the banking system as a whole (in the manner described in the last chapter).

Although the Federal Reserve Banks are not required to lend to member banks upon application, they have almost invariably been willing to do so provided that satisfactory collateral is offered. Consequently, an important method by which the System is able to encourage or discourage borrowing by the banks is through adjustment of the rediscount rate. Lowering this interest rate tends to make borrowing by the banks more profitable, whereas raising the rate discourages bank borrowing.

When the Federal Reserve System was established in 1913, it was thought that the rediscount rate would be a powerful device in the hands of the central-banking (Federal Reserve) authorities, permitting them to check the expansion of bank credit, and consequently the money supply, in periods of inflation and to encourage the expansion of commercial loans when deflation threatened. In part, this expectation has been fulfilled, but it has been found to be more difficult to encourage expansion of credit by this device than to inhibit credit extension. When excess reserves of the banking system are large, as they were during the 1930's, the rediscount rate is of little significance, since banks do not need to borrow. In addition, the large volume of "near reserves" acquired by the banks during and after World War II in the form of government securities diminished their need to borrow and hence reduced the importance of the interest rate charged by the Federal Reserve Banks, as will subsequently be explained. During the 1950's, with excess reserves smaller, there has been some revival of the efficacy of the rediscount, or borrowing, rate as a control device. Also the volume of near reserves has been reduced since the war. In December, 1945, commercial banks held over $90 billion in U.S. bonds; in December, 1957, the total was about $58 billion.[1]

Changes in Legal Reserve Requirements

It should be easy to see from the analysis of the previous chapter that a very direct and powerful method of government control of the supply of bank money is the changing of the percentage reserves required to be held against deposits. If the commercial banks have large excess reserves on deposit with the Federal Reserve Banks, and hence are in a position to make loans and investments in large volume, the authoritative raising of reserve requirements can wipe out millions of dollars in excess reserves at the stroke of a pen.

The power of the Board of Governors to change legal-reserve ratios is limited by Congressional authorization. As of May, 1958, reserve requirements in relation to demand deposits were 18, 16½, and 11 per cent, respectively, for Central Reserve, Reserve City, and Country Banks. New York and Chicago constitute the Central Reserve cities, and cities of medium size are designated Reserve cities. Banks in small cities and towns comprise most of the Country Banks, but actually some banks in the large cities (*e.g.*, Chicago) are so classified. Historically, required ratios have almost doubled; they were 13, 10, and 7 per cent, respectively, in 1917; these percentages correspond with the minimum ratios which the Federal Reserve Board could now legally impose. The maximum reserve ratios which have been authorized by Congress are 26, 20, and 14 per cent for the three categories of banks.

The changing of required reserves is a device which is used infrequently. Congress is not always willing to authorize the changes in maximum reserve ratios which Federal Reserve authorities deem desirable. Even apart from the matter of Congressional authorization, there remains the problem of the uneven

[1] *Federal Reserve Bulletin,* February, 1958, p. 172.

status of the various commercial banks within each of the three categories. At the same time that some banks have large excess reserves, others may have little more than the minimum needed against their deposits. A raising of legal ratios then places the latter banks in a difficult position, necessitating such measures on their part as the liquidation of securities or borrowing from the Federal Reserve Banks. The Federal Reserve authorities are generally reluctant to impose controls which have a very uneven impact on the operation of different banks. The raising of legal-reserve ratios is consequently not so practicable a measure as it at first appears to be. At times, however, it has been employed effectively. There are no comparable problems in lowering reserve requirements, but, if banks generally already have excess reserves, this action may have little influence upon the expansion of credit.

Open-market Operations

The most interesting, and in recent years probably the most important, method by which the Federal Reserve System through its Open Market Committee exercises control over bank credit is the purchase and sale of government securities in the "open market" (*i.e.*, in the ordinary markets in which existing securities change hands). The Federal Reserve Banks usually do not buy new government issues directly from the United States Treasury.[1] However, their investment portfolio included about $23 billion of United States securities in early 1958, the bulk of which were purchased in the open market for securities.

When the Federal Reserve authorities wish to encourage the further expansion of bank loans and consequently of the money supply they can do so by *buying* bonds on the open market. Suppose they buy bonds directly from a member bank: the Federal Reserve Bank simply credits the selling bank's reserve account with the proceeds, placing that bank in an improved position to create new deposits by means of loans or investments. (The banking system is then able to engage in total-deposit expansion to a multiple of the newly created reserve if a sufficient demand exists for bank credit.) If a Federal Reserve Bank buys government bonds from private owners, the result is the same. Normally, the

---

[1] During World War II, however, the Federal Reserve authorities bought a large volume of bonds directly from the Treasury. The inflationary effect is about the same whether the Federal Reserve System buys new or "second-hand" bonds.

seller will deposit the Federal Reserve check or Federal Reserve notes (paper money) which he receives for his bonds in his account at a commercial bank. When his bank, in turn, deposits the Federal Reserve check or notes in its own account at the Federal Reserve Bank, it will build up its excess reserves and be in a position to make further loans. Open-market purchases by the Federal Reserve System thus encourage bank-credit expansion, since their result is to convert United States government bonds held by commercial banks, business enterprises, and individuals into reserves of the banking system.

If the Federal Reserve authorities wish to tighten up on bank credit (curb the creation of money by the commercial banks), they can do so by *selling* United States government bonds or other assets. If commercial banks buy these securities, their reserve accounts are directly reduced by their market value. If individuals and firms buy them, they normally pay by means of checks drawn against their deposits in commercial banks. When such a check clears through the Federal Reserve Bank, it becomes a charge against the reserve account of the bank upon which it was drawn. This reduces the bank's reserve and places the commercial bank in a poorer position to make loans. New applicants for bank loans are more likely to be turned down, some old borrowers may be unable to renew their loans as they come due, and those who are able to secure loans may have to pay a higher rate of interest. As was seen in the previous chapter, a one-billion-dollar reduction in bank reserves, for example, can necessitate something like a five-billion-dollar decrease in demand deposits and hence in the supply of money. This occurs, however, only if banks have loaned to the limit prior to the open-market sales, *i.e.*, if excess reserves were negligible.

Federal Reserve Support of the United States Treasury

The general mechanics of open-market operations have been discussed, but the student cannot understand recent Federal Reserve policy without studying the place of the United States Treasury in the banking picture. A very important job of the Treasury consists in administering the huge national debt ($275 billion early in 1958), that is, selling new United States securities, paying off those which mature (or are redeemed before maturity, in the case of Series E savings bonds), and making interest payments on the public debt (over $7 billion per year). While the Treasury made a strong effort during and after World War II to place United States securities in the hands of individuals, firms, and nonbanking institutions, it was found necessary to sell a very large volume to the commercial banks and to a much lesser extent directly to the Federal Reserve Banks.

When commercial banks buy newly issued government bonds, they are extending credit to the United States Treasury in the same way that they regularly extend credit to businessmen. In exchange for the United States bonds, the Treasury secures demand deposits against which it can draw checks to pay its bills. These Treasury deposits may be in either the Federal Reserve Banks or the commercial banks.

To illustrate the process by which the commercial banks acquire government bonds, suppose the ABC National Bank, which we assume is subject to a 20 per cent legal reserve requirement, has excess reserves of $0.2 million and is consequently in a position to make further loans to business or government. The important accounts might look like this:

ABC National Bank
(In millions of dollars)

Federal Reserve account........$1.2	Demand deposits................$5.0
Loans and securities............ 4.0	

Suppose now that our bank wishes to buy additional newly issued United States securities in the amount of its excess reserves. It may do so through the Federal Reserve Bank in its district. The Federal Reserve Bank simply shifts $0.2 million from the ABC Bank's account to the Treasury's account and turns over the new United States securities to the ABC Bank. The key accounts in our bank's balance sheet will then look as follows:

ABC National Bank
(In millions of dollars)

Federal Reserve account........$1.0	Deposits......................$5.0
Loans and securities............ 4.2	

As the United States Treasury pays its bills by drawing down its new $0.2 million in deposits at the Federal Reserve Bank, its checks will be deposited in various banks which will then find themselves with excess reserves in the manner described in the previous chapter. They can then make additional loans to businessmen or to the United States government: to the extent that they lend to the government they will acquire additional United

States securities. Thus a maximum of about $1 million in government securities might be acquired by the commercial banks as a whole based on the original credit extension to the government by the ABC National Bank. This illustration indicates the process by which the banks have simply created much of the money with which they have acquired over one-fifth of all U.S. government securities.[1] This has been made possible by the fractional-reserve banking system and, of course, by the deficit financing on the part of the United States government during the decades of the forties and fifties.

The Federal Reserve Banks during the war and for some years after stood ready to buy all United States securities offered for sale on the open market by banks and others at definite prices which were seldom allowed to change. Why did the Federal Reserve authorities support the United States bond market in this way? They did so in order to aid the Treasury in its tremendous job of debt management. By supporting government-bond prices, the Federal Reserve Banks held down interest rates both on existing bonds and on new bond issues. If U.S. bonds had been permitted to fall in a free market they would have yielded higher rates of return to buyers, and these higher interest rates would have had to be matched by the United States Treasury in selling new bonds.

In addition to the Treasury's desire to keep down interest rates, there is pressure from owners of government bonds to keep their prices from dropping. Bond owners do not wish, of course, to suffer capital losses on securities which they hold, and if such losses are threatened they may be reluctant to subscribe to new government-security issues.[2] During and after World War II, the Federal Reserve System found itself operating a price-support program somewhat akin to the farm-price-support program—it was forced to acquire a large inventory of government securities in much the same way that the Commodity Credit Corporation acquires stocks of farm products which no one else wishes to own.

---

[1] In our example we have assumed that the commercial banks initially had excess reserves. It should be pointed out, however, that even if this were not the case, excess reserves could have been easily created by the sale of securities to the Federal Reserve Banks. This was, in fact, one of the reasons for the sale of new securities to the Federal Reserve System during World War II.

[2] When interest rates rise and bond prices fall, bondholders suffer actual capital losses only if they choose to liquidate their holdings prior to maturity. Regardless of the fluctuations in bond prices, no owner suffers a capital loss if he holds his bonds until the stipulated maturity date, when the Treasury will pay off at full face value. Thus actual capital losses are suffered more often on long-term bonds than on short-term securities.

United States Treasury and Federal Reserve officials reached a highly publicized "accord" in March, 1951, which permitted the Federal Reserve System to operate with a greater degree of independence. The result was a general (though modest) rise in interest rates on Federal securities and private loans as the Federal Reserve more nearly allowed United States securities to seek their own (lower) price levels. A general rise in interest rates on government (and other) bonds began in late 1954 and continued until late 1957 when business activity slowed down. During the early weeks of 1958 interest rates continued to fall, aided by Federal Reserve relaxation of monetary restraint.

Moral Suasion

The fourth type of Federal Reserve control, frequently called "moral suasion," consists in the occasional Federal Reserve practice of requesting that member banks exercise more or less restraint in the granting of business loans. The American Bankers Association cooperates in requesting banks' compliance with such requests.

Like other voluntary controls sometimes attempted by government, moral suasion is often relatively ineffective, since the desired action may be contrary to the profit-seeking ends of the member banks. The exercise of certain types of government economic control over individuals and firms is frequently questionable as a matter of policy. If controls are imposed, however, they should be mandatory, uniform in their operation with respect to similarly situated firms, and adequately enforced. Moral suasion on the part of the Federal Reserve authorities fails to meet these tests, especially because some bankers may try to comply with the request while others disregard it. Nevertheless, moral suasion cannot be written off as being entirely impotent, particularly when it is backed by a threat of more direct action such as the denial of loans to noncooperating banks.

Selective Controls

The controls discussed so far are all *general* credit controls, in that their basic purpose is to affect the commercial banks' capacity to make loans for all sorts of purposes and hence their capacity to create or destroy money. During and after World War II, *selective* credit controls were frequently used by the Federal Reserve System. These selective controls specify credit terms upon which banks may make loans for particular purposes, especially for financing installment purchases by consumers.

Wartime regulation W of the Federal Reserve System imposed a twofold restraint: It specified minimum percentage down payments on listed articles and maximum periods within which loans had to be repaid. The purchaser of an automobile, for example, had to make a one-third down payment and pay the balance within eighteen months. Consumer-credit restrictions applied also to lenders outside the banking system. Personal-loan companies, department stores, appliance dealers, and others who might grant consumer credit were subjected to Federal Reserve regulations. Selective credit controls were terminated November 1, 1947, reimposed in 1948, and removed again in 1949. They were reimposed in 1950 after the outbreak of warfare in Korea, and again were terminated in 1952.

To the extent that selective credit controls curtail bank loans, they tend to hold down the total supply of money. This is not their primary purpose, however. They are designed to restrict consumer demand for the particular articles to which they apply. This has a twofold result: (1) it reduces the upward pressure on the prices of houses, automobiles, household appliances, and similar "hard" goods which is likely to exist during a period of national emergency; and (2) it tends to shift resources out of these consumer-goods fields into munitions production by reducing the profitability of the civilian items to producers. The saving in civilian consumption of such metals as steel, copper, and aluminum is especially important because of their heavy use in war production. It should be noted, however, that selective credit controls are a less certain device for limiting civilian output and forcing a redirection of resources toward the munitions fields than are such non-Federal Reserve controls as limitation orders, priorities, and material allocations.

Another type of selective control administered by the System is that over margin requirements for stock purchases. The basic purpose is to limit the use of bank credit for security speculation. During the 1920's, speculators could purchase stocks on as little as 10 per cent margin, borrowing the remaining sums from brokers (who, in turn, borrowed from the banks). This practice has been held partly responsible for the great price boom in securities and the devastating 1929 crash. Stock prices also rose during World War II, causing the Federal Reserve authorities to impose 50 per cent, then 75 per cent, and finally 100 per cent margin requirements. The margin requirement was dropped to 75 per cent in February, 1947, and to 50 per cent in February, 1953. Subsequently it was raised again to 60, then 70 per cent but was reduced to 50 per cent in January, 1958, to bolster a stock market which was feeling the effects of economic recession. In the summer of 1958 the requirement was raised to 70 per cent.

Federal Reserve Notes

So far the discussion has been concerned chiefly with Federal Reserve control over the volume of demand deposits; little notice has been taken of Federal Reserve notes, which constitute most of our supply of currency. Demand deposits and their fluctuations are of much greater importance in the total money supply, but changes in the volume of currency are not without significance.

Federal Reserve notes are paid out by the twelve Federal Reserve Banks to member banks whenever the latter require more cash. Reserve accounts of the member banks are charged for the amount of notes paid out; one sort of Federal Reserve liability is substituted for another type of liability. The only limitation on the issue of Federal Reserve notes is that the Federal Reserve Banks must have on hand gold certificates amounting to at least 25 per cent of the combined total of notes and deposits. Government bonds and other assets owned by the Federal Reserve Banks serve as the additional collateral behind Federal Reserve notes. The 25 per cent reserve requirement does not actually constitute an important check on either the issue of Federal Reserve notes or aggregate deposits (and hence member-bank reserves), since the Federal Reserve Banks have a large excess of gold certificates and since in any event Congress can readily lower the required reserve ratio—and has done so in the past.

In summary, Federal Reserve notes—which constitute our basic hand-to-hand currency—are "backed" principally by government securities, *i.e.*, by national debt, although gold certificates play a secondary and changeable role. The quantity of notes which circulate depends mainly on the need of the country for currency as gauged by the commercial banks. Since the commercial banks secure additional Federal Reserve notes at the cost of reducing their reserves, they have an incentive not to demand unnecessarily large amounts of currency from the Federal Reserve Banks. Also, they have the necessary incentive to turn in Federal Reserve notes which they acquire in excessive volume, since this action will build up their reserve accounts, or, alternatively, pay off debts which they have contracted by borrowing from the Federal Reserve Banks.

Gold and the Federal Reserve System

Since 1934 the United States government has followed the policy of paying $35 per ounce for all gold bullion offered to it for sale. This represents a sharp increase above the value of approximately $21 per ounce which prevailed while the country was on a full gold standard prior to that year.[1] Much of the gold newly mined in this country is sold to the United States Treasury to be buried (again) at Fort Knox, Kentucky. Much new gold from South African, Canadian, and other foreign mines is also sold to the Treasury. Gold movements between countries are one means of settling international balances. When private firms in this country receive gold from abroad, they are also obliged to sell it to the United States Treasury at $35 per ounce.

It is important to see how the Treasury's purchase of gold affects the banking system. When the Treasury buys gold, it pays with a check drawn against its account at a Federal Reserve Bank. It then issues gold certificates against the gold and deposits them in the Federal Reserve Bank in order to replenish the Treasury account there.[2] The United States government thus virtually acquires the gold "for nothing," but this should not be surprising, since a central government can always issue money in order to buy what it wishes. From a broader point of view, however, the gold is not free, since its sale gives gold sellers command over real goods and services produced in the United States. Its artificially maintained price gives producers a continuing subsidy to the extent that gold sells at a price above what it would sell for if it were not government supported. (The $35 price no longer looks so high, however, due to the great rise in prices in general since 1934.)

Ordinarily, the gold seller deposits the Treasury's check in a commercial bank, which in turn sends it to the Federal Reserve

---

[1] The price of gold was raised in part because of the peculiar belief of those in authority that raising the dollar price of gold would raise the price of all commodities above their depressed levels. It was also designed to stimulate United States exports by cheapening our dollar relative to foreign monies and to "export unemployment" to foreign countries.

[2] To save the cost of printing actual gold certificates, the more common practice is actually merely to give the Federal Reserve Banks credit on the Treasury Gold Certificate Book.

Bank and secures a corresponding addition to its reserve account. Thus the gold purchase increases both deposits in commercial banks and their deposits in the Federal Reserve Banks. Under the system of fractional-reserve requirements, this builds up excess reserves upon which the banking system can base an expansion of deposits to a multiple of the value of the gold purchase.

The effect of gold purchases by the United States Treasury is thus similar to that of open-market purchases, loans by the Federal Reserve Banks to member banks, or the deposit in banks of cash previously hoarded by individuals. In years when a large inflow of gold from abroad occurs, the control job of the Federal Reserve authorities is made more difficult, since this is a money-creating force outside of its jurisdiction. At times the Federal Reserve Banks have been able to offset the gold inflow by means of open-market sales. The raising of reserve requirements to offset the effect of a gold inflow can only occasionally be resorted to, as pointed out earlier, and the raising of interest rates charged member banks is not very effective, since banks rely less on such borrowing than they did during the first decades of the Federal Reserve System.

Federal Reserve Accounts

It may be useful by way of summary to examine a highly consolidated balance sheet for the twelve Federal Reserve Banks (Table 17.1). Inspection of the asset side shows gold certificates held by the Federal Reserve Banks amounting to $22.1 billion. It should be remembered that they must hold gold certificates equal

Table 17.1. Combined Federal Reserve Banks Consolidated Balance Sheet
as of January 29, 1958
(In billions of dollars)

Assets		*Liabilities and capital*	
Gold certificates	$22.1	Federal Reserve notes	$26.7
U.S. government securities	23.4	Deposits:	
Discounts and advances	0.3	Member bank reserves	19.0
Other assets	6.1	U.S. Treasury	0.5
		Foreign and other	0.5
		Other liabilities	3.9
		Capital paid in	0.3
		Surplus	1.0
Total assets	$51.9	Total liabilities and capital	$51.9

Source: *Federal Reserve Bulletin*, February, 1958.

to at least 25 per cent of notes and deposits. The latter accounts, as can be seen on the right-hand side, totaled $46.7 billion. Hence the value of the gold certificates was actually more than 47 per cent of notes and deposits. This illustrates the difference between Federal Reserve and commercial banks' operations. The Federal Reserve System, which makes no attempt to maximize profits, generally has large excess reserves. The member banks, on the other hand, frequently carry small excess reserves. Member-bank reserves of $19.0 billion, as shown among the liabilities of the Federal Reserve Banks, were only about $0.5 billion in excess of the amount actually needed to be held against demand and time deposits. It is not profitable for the commercial banks to carry substantial excess reserves, since they receive no interest on their deposits in the Federal Reserve Banks. Federal Reserve assets included $23.4 billion in United States government securities. Discounts and advances were much smaller in magnitude ($0.3 billion), but loans to banks included in this figure are of somewhat greater importance than they were a few years ago.

Federal Reserve notes outstanding of $26.7 billion represent the largest single liability of the system. The volume of such notes increased sharply during the war years and was maintained in the postwar period. The increase in notes compared with prewar years reflects in large part the need for more hand-to-hand currency because of price inflation. To a lesser degree, the increase in such currency has itself been a cause of the inflation.

The final item of particular interest is the United States Treasury deposit ($0.5 billion). The modest amount of this item may be misleading, since it does not reflect turnover (velocity). As was pointed out earlier, the Treasury usually pays for gold by drawing checks against its Federal Reserve accounts, and replenishes these accounts with gold certificates. The Treasury maintains the bulk of its demand deposits in designated commercial banks and as a rule maintains only a minimum operating balance at the Federal Reserve Banks. Usually its deposits in commercial banks are transferred to the Reserve Banks as they are needed, and checks are drawn against them there.

Summary

In this chapter we have noted that substantial changes have taken place in the types of control operations emphasized by the Federal Reserve System. After more than four decades the System

remains an important institutional device through which a measure of central control can be exercised over the nation's money
supply. The Federal Reserve Board's performance of this function
has been greatly complicated, however, by the great growth in
the national debt, by the vast security holdings of the commercial
banks, and by the United States government's policy of buying
gold at a fixed price. Perhaps the most important danger which is
involved in the huge national debt is to be found in the restrictions
which it tends to place on the power of Federal Reserve authorities
to control inflation. In recent years, however, the Federal Reserve
System has operated with greater independence than in the years
just after World War II. Without such independence it cannot
fulfill its major role of controlling the money supply by affecting
the availability of credit in the commercial banking system.

18

MONETARY POLICY

The two preceding chapters have discussed the monetary institutions of the United States. The discussion of the Federal Reserve System considered the possible controls which might be exercised over the supply of money and credit. The emphasis in the preceding chapter was upon the mechanics of Federal Reserve or central bank controls. In this chapter, we shall discuss the use of these controls in the more normative sense. We shall discuss the efficacy, the appropriateness, and the criteria for application of central bank controls over the supply of money and credit. This complex of topics is generally referred to as "monetary policy."

We may first attempt to provide a more specific definition. "Monetary policy" is defined as any operation by the government (or the central bank) which affects the stock of money, its rate of turnover, and/or the volume of close money substitutes (near monies). So defined, monetary policy includes Federal Reserve or central bank action in modifying rediscount or loan rates, changing reserve requirements, buying or selling government securities in the open market, and using other more selective control devices which may, under certain conditions, be within the discretionary power of the authority (such as the regulation of margin requirements for the purchase of securities). Monetary policy in the sense considered here may also be exercised directly by the Treasury Department. Treasury action in refinancing maturing issues of the national debt constitutes a powerful weapon of monetary policy. By refinancing maturing short-term issues at long term, the Treasury is reducing liquidity in the economy, and vice versa. By paying off debt held by the Federal Reserve Banks through the sale of debt to individuals the Treasury is reducing the money supply, and vice versa. The Treasury Department also carries out monetary policy in other ways. By its power of action relative to the utilization of gold purchases, its decisions concerning cash balances, and in many other ways, Treasury Department policy must be considered as an important part of the whole complex which we define as "monetary policy." Congress itself directly carries out monetary policy. It does so when it varies the limits within which the Federal Reserve Board can modify reserve requirements, when it expands or contracts the discretionary power of the Federal Reserve in exercising selective controls of various sorts, and when it sets up special governmental agencies or regulations designed to modify, in any way, the working of the monetary and credit system.

Criteria for Policy

An outstanding fact which should have been made clear by a study of Chapters 13, 14, and 15 is that there is no automatic mechanism in the real-world economy which guarantees ideal stability, however this may be defined, in the aggregative, or overall, sense. The level of income is determined by the spending and saving decisions of individual families, business firms, and government. These decisions may or may not interact to produce an income that is high enough to produce reasonably full employment without at the same time producing pressures toward inflation. The same conclusion appears if the economy is discussed in terms of the price level. The price level is determined by the stock of money, its rate of turnover (velocity), and the amount of work this money is required to do. There is no assurance that these independent factors will generate a stable price level, even if the stock of money should remain constant.

This leads directly to the conclusion that, given the existing monetary framework, some deliberate action should be taken by the government to ensure "desirable" economic stability. There is immediately introduced, however, the definitional issue. What do we mean by "stability"? Taken independently, the stabilizing of employment at some level at which substantially all able-bodied persons desiring work can find work seems highly desirable. Involuntary unemployment is so obviously undesirable as to require little elaboration of this point. On the other hand, reasonable stability in the value of the monetary unit (the reciprocal of the price level) seems essential for a free society. It seems questionable whether free society can survive continued deterioration in the purchasing power of its monetary unit without disastrous consequences. Stability in both employment and prices may be taken as desirable social goals, and governmental policy should be aimed at the accomplishment of these objectives.

There may be difficulties, however, in attaining both these goals at once. Governmental policy aimed at maintaining full employment may generate inflation. And governmental policy aimed solely at keeping the value of the dollar stable may not be sufficient to guarantee satisfactorily full employment. For society, and thus for government, a choice may have to be made between these possibly conflicting goals before definitive criteria for either monetary or fiscal policy can be established.

FULL-EMPLOYMENT GOAL

Let us see how these two objectives, each desirable in itself, may come into conflict when both are set up as direct goals for policy. Let us suppose that the government adopts the policy of guaranteeing full employment of the labor force at all times. It plans to accomplish this objective by keeping aggregate total expenditures at whatever level is required to do the job. Assume that the government accomplishes its declared task in any given year so that total expenditures on goods and services—*i.e.*, consumption, investment, and government—are sufficient to employ approximately all the available labor[1] at the prevailing level of wages. Now suppose that the strongly organized labor groups exert pressure for wage increases in excess of the increases which have occurred in labor productivity and that these groups are successful. This will raise labor costs for business firms, which will be forced to lay off workers unless the demand for their products also in-

[1] Excluding those who are in the process of shifting jobs at any given time. This type of unemployment is called "frictional," and could never be eliminated in a free society, even should its elimination be deemed desirable.

creases commensurately. Workers will tend to be forced into unemployment as a result of the wage increase. But here the government will again enter the picture, for it has adopted the policy
objective of maintaining full employment. It will cause expenditures to expand (via either fiscal or monetary policy or both).
This increase in total expenditures will increase demand for goods
and services sufficiently to allow firms to reemploy all the labor
previously laid off. But the expansion in demand will also have
increased the level of product prices. Full employment will have
been secured only at the expense of a rising price level, *i.e.,* inflation.

PRICE-LEVEL STABILITY AS A GOAL

On the other hand, let us assume that the government adopts a
policy of keeping the price level, or the value of the dollar, roughly
stable. Now suppose, as before, that strong labor groups are successful in securing wage increases in excess of the increase in labor
productivity. This would increase costs to business firms, and,
again, they would be forced to lay off workers unless the demand
for their products were correspondingly raised to offset the increase in costs. But under the policy of keeping the price level
stable, the government would not increase expenditures in this
situation. Hence, the demand for products would not increase,
and the layoffs would be turned into permanent unemployment
as long as the wage rate remained at the high level. A policy of
price-level stability, accordingly, may be consistent with less than
full employment, and a policy of full employment may be consistent with a constantly rising price level. This conflict will be
present as long as the economy is characterized by strong monopoly pressures among labor groups which are able to force wages
above competitive levels. The inherent policy conflict may be
summed up in the statement that society can have any two of the
following: (1) full employment, (2) a stable level of prices, and
(3) strong monopoly labor groups.[1] It cannot have all three. It must
decide which of the three it will abandon and which it will retain.
If wages are allowed to move up only in accordance with productivity as would tend to be the case in free input markets, full em-

[1] Monopoly in the labor market is significant here because "full employment" primarily implies full employment of the labor force. Of course, monopoly in other segments of the economy will alter both the allocation of resources and the distribution of income and, in so doing, may make "full
employment" more difficult to achieve.

ployment and a stable price level do not conflict as policy alternatives. If union pressures are not checked and wages are allowed to move upward at a faster rate than this, a governmental policy of full employment will be attained at the expense of a rising price level, that is, a continually falling value of the dollar. This appears to be the probable alternative which our society will adopt, although clearly the more desirable policy would be one aimed at limiting the monopoly power of unions[1] along with, of course, a more general attack on monopoly in all forms. Here we find yet another reason for seeking to maintain competition in all markets. Monopoly not only is harmful in distorting the allocation of economic resources among various uses but also serves to interfere with the accomplishment of other desirable social goals for the whole economy.

RECENT EXPERIENCE AS AN ILLUSTRATION

The policy dilemma confronting the United States in respect to these two desirable, but conflicting, objectives is well illustrated by recent experience. The recession of 1957–1958 was characterized by increasing unemployment and declining production accompanied by increasing product prices, especially in the nonagricultural sectors of the economy. The Federal Reserve Board, properly concerned with the dangers of continued long-run inflation, included price-level stability as an important aspect of its policy criterion. The Board continued to exert pressures against the expansion of the money and credit supply; "tight money" continued until November, 1957. On the other hand, other individuals and groups, including many in high governmental positions, were looking more directly at employment and production indexes which began to decline midway in calendar year 1957. These groups, implicitly giving production and employment more weight and price-level stability less weight in aiming at some criterion for monetary policy, were urging a relaxation of "tight money" policies several months prior to Federal Reserve action.

[1] Some students of this problem believe that, upon adoption of a genuine employment-stabilization policy by government, union officials will see that it is to their own interest to keep wage increases approximately in line with productivity increases. Should this happen, we might have all three of the things listed, but the monopoly power of labor would be left unused. Other students of this problem (notably Professor A. P. Lerner) have recognized the inherent policy conflict and have proposed schemes for government regulation of wages to keep them in line with productivity. See A. P. Lerner, *Economics of Employment* (New York: McGraw-Hill Book Company, Inc., 1951), Chap. 14.

Expansive Monetary Policy

In the preceding section we have discussed, but we certainly have not solved, the problem of determining appropriate criteria for stabilization policy. It is now time to assume the criteria problem away and to examine the mechanics of monetary policy. If income, employment, and the price level are all falling, the question of conflicting goals disappears. Antidepression action is indicated on all policy fronts, both monetary and fiscal. The Federal Reserve Board should proceed to adopt expansionary measures of various kinds. First of all, reserve requirements for member banks should be lowered; secondly, the rediscount or borrowing rate should be reduced. And, finally, government securities should be purchased in open-market operations. Selective controls, if they are present, should also be relaxed.

Each of these steps will have the effect of increasing the excess reserves of commercial banks. Banks may be placed in a favorable reserve position, but this action in itself will promote recovery only if individuals or firms borrow the newly available funds and subsequently spend these funds on goods and services. The purchase of government securities by the Federal Reserve Banks may drive interest rates down, but the attractiveness of low rates and ready availability of credit may not be sufficient to encourage prospective borrowers. In a period of unfavorable business expectations, firms may respond rather little to small shifts in interest rates. This difficulty of monetary policy in promoting recovery from a depression has given rise to the phrase "you can't push on a string."

For monetary policy to prove positively effective, it must directly encourage increased spending. Open-market purchase of securities will accomplish some direct effect. By replacing securities with cash in the portfolios of individuals and firms, liquidity in the economy is increased and spending is encouraged. But even for those groups continuing to hold securities, bond prices are increased. Net worth is increased in so far as these assets are not offset directly by liabilities. And since individual taxpayers are rarely cognizant of their own liability inherent in public debt, open-market purchases of government bonds are especially likely to be influential in this respect. Individuals who hold marketable government bonds become wealthier as the pattern of interest rates falls (bond prices rise), and they will tend to increase spending on real goods and services.

The Treasury Department, faced with problems of debt re-financing during a depression, should pay off as much individually held debt as possible and replace this with debt held by Federal Reserve Banks and commercial banks (to the extent that the latter have excess reserves). This action on the part of the Treasury would be equivalent in result to Federal Reserve purchase of government securities from the public in the open market. This sort of Treasury policy would amount to "monetizing" a portion of the debt held by the public. And by the replacing of securities with the more liquid asset, cash, people will be encouraged to increase spending. If conditions warrant, this process of debt monetization can be accomplished without difficulty since the Treasury will constantly be faced, during the late 1950's and the 1960's, with major problems of maturing issues of the national debt. Merely by replacing maturing issues held by individuals and nonbanking institutions with securities sold to the banking system, a substantial monetization of the debt might be effected.

Restrictive Monetary Policy

If the economy is characterized by rising prices and substantially full employment, some restrictive monetary policy is indicated in order to promote stability in the price level. A "tight money" policy is appropriate in such situations. Restrictive policy taken in 1955 and 1956 was motivated properly in this respect.

In periods of threatening, or actual, inflation the Federal Reserve Board should increase reserve requirements for member banks, increase the rediscount or borrowing rate, and direct Federal Reserve Banks to sell securities in the open market, and perhaps impose selective qualitative controls on certain types of credit extension. The action is the reverse of that undertaken in depression. Here the phrase "you can't push on a string" must be supplemented with "but you can pull." For each of these policy steps tends to put pressure on banks' reserve positions or, in the case of qualitative controls, to restrict the demand for loans. Banks will be encouraged to restrict lending and to increase interest rates. While low interest rates are not alone sufficient to encourage expanded investment in depression, high interest rates can be sufficient to deter some investment during periods of threatening inflation.

The sale of securities in the open market by the Federal Reserve System will also have direct effects on spending apart from those generated through a contraction of bank reserves. As people are induced by higher interest rates to give up the more liquid cash for the slightly less liquid but more productive government securities, private spending will tend to be reduced.

Treasury management of the public debt can supplement Federal Reserve action in combating inflation. During such periods, the Treasury should attempt to shift debt out of the hands of the Federal Reserve Banks (and perhaps of the commercial banks) and into the hands of individuals and nonbanking institutions. By retiring debt held by the Federal Reserve Banks and refinancing this debt by sales of securities to individuals, the Treasury can create effects equivalent to Federal Reserve open-market sales of government securities to the public. If new debt is created during such periods (by deficit financing) which would, of course, represent a fiscal policy just opposite to the proper one, the new issues of government securities should obviously be sold to the nonbanking public where the total effect will be less inflationary than elsewhere. Deficit financing during an inflation is not an unusual case, as has been indicated by the Korean War experience.

General Evaluation of Monetary Policy

Monetary policy was prevented from being effective during the years of postwar inflation, 1946–1951. The Federal Reserve Banks were obliged by the Treasury to maintain prices of government securities during this period, and consequently, the power to restrict the expansion in the supply of money and credit was curtailed. This support-price policy was abandoned after March, 1951, when the Federal Reserve Board exerted its independence from Treasury Department domination.

Owing to a combination of wise policy and accidental circumstances, the years following 1951 were characterized by a high degree of stability in both prices and employment. Except for a minor recession in 1953–1954, which was quickly reversed, the economy operated over the 1951–1954 period at substantially full employment without noticeable or serious upward pressures on the price level. Somewhat understandably, therefore, considerable reliance, perhaps too much, came to be placed on monetary policy as the device with which to promote economic stabilization.

Upward pressures on prices began to be exerted in the years 1955, 1956, and early 1957. The Federal Reserve Board, with full support of the national administration, responded by adopting more stringent measures. "Tight money" came into existence as a commonly used term. The higher level of interest rates and the general shortage of credit tended to slow down the rate of spending, and the policy was effective for a time in checking or preventing general inflation. But, as with all policy, certain groups in the economy were affected more than others by the credit stringency. Funds for guaranteed mortgages became scarce, and the residential construction industry was acutely slowed down in its activity. States and local governments, in their attempts to undertake substantial expansion in schools, roads, and other capital projects, found themselves unable to market securities at previously acceptable prices. Small business firms, having little access to external financing through direct issue of securities, found themselves unable to borrow on what they considered favorable terms. Although the legitimacy of the claim may be questioned, these groups argued that the "tight money" policy discriminated against them in favor of large corporations who possessed ready access to both internal financing out of retained earnings and external financing through direct security issue.

The public dissatisfaction with the continued policy of restriction became more pronounced after mid-1957 when spots of unemployment began to appear in isolated sectors of the economy, and rates of production in basic industries began to slow down. Articulate support was given to the view that the restrictive monetary policy was not preventing inflation; it was merely slowing down the rate of economic growth.

Several proposals were made in 1957 to undertake a searching reexamination of all United States monetary institutions. Bickering between the administration and Congress prevented decisive action from being taken. Finally, in the late fall of 1957, the Committee for Economic Development, a nongovernmental private group, announced its plans to sponsor (with Ford Foundation support) the organization and work of a National Monetary Commission. This Commission was charged with the responsibility of undertaking the most exhaustive study of the monetary structure which has been made in a half-century.

It may be useful to speculate on the problems which will arise in the course of the Commission's work. We have already discussed the question of criteria for action. In the United States economy of 1960, the goals of full employment and price-level stability are not compatible. They can be made so only upon courageous and vigorous action in the field of wage and price setting, action taken to restore some semblance of effective workable competition.

Failing this, the economy will likely be faced with a continuing choice between rapid short-run growth accompanied by inflation and somewhat slower growth accompanied by reasonable stability in the value of the monetary unit. Many reasonable people are likely to favor the first alternative. But the advantages may well be illusory. The economy can, no doubt, grow more rapidly over short periods (given the current institutional structure) if the inflationist policy is accepted. But sustained, or long-run, growth seems likely to be threatened by a deliberate abandonment of price-level stability as a policy goal. It seems highly questionable whether or not "moderate" inflation can be prevented from generating runaway inflation, with its acknowledged disastrous consequences.

The problem of devising appropriate stabilization criteria in the modern economy is indeed basic. But in one sense this problem itself reflects a more fundamental issue which the Commission, or anyone looking at the monetary-fiscal picture, must examine. The fundamental issue is the one of *rules versus discretionary authority* in stabilization policy. Regardless of the criteria adopted, policy measures must be largely unpredictable so long as policy is to be exercised by discretionary authority. It is impossible to predict what the Federal Reserve Board will do in a particular situation, and a study of the record will provide little or no assistance in this respect. This represents no reflection on the Board. The Board may consist of the wisest men in the land. But as long as there remain men who are empowered by law to take action, *at their own discretion,* the particular shape of their action cannot be predicted. This gets to the root of the difficulty. Discretionary authority can always be subjected to criticism by specific individuals and groups. Any policy step, even if it involves no action, must benefit certain groups and harm other groups in the society. Therefore, the discretionary authority must always be subjected to criticism, as, indeed, the Federal Reserve Board has been throughout its existence.

The alternative to discretionary authority is fixed and definable monetary rules. It is undoubtedly possible to devise a monetary system which will operate in accordance with a set of rules which are written down in law. Under this alternative, predictability is restored and pressures are toward changing the law rather than changing the men. The great difficulty in establishing a modern monetary system on the basis of rules lies, of course, in securing some general agreement among the groups in society on the basic content of the law in the first place, and some tacit consent to abide by the rules once made.

19

FISCAL POLICY

Monetary policy, discussed in Chapter 18, is not the only means through which the goals of economic stabilization may be achieved. Fiscal policy provides an additional means. For purposes of the following discussion we may define *fiscal policy* as including any operations on the budget of government which are deliberately aimed at promoting stabilization objectives. In this way we are able to distinguish *fiscal policy* from the more general financial policy of government, the latter being defined as the raising and spending of revenues for the purpose of accomplishing specific social or collective aims. Financial operations may or may not be accompanied by deliberate fiscal policy. For example, a decision to expand Federal spending on highway construction may be based solely on the desire to get better highways. In this case, no fiscal intent, as such, would accompany the purely financial operation which involves the raising of revenues and spending them on highways. On the other hand, the desire for better highways may be accompanied by the desire to expand aggregate demand for goods and services in order to expand employment and real income. In this circumstance, the purely financial aspects of the operation are accompanied by *fiscal-policy* aspects. In this chapter we shall discuss only the fiscal-policy aspects of government financial operations.

The Balanced Budget

Fiscal tradition and convention incorporate the balanced-budget rule. This rule states that governmental revenues and expenditures should be kept in approximate equality. The rule has a certain legitimacy in that adherence to it, or rather faith in its validity, serves as an important check to irresponsible action. Political support for expanded government spending and reduced taxation is almost always easy to secure in democratically elected legislative assemblies. The legislator is likely to be motivated by two pressures: first, a pressure to increase the number of government projects (veterans' hospitals, drainage canals, Air Force installations, etc.) in his district, and, second, a pressure to reduce the taxes paid by his constituents. Complete abandonment of the balanced-budget rule in the interest of securing more flexible, and more effective, fiscal policy in the stabilization sense might lead to the necessity of imposing some additional or supplementary constitutional restraints on legislative behavior in fiscal matters. Yet, as we shall see, abandonment of the balanced-budget rule has been widely advocated since the great depression of the 1930's. This is one more area of economic policy in which reasonable arguments can be made on opposing sides. The desirable control features implicit in widespread acceptance of the balanced-budget rule must be offset against the desirable stabilization objectives which may be promoted by deliberate unbalancing of government budgets. Certain compromise solutions have been proposed, and we shall now examine some of these.

BUDGET BALANCE AT HIGH EMPLOYMENT

One of the proposals which has been advanced with a view toward combining the advantages of the balanced-budget rule with those of countercyclical flexibility may be classified as the rule of budget balance at high and suitable levels of income and employment. This proposal has been associated with the Committee for Economic Development in its more practicable form and with Professor Milton Friedman of the University of Chicago as its theoretical propounder.

This proposal is based essentially on the proposition that under conditions of desirable economic stability, that is, during situations characterized by substantially full employment of economic resources and price-level stability, the budget of the national government should be balanced. Revenues should equal expenditures on a normal basis, and leaving out of account extraordinary capital outlays.[1] The proposal is that decisions as to whether or not additional public expenditures are to be undertaken and additional taxes levied should always be made on the assumption that the full-employment level of national income prevails. In other words, both revenue and expenditure estimates should be made on the hypothesis that full employment will prevail, and any newly proposed expenditure items must be matched by sufficient newly imposed taxes to maintain budget balance. However, sufficient flexibility should be built in, on both sides of the budget, to ensure that, should the full-employment–stable-price-level situation not prevail, more or less automatic stabilizing forces would be brought into play.

The way such a budget would work may be quite easily explained. Let us suppose that, on the presumption of a high-employment–stable-price-level situation, the Federal government's budget is balanced at $75 billion on an annual rate basis. Now assume that, for some reason, a slight recession should occur. With the onset of recession, personal and corporate incomes will fall, reducing the revenue yield from the personal and corporate income tax. Therefore, tax revenues will be less than estimated, let us say $70 billion. On the other side, the recession, accompanied by some unemployment, will cause social-security benefits, unemployment compensation, and other expenditure items to be larger. Total expenditure will be larger, or at least no smaller, than estimated, let us say $77 billion. A budgetary deficit (in our example $7 billion) will in this way be generated automatically by the recession, and this deficit will act to reverse the adverse shift in national income. If the recession should get worse, the automatically generated deficit would be continued and increased in size. The money supply would be expanded through the financing of the deficit, and aggregate de-

---

[1] Certain proposals have been advanced which suggest that, even under such conditions, the balanced-budget rule should be modified to allow for loan financing of public-investment projects which are expected to be nonrecurrent in nature, the benefits from which are expected to accrue over a reasonably long time period. These proposals, which involve the creation of a separate capital budget, warrant serious consideration, but space does not permit a lengthy discussion of the issue at this point.

mand would be increased. Eventually, the equilibrating forces would become more powerful than the contractionary forces, and national income would begin to move upward.

The equilibrating mechanism is also set in motion to correct inflationary tendencies. As inflation develops, more revenues are taken in through taxes, and, to some extent, expenditures are not changed, or are reduced. Budgetary surpluses are generated which act to reduce aggregate demand and to reduce the money supply. The inflationary forces will eventually be overcome and national income will tend to move toward desirable levels.

The rule of budget balance at high employment represents a substantial improvement over either the older rule of simple budget balance or the rule of complete flexibility in fiscal policy. It does provide a rule which, if followed, would ensure adequate fiscal discipline or control while at the same time providing a powerful force toward promoting economic stability. But the fundamental questions are: Would such a rule be followed? Is such a rule practicable in the context of democratic decision-making? For this rule, to be effective, requires a high degree of sophisticated thinking on the part of legislators and the public. It requires deliberate abstention from practices which economic pressures dictate and economic arguments support. Congress must refuse to expand expenditures, without accompanying them by additional taxation, even in times of economic recession. And it must also refuse to cut taxes in times of inflation even though surpluses are accumulated, unless it is willing to reduce the scope of governmental activity. The hypothetical budget which is to be balanced must be distinguished from the actual budget which may not be balanced. All of these problems should at least be recognized when considering this rule. Appropriate economic education and farsighted statesmanship may create situations in which the rule is politically workable, but at this stage the political problems involved appear difficult.

THE BALANCED-BUDGET MULTIPLIER

The government budget may have stabilization effects even though rigid balance between revenues and expenditures is maintained. A change in the size of the budget may have important effects on the level of economic activity. The discussion of these effects may be included under the classification of *the balanced-budget multiplier*.

If the government spends directly for real goods and services in the domestic economy, this spending constitutes a direct addition to the income stream by the full amount of the expenditure. The tax levy necessary to finance this spending does not reduce income by as much as the spending increases it because a portion of the funds paid to government in taxes would have been saved if they had not been collected as taxes. The forgoing of this saving, because of taxation, does not directly reduce the income stream. Therefore, an increase in the size of the government's expenditure on domestically produced goods and services will increase national money income. A decrease in the size of this expenditure will decrease income.

This proposition can be illustrated by a numerical example, although care must be taken not to read too much into the arithmetical values derived. For example, let us assume an increase in government spending on real goods and services of $10 billion. This is financed out of taxation. The marginal propensity to spend out of income is $9/10$: of each extra dollar of income individuals spend 90 cents. Hence, the $10 billion additional taxes will reduce spending by only $9 billion. The net increment to total spending brought about by the budgetary change is $1 billion. This will have multiplying effects on national income as suggested by the ordinary income multiplier. Under the assumption of this example, this one-billion-dollar net increment to total spending will generate a tenfold increase in national money income, or $10 billion. The increase in tax-financed expenditure by $10 billion generates a $10 billion increase in national money income. In this way, the balanced-budget multiplier, having a value of unity, may be derived, regardless of the value of the propensity to spend.

The seemingly magic value of unity for the balanced-budget multiplier must be carefully qualified. First, the analysis works only for government expenditure on domestically produced real goods and services. It tells us little about a change in the size of the budget as normally conceived. Second, the analysis assumes taxation to reduce personal incomes directly as would be done by the personal income tax, when this may not be true, as in the case of excise and inheritance taxes. Third, the marginal propensities to spend must be equal for all relevant groups. Last, investment spending must remain unchanged. These qualifications narrowly restrict the analysis. About all that remains is an indication as to the directional effect which a change in the government's budget has upon national money income. It seems certain that an increase in the balanced budget, within reasonable limits and under normal circumstances, will generate upward pressures on national money income and that a decrease will generate downward pressures.

The onset of cold peace in lieu of cold war might allow for substantial reduction in defense spending. Even if taxes are reduced dollar-for-dollar with spending, as would almost certainly be the case, national money income would tend to fall. Prices would fall, and as price rigidities appeared, some unemployment would develop in the short run. In such circumstances, a strong argument could be advanced for reducing taxes more than spending, that is, for deliberate budgetary unbalance over a transitional period.

On the other hand, the race for military supremacy in the space age seems almost certain to create pressures for ever-larger Federal spending programs. This suggests that, in order to prevent inflation from getting out of hand, either surpluses must be deliberately planned (a rather naïve hope) or that the fiscal impact must be offset by "tight money" policy.

The Flexible Budget: Depression Policy

If we may disregard for a moment the problems involved in implementing flexible budgetary rules, it will be useful to discuss fiscal policy on the assumption that the balanced-budget rule is wholly abandoned, and, in its stead, some "functional-finance" rule is adopted. Functional finance means the purposeful manipulation of the government budget with a view toward achieving economic stabilization objectives. We may first discuss the appropriate fiscal policy in depression, followed by a discussion of fiscal policy in inflation.

EXPENDITURE INCREASE

In periods of deep depression, deliberate unbalancing of the government budget in the direction of creating a deficit is indicated. This unbalancing can be accomplished in either of two separate ways, or by some combination of the two: (1) expenditures may be raised, or (2) taxes may be decreased. We shall examine the first alternative.

Let us suppose that the government decides to create a deficit by expanding expenditures without raising taxes. (The precise manner in which the extra expenditure is made, whether for satellites, bridges, or school lunches, for flood control or unemployment relief, is an important factor in determining the aggregate effect, but these differences may be neglected in this initial discussion.) This will increase total spending by the amount of the deficit. The increase in total spending will increase national income. But the increase in national income will be larger than the amount of the deficit, especially if the deficit is maintained during several spending periods. The ratio of the increase in income to the initial increase in spending, is, of course, the income multiplier, and it depends for its value on the marginal propensity to spend, *i.e.*, the ratio of additional spending to an additional increment of income.

TAX REDUCTION

As one alternative to the expenditure-expansion policy, the government may leave its spending unchanged and lower taxes. This will also create a deficit. The disposable income of private individuals and firms will be increased by the tax reduction, and with a higher income, spending by these units will be increased. But it is probable that the deficit required to generate a given increase in national income will be greater in this case than in the case of public-expenditure expansion. This is true, since some of the addition to disposable income resulting from the tax reduction will be saved, *i.e.*, not spent, and accordingly total spending in the economy will not increase by the full amount of the deficit. The exact amount of the increase depends again on the marginal propensity to spend. If, for example, national money income is twenty billion dollars less than the desirable "full-employment" level, and if the marginal propensity to spend is $4/5$, a tax reduction of five billion will cause a four-billion-dollar increase in spending by individuals. This four-billion increase in spending will ultimately generate the required increase of twenty billion through the multiplier effect (if the marginal propensity to spend is $4/5$, the multiplier will, of course, be five). Thus, a five-billion-dollar deficit would be required to generate a twenty-billion-dollar increase in national income in the tax-reduction case, whereas only a four-billion deficit would be required in the expenditure-expansion case. This conclusion assumes, however, that investment plans are the same in the two cases. There seems to be some reason for believing that business firms will react more favorably to tax reductions by government than to an expansion of public expenditures. If this is true, the marginal propensity to spend will be higher in the tax-reduction case, and the necessary deficit may be no larger, and perhaps even smaller, than in the expenditure-expansion case.

The reduction of taxes is, in some respects, a more desirable weapon of antidepression fiscal policy than increased government spending. First of all, taxes can be adjusted more quickly than can public expenditures. Second, the area of government activity is kept within sharper limits, always a desirable feature in a freedom-loving society. It is true, however, that the real costs of government services are much lower than during depression periods when there is widespread unemployment, and this is a point in favor of expenditure expansion. The appropriate antidepression fiscal policy, therefore, would seem to be one of using both expenditure expansion and tax reduction as weapons in increasing total spending in the economy.

WAYS OF FINANCING A DEFICIT

If the government is to spend more than it collects in tax revenues, it must secure additional purchasing power from some source. The Federal government could simply create the money. Congress could legally authorize the issuance of paper money without limit if it chose to do so. There are, however, certain traditional beliefs and myths surrounding money which have evolved in our society. One of these seems to be that money should have some connection with gold. It does not appear likely, therefore, that outright currency issue would be resorted to in this country as the sole means of financing a deficit.

The same results may be achieved by government borrowing from Federal Reserve Banks. The government would merely transfer instruments of debt (Treasury bills, certificates, or bonds) to the Federal Reserve Banks in exchange for a Treasury deposit account. The Treasury would then cover that portion of its expenditures not covered by taxation by drawing down these deposit accounts. Additional purchasing power in the amount of the deficit is pumped into the economy by this operation with precisely the same effects that would follow the outright creation of currency by government. The effects on bank reserves are also equivalent. The outright issue of currency would, when the money is spent by government and redeposited by individuals in commercial banks, cause bank reserves to increase by the full amount of the issue, allowing a possible multiple increase in loans and deposits. A reduction in Treasury balances at the Federal Reserve Banks is no different in this respect. As the Treasury draws down its account, individuals receiving government checks deposit them with commercial banks. Upon clearance, these checks increase member-bank reserves in the full amount of the deficit, allowing a multiple expansion in bank loans and deposits. Thus, the budget deficit may be said to generate inflationary effects in two ways. First, there is an income multiplier resulting from the increase in total spending. Second, the increase in bank reserves tends to lower interest rates and to increase the availability of bank credit to businessmen and householders. Higher investment and consumption spending would thereby be promoted. The inflationary fiscal policy would also tend to generate inflationary monetary effects.

The deficit could also be financed by government borrowing from the commercial banks. If banks hold excess reserves, this method of financing the deficit also becomes equivalent in effect to an outright creation of currency. The utilization of excess reserves by banks to purchase new government securities allows the banking system to purchase securities in some multiple of the excess reserves because, as the Treasury spends the proceeds, its checks are redeposited in commercial banks thus rebuilding their reserves. Even if banks do not hold excess reserves, these can be readily created by the government's selling a small fraction of its new securities to the Federal Reserve Banks in the manner outlined in the preceding paragraph; when these funds are spent by the government, member-bank reserves are built up. This was the procedure followed during the deficit financing of World War II. In summary, it may be concluded that government borrowing from either Federal Reserve Banks or commercial banks is equivalent to the outright printing of paper money. The only difference is that the government interest-bearing debt is increased in the process, whereas in the direct issue of currency this would not be the case.

The deficit may also be financed by borrowing from individuals and nonfinancial business institutions. This method is obviously different from an issue of currency; indeed, it more closely resembles taxation. Borrowing from individuals reduces disposable incomes, and this in turn tends to reduce private spending. Borrowing does not, however, reduce private spending to the same degree as taxation. The essential difference is that lending is voluntary while taxation is compulsory. However, some of the money spent in the purchase of government securities would otherwise probably have been spent for the purchase of goods and services; not all of it would have been saved. Therefore, the antidepression impact of deficit financing is largely destroyed if the funds are borrowed from individuals. The maximum effects on total expenditures are clearly forthcoming when the deficit is financed by borrowing from banks. The sale of government securities to individuals really belongs in the realm of anti-inflation fiscal policy, and should be employed in this fashion. As we have seen, one of the most potent antidepression weapons of monetary policy is the *purchase* of government securities from the people by the central-banking system.

The Flexible Budget: Inflation Policy

Ideally, fiscal policy during periods of inflation should be exactly the reverse of that followed during periods of deflation and unemployment. If the savings and spendings decisions of private individuals interact to generate a national income in excess of that necessary to maintain approximate stability in the level of prices, the budget should be adjusted so as to reduce total expenditures (the sum of private and public spending).

This reduction may be accomplished in ways just the reverse of those cited as antidepression measures. To combat inflation, a budgetary surplus needs to be generated. This may be done by (1) lowering expenditures, or (2) raising taxes, or by some combination of the two.

The mechanics of anti-inflation fiscal policy are also similar, in reverse, to those of antidepression policy. Suppose that national money income is predicted to be twenty billion dollars above that thought to be desirable and that the marginal propensity to spend is again $\frac{4}{5}$. How much should fiscal policy attempt to reduce total spending (private and public) in order to generate the twenty-billion-dollar reduction in national income? The negative multiplier also being assumed to be five, the answer is four billion. Again the method of expenditure adjustment while taxes are kept constant requires a smaller departure from budget balance than that of tax adjustment. If government expenditures are reduced by four billion dollars, and this reduction is maintained for several spending periods, income will eventually fall by twenty billion dollars. (This assumes that private investment is not directly affected.) If, however, taxes are increased and expenditures are left unchanged, a tax increase of five billion dollars will be required. For not every tax dollar would have been a spendings dollar if left in private hands. Also, as in the opposing case, the second method, that of a budget balanced at a lower level, requires a very considerable reduction in the size of the budget. This may be very difficult to effect, especially when the budget is made up largely of such items as defense expenditures, veterans' benefits, and interest on the public debt.

The most appropriate over-all scheme for anti-inflation fiscal policy should combine government-expenditure reduction and tax increases. Selectively, those expenditures having the greatest income-multiplying effects should be first reduced, and those taxes reducing spending most should be first increased.[1]

DISPOSITION OF A SURPLUS

If appropriate anti-inflation fiscal policy is pursued via the over-balanced-budget method, there is a problem of the disposition to be made of the excess revenue collected. (Just as we have discussed the financing of the budget deficit, we must now discuss the disposition of the budget surplus.) If the government creates a surplus by collecting greater amounts in tax revenues than it spends, the full anti-inflation effects of this budget position will be realized only if the surplus money does not somehow find its way back into the income or spendings stream. The simplest method of ensuring this full effect would consist in the government's "burning up the money" not needed to meet expenditures. But just as the government's rolling of the printing presses is not politically practicable in the deficit case, actual government destruction of surplus money is not practicable here. The government may accomplish the same desired result by using the surplus to build up its balance at the Federal Reserve Banks. If a larger balance is kept in the Treasury account, the surplus is effectively neutralized. It does not return to the spendings stream.

With a Federal debt of almost 280 billion dollars, however, it would seem that any budgetary surplus of revenues over expenses should be used to pay off some of the enormous debt. We must then examine this possibility and inquire whether or not the government can use surplus funds to retire debt without at the same time destroying the anti-inflation effects of the surplus.

The ownership of the Federal debt may be broken down into a few major categories. These include United States government agencies and trust funds, Federal Reserve Banks, commercial banks, insurance companies and mutual savings banks, and individuals and other investors.[2] Let us trace through the effects of using a government surplus to retire government securities held by each of these

---

[1] Throughout the discussion in this chapter, we are concentrating upon the stabilization aspects of the fiscal policy to the neglect of effects on resource allocation and income distribution.

[2] The distribution of ownership in May, 1958, was as indicated in the following table (in billions of dollars):

U.S. government agencies and trust funds	$ 55
Federal Reserve Banks	24
Commercial banks	63
Insurance companies and mutual savings banks	19
Individuals and other investors	112
Total	$274

major groups. Government agencies and trust funds may be neglected here. These hold special issues of debt for the most part, and
there would be little reason for retiring such debt since reserves are
required to be in the form of government securities.

Government repayment of debt obligations held by the Federal
Reserve Banks does provide an effective way in which the surplus
may be used to reduce the debt without destroying its anti-inflation
effects. In any analysis of debt repayment, both the tax-collection
side and the debt-repayment side must be considered. In creating
the surplus, tax revenues are collected but not spent. Thus, on the
tax side, the net effect is clearly deflationary. Disposable incomes
are reduced; consumption spending is reduced. But the effects of
taxation on bank reserves must also be considered. To pay the taxes,
individuals and business firms draw down their deposit accounts. If
the government spends the tax money, this tends to build these
deposits up again, and there is no substantial net effect on the
banking system. If, however, the government uses the funds collected in taxes to repay debt held by Federal Reserve Banks, the
money will not find its way into the reserves of commercial banks,
and reserves will therefore tend to be reduced by the full amount
of the reduction in deposits. The net effect is that member banks'
accounts with the Federal Reserve Banks are decreased and the
Federal Reserve Banks' cash accounts are increased. If member
banks hold no excess reserves, their reserve position will be endangered, and they will be forced to curtail loans and investments.
When surplus funds are used to retire Federal Reserve-held government debt, accordingly, not only is the negative income multiplier
working to reduce inflationary pressures but, in addition, the deposit multiplier is set to work in a deflationary direction. Both of
these effects would also be felt if the surplus were used to build up
Treasury balances at the Federal Reserve Banks.

If, however, the government surplus is used to retire debt owned
by any of the remaining groups of security holders, the effects of
the repayment itself tend to work in the opposite direction from
those of the surplus creation. Consider now the repayment of debt
held by the commercial banks. The initial collection of taxes reduces bank deposits, but the government in turn uses the nonex-
pended funds to retire bank-held securities. On the bank's balance
sheets, the net effects will consist of a reduction in demand deposits on the liability side and an equivalent reduction in the gov-
ernment-securities item on the asset side. The reserves held by commercial banks are not finally affected, but their reserve position is

strengthened. This is true because total deposits have been reduced, and thus some reserves which were previously required are now excess. The banks may proceed to expand loans and deposits in some multiple of the excess amount.

To illustrate this point by an arithmetical example, let us assume that the government creates a surplus of ten billion dollars and uses this to retire government securities held by commercial banks. When taxpayers pay their tax bills initially, bank deposits are reduced by approximately the amount of such payments. The surplus, we are assuming, is used to retire bonds, bills, and certificates held by the banks. The banking system's total holdings of government securities are thus reduced by ten billions. No change is effected in the actual reserves of banks, but deposits are down by ten billion dollars. Thus, if banks are operating under a legal reserve requirement of 20 per cent, they now need two billion dollars less for reserves. Excess reserves appear in the amount of two billion dollars. As the deposit multiplier works itself out, this allows a potential expansion of loans and deposits of ten billions. The repayment of the government debt in this case makes possible a deposit-multiplier effect which is in the opposite direction from the original effect of the surplus. It may be concluded that the total impact of a policy of surplus financing to repay commercial-bank-held debt is probably deflationary, since the negative income-multiplier effects are probably more powerful than the positive deposit-multiplier effects.[1] But the total impact is less deflationary than the policy of surplus financing to repay Federal Reserve-held debt or to accumulate Treasury balances.

The use of surplus revenues to repay government debt held by nonbanking holders also generates opposing effects on the tax-collection and the debt-repayment sides. As taxes are collected, bank deposits are reduced. But as the government retires securities held by individuals or corporations, bank deposits are again increased. The net effect is probably deflationary, but the deflationary impact is slight relative to repayment of debt held by Federal Reserve Banks or even by commercial banks. The only deflationary effect here stems from the fact that the marginal propensity to spend is perhaps slightly greater for taxpayers in general than for bond-holders.

[1] This conclusion is reinforced when the effects on liquidity positions are considered. The full replacement of government debt by private debt, which would be necessary if the tax and retirement sides were to be fully offsetting, might reduce liquidity in the economy. Therefore, private debt expansion is not likely to be fully compensating.

There will be more significant effects on the pattern of spending, however. Some portion, perhaps a large portion, of tax revenues would have been spent for consumption goods if the money had been left in private hands. Public-debt repayment to individuals and corporations serves to increase their spending for outstanding government and corporate securities. This drives down interest rates and tends to increase investment spending by firms. In total, a policy of surplus financing to retire debt held by individuals and nonbank business firms tends to encourage investment relative to consumption.

Problems of Implementation

Strong political arguments support the adherence to a rule of budget balance, or at least, some modification on this rule. Strong economic arguments support a policy of flexibility in government budget-making. Political factors must be given particularly strong weight in budgetary discussions; the traditional protection of the people against tyranny by bureaucracy lies in the power of the purse, the power to tax and spend. Broad fiscal decisions can never be left to the responsibility of discretionary authority, as are decisions regarding monetary policy. Nor can wise fiscal decisions be incorporated readily into rules of law such as might conceivably be achieved with an appropriate monetary framework. Decisions concerning the rate of spending by government and the rate of taxation must continue to be made by legislative bodies. And legislative bodies represent the public interest by means of an interplay of group interests and pressures. The nature of the choice process is such as to make the deliberate generation of a budgetary surplus extremely difficult to secure, as our postwar experience demonstrates. On the other hand, deficit financing will more or less automatically arise if the rule of budget balance ceases to exert some considerable influence on individual decisions of legislators.

Fiscal policy seems, therefore, to contain a built-in bias toward the promotion of inflation. Legislatures will generate budgetary deficits to combat deflation, but they will go no further than budget balance during periods of threatened inflation. To some extent, this bias may be offset by an opposing bias of monetary policy, which seems to be more effective in preventing inflation than in encouraging recovery from recession.

Deliberate manipulation of government budgets to accomplish economic stabilization objectives also has other drawbacks. As fiscal decisions must be made, adjustments in policy to economic changes can only be produced after considerable time lags. And, by the time action is taken, the economic situation may have changed. In addition, decisions, once made, are not readily reversible despite changes in the economic climate.

An example may illustrate this point. The 1959 budget, the largest in United States peacetime history, was accepted without a great deal of controversy because in early 1958, when it was presented, the economy was undergoing a rather severe short-run recession. Additional Federal expenditures, quite apart from their intrinsic merit in accomplishing specific purposes, seemed useful in order to stimulate employment. However, by the time that the spending actually occurred, the economy was again threatened with inflation and the extra Federal spending added yet another inflationary force.

Many features of the economy suggest that a depression comparable with that of the 1930's is not likely to occur. Should this prediction prove false, and long and continued recession take place, fiscal policy would assume major significance. Deficit financing might prove necessary, and, in such situation, clearly would be implemented. However, if the economy should escape major slumps, that is, if recessions of the degree of those of 1949 and 1953 should be the order of severity encountered, deliberate departure from the general rule of annual budget balance does not seem appropriate. Reliance upon monetary policy seems indicated.

If, as seems much more likely, the long-run danger is serious and continued inflation, little help can be expected from fiscal policy. Strict adherence to the rule of budget balance seems all that can be hoped for, and monetary policy must largely carry the burden of achieving stabilization.

20

COMPARATIVE ADVANTAGE

We have assumed until this point that the economy has no commercial intercourse with other nations; that is to say, we have been concerned with what is sometimes referred to as a "closed" economy. The fact is, of course, that both consumers and domestic firms often purchase inputs from abroad, and many producers sell a part of their outputs in foreign markets. It is appropriate that we consider the effects of international trade, not only because in the real world trade across international frontiers does exist, but because, in addition, international trade changes the whole pattern of economic life and enables wants to be better satisfied than they could be in a state of isolation. If foreign trade is a significant factor affecting the allocation of an economy's resources, it is important that it not be left out of account.

In embarking upon the study of international trade the student should keep in mind that the essential principles which underlie this branch of economics are not fundamentally different from those which apply to the domestic economy. Trade between nations is similar in most respects to trade between regions within a country, *e.g.*, the East and the West, and, like internal trade, it is a natural application of the principle of specialization. Any exchange of commodities or services between individuals can usefully be considered a means whereby each individual *indirectly* produces the commodity which he receives in trade. Usually it is more economical for the individual, region, or nation to specialize in producing a limited number of goods, or even the fractional part of one good, and to secure other needed goods by means of trade. The economic unit can, by specialization and trade, usually produce directly and indirectly a larger volume of goods than would be possible if it attempted complete self-sufficiency.

The question as to the nature of the "gains" to the country as a whole which result from participating in foreign trade raises complex issues which have received attention from writers on economic matters ever since the time of the mercantilists, a group of writers who dominated economic thinking and policy in Europe and America during the three centuries from Christopher Columbus to George Washington. The mercantilists assumed that what one nation gains from trade another nation must lose, and they extolled the virtue of maintaining a "favorable balance of trade," *i.e.*, they felt that to be powerful and prosperous a nation should export more than it imported. The classical economists were able to demonstrate the fallacy in the mercantilist position and to show that the real basis for trade, either foreign or domestic, is the mutual advantage which can be secured. Ideas are long-lived, however, and mercantilist fallacies still pervade much popular thinking on matters of international economic policy. To refute such fallacies a demonstration of the mutual gains which may arise from trade seems to be in order. This chapter will be devoted, accordingly, to a consideration of the effects on the domestic economy of engaging in international trade.

Trade as a Substitute for Factor Mobility

If there were no restraints on the free movement of productive factors from one region to another, or from one nation to another, the total world production of goods and services would be maximized when the marginal products (in value terms) of similar units of each productive factor were equal in all uses and in all places. If the marginal revenue product of labor, for example, were less in sheep raising than in wheat growing, total production would be increased by taking some units out of sheep raising, where the loss would be relatively small, and adding them to wheat production, where the gain would be relatively great. Within a single economic

system, the payment to owners of resources in accordance with
marginal revenue productivity tends to ensure that such movements
do, in fact, take place. If similar workers produced more in wheat
farming than in sheepherding in the United States, for example,
wage rates on the wheat farms would tend to be above those on
sheep ranches, and workers would be attracted to wheat farming
and away from sheepherding. The same sort of allocative process
tends to take place among different geographical areas within the
same economy. Resources are attracted to areas where they are
most productive, and the total output of goods and services is maximized when similar units of resources produce marginal products
of equal value in all regions. From this it is easy to see that if the
whole world were considered as the economic unit and the maximization of world production were accepted as the appropriate
policy goal, the same principles would apply. This means, of course,
that the total world production of goods and services could be increased by a migration of coolie laborers from East Asia to the
United States. The marginal product of such labor would clearly be
greater in this country than in the Orient. Even from a "one-world"
outlook, however, the maximization of world output resulting from
the free movement of labor might not prove to be an acceptable
goal since the drastic redistribution of income that would take place
might generate disruptive social, political, and cultural problems.

The fact that the international mobility of productive factors
would serve to increase total production of goods and services (if
we ignore the possible indirect effects on production resulting
from such mobility) may be illustrated geometrically in Figure
20.1. Let us assume a two-country world, Country I and Country II.
Let us further assume that labor is the only mobile productive factor.
The x axis for Country I is read in the conventional way, but the
x axis for Country II is read from right to left. MRP_I is the marginal
revenue product curve for labor in Country I, and MRP_{II} is labor's
marginal revenue product curve in Country II. It is assumed that
perfect competition prevails in both countries, that all workers are
identical, and that the countries have a common currency. The total
number of workers in both countries taken together is equal to
OO', ON being situated in Country I and $O'N$ being situated in
Country II. Under these circumstances the wage rate in Country I
will be NS, and in Country II it will be NT, since the wage rate
will tend to equal the marginal product of labor under competitive
conditions. The value of the total product in Country I, *i.e.*, the
area under the MRP_I curve, is $OLSN$, and the value of the total

FIGURE 20.1. INTERNATIONAL FACTOR MOBILITY
—Would Bring Net Gain in Total Production

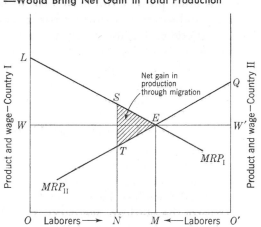

product in Country II is $NTQO'$.[1] If MN workers migrated from Country II, where wages are lower, to Country I, where wages are higher, the marginal revenue product of labor, ME, would be equal in both countries. The value of the total product in Country I would be increased by an amount equal to $NSEM$, while the value of the product in Country II would be diminished by $NTEM$. Since the gain from the migration is greater than the loss, the aggregate output of the two countries would be increased, in this instance by an amount equal to TSE. The combined total product of the two countries would now be $OLEQO'$, and this total could not be increased by further migration.

Even if there were perfect mobility of productive factors, trade between nations would take place because of climatic or other natural advantages for certain types of production in particular regions. In addition, even if no such natural advantages were present, countries would perhaps find it economical to specialize to some extent in particular lines of production and to trade with other countries in order to secure the cost savings which are often inherent in large-scale production. In this way all countries taken together would produce more than if no international trade were to take place.

In the real world, however, productive factors do not move readily

---

[1] The area under any "marginal" curve is the total for the variable under consideration. For example, the area under a marginal physical product curve is total physical product, and the area under a marginal cost curve is total variable cost.

across international boundaries. This applies especially to labor; immigration restrictions often prevent the movement of laborers into and out of a country, and sometimes cultural barriers are nearly as effective as legal restrictions. Capital tends to move much more freely, although it too has been subject to restrictions in recent years. The immobility of productive factors among nations has been one of the features which distinguish the study of international trade from that of domestic trade. The distinction is not so sharp, however, as it might at first appear. Even within the same country mobility is far from perfect. Laborers often do not move readily from low-wage regions to high-wage regions either because of inadequate information, high costs of moving, or reluctance for non-economic reasons to leave home. And in spite of immigration restrictions laborers do move across international boundary lines, especially between contiguous areas. The case of the Mexican "wetbacks" provides an excellent example; in spite of immigration restrictions, coupled with the efforts of both the Mexican and United States authorities to enforce them, thousands of Mexican workers cross the Rio Grande into this country each year, attracted by the higher American wage rates.

In so far as productive factors cannot, or will not, move across national or regional borders in response to economic rewards, the impetus for trade in goods across such borders is increased. For differences in the efficiency and in the proportions of labor and capital make it profitable for nations and regions to specialize in the production of those goods and services for which the resource situation is most advantageous. Interregional and international trade resulting from geographical specialization, therefore, represent something of a substitute for the movement of productive factors from place to place.

The Gains from Trade

David Ricardo, a famous British economist of the classical school, was the first to demonstrate numerically the gain which accrues to both countries which engage in trade. The following model, which has been used by a modern British economist,[1] is constructed in much the same manner as Ricardo's original demonstration: a unit of commodity *A* and a unit of commodity *B* have been defined in such a way that the cost of each is the same in Country I. In Country II a unit of *B*, as so defined, costs twice as much to produce

[1] R. F. Harrod, *International Economics* (London: Cambridge University Press, 1933), p. 17.

as a unit of *A*. It does not matter whether the method of measuring costs is the same in the two countries; cost might be measured in man-hours of labor in one country and in dollars in the other. The only important point for our purposes is that whereas the ratio of production costs for the two commodities is one to one in Country I, it is one to two in Country II. The two commodities are assumed to be the only ones produced.

Table 20.1. Comparative Advantage

	Costs of production	
	In Country I	In Country II
One unit of commodity *A*..............	x	Y
One unit of commodity *B*..............	x	$2Y$

Under conditions assumed in the model it will be desirable for Country I to specialize in the production of commodity *B*, for Country II to specialize in the production of commodity *A*, and for the two countries to trade with one another. Country I has a comparative advantage in the production of commodity *B* since it can produce *B* at the same cost it can produce *A*, whereas in Country II it costs twice as much to produce a unit of *B* as it does to produce a unit of *A*. Country II has a comparative advantage in the production of commodity *A* since it can produce a unit of *A* at half the cost it can produce a unit of *B*, whereas it costs Country I as much to produce a unit of *A* as it does to produce a unit of *B*. If we assume transportation between the two countries to be costless, trade between them to be free (*i.e.*, no tariff or other legal barriers), and pure competition to exist within both countries, it will not only be desirable for the countries to specialize as indicated, but it will be necessary for them to do so. This is the case because the prices of input factories in Country II, for example, will be based on their marginal revenue productivity in their best use, which is the production of commodity *A*. Thus any firm attempting to use these inputs to produce commodity *B* in that country could not do so profitably. This is the same principle that was discussed in Chapter I to show why it would be unprofitable to produce sugar beets in Iowa; *i.e.*, the "corn" use of land and labor would make rentals and wages so high as to make sugar-beet production economically infeasible.

If Country I specializes in the production of commodity *B* and Country II produces nothing but commodity *A*, it will be necessary for traders to arrive at some exchange ratio between the two goods. This exchange ratio will have to fall somewhere between the limits of 1 of *B* for 1 of *A* and 1 of *B* for 2 of *A*. Since if Country I did not trade with Country II but produced both commodities for its own consumption, it could get 1 unit of commodity *A* by giving up 1 unit of *B* (by shifting resources from the production of *B* to *A*), it would be unwilling to trade with Country II if it had to give up more than 1 unit of *B* in exchange for 1 unit of *A*. Similarly, if Country II did not engage in international trade, it could get 1 unit of *B* by giving up 2 units of *A*. Country II will not, accordingly, pay Country I more than 2 units of *A* for 1 of *B*.

THE TERMS OF TRADE

Since Country I is specializing in the production of commodity *B*, the closer the actual exchange ratio approaches the limit 1 of *B* for 2 of *A*, the more favorable are the "terms of trade" to Country I. Similarly, since Country II is specializing in the production of commodity *A*, the closer the exchange ratio comes to the other limit, 1 of *B* for 1 of *A*, the more favorable are the terms of trade to Country II. The actual exchange ratio which is arrived at by the traders of the two countries will depend on the relative *demands* for the two goods. Any shift in demand would cause the terms of trade to become more favorable to the country which produces the good for which the demand increases relative to that of the other. If we assume that Country I is specializing in cloth and Country II in beer, a cold winter might turn the terms of trade in favor of Country I, while a hot summer might make the exchange ratio more favorable to Country II.

Suppose that the actual exchange ratio between commodities *A* and *B* in our model turns out to be 1 of *B* for $1\frac{2}{3}$ of *A*. Both countries will gain by trading. Country I will produce a unit of *B* at a cost of 1 and receive for it $1\frac{2}{3}$ units of *A*; she is getting for a cost of 1 what without trade it would have cost her $1\frac{2}{3}$ to produce domestically. And Country II gets 1 unit of *B* at a cost of $1\frac{2}{3}$, whereas it would have cost her 2 to produce *B* domestically. Country I, therefore, saves $\frac{2}{3}$ of a cost unit on each unit of *A*, and Country II saves $\frac{1}{3}$ of a cost unit on each unit of *B*.

The highly simplified model which we have examined is designed to emphasize an important point, namely, that by specializing in the commodities for which it has the greatest comparative advantage and trading part of its output with other nations a country can produce a greater volume of goods and services than if it attempted to be self-sufficient. It is more economical to produce many commodities *indirectly* through international trade than to produce them *directly* at home. The specialization on those commodities in which a nation has the greatest comparative advantage, however, does not imply that a country may not produce a part and import a part of its requirements of a given commodity. The United States, for example, imports large quantities of wool, but some sections of this country are well adapted to the production of this commodity, and a significant part of our wool requirements are met from domestic production.

DEMAND AND SPECIALIZATION

So far we have neglected the effect of demand in the determination of which commodities a country will find it desirable to specialize in producing. In order to see this effect more clearly let us expand our model by considering a world consisting of only two countries in either of which any of six commodities can now be produced—in quantities which are limited, of course, by available resources. We may again designate the countries as I and II and the commodities as a, b, c, d, e, and f. We shall define a unit of each commodity as the amount which can be produced by a given amount

Table 20.2. Two-country Six-commodity Model

Commodity	Cost of production	
	Country I	Country II
a	x	Y
b	x	Y_2
c	x	Y_3
d	x	Y_4
e	x	Y_5
f	x	Y_6

of resources in Country I; this cost will be designated as x. In Country II, on the other hand, each commodity is produced at a different cost—whether at a greater or smaller cost than in Country I is immaterial. These cost data are summarized in Table 20.2. We may assume that the six commodities are arranged in order of increasing cost in Country II, that is, Y_2 is greater than Y, Y_3 exceeds Y_2, etc. Tariff barriers are assumed not to exist, and transportation between the two countries is assumed to be costless.

Country II clearly has a comparative advantage in the commodity at the top and Country I in the commodity at the bottom of the list. We can be sure that if trade occurs between the countries, Country I will export *f* while Country II will export *a*. But without knowing the nature of the demand for the several commodities, it is impossible to determine which country will produce the intermediate commodities. Each country will have to pay for its imports with its exports. If the demand in Country II for *f* is sufficiently great, it is possible that Country I could produce only this commodity and pay for its imports of *a, b, c, d,* and *e* by exporting *f*. Or Country I may produce and export *d, e,* and *f* and import *a, b,* and *c*. A knowledge of the demand side of the international market is necessary for determination of the nature of the commodity specialization as well as the terms of trade. Brazil, for example, exports considerable quantities of cane sugar and citrus fruits in addition to coffee. If, however, the world demand for coffee should increase sufficiently, Brazil might give up the production of sugar and citrus fruits and pay for her imports by exporting only coffee.

It should be kept in mind that the above model is constructed using only assumptions as to the relative costs of the six commodities *within* each country; no intercountry cost comparisons are involved. Country I may have a large and poorly paid labor force so that in spite of a small supply of capital per worker as compared with Country II it can in absolute terms produce all commodities at lower costs than Country II can. Yet Country II will be able to trade with Country I because Country I will find that it can enjoy a greater volume of the six commodities by specializing in one or a few in which it has the greatest comparative advantage and securing the others by trade. Country II, whether it is relatively rich or poor in resources, can maximize its own real income by producing the goods for which its resources are best adapted and securing other goods by trade. Neither country will find it advantageous to produce directly those goods which can be obtained more economically indirectly by trade.

The models used in this chapter to illustrate comparative advantage have been purely hypothetical and highly simplified. They help, however, to answer some important real-world questions. Is the American standard of living endangered, for example, by free trade with Japan? The answer is clearly no. Such trade permits us to concentrate to a greater degree on the commodities for which our labor and capital are particularly well adapted and to secure from Japan items for which they have a comparative advantage. Toys which require a great deal of hand labor, for example, have long been a commodity for which Japan is highly suited. While American toy manufacturers and their employees might like to prevent their importation, this action would make it necessary for us to divert resources from uses where they are more efficient to uses where they are less efficient, and this would do its bit to lower the American standard of living, and it would also, of course, work to the detriment of Japan.

As a long-run matter all countries gain from international trade because of the superior allocation of resources possible with trade as compared with what would obtain without trade. As a short-run matter, changes in the demand and supply conditions under which international trade is carried out can require difficult readjustments. (This, of course, is also true of purely internal trade.) If, for example, a commodity which is imported is suddenly reduced sharply in price to American consumers because of a drop in the dollar price of a foreign currency, domestic producers of the same good or of close substitutes will find their sales volume reduced. This will have adverse effects on investors and laborers in the affected domestic industry, and they may press for a tariff or other restrictions on imports. (These matters of political economy will be considered in Book Two.) But it is generally not wise to allow the short-run interests of any producer group to dominate the allocation of resources. To do so reduces the national real income, and it is likely to be harmful to international political relations as well.

21

ECONOMIC GROWTH

Writing over three decades ago a prominent American economist observed, "Few problems are more fascinating, more important, or more neglected than the rates at which development proceeds in successive generations in different countries."[1] During recent years economists and other social scientists as well as politicians and the public generally have become seriously interested in economic growth, particularly with reference to the underdeveloped countries. This interest has been manifested in the form of numerous official statements by the governments of the leading industrial nations of the world, in the Charter of the United Nations, in the Atlantic Charter, in the Articles of Agreement of the International Monetary Fund and the International Bank for Reconstruction and Development, in the Havana Charter of the proposed International Trade Organization, in former President Truman's famous "Point Four" program, and in numerous scholarly and popular books and articles on the subject. It is readily apparent to the casual observer that some nations now enjoy high standards of living while in others

[1] Wesley Clair Mitchell, *Business Cycles* (New York: National Bureau of Economic Research, 1927), p. 416.

extreme poverty is widespread if not virtually universal.[1] But what is meant by economic growth, and how is it measured? Why have some geographical areas of the world made marked economic progress while others have remained little above the bare subsistence level? Should the more advanced countries attempt to help the underdeveloped nations, and, if so, what can be done? Are there hazards in attempting to push economic growth at too rapid a rate? It will be the purpose of this chapter to consider these and related questions, though to some of them there are at the present time no definitive answers, and in this entire area much work remains to be done.

Meaning of Economic Growth

For our purposes we shall identify economic growth with increasing output per head. Like most definitions, this one is largely arbitrary, and for some uses other measures are undoubtedly better. Suppose, for example, that output per man-hour increases, but workers elect to work fewer hours so that annual per capita output remains constant. Does this not represent economic growth? Or if total output doubles as population doubles, is it appropriate to argue that there has been no economic growth? We might measure economic growth in terms of total output, but this definition also has its limitations. Suppose that in a country such as China, where there is a very large population relative to other resources, 50 per cent of the population die as result of famine and pestilence but total national real income diminishes by only 25 per cent. Can it not be argued with some point that the country has experienced economic growth in spite of the decline in national income, and that, indeed, a reduction in population may very well be a prerequisite to economic growth in a nation that is overpopulated?[2]

Whether economic growth is measured in terms of total national income or per capita output (and more often than not the two are likely to move in the same direction), it is important to keep three points in mind:

[1] In 1949 the per capita income in the United States was $1,453, while in Indonesia it was only $25, according to United Nations estimates. In that year 54 per cent of the world's population lived in countries with less than $100 per capita income, while only 7 per cent lived in a country with over $1,000 per capita income. Statistical Office of the United Nations, "National and Per Capita Incomes of Seventy Countries—1949," *Statistical Papers Series E, No. 1,* New York, October, 1950, pp. 14–16, 29.

[2] For the case against using per capita real income as the measure of economic growth see Gerald M. Meier and Robert E. Baldwin, *Economic Development* (New York: John Wiley & Sons, Inc., 1957), pp. 4–8.

1. Economic growth, as the term is used here, and welfare are not synonymous. It is quite possible for total output to be increasing at a faster rate than population with each person having a command over more goods and services than before, but at the same time the total utility or satisfaction of the community may not be increasing. Unless one identifies income and welfare, he must also distinguish between economic growth and growth of welfare. We usually assume that the marginal utility of any given commodity for the consumer is positive, and that an increase in the quantity of the good available for consumption will, accordingly, increase the consumer's total utility. But consider a community in which workers, due to ignorance, are induced to labor under dangerous or unhealthful circumstances. The total income of the community as well as the per capita output will, we may assume, be increased, but it does not follow that there has necessarily been an increase in total satisfaction or welfare.

2. Economic growth must be distinguished from an increase in consumption. The increase in output may not result in higher standards of living. Soviet Russia, for example, made significant gains in total (and per capita) output during the years following World War I, but the increased productivity took the form of more industrial equipment and war materials with living standards very little improved. But it would be idle to argue that Russia has not experienced great economic growth; it is because of the growth that Russia is a serious threat to the free world today.

3. Economic growth does not imply an equitable distribution of the gains from the increased output. It is possible that the increased output may have been the result of the exploitation of ignorant and impoverished workers, so that the net result is that the rich have become richer while the poor were getting poorer. How income is distributed may well affect output, but growth and distribution are separate if related problems.

Causes of Economic Growth

Economic growth has moved at widely differing rates in different times and places. Table 21.1 indicates the wide range of per capita incomes in selected nations for the year 1948. In many countries the data are incomplete and unreliable, but the range from poorest to richest is indeed broad. Why have some nations attained relatively high incomes while many others have not? There is no single simple answer to this question, and factors which

seem to have contributed to high levels of income in some regions
have not done so in others. With respect, for example, to the relationship between rates of growth of population and per capita
product we find these combinations: (a) high rate of population

Table 21.1. National Income: Selected Countries, 1948

Country	Population, in millions	National income, in millions of U.S. dollars	Per capita income, in U.S. dollars
United States	146.6	$223,500	$1,525
Switzerland	4.6	4,365	950
New Zealand	1.9	1,755	933
Canada	12.9	11,538	895
Australia	7.7	6,256	812
Sweden	6.9	5,600	805
Denmark	4.2	3,280	781
United Kingdom	50.0	39,000	777
France	41.5	17,336	418
Germany:			
Western	41.7	15,000	360
Eastern	26.0	7,800	300
Italy	45.7	10,900	225
Jamaica	1.3	262	201
U.S.S.R.	193.0	35,000	181
Panama	0.7	125	179
Japan	80.2	11,523	143
El Salvador (1944)	1.9	217	114
India (1946)	346.0	26,000	75
Pakistan (1949)	74.4	5,000	67
Philippines	19.4	799	41
Ecuador	3.4	134	40
Belgian Congo	10.9	380	35

Source: W. S. Woytinsky and E. S. Woytinsky, *World Population and Production* (New York: Twentieth Century Fund, 1953), pp. 392–393.

growth and high rate of per capita income increase, *e.g.*, United
States and Japan; (b) low rate of population growth and high rate
of per capita income increase, *e.g.*, Sweden; (c) high rate of population growth and low rate of per capita income increase, *e.g.*, Italy;
and (d) low rate of population growth and low rate of per capita
income increase, *e.g.*, France. In some countries there appears to

have been a combination of relatively high proportions of savings and capital formation with high rates of growth, *e.g.*, Japan; in other countries there seems to have been a combination of moderate proportions of capital formation and high rates of growth, *e.g.*, Sweden; and there have been periods when there has been a relatively high proportion of capital formation with moderate rates of growth, *e.g.*, Great Britain from 1870 to 1914. There has been a diversity among countries in the extent of their reliance upon foreign trade and capital imports; in the abundance of natural resources and the rate of growth attained; in the nature of the industries that lead in the process; and in the nature of the dominant social institutions and the social heritage of the several nations which have attained relatively high per capita outputs.[1]

The factors which affect growth are so diverse that casual observations as to why the United States has a relatively high standard of living or why the Southeastern states of the United States are relatively poor or what Ecuador needs to do to increase its per capita output are likely to have little more validity than the old timer's explanation of why he has lived to such a ripe old age. The existence of certain institutions in high-income countries does not mean that those institutions have caused the high rate of productivity, and even less does it mean that the imposition of those institutions upon a low-income country would have salutary effects. There are no buttons to push which will overnight transform a poor into a wealthy nation; if the formula for increasing per capita output were simple, no nation or region would long remain poor. In investigating the causes of economic growth we must, at least in the present state of our knowledge, move slowly and with caution.

One of the leading students of economic growth has listed the following as the principal proximate causes of growth: (1) the effort to economize; (2) the increase of knowledge and its application; and (3) the increase of capital or other resources per head.[2] If we

---

[1] Simon Kuznets, Comment on Moses Abramovitz, "Economics of Growth," in Bernard F. Haley (ed.), *A Survey of Contemporary Economics*, Vol. II (Homewood, Ill.: Richard D. Irwin, Inc., 1952), p. 179.

[2] W. Arthur Lewis, *The Theory of Economic Growth* (Homewood, Ill.: Richard D. Irwin, Inc., 1955), p. 11. Professor Abramovitz organizes the central questions in the theory of growth around the following headings: 1. The supply of the factors of production. 2. Psychological and other qualitative attributes of the population. 3. Industrial, commercial, and financial organization. 4. The legal and political framework of economic life. 5. Discovery and exploitation of knowledge. Abramovitz, *loc. cit.*, pp. 135–144. For a list of nineteen determinants of growth see J. J. Spengler, "Theories of Socio-Economic Growth," *Problems in the Study of Economic Growth* (New York: National Bureau of Economic Research, 1949), pp. 52–53.

go behind these causes and look for the causes of the causes, we become involved in matters well beyond the scope of economics: Why is the effort to economize so much stronger in some countries than in others? Why does knowledge increase at a more rapid rate in some places than in others, and why do some people put their knowledge to more effective use than others? Why does capital accumulation proceed at a much faster rate in some regions than others? What environments are most suitable to the encouragement of the forces which promote growth, and how do the institutions which facilitate growth come to be established? The answers to these questions require the knowledge and wisdom of the sociologist, the anthropologist, the historian, the social psychologist, and the geographer as well as the best talents of the economist.

Although, as we observed earlier, it was not until recent years that economists engaged in extensive studies of growth, many earlier writers made incidental reference to the subject, and a number of them developed clearly defined theories of development. Adam Smith, for example, felt that the key to economic growth was the proper institutional framework; given the appropriate institutions, the other requisites of growth would be forthcoming. Malthus was concerned with the problem of inadequate demand, or what we today describe as a low evaluation of income in relation to leisure. Former President Truman's Point Four program points to the lack of technological skill as *the* bottleneck for the economic growth of underdeveloped countries. Others have insisted that lack of capital is the bottleneck, and with adequate capital all other restraints upon growth will become inconsequential. And finally, there are those who believe that natural resources are the key; given adequate resources, the necessary capital and institutions will be forthcoming.[1]

Characteristics of Underdeveloped Areas

Although the causes of economic backwardness appear to be diverse and not uniform from region to region, the characteristics of underdeveloped areas are sufficiently similar that fairly accurate generalizations can be made. A glance at the list of the underdeveloped countries in Table 21.2 is sufficient to suggest a number of uniformities that can be detected. These are, by definition, very poor countries, many of the people living at the bare subsistence level. In most of these countries a high proportion of the popula-

[1] Lewis, *op. cit.*, p. 19.

Table 21.2. Countries Grouped by Level of Economic Development

I. HIGHLY DEVELOPED COUNTRIES (ABOUT 400 MILLION PEOPLE)

In the Americas	*In Europe*
Canada	Belgium
United States	Denmark
	France
	Germany
	Netherlands
	Norway
	Sweden
	Switzerland
	United Kingdom

II. INTERMEDIATE COUNTRIES (ABOUT 500 MILLION PEOPLE)

In Africa	*In Europe*
Union of South Africa	Austria
	Czechoslovakia
In the Americas	Finland
Argentina	Hungary
Cuba	Ireland
Chile	Italy
Puerto Rico	Poland
Uruguay	Portugal
Venezuela	Spain
In Asia	*In Eurasia*
Israel	U.S.S.R.
Japan	

III. UNDERDEVELOPED COUNTRIES (ABOUT 1.7 BILLION PEOPLE)

In Africa	*In Asia*
Algeria	Afghanistan
Angola	Borneo
Belgian Congo	Burma
Cameroons	Ceylon
Egypt	China
Ethiopia	Formosa
French Equatorial Africa	India
French West Africa	Indo-China
Gold Coast	Indonesia
Kenya	Iran
Liberia	Iraq
Libya	Jordan
Madagascar	Korea
Morocco	Lebanon
Mozambique	Malaya

Nigeria	Nepal
Nyasland	New Guinea
Northern Rhodesia	Pakistan
Ruanda-Urundi	Philippines
Sierra Leone	Saudi Arabia
Southern Rhodesia	Syria
Sudan	Thailand
Tanganyika	Turkey
Tunisia	Yemen
Uganda	

In the Americas	*In Europe*
Bolivia	Albania
Brazil	Bulgaria
British West Indies	Greece
Colombia	Rumania
Costa Rica	Yugoslavia
Dominican Republic	
Ecuador	
El Salvador	
Guatemala	
Haiti	
Honduras	
Mexico	
Nicaragua	
Paraguay	
Peru	

Source: Eugene Staley, *The Future of Underdeveloped Countries* (New York: Harper & Brothers, 1954).

tion, usually from 70 to 90 per cent, are engaged in agriculture. If the economy is barely able to sustain its population, a very large part of the workers will be engaged in the production of necessities and near-necessities. Housing and conditions of health and hygiene will be poor. For the most part production will be for domestic consumption and the quantity of foreign trade on a per capita basis will be low. When exports are large, they are likely to be of a single-crop nature such as rubber, cocoa, and sugar cane. The low living standards will encourage child labor, and educational facilities are likely to be poor. Savings will be low, and if credit is available the people are likely to be in debt. Agricultural yields per man may be expected to be low, and frequently the yield per acre is low.[1]

[1] But yields per acre in some underdeveloped countries are higher than in some more advanced countries. For example, wheat yields are higher in Egypt than in Canada but lower than in Denmark, Belgium, Holland, and the United Kingdom. W. S. Woytinsky and E. S. Woytinsky, *op. cit.*, pp. 546–547.

The concentration of workers in agricultural industries often results in an absolute overpopulation in these fields, that is, the number of workers in agriculture could be reduced without reducing agricultural output. The amount of capital per worker is low, and the agricultural output consists predominantly of cereals and raw materials with little production of meat products; this comes about because an acre of land devoted to cereal production will produce substantially more calories than the same amount of land devoted to cattle production. Such tools and equipment as are available are likely to be crude and inefficient, and the small size of plots would make the use of modern capital equipment uneconomic in any event. In those areas where there are large landowners, such as India, modernized agriculture is handicapped by inefficient means of transportation and inadequate local markets. Since short-run survival is the primary objective of the small landholders, the soil is frequently depleted with little attention being given to crop rotation and fertilization.

Most underdeveloped nations have high birth rates, high mortality rates, and low life expectancies at birth. Women usually hold positions of low status, and the behavior of the population is largely determined by tradition. Communication and transportation facilities are inadequate, particularly in the rural areas, literacy rates are low, technology is crude, and there are poor training facilities for technicians and engineers.[1]

Economic growth does not proceed at the same rate even in different sections of the same country or at different times in the same region. It is not surprising, accordingly, that we find a tremendous diversity in the level of economic achievement attained by the several countries of the world. There are significant differences in the degree to which economies seek out and exploit economic opportunities. Attitudes toward wealth differ. We are accustomed to associating wealth and power and social status, but these are not universal attitudes. In the days of early Christianity the merchant and the money-lender were despised while asceticism was greatly admired. In other societies the priest, the learned man, or the soldier held the place of highest honor. As recently as the 1940's Mahatma Gandhi, the great Hindu nationalist leader who was educated in England and was intimately acquainted with the nature of Western economic advances, decided that the imposition of modern industri-

---

[1] For a list of the characteristics of underdeveloped areas see Harvey Leibenstein, *Economic Backwardness and Economic Growth* (New York: John Wiley & Sons, Inc., 1957), pp. 40–41.

alism upon the economy of India would be a tragic mistake. In some areas where there is an interest in improving productivity, available resources may be inadequate or institutions which encourage production and provide rewards to the workers may be lacking. In some of the more remote corners of the world incentives to effort have been lacking as result of limited horizons; there has been little knowledge of how the more prosperous part of the world lived. American movies and the American GI have done much to provide to the rest of the world a picture, sometimes badly distorted, of life in the United States, and this appears, perhaps somewhat surprisingly, to have provided a number of countries with an incentive to emulate the American way of life.

In some places there appears to be a desire for higher living standards, but the cost seems to be too great. For most people work is irksome, but for people in a depressing climate, afflicted with disease and malnutrition, the effort necessary to provide anything beyond the bare necessities is too great to make it worth while. Even in our own country it has been charged that with certain laborers the problem of absenteeism becomes more serious as pay rates increase. Modern industrialism requires a spirit of adventure and enterprise that is largely lacking among some peoples. To make marked economic progress there must be a degree of freedom from convention and taboo. Attitudes toward the sacred cow, the kind of work women may do, birth control, and willingness to trade with strangers may have an important effect upon the rate of economic progress. Economic development requires risk-takers. Some people enjoy taking risks—creating them if none develop in the natural course of events; these are the gamblers. Other people seem to make the avoidance of risk their chief occupation. Some people cannot afford to take risks; the wealthy farmer can experiment with new seed or new methods, but the bare-subsistence farmer is forced to stick to established techniques and procedures. Tradition often slows down the rate of progress. A willingness to change occupations is a requisite to development, but a caste system renders such changes virtually impossible.

It is clear that a program to assist the underdeveloped areas achieve higher living standards must be prepared to cope with complex and diverse problems. Strictly economic assistance must be largely limited to providing additional capital and technical knowledge. But before we can determine what we might be able to do, it is well to know why we are interested in doing anything at all. Are we interested in raising living standards in underdeveloped areas for strictly humanitarian reasons? Or are we ready to offer help in order to assure ourselves friends abroad? Or are we trying to improve our military position? Or do we want to have a hand in influencing the foreign policies of other countries in such a way as to make them more congenial to our interests? Or do we think that by being helpful we can encourage the backward countries to resist communism more effectively? Or do we believe that by raising standards of living in these areas we will make them better customers and thereby help ourselves?

It is probably true that none of these is a satisfactory base for foreign aid on a large scale. We have already learned that making gifts to foreigners does not necessarily make friends of them; some of them have said that what they want is trade, not aid. The military assistance that many of these countries could provide would be insignificant; some of them are barely able to maintain a semblance of law and order at home. If foreign aid is offered as a bribe to establish institutions which are agreeable to us, the project would seem to be doomed to failure from the start. As the general level of literacy increases there is likely to be more rather than less political unrest, and there is no assurance that a better fed people will shun socialism and cleave to capitalism.

In spite of the many-sidedness of the problem of foreign aid to underdeveloped areas, it appears that a case can be made for such a program, and, although there is a limit to what any outside nation can do, there does appear to be something that the United States can do. But if such a program is to be successful, we need to know what we can do, why we are attempting to do it, and what each of the underdeveloped nations must be expected to do for itself. A brief survey of these matters will be considered in Chapter 36, "Economic Aid for Underdeveloped Areas."

Book Two
Allocation of Resources

Part **1**

THE MARKET ECONOMY

22

THE NATURE OF ECONOMIC ANALYSIS

The first half of this book has covered a variety of topics, some of which may have appeared to have little relationship to each other. It is somewhat tempting to begin the second half with a simple promise of "more of the same." Inherent in the study of elementary economics is a sense of grappling with a lot of loose ends which do not seem initially to form a common pattern. The unity of subject matter which characterizes some disciplines seems absent. About all that can be done at this stage is to state rather categorically that a unity does exist, that the various loose ends do fit together, and that, if he has faith and perseveres, the student will begin to appreciate this. If a student is at the point where he can, in fact, see the organic unity of economics, the subject field becomes relatively simple. The difficulty is that the student is not normally equipped to grasp this unity until he has been subjected to considerable exposure.

It will be useful, however, to back away briefly from the discussion of particular problems in economic analysis or economic policy and, at the beginning of Book Two, introduce the subject matter all over again. In a real sense, this chapter is an introduction to the study of elementary economics. Many textbooks include the material discussed here in the very first chapter with the result that students are introduced to something with which they are wholly unfamiliar and the introduction is likely to be largely meaningless. But now that the first half has provided a flavor of the actual discipline, we may stop and combine a belated introduction with a progress report.

Let us review briefly what we have discussed in Chapter 1. The very word "economics" can best be understood from the verb form "economize" in its everyday or common usage. We speak of economizing on many things, money, time, effort, etc., in the ordinary pursuits of personal life. Why is it necessary to economize at all? We come immediately to the reality of *scarcity* when we try to answer this question. Economizing is necessary only because something is *scarce*. And scarcity is the fundamental characteristic of any economic problem.

Technological and Economic Choices

Economizing as a process embodies two separate operations which, for purposes of clarification, we may call the *technological* and the *economic*. In its broadest, or economic, sense, economizing means choosing among alternatives. But prior to the ultimate choosing among separate alternatives, the set of best possible alternatives must be selected. And this selection embodies the *technological* process of choice. Let us illustrate by a simple example. Suppose that an individual has $10 to be spent on beans and bread. The *technological* problem is that of choosing, from among the infinite variety of beans, that particular variety which provides the desired qualities at the lowest cost. For example, suppose that a famous brand name costs 25 cents a can, but that the consumer knows that the same beans are also sold under another label for 15 cents. His choice of the 15-cent beans is a *technological* one. By a similar process, all brands of bread except the most "efficient" are eliminated from his consideration. Having solved his purely technological problem, the consumer finally makes his *economic* decision. He allocates $3 to beans and $7 to bread. To be sure, many economizing decisions involve both types of choice in one and the same operation. But it is helpful to separate the two, for they involve quite distinct characteristics. If there is only one thing desired, but the means for attaining it are scarce (because there exist alternative uses), the problem becomes that of stretching the available means as far as is possible. The technological problem may be stated in two ways. First, if the goal is absolutely fixed, technological economizing becomes the process of minimizing the cost of accomplishing this goal, that is, utilizing the least amount of resources possible while still getting the job done. To return to our example, if the dietician should specify the precise amount of nutritive value which the consumer must attain from beans, the technological problem becomes that of choosing the particular quality and amount of beans which will provide this nutritive value at the lowest cost. Or consider an example drawn from military experience. Let us suppose that the decision is independently made to place a satellite of certain specifications into orbit. This decision definitely fixes the end to be accomplished; no choice is involved on this side of the problem. Economizing reduces to minimizing the costs of accomplishing this given task. Decisions must be made; choices must be exercised. Some one must choose the single "best" or "cheapest" way of getting the satellite into space, the one best way from among an almost infinitely large number of possible ways.

Alternatively, the technological problem may be stated as follows. The means may be fixed while the single end or goal is quantitatively variable. Here the question reduces to *maximizing* output or payoff from the available means (resources). Again a military-scientific example will be useful. Suppose that the Department of Defense is provided with a budgetary supplement of $5 billion and is directed to utilize this sum solely in putting a satellite into space. The choice problem here consists in choosing among the alternative forms of satellites which might be put into space for this expenditure, choosing that one which will provide the most effective combination of size, data collecting, etc. This is a payoff-maximizing problem; the previous example was a cost-minimizing problem.

There is choice, decision-making, in either the cost-minimizing or the payoff-maximizing problem. But the necessity of choosing is imposed by the larger *economic* problem created by the scarcity of resources. If alternative uses for resources were not available, there would be no need to economize on costs. Then we could build the most expensive satellite from among the set of those technically possible. The resource limitation (cost limitation) sets the bounds within which the whole technological problem must be solved.

These technological choices are essentially the task of the pure scientist or the engineer. The decisions are purely technical or scientific. This definition may be clarified as follows. Because the end product is predetermined, there exists only one efficient optimum or best solution. Competent scientists (engineers or technicians) should, if they have access to the necessary information, be able to reach rather full and complete accord on the nature of the optimum. All choice problems which are characterized by a single, well-defined goal may be classified as *technological* rather than *economic*.

Many other examples may be introduced. Let us assume that a business firm seeks to maximize profits (more correctly, some present value of a net earnings stream over time) and that all other considerations are wholly irrelevant. This is a quantitatively determinate goal. The decisions which must be made in the organization of production, the sale of output, etc., are technological. If complete certainty were present along with perfect foresight, any competent analyst could, given the proper information, tell a firm precisely how "profits" could be maximized. And other experts should approximately agree.

On the other hand, we sometimes say that individuals seek to maximize satisfaction or utility. Included in this catch-all term is the attainment of many more concrete, or measurable, goals such as stimulating work, adequate leisure, high living standards, good friends, socially acceptable position, etc. These separate components of a single individual's utility complex may come into sharp conflict. For example, a poet who prefers to enjoy the beauties of nature may find it necessary to undertake college teaching in order to earn money. Yet another ascetic may sacrifice the material pleasures for the leisure of contemplation. It becomes quite clear that an efficiency expert or analyst could not objectively determine the way in which an individual should act so as to maximize utility. The choice here is essentially subjective, and the relative importance of satisfying the mutually conflicting goals will vary greatly from individual to individual.

We say that the individual is faced with an economic problem. He must choose some allocation of his scarce means (time, money, energy, opportunity) among alternative ends or uses. These compete with each other for the means. This decision is much broader than the one which we discussed above as technological. There is no one best allocation of resources, that is, no one upon which detached and independent experts could agree. The individual subjectively determines a best course of action, but this choice is entirely subjective. Utility as a single end is not subject to objective measurement.

The existence of alternative ends, each desirable in itself but mutually conflicting, characterizes an *economic* problem. Diminishing returns must be present in order that a choice be made. We see here that the law of diminishing returns has universal applicability. Its usage and importance are far beyond those suggested in Chapter 8. We may clarify the generality of this familiar law by reference to an example. The ultimate scarce resource is time. Assume that a particular individual, a college student before Sputnik I, considers the most satisfactory moments of his day to be those spent in sleeping. If the incremental additions to his utility do not diminish as more time is spent in the sack, he will sleep the whole twenty-four hours. This student would face no choice. But people do not act in this way. Diminishing returns do exist, and the incremental satisfaction from additional hours spent sleeping becomes less and less relative to that derived from other uses of time as more sleeping time is added. Choice becomes necessary when diminishing returns appear.

Although we say that the individual is confronted with an *economic,* as opposed to a technological, problem, the central body of economics as a scholarly discipline is not devoted to the study of individual choice at the subjective level. Economics is a *social science* or a *social study,* and its primary content embodies the consideration of a particular aspect or form of social organization. To be sure, society does not make decisions independently of the individuals within it. But it is with individuals as they play their roles in the social organization of economic activity that we are fundamentally concerned. The purpose is that of securing an understanding of how the economic organization works.

The Study of Economics

Economics then is, basically, a study of how society or the social group makes its decisions or choices. The group of individuals or families composing what we call society is faced with a genuinely *economic* problem. There are always limited resources, even in the Zeta age, and there exist almost an infinite number of uses to which these resources may be put. Included in this allocation problem is the distribution problem of how much of the total product goes to each of the cooperating factors of production.

It would be possible to study the economic problem and the decision-making of a centrally organized society such as that of the Soviet Union. We could study the way in which criteria for choice are determined, and once these criteria are fixed, we might begin to talk about better or worse solutions in something akin to the technological sense. But a free-enterprise economy is not centrally organized; indeed the absence of centralized authority is its essential characteristic feature. The study of the economics of a competitive or free-enterprise system becomes a study of the way in which the many separate decisions of private individuals and private firms fit together in order that the larger decisions for the whole economy can be made. For it is literally true that aggregative choices are made without a single choosing agent. The United States economy produces a determinate number of shoes each year without some bureau or commission having decided on a target or plan. Social decisions become composites of private decisions, and the genius of Adam Smith was that of emphasizing and popularizing this fundamental truth. No economy, as it actually exists, is purely centralized or purely free. There are elements of a market or competitive economy in the Soviet Union just as there are many elements of the controlled economy in the United States. Governmental decisions may not be explicitly necessary to determine the number of shoes, but they do determine the number of satellites. The difference is one of degree, but this is an all-important difference.

What then does the study of economics involve? It includes the study of individual and institutional behavior with a view toward securing an understanding of how such behavior functions in the whole economy. In this way, we study demand, which introduces the range of problems connected with consumer decision-making. But we study consumer choices, not to be able to advise particular consumers, but to see how consumer desires can make themselves felt in the final social choices which the economy implements. We also spend considerable time discussing the economics of the individual business firm or enterprise. We do not study the firm in order to train students to go out and make large profits in business (except in so far as any understanding of the environment within which business operates will help him). We study the firm in order to understand its role in supplying goods and services and in demanding productive services, the first in response to consumer demands, the second in the nature of a derived response to the same demands.

The economy is organized into markets, and we must examine the roles and behavior of individuals and firms as they participate in market activity. Breaking down the economy into the separate markets provides us with a useful starting point. We talk about the market for productive services and the market for final products. More particularly, we talk about the labor market, the money market, consumer durables market, capital market, bond market, stock market, produce market etc. But markets do not exist in a political vacuum. The economic organization operates in accordance with certain rules, not necessarily explicit, as must all social orders. It might just be possible to examine the workings of a completely anarchistic economy, if, indeed, one could exist. But such a study would be wholly academic since real-world economies, as we know them, operate within the framework of a system of laws and rules which have been imposed politically or accepted through custom.

The most fundamental or basic of these rules provide legal protection for life, property, and contract. Your neighbor cannot satisfy his needs for meat by butchering your livestock. Nor can he satisfy his vegetarian needs by picking from your garden. And if he has obligated himself to repay you a debt, he must do so or face legal action. The legal framework of Western societies provides for severe sanction against those who try to violate these essential rights.

These rules provide that the interpersonal satisfaction of wants must take place through voluntary exchange or trade, that is, a transaction which is mutually agreeable to all parties. But at this point additional rules or constraints may impinge to prevent completely free exchange. A man is not allowed to sell himself into slavery, for example, and one is not freely allowed to purchase narcotics or firearms. Rules may also be imposed to prevent undue concentration of power on either side of a market. Common law prohibitions against forestalling have evolved into the modern laws regulating monopoly.

Markets function in the modern world only through the employment of some commonly accepted, and legally approved, medium of exchange. Rules and regulations regarding money clearly must be introduced to provide orderly procedure. The social group also demands that a certain share of resources be devoted to public rather than private uses. Taxation and public expenditures represent the two sides of the public economy which both supplements and competes with the private economy in its demands on economic resources.

In addition to these rather universal rules concerning the protection of basic rights, market power, money, and governmental usage of resources, the social group may impose an almost infinitely variable set of other constraints on the workings of the economic mechanism. These additional constraints may be imposed for almost any reason. Attempts may be made to control prices, to hold them above or below equilibrium or market clearing levels. Minimum wage laws may be passed. Zoning ordinances may be widely adopted. Discriminatory licensing arrangements may be popular. Tariffs may be placed on imported goods. Subsidies may be placed on other goods.

The study of economics should provide an understanding of the way in which the economic organization, as it exists, solves its choice problems. But, when we consider the whole set of legal constraints which may surround the workings of any particular economic structure, or even of any one specific market within the structure, it is necessary that we abstract from many of the peculiar or characteristic features and consider *models* of economic organization. Only by first understanding the way in which a *model* of an economic organization works can we begin to understand how the actual organization functions. In this, economics is precisely equivalent in its method to the physical sciences which, too, must begin with very abstract or simplified models.

Models of Economic Behavior

The most familiar of these models, and the one which is central to the study of economic analysis, is the *competitive model*. We have stated that the American economy is based on competition as an organizing principle, although departures from competition exist in all forms. The *competitive model* is designed to provide an understanding of the way in which the economy would work if competition were, in fact, universal, and the idealized legal framework appropriate to this sort of economy did, in fact, exist. This model includes many heroic assumptions: all buying and selling units must be small relative to the markets in which they participate; all prices must be flexible; resources must be mobile between different employments; and the monetary framework must adjust appropriately to provide over-all stability.

This is the model which has been used, more or less implicitly, in the discussions of demand and supply and price formation in the earlier chapters. Essential to economic analysis is a genuine understanding, indeed an appreciation, of how such an ideal-type economic organization would carry out the social functions required of it. The student should learn how this sort of system would determine what is to be produced, how production is organized, and how the final product of the system is to be distributed. Since these *social* functions are carried out through the interaction of *private* decisions, it is necessary to study individual and firm behavior.

But economic analysis is far from complete when an understanding of the competitive model is mastered. This represents only the beginning toward an understanding of the real-world economy. The next step is that of seeing how the various departures from the competitive assumptions affect the operations of the system. Since not all buying and selling units are small relative to the markets in which they operate, some analysis of monopoly power must be a part of the total. Since many prices are not flexible, and the monetary framework as it exists does not provide for over-all stability, we must introduce macroeconomic models to understand a little more about the determinants of national income, employment, and the price level.

Economics, by providing some understanding of the actual workings of the system, should enable the student to make a few rough-and-ready predictions concerning what will happen when certain properties of the system are modified. For example, suppose a particular law is modified, say, a rent control law. The student of economics should be able to predict the consequences in general terms. The major problem here, even for the student who has mastered economic analysis in the formal sense, is that of choosing the appropriate predictive model. If the competitive model is used, one set of results may come up. If a monopoly model is employed, a different set is reached. The choice among separate analytical models here, as in all sciences, must be essentially pragmatic. And the appropriateness or inappropriateness of the model will finally be determined by the truth or error in the final prediction, and by little else.

Economists have long debated these points. Some economists, while recognizing the many departures from competition which exist in the real world, hold that, by and large, the usage of the competitive model to reach predictive conclusions concerning the American economy provides superior results to any alternative model. Other economists, looking perhaps more closely at the lack of correspondence between the competitive assumptions and the apparent realities of markets as they exist, hold that some monopoly or power bloc model should yield better predictive results. This second position is appealing, but it is weakened by the fact that no one has yet developed a fully satisfactory model for the workings of a whole economy based on monopoly or power bloc assumptions.

We should not forget, however, that this book is an elementary text. It is designed to provide the student with an introduction to economics. Quite obviously elementary economics can go but a small way toward providing the type of understanding discussed above, and it must exclude altogether considerations such as that mentioned in the last paragraph. Just as in all other scholarly fields, it takes considerable study and effort to make one expert, although economics is singular here in that almost any man on the street presumes himself to be an expert in economics, something which he would never do in physics.

Plan of the Book

The first half of this book has covered the whole field of economics with an exceedingly broad brush. The second half will begin to explore some, but by no means all, of the finer points of detail. The first two chapters following this one introduce once again the behavior of individual firms in supplying output. Here we try to explain a few of the problems more or less assumed away in the discussion of earlier chapters. Chapters 25, 26, and 27 reexamine the competitive model and its market imperfections. Chapter 29 introduces a major problem, that of uncertainty and risk, thus far ignored. Chapter 30 introduces the natural monopolies, a singular sort of departure from the competitive model.

In Chapter 31 we examine the distribution of income and wealth, then we go on to discuss the public or government economy in its actual operation at mid-twentieth century. Following this we look somewhat more carefully at the problems posed by the relationships among the separate national economies. And, finally, in Chapter 37 we try once again to provide the student with some sense of the underlying unity of the discipline.

23

SUPPLY AND SHORT-RUN COST

The role of the firm in a private-enterprise economy is to buy or hire productive factors and transform them into goods and services which will be offered for sale in the market. Such an undertaking involves a variety of risks. The risks are assumed by the management of firms in the hope of making profits. Although there are other incentives, the profit motive is by far the most important, and we shall consider it to be the force which impels businessmen to undertake business risks. We shall go further and assume that not only are businessmen in business to make profits, but that they are also trying to maximize profits. This, too, is something less than a perfect description of economic behavior, but it is the best single assumption that can be made, and it lends itself to an analysis of the workings of the economy that would not be possible in any other way.

The firm's profits are the difference between its revenues, which result from the sale of products, and its costs, which result from the purchase of productive factors.[1] Profits are, of course, closely tied to

[1] The terms "factor," "factors of production," "productive services," and "inputs" are used to refer to the things which the firm buys; the terms "product" and "output" refer to the things which the firm sells. The product of one firm may be a factor of another. Sheet steel, for example, is a product of the steel industry and a factor of the automobile industry.

prices; other things being equal, an increase in demand with the resultant rise in price will make production more profitable. The profits of the firm are not, however, determined exclusively by the prices of the products it offers for sale. Since firms are buyers as well as sellers, the prices of the input factors which they buy are quite as important in determining their profit positions as the prices of their products. Before the behavior of firms can be analyzed effectively, accordingly, it is necessary to understand in some greater detail certain aspects of costs.

The Nature of Costs

Cost in its everyday usage means a sum of money that must be given up to acquire a unit of a commodity. If it takes $15 to buy a new hat, we say that the hat costs $15. Upon closer examination, however, the idea of cost is a much more fundamental one than simply the giving up of a sum of money. What is really given up when $15 is paid out for the new hat? The answer is that the purchaser of the hat is sacrificing $15 worth of something else which he could have purchased if he had not bought the hat. The real cost of the hat is the pair of shoes which could have been bought with the $15 but which now cannot be bought. Fundamentally, cost is the alternative good or service sacrificed in the process of acquiring another good or service. The concept may be extended to the whole economy as well as to the single purchaser. Just as the buyer foregoes the purchase of a new pair of shoes to be able to buy a new hat, the whole economy also foregoes something in order to get the hat produced. The real cost to society consists in the alternative goods and services which could have been produced with the resources which went into the production of the hat. Perhaps the wool that was used in making the hat could have been used instead to make a pair of gloves. Or the labor might have been used to produce milk shakes and the machinery to produce toy soldiers. Whatever the productive resources which went into the production of the hat could otherwise have produced may be considered as the real cost of the hat. Productive services cost something in money terms to business firms precisely because these resources could produce alternative products elsewhere in the economy. In order to purchase inputs for the production of any commodity, the firm must compete with other potential users of the inputs, and this competition determines input prices. A firm's costs actually derive from the alternative production possibilities of the inputs which it uses.

TOTAL COST AND TOTAL REVENUE

It appears to be useful at this point to reexamine the concepts total costs and total revenue which were used in Book One. The total costs of a firm represent the payments made by it to owners of factors of production. These include, among others, payments in the form of wages to laborers of various kinds and skills; purchase of raw materials and power; rent on land and buildings; salaries to the company executives; interest on borrowed funds; advertising and selling costs; and depreciation of tools, machines, and other physical equipment. The several cost elements must be classified for purposes of analysis, and the kind of classification employed depends upon the purpose of the analysis. The economist classifies all costs into two broad categories: fixed costs and variable costs. Fixed costs are those which do not change in total as output changes; these are the costs which the firm would have to bear even if the plant were completely closed down for a time. Rent and the salary of the corporation president are examples of fixed costs. Rent must be paid to the landlord whether nothing, little, or much is produced, and the amount of the rent paid will ordinarily not be affected by the size of the output. Variable costs, on the other hand, are those which do vary as output changes. Variable costs are illustrated by wages paid to laborers and the cost of raw materials. If a shoe factory produces 200,000 pairs of shoes in a month, the cost of the leather used will be greater than if the monthly output is only 150,-000. By definition, the total fixed costs remain constant as output increases, but total variable cost increases with an increase in output.

The nature of total costs is illustrated graphically in Figure 23.1. The *TC* curve represents the total costs of a firm for the various outputs as measured on the *x* axis. If the output is *OL*, for example, total cost will be *LA*; if output is greater, say *OM*, total cost will be greater, in this case, *MB*. It will be noted that when output is zero, total cost is *OF*. This, then, is total fixed cost. When output is *OM*, the total cost of *MB* consists of a fixed cost of *MH* (which equals *OF*) and variable costs of *HB*. The vertical distance between the *FF'* line and the *TC* curve measures total variable cost at any output.

The *TR* curve in Figure 23.1 represents the firm's total revenue. As output increases, it is assumed here that the firm's revenue increases proportionately, *i.e.*, the firm is selling in a perfectly competitive market. At an output of *OL*, the total revenue is *LA*, and at an output of *OM*, the total revenue is *MJ*. It will be noted that

FIGURE 23.1. BREAK-EVEN CHART

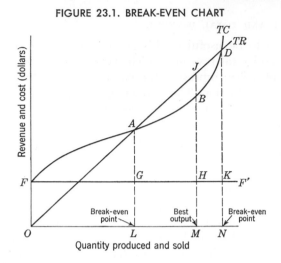

in the figure total cost and total revenue are equal at outputs *OL* and *ON*. These points are known as "break-even" points.[1] The firm depicted in Figure 23.1 must be able to sell at least *OL* units of its product per time period, or it will incur losses. For outputs between *OL* and *ON*, total costs are less than total revenue; that is, the firm can operate within this range and make a profit. For outputs greater than *ON*, the firm would again incur losses. On the assumption that the management wishes to maximize profits, the firm must operate somewhere between output *OL* and output *ON*. The particular output where profits are greatest will be where the vertical distance between the *TR* and *TC* curves is greatest. In this figure this is at output *OM*, where total cost is *MB*, total revenue is *MJ*, and profit is *BJ*.

It is clear that if a firm actually had sufficient data to draw its total cost and total revenue curves, it would be a simple matter to determine the output at which profits would be maximized. In practice they do not, of course, have precise data of this sort. We may assume, however, that the firm's officers are actually attempting to make as accurate estimates as possible concerning costs and revenues. To a considerable extent the firm's policy makers are required to make "educated guesses," but the break-even chart in-

---

[1] In some situations there is only one break-even point. It is taken as a rule of thumb, for example, that it requires 100 performances for a Broadway play to make expenses; there will be no second break-even point as long as the performance draws a good house. When businessmen refer to *the* break-even point, they refer, of course, to the first one.

dicates what they are guessing at, and such charts are becoming increasingly popular with managers of firms.

AVERAGE AND MARGINAL COSTS

It is frequently helpful to think in terms of average costs rather than total costs; this allows costs to be directly related to prices. Corresponding to the concepts of total cost, total variable cost, and total fixed cost, we have average total cost, average variable cost, and average fixed cost, *i.e.*, the total, variable, and fixed costs per unit of output. The average total cost is the sum of the average variable and the average fixed cost. The relationship between total and average costs is indicated in Table 23.1.

Table 23.1. Production Costs of a Hypothetical Firm

(1) Output	(2) Total fixed cost	(3) Total variable cost	(4) Total cost	(5) Average fixed cost	(6) Average variable cost	(7) Average total cost	(8) Marginal cost
1	$50	$ 20	$ 70	$50.00	$20.00	$70.00	$20
2	50	39	89	25.00	19.50	44.50	19
3	50	57	107	16.67	19.00	35.67	18
4	50	74	124	12.50	18.50	31.00	17
5	50	90	140	10.00	18.00	28.00	16
6	50	105	155	8.33	17.50	25.83	15
7	50	120	170	7.14	17.14	24.29	15
8	50	136	186	6.25	17.00	23.25	16
9	50	154	204	5.56	17.11	22.67	18
10	50	174	224	5.00	17.40	22.40	20
11	50	196	246	4.55	17.82	22.36	22
12	50	220	270	4.17	18.33	22.50	24
13	50	246	296	3.85	18.92	22.77	26
14	50	274	324	3.57	19.57	23.14	28
15	50	304	354	3.33	20.27	23.60	30
16	50	336	386	3.12	21.00	24.12	32
17	50	370	420	2.94	21.76	24.70	34
18	50	406	456	2.78	22.56	25.33	36
19	50	444	494	2.63	23.37	26.00	38
20	50	484	534	2.50	24.20	26.70	40

The output, total fixed cost, and total variable cost columns are assumed to be given. Column 4, total cost, is simply the sum of total fixed cost and total variable cost for each output. Column 5

FIGURE 23.2. SHORT-RUN COST CURVES
OF HYPOTHETICAL FIRM

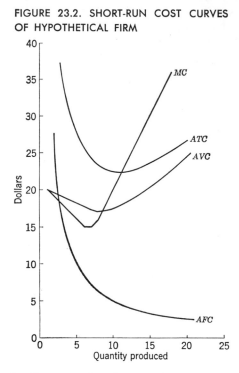

is the average fixed cost and is derived by dividing total fixed cost by output. Average variable cost, column 6, is the variable cost per unit of output, and it is determined by dividing total variable cost by output. Column 7 is the total cost per unit of output, and it may be derived either by dividing total cost by output or by adding average fixed cost and average variable cost.

Marginal cost, column 8, is neither a total nor an average cost. It is the *additional* cost incurred as a result of producing an additional unit of output. The total cost of producing 10 units of output, for example, is $224. If output is increased to 11 units, the total cost will be $246. The additional cost incurred as a result of producing the eleventh unit is, accordingly, the difference between $246 and $224, or $22, which is the marginal cost at that output.[1] Marginal cost, as we shall soon see, is a very important concept in economic analysis, and we shall also meet other marginal concepts which are important devices in the economist's kit of tools.

[1] Since variable costs are the only costs which change as output changes, marginal cost is also the difference between successive total variable costs. When output is 10, total variable cost is $174, and when output is 11, total variable cost is $196. The difference, $22, is marginal cost.

The same relationships demonstrated in Table 23.1 are shown graphically in Figure 23.2. The way in which average fixed cost, average variable cost, average total cost, and marginal cost vary as output changes is shown in the four fundamental cost curves.

The average fixed cost curve shows that fixed cost per unit decreases continuously as output increases. Since it is derived by dividing the total fixed cost of $50 by the output, the fixed cost per unit of output will become smaller and smaller as the output increases. If output were 10 units, for example, average fixed cost per unit would be $5; if 1,000 units were produced, the average fixed cost would be 5 cents. As output increases, the average fixed cost approaches but never reaches zero. The decline in average fixed cost is a matter of particular significance in those industries where fixed costs are relatively high. If a die for the right rear fender of a Chevrolet, for example, costs $1,000,000, the die-cost per automobile will be $1,000 if only 1,000 Chevrolets are produced, but it will be only $1 per unit if 1,000,000 cars are produced. Businessmen recognize the relationship between output and average fixed cost by the use of such terms as "spreading the overhead."

It will be noted that the average variable cost curve indicates that variable cost per unit of output decreases, then reaches a minimum value, and thereafter increases. The initial decline in average variable cost may be attributed to the fact that within this range more units of the variable factors are needed to utilize the fixed equipment effectively. For example, the efficiency of a garbage truck may be more than doubled by the addition of a second man. This is the same as saying that the variable costs per ton of garbage collected decrease as the amount collected per truck increases over this range. But it is also likely that the efficiency of the garbage truck operation will not be proportionately increased by the addition of a third man. Average variable costs begin to increase with the third man and continue to increase as more men are added. In graphic terms, the average variable cost curve is of a general U shape.

The average total cost curve is the summation of the other two. It is also seen to be U-shaped, with its minimum value appearing at a greater output than that at which average variable costs are at their lowest level. For very small outputs both average fixed costs and average variable costs are decreasing as output increases, and the sum of the two is, accordingly, decreasing. As output continues to decrease, the average fixed cost becomes a smaller and smaller part of average total cost, and the increase in average variable cost ultimately more than offsets the decrease in average fixed cost, with the result that average total costs begin to increase as output increases.

The marginal cost curve indicates the rate of change in total costs as output increases. It will be noted that the marginal cost curve declines, reaches a minimum, and then rises. The shape of the marginal cost curve reflects the fact, illustrated in Figure 23.1, that total cost at first increases at a decreasing rate and then increases at an increasing rate. It can be seen in Figure 23.2 that the marginal cost curve intersects both the average variable cost curve and the average total cost curve at their lowest points. As long as average variable cost is decreasing as output is increasing, the additional cost of producing an additional unit must be less than the average in order to bring the average down. If average variable cost is unchanged as output changes, marginal cost must equal average variable cost. And if average variable cost increases as output increases, marginal cost must be greater than average variable cost in order to bring up the average.

Similarly, the marginal cost is less than average total cost as long as average total costs are decreasing, equal to average total cost when average total costs are constant, and greater than average total costs when they are increasing. The marginal cost curve will, accordingly, lie below the average variable cost curve as long as the average variable cost is decreasing, intersect it at its minimum value, and lie above it when it is increasing; the marginal cost curve will also lie below the average total cost curve as long as the average total cost curve is decreasing, intersect it at its minimum value, and lie above it when it is increasing as output increases.[1]

Marginal Cost and Supply

All firms must make three basic decisions: (1) what to produce, (2) how to produce, and (3) how much to produce. These are the only decisions which must be made by the firm selling in a per-

[1] A common-sense notion of the relation between average and marginal concepts may be gained from the observation of a baseball player's batting average. Suppose that after the July 1 game a player's average for the season is .252, but after the July 2 game his average has fallen to .250. It is clear that during the July 2 game he must have batted less than .250—he probably went hitless—since the last or "marginal" game has brought the average down. Suppose that after the July 3 game his season's average remains at .250. It is clear that he batted .250 on July 3—probably one hit in four trips to the plate; *i.e.*, when average did not change, marginal must have equaled average. After the July 4 double-header our hero had boosted his season's average to .255. In this case marginal must have been greater than average to have brought the average up.

fectly competitive market; it does not have the additional decision of determining what price to charge. Once having decided what to produce and how input units are to be combined to produce its product, the firm adjusts its output to the given market price. As the market price changes, the firm will try to change its output so as to move toward a position in which profits are greatest.

Profits are greatest, of course, at that output where total revenue exceeds total cost by the largest possible amount. This *maximum-profit output may be reached by expanding output as long as the addition to revenue resulting from the sale of additional output is greater than the addition to cost caused by producing the extra output.*

If a firm is selling its output competitively, the addition to total revenue resulting from selling one more unit of output is equal to the price of a unit of output, since the perfectly competitive firm can, by definition, sell as much as it wants to without affecting the price of its product. The addition to total cost resulting from the production of an additional unit of output is marginal cost. Another way of defining the maximum-profit output for the purely competitive firm is to say, accordingly, that it is that output for which *price equals marginal cost.*

A competitive profit-maximizing firm will, therefore, tend to adjust output to the point at which marginal cost equals price.[1] But producing at this point does not imply that the firm will always make a profit. Whether or not there are profits depends on the relation between total cost and total revenue or between average total cost and price. The equality between price and marginal cost guarantees that a maximum profit *or* minimum loss has been attained, but it does not provide any information concerning the firm's absolute profit or loss position.

If a firm has made the basic decisions concerning what to produce and has constructed a single plant to embody a certain quantity of physical resources, its ability to change output in the short run is limited. It can change the number of inputs employed and thus adjust output somewhat, but it cannot change the over-all scale of its operations, since that would require changing fixed as well as variable factors. The marginal cost function represents the rate of change in total cost as output is changed within the limits of a

[1] Even this statement must be qualified. It is true only if marginal costs are rising. The equality of price and marginal cost will not represent the position of maximum profit or minimum loss if marginal cost is falling. For then it would be possible to improve the firm's position by expanding output since price would exceed added cost.

FIGURE 23.3. THE MARGINAL COST CURVE—Is the
Short-run Supply Curve

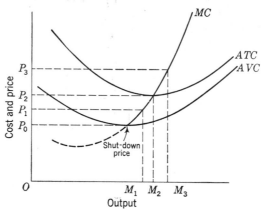

given scale of plant. Since for the individual seller in pure competition price does not change as his output varies, the equation of
price and marginal cost is reached by an output, rather than by a
price, adjustment. The marginal cost curve, therefore, indicates the
quantities which the firm will produce at all possible prices; the
marginal cost function is the supply function for the competitive
firm in the short run. This is illustrated in Figure 23.3. At a price of
OP_3, the firm will supply an amout equal to OM_3, at price OP_2
an amount OM_2, and at OP_1 an amount OM_1.

Some qualification must be made here, however; the marginal
cost curve represents the firm's supply curve only above a certain
minimum price. If the price is so low that a firm cannot cover its
variable costs, it should shut down in order to minimize its losses. If
the firm padlocks its plant, its total loss will be equal to its total fixed
cost, which the firm will have to pay even at output zero. But if
price is less than average variable cost, the firm's loss will consist
of its fixed cost plus that part of its variable cost not covered by its
total revenue. This is seen in Figure 23.3. If *AVC* represents the
average variable cost curve of the firm, no quantity would be produced at any price below OP_0. If the price fell below this point, the
firm would close down, and OP_0 can conveniently be labeled the
"shut-down" price. The marginal cost curve is the firm's supply
curve at all prices above OP_0. As long as price is above OP_0, the
firm will continue to operate even if it is not covering total costs
since it will be more than covering variable costs; *i.e.*, it will be
making some return on its fixed investment, whereas it would lose
the entire amount of its fixed costs if it did not operate at all.

If we include an average total cost curve, ATC in Figure 23.3, it can be seen that between prices OP_0 and OP_2 losses would be incurred since price is less than average cost, and total revenue, accordingly, is less than total cost. At price OP_2 the firm would break even, and at prices above this level it would make positive profit.

The short-run supply curve for a whole industry of competitive sellers is derived by the summation of that part of all the firms' marginal cost curves which lies above the minimum points on their average variable cost curves. If a hypothetical competitive industry consists of 100 identical single-plant firms, one of which is pictured in Figure 23.3, the industry would supply an amount equal to 100 OM_1 at price OP_1, 100 OM_2 at price OP_2, and so on. This industry supply function and the market demand function would determine, by their intersection, the short-run competitive price, as will be explained in more detail in Chapter 25.

24

LONG-RUN SUPPLY
AND COMPETITIVE PRICE

The short run has been defined as a period of time sufficiently long to allow the firm to adjust its output by increasing or decreasing the number of inputs employed, thereby changing the proportions of fixed and variable factors utilized in the productive process. The long run is a period of time sufficiently long to permit changes in the fixed as well as the variable factors. In the long run, accordingly, all factors are variable, and none are fixed. In the preceding chapter we saw that that part of the firm's marginal cost curve which lies above the average variable cost curve is its short-run supply curve; the short-run supply curve for the entire industry is the summation of the supply curves of the firms which comprise it. In this chapter we shall explore the nature of cost and supply over a long-run period. This will involve two separate but related matters: (1) the output adjustments of the firm made in the long run in response to changes in demand, and (2) the nature of the long-run supply curve for the industry as a whole.

The Firm in the Long-run Period

In considering the long-run adjustments made by the firm we are concerned with problems of scale. We seek answers to the following questions: How do costs change as the whole scale of the firm's operations changes? Will operation on a larger scale necessarily lead to more efficient production? Or is there an optimum or most efficient size for a business firm? In this connection it is important to distinguish between the single-plant firm and the multiple-plant firm. Let us consider the single-plant firm first.

It seems evident that if a plant is too small it is likely to be inefficient, *i.e.*, high cost, in almost any line of production. The production unit in this case is too small to take full advantage of the use of specialized labor and equipment. A good example of inefficient single-plant firms is provided by very small farms. They have proved to be inefficient relative to larger farms because they are not big enough to utilize mechanized equipment effectively. It would hardly pay a wheat farmer with a 10-acre plot to purchase the combine that the farmer with a 1,000-acre farm would use. But it seems equally clear that firms operating very large plants are also likely to be inefficient in almost any line of production. The production unit may become too large for the job to be done properly. An ocean-going freighter, for example, would be inefficient if used as a shrimp boat, and an auditorium is of little use as a classroom. We may conclude, therefore, that average total costs for the single-plant firm will fall for a range as the plant size is increased, reach a minimum, and then increase as the plant gets larger.

The efficiency or inefficiency stemming from the size of the plant may not be the main consideration determining the appropriate scale of operations for the multi-plant firm. All of the plants operated by the firm might be of the optimum size, but the question remains as to the number of plants the firm should operate. Extremely small firms operating only one plant, even if this plant is of the optimum size, are often less efficient than firms operating several plants. An example is provided by the movie-theater industry. The single-theater firm seems clearly less efficient than the many-theater firm, as evidenced by the latter type of firm in the industry. The advantages of scale here are perhaps largely those of booking and scheduling. Another example is provided by the emergence of the grocery chains, where the advantages of centralized purchasing and distribution are the important considerations. For many industries it seems probable that the number of plants that a firm operates has little effect on its efficiency over a rather wide range. In the fishing industry, for example, the firm operating several boats has little, if any, cost advantage over the firm operating a single boat (plant). It is clear, however, that once a firm operates a great many plants, even if they are all technically efficient, the problems of coordinating the firm's activities begin to loom large. It has been noted, for example, that as universities become larger the administrative costs tend to become a larger part of the total budget. So, just as in the case of the single-plant firm, the multiple-plant firm becomes inefficient once it gets too large. The amount of paper work involved sometimes becomes inordinately burdensome, and the number of employees who are not actually producing goods or services but simply check on those who do becomes so great as to increase the costs of production. After a point the economies of large-scale production are more than offset by the diseconomies of scale.

In summary we may say that for both the single-plant firm and the multi-plant firm average total costs tend to decrease over a certain range as the scale of operations is increased, ultimately to reach a minimum, and then to increase as the scale of operations becomes too large. Since the same conclusions apply to the two types of firms, we will find it convenient to concentrate on the single-plant firm in the more detailed discussion which follows.

The nature of the long-run cost concept may be understood more easily by a study of Figure 24.1. Curves a_1, a_2, a_3, and a_4 represent short-run average total cost curves for plants of alternative sizes, a_1 representing the plant with the smallest capacity and a_4 representing the largest of the four plants. If the firm is considering the construction of a new plant—a long-run consideration—it must determine what size plant to build. If it is anticipated that demand conditions will justify only a small output, such as OL, the a_1 plant will be the appropriate size. If, however, it is anticipated that the plant will need to produce an output of OM, that output can be produced at a lower cost with plant a_2 than with a_1. Plant a_3 represents the "optimum-sized" plant; any smaller size fails to take full advantage of the economies of large-scale production, and larger plants suffer from diseconomies of too large size. If output ON is produced with plant a_3, the optimum output is being produced by the optimum-sized plant; the average total cost is then NG, and this is less than the amount for which any other output can be produced. If, how-

FIGURE 24.1. LONG-RUN AVERAGE COST

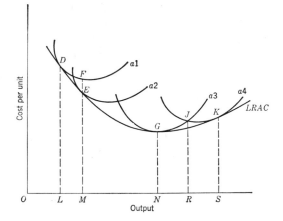

ever, an output greater than *OR* is to be produced, it can be produced at a lower unit cost with plant a_4 than with a_3. The envelope
curve *LRAC*, which is tangent to each of the short-run average total
cost curves, is the long-run average cost, or "planning," curve; *it
indicates the lowest cost at which any output can be produced on
the assumption that sufficient time is allowed to permit the construction of the appropriate-sized plant* and, further, that a plant of any
size can be constructed. Considerations of this sort are important
when firms are contemplating the building of new plants. The construction of a plant which in relation to the market demand is
either too large or too small will result in reduced profits and may
bring financial failure. For long-range planning, as we have seen,
there are no fixed costs; the amount invested in "fixed" input factors
will vary depending upon the size of the plant that is to be built.
After the appropriate size has been decided upon and the plant is
constructed, however, the decisions of the firm's management become short-run decisions, and fixed costs are clearly distinct from
variable costs. To summarize: the day-to-day decisions of management are short-run decisions; but periodically, when the construction of a new plant or the abandonment of the old plant is contem-
plated, important long-run decisions must be made.

An illustration may be useful in showing the difference between
long-run and short-run considerations. Suppose a young man wishes
to go into the business of producing concrete blocks. He can erect
a plant which could turn out a maximum of anywhere from 1,000
to 20,000 or more blocks a day, depending on the number and
size of the block-making machines utilized. The average cost per

block would be somewhat higher in the smallest plants. If he can raise enough capital, he will probably want to erect a plant which could turn out 5,000 or 10,000 rather than 1,000 or 2,000 blocks a day. If he were to acquire a plant capable of turning out 50,000 blocks a day, however, his average cost might go up again. Such a plant requires highly skilled supervision, accurate planning of receipts and shipments, and skilled handling of inventory.

Suppose he settles this long-range problem and erects a plant to turn out blocks on the most economical scale, say 10,000 per day. His short-run average cost curve could be represented by a_3 of Figure 24.1. An output of 10,000 a day would be the quantity ON. At this output he would be minimizing both long-run and short-run costs; the former would have been achieved by selecting the best-sized plant and the latter by operating it at the most efficient rate. At a daily output of 8,000 or 12,000 blocks, for example, his short-run average cost would be somewhat higher than at the optimum rate. The firm might or might not make a change in the size of its plant at some later date; it would, however, constantly be faced with the short-run problem of deciding upon the appropriate daily output.

Long-run Supply

In order to indicate the nature of industry's long-run supply curve it will be convenient to refer to the very short-run, the short-run, and the long-run period analysis described in Chapter 3. In the very short run, it will be recalled, the firm does not have time to make any output adjustments. It has a stock of goods on hand, and, in the case of perishable goods, it must sell what it has produced at whatever price the market will bring. In the very short run costs of production do not enter into the firm's calculations at all. The very short-run supply curve is a vertical line, and price is determined by demand. An increase in demand is followed by a sharp rise in price but no change in the amount offered. The short-run period, however, is sufficiently long to allow the firm to make limited output adjustments. If price rises, the firm will in the short run increase output to the point where price equals marginal cost. The new short-run equilibrium price will be higher than the price before the increase in demand, but not as high as the very short-run price, and output will be greater in short-run equilibrium than it was before the increase in demand. Finally, in the long run firms have had time to expand their plants and build new plants, and new

FIGURE 24.2. LONG-RUN SUPPLY—In a
Constant-cost Industry

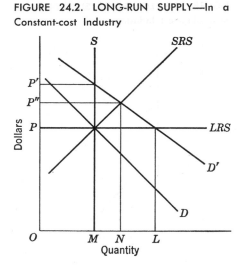

firms have had time to enter the industry. In the long-run equilibrium, price will be established at a lower level and output at a higher level than in the short-run position.

The nature of the process by which a firm moves from one long-run equilibrium position to another is illustrated in Figure 24.2. We begin with price at *OP* and quantity offered at *OM*. *S*, a vertical line, is the very short-run supply curve, and *SRS* is the short-run supply curve, which represents the summation of the marginal cost curves of the firms which comprise the industry. *LRS* is the long-run supply curve. Since *LRS* is represented as a horizontal line, this is a constant-cost industry, Now suppose that demand increases from *D* to *D'*. In the very short run price will rise sharply from *OP* to *OP'*. Since in the very short run the firms can sell only what they have already produced, the total amount offered for sale will remain at *OM*.

As soon as the firms can adjust their outputs to the higher price, they will expand output to the point where price equals marginal cost. Short-run equilibrium will be reached at price *OP''* and output *ON*. In the long run new firms will enter the industry, the total output of the industry will increase, and the price will fall. In the case of a constant-cost industry the new equilibrium price will be the same as the original equilibrium price, and the long-run supply curve will be a horizontal line.

Under what circumstances will the long-run supply curve be horizontal? Clearly, as the number of firms in the industry increases

FIGURE 24.3. LONG-RUN SUPPLY—In an
Increasing-cost Industry

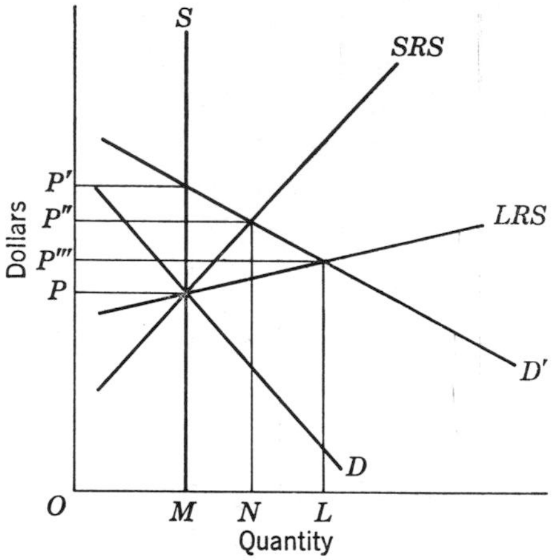

there will be an increased demand for the inputs employed by the industry, and if the prices of these inputs increase as the industry expands, the new long-run equilibrium price will be higher than the old one. A constant-cost industry, accordingly, must be one which uses the same kinds of inputs that other industries use, and the demand of this industry for those inputs must be a very small part of the total demand for them. The paper-doll industry might be a case in point. This industry uses such a small part of the paper produced in a year that a sharp increase in the output of paper dolls would have no perceptible effect on the price of paper. Similarly, the increased demand for labor in the paper-doll industry would not have the effect of raising the wages of labor generally. An increase in the demand for paper dolls would not, therefore, be expected to raise the price of paper dolls in the long run.

The case of an increasing-cost industry is illustrated in Figure 24.3. An increase in demand would increase price from *OP* to *OP′* in the very short run. In the short run price would fall from *OP′* to *OP″* and the quantity offered for sale would increase from *OM* to *ON*. In the long run price would fall from *OP″ to OP‴*, and output would expand to *OL*. The new long-run price, *OP‴*, is higher than the original equilibrium position, reflecting the increasing costs to the firms in the industry as the demand for inputs increased.

It is conceivable that an industry might enjoy decreasing costs due to what are termed "external" economies of increasing production. A young industry in a new territory, for example, might be handicapped by poor transportation, communication, and marketing facilities. An expansion of the industry might make feasible an improvement in these facilities, with the result that in the long run production costs would be reduced. In this less usual case, the long-run supply curve would be negatively inclined, and the new long-run equilibrium price would be lower than the original.

By way of summary it may be noted that the long-run average cost curves of both the plant and the firm are U-shaped. As the firm expands in size, by increasing the capacity and/or the number of plants, it encounters both economies and diseconomies of large-scale production. Among the economies which tend to reduce unit costs as the size of the firm is increased are the following: improved ability to borrow capital funds at lower costs, higher degree of division of labor among workers and capital equipment, greater resources for research and selling activities, ability to buy factors at discounted prices, and greater diversification of products. If, however, the firm becomes too big, administrative costs are likely to increase at a disproportionate rate with the result that unit costs after a point are likely to increase. What constitutes the optimum size of the firm varies greatly from industry to industry; in the cotton textile industry it appears that the optimum-sized firm is relatively small, whereas in the steel industry it is quite large. The shape of the firm's long-run average cost curve is also subject to a wide degree of variation; for some industries the curve may be relatively flat on both sides of the minimum point, while for others the decreasing-cost segments of the curve may be quite steep. The important thing to observe is that there is an optimum size for both plant and firm, and goods are produced at the lowest possible cost only when the optimum-sized firm is operating its optimum-sized plants at optimum outputs.

Industries vary in their long-run response to increases in demand. If the given industry utilizes little highly specialized labor and capital and its demand for inputs represents but a small fraction of the total demand for these resources, it is likely to be a constant-cost industry, and the new long-run equilibrium price following an increase in demand will be at approximately the same level as the original equilibrium price. If, however, the industry's demand for inputs is a sufficiently large part of the total demand for those resources that an increase in the industry's demand for them would

FIGURE 24.4. LONG-RUN EQUILIBRIUM—Of the
Competitive Firm

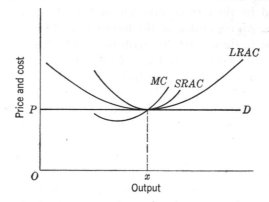

cause their prices to rise, the new equilibrium long-run price will be
higher than the original, and the industry is characterized by increasing costs.

The long-run equilibrium position for an individual firm in a
competitive industry is represented in Figure 24.4. Price is equal to
marginal cost so that in the short run profits are maximized. Marginal cost equals short-run average cost, since the firm is operating
at the most efficient output. Short-run and long-run average costs
are equal at the lowest-cost point, since the firm is of the most
efficient size. Price is equal to short-run average cost, since the firm
is just covering its costs of production, including the approximate rate
of return on capital which it could earn elsewhere; it has, therefore,
no incentive to contract or expand. New firms have no incentive
to enter the industry since there is no abnormal return being made
to attract them. Although the position represented is purely an imaginary one toward which the market forces tend to push the individual firms, it is extremely useful as a starting point in the analysis of particular problems. It may be helpful to take a highly competitive industry and trace through the changes resulting from the
movement from one such long-run equilibrium to another.

Competitive Adjustment in the Fishing Industry

We have selected for this purpose commercial fishing which,
as it is practiced along the South Atlantic and Gulf coasts, is probably one of the best examples of perfect competition (on the selling side) in the United States today. In some cases even this in-

dustry is dominated by a few large companies or characterized by the organization of the fishermen, but for the most part it corresponds very closely to the economist's conception of pure competition as far as the catching and initial sale of fish are concerned. The processes of distribution are usually less completely competitive.

The plant (boat, nets, and other gear) is small for operations near the shore where fishing is carried on. This is conducive to small-sized firms, which often consist of two-man partnerships. A small firm is large enough to own one efficient plant, which is quite different from the situation in an industry like steelmaking, where a plant of economical size is so large that a steel company must be large to own even one plant. Further, the fishing industry is not normally characterized by important advantages of multiplant ownership such as exist, for example, in the food-retailing business. Firms owning only a single satisfactory fishing vessel are normally at no disadvantage compared with those owning several. The firm of optimum size, represented in Figure 24.4, is relatively small. It is quite possible that fishing firms ranging quite widely in size are of equal efficiency. The *LRAC* curve of Figure 24.4 would then be horizontal over this range. If the firm is very small, however (*e.g.*, only large enough to own a rowboat), it is clear that efficiency will be reduced. Above a certain size, efficiency of the firm may be diminished by a diffusion of managerial skill in the coordination of activities of a large fleet.

The fishing industry also satisfies the requirement of perfect competition that firms may enter and leave at will. Only small capital and moderate skill are required to set oneself up in the fishing business along many of our shores. Indeed, entry is so easy that a successful sports fisherman can usually sell to a shore dealer any part of his salt-water catch which he wishes to dispose of.

It is also necessary that there be many buyers as well as many sellers in order to render competition fully effective. Generally this condition is also met. In most localities fishermen have a considerable choice of shore dealers to whom they may sell their catch. This is a result of the simplicity of the dealer's business and the rather small capital investment necessary for the erection of landing piers and sheltering structures.

When a fisherman lands his boat at the shore dealer's docks, he finds posted a single price per pound for each variety of fish normally caught in those waters. He can sell as much as he has caught at that price, but he can sell none at a higher price. This is the

meaning of the horizontal demand curve for the perfectly competitive firm. The price is established in accord with the over-all
supply and demand situation for each variety of fish and is changed
frequently as these conditions change. No fisherman feels it necessary to advertise. The boats do not carry signs to the effect that
one should "Buy Mac's Mackerel," "Purchase Pete's Pompano," or
"Try Tony's Trout."

Each fishing firm is unable to affect price; all it can do is to
adjust its own operations to the prevailing market prices. When
prices are favorable, fishermen generally work longer and harder
in order to take advantage of this situation. To some extent it is
possible for them to consider relative prices of fish, modifying gear
and tactics in such a way as to increase the proportionate catch of
the kinds of fish which have become more profitable. In the main,
however, fishing by net is unselective, and the principal short-run
response to price changes consists in altering the number of hours
of work. During World War II, when fish prices were high, it was
common for fishermen to work seven days a week.

"Long-run" adjustments take place much more quickly in commercial fishing than in most other types of production. The number of plants utilized can be increased rapidly by simply pressing
certain types of pleasure boats into this use or by bringing fishing
boats from other territories where conditions are less favorable.

Suppose the commercial fishing industry of a coastal region is in
a position of long-run equilibrium in the sense that the number
and size of fishing enterprises are appropriately adjusted to the
prevailing demand and cost conditions. Fishermen will be receiving normal wage rates for their labor, and capital invested in boats
and gear will be earning a normal return. On the left side of
Figure 24.5, the industry is first assumed to be fully adjusted in
both size and rate of operation to demand D_1; consequently, the
short-run supply curve and the demand curve intersect at a price
which is equal to long-run supply price OP_1. (The long-run supply
curve has been assumed to be horizontal because the fishing industry does not purchase large quantities of any factor which is
likely to change permanently in price because of either larger or
smaller purchases by fishermen.) Equilibrium output for the industry is OA.

A single firm in the same industry is represented on the right
side of Figure 24.5. At the market price OP_1, determined by the
over-all supply-demand conditions pictured, the firm can sell all
that it produces. Its best rate of operation is Oa, where marginal

FIGURE 24.5. DECLINE IN DEMAND FOR FISH—Causes Short-run and Long-run Adjustments

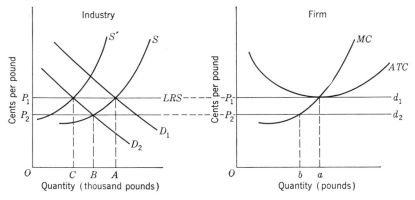

cost equals price. The firm which is pictured is of the most efficient size as is indicated by its operation at the point of lowest average cost in this industry equilibrium situation. The industry is assumed to be made up of 1,000 such firms, requiring that the scale in which quantity is measured be thousands of pounds for the industry and pounds for the single enterprise.

Suppose a decrease in the demand by consumers for fish now occurs, caused, for example, by a substantial fall in the price of beef. This results quickly in a lowered demand by shore dealers, represented by D_2 in the industry diagram, and the dealers will lower the price which they will pay for fish. The disappointed fishermen will respond by working less, reducing output of the typical firm to Ob, at which output marginal cost is again equal to price. The sum of these actions will be similarly reflected in the industry diagram at the left where total output will be reduced from OA to OB, determined by the intersection of curves S and D_2.

Fishing boats and gear will now be used less intensively, and the return to capital and labor will fall off. The decline in the attractiveness of fishing will cause some firms to leave the industry. The egress will take some time but, as already mentioned, much less time than a comparable adjustment would require in most industries. The ultimate effect of the decline in demand will be a reduction in the number of firms in the business of catching fish, but the size of the remaining organizations should be no smaller than before. The rate of fish catching will be diminished by the exit of firms, that is, the industry supply curve will shift to the left, and price will respond by gradually rising again to the previous level, OP_1. As firms leave the industry, the typical remaining firm will gradually increase its rate of operations back to Oa. Thus its own position will eventually be the same as before the decline in demand. The industry will be smaller than before; hence the new industry supply curve S' will meet the demand curve D_2, rather than D_1, at the original price OP_1. The industry short-run supply curve has moved to the left reflecting the fact that fewer than the original 1,000 firms are now in the industry.

The foregoing discussion of a movement from one long-run equilibrium position to another has assumed that sufficient labor and capital will leave an industry when rates of return fall below those which can be earned in alternative employment; that is, it has assumed some degree of mobility of productive factors. To the extent that lack of knowledge or inertia prevents such a shift, the number of firms may not decline in the manner indicated in response to a decrease in demand. In that event the price of fish would be permanently lowered by the reduced demand since supply would not be contracted sufficiently, and labor and capital employed in this industry would receive less than the going return in other industries. This analysis is also dependent on the assumption that prices of all input items (*e.g.*, gasoline) remain constant throughout the period required for full adjustment to the new demand conditions.

Summary

We have in this chapter examined some of the workings of purely competitive markets. It has been shown that competition among sellers tends to keep output prices in some relation to costs of production. For the profit-maximizing firm output prices will tend to equal marginal costs of production in fully competitive industries. The equality between price and marginal cost means that the consumer is required to pay for a product an amount equivalent to the additional cost incurred in producing an additional unit of that product. This cost represents the value of the goods which could have been produced elsewhere in the economy by the resources that are used up in the production process. Output prices in the short run may be above, equal to, or below average costs of production. Competition ensures that firms in expanding industries enjoy abnormal profits and that firms in declining industries incur losses. This forces firms to move to those areas of production indicated as desirable by consumer demand.

In the long run, prices tend to equal average costs of production. Furthermore, average costs of production tend to be forced to the minimum level by the pressure on the firm to operate at the most efficient scale. In this way competition makes for the optimum allocation of resources and the production of goods at the lowest possible costs. Alternately, it can be stated that competition tends to secure for the economy as a whole the maximum real income which is attainable with the given available resources.

25

THE COMPETITIVE MODEL

In earlier chapters frequent reference has been made to perfectly competitive markets, and the nature of the competitive firm's reaction to changes in demand and changes in costs both in the long and short run have been described in some detail. It has been observed that in the real world perfectly competitive markets are relatively rare, and monopolistic forces of greater or lesser degree are present in most industries. The interest of the economist in the perfectly competitive case is clearly out of proportion to its importance as a description of reality. And the curious fact has been noted that although it seems generally agreed that competition should be encouraged and monopoly restricted, agencies of government are concurrently restricting monopoly through antitrust laws and otherwise and encouraging it through such devices as fair-trade laws and parity-price supports. It is the purpose of this chapter to indicate somewhat more fully than has been done heretofore the nature of perfect competition, the significance of this model for purposes of economic analysis, and the several equilibrium conditions implied by the concept. This will involve the review of several points previously made as well as the introduction of some new material.

306

The Idea of Perfect Competition

The idea of perfect competition is not presented as a description of reality. There are industries which approach fairly closely the conditions of perfectly competitive markets, but usually the economist concerns himself with this concept by raising such questions as "What would happen if the industry were perfectly competitive?" It is necessary to keep economic analysis separate and distinct from description. Economic principles are designed to serve as a set of tools which will assist in the process of understanding the workings of a free-enterprise economy. For this purpose more is required than factual description. One of the most valuable tools in all of economics would be lost if we dismissed the case of fully competitive markets as unimportant simply because in the real world such markets are rare. This analysis is important for several reasons. First, competitive markets represent a normative ideal. We are interested in how the free-enterprise system would work if there were no monopoly elements present since proper public policy must generally imply an attempt to make the system tend more toward, rather than away from, the competitive position. Second, many real problems simply cannot be solved within any analytical framework other than that of perfectly competitive markets. Even when industries are composed of imperfectly competitive firms, many problems affecting the whole industry can best be solved if the departures from pure competition are ignored. And finally, a thorough knowledge of the theory of price formation in competitive markets will greatly facilitate the understanding of the theory of noncompetitive behavior, the topic to which we turn in the next chapter.

CHARACTERISTICS OF PERFECT COMPETITION

There are four fundamental characteristics of perfectly competitive markets.

1. There must be a large number of sellers in the industry. A perfectly competitive market is one in which no one seller or small group of sellers can affect price. The power to set prices is a monopolistic power; if the seller can determine the price of his own product even within narrow limits, he has some degree of monopoly power. If there is only one seller in the industry, the market is characterized by pure monopoly, and although one price will be more profitable than any other, the monopolist can set

prices throughout a broad range. If there are only a few sellers in the industry, the market is characterized as being an oligopoly (from the Greek, *oligo,* meaning few); since the number of sellers is few, what one firm charges is of importance to the other firms in the market, and no firm will set a price without taking into account what the reaction of other firms will be, but each firm does have some control over what price it will set. In order for the industry to be perfectly competitive there must be so many firms that none of them is sufficiently important to affect market price; each firm can sell as much as it has at the going price, but none of them can sell any at all at any price even slightly higher than the current market price. The chicken farmer is a case in point. If the supply and demand forces of the market have set a price of 35 cents per pound for broilers, the farmer can sell part or all of his inventory at that price, but if he holds out for 36 cents he won't be able to sell any at all.

2. If a market is perfectly competitive, there must be a large number of buyers so that no one of them can affect the price of the good or service which it is buying. If there is only one buyer in a market, the industry is called a pure monopsony. An industry with only a few buyers is an oligopsony. Either the monopsonist or the oligopsonist has some control over the prices he pays; he can lower the price he is willing to pay without forcing himself completely out of the market. In a perfectly competitive market, however, the price is set by the forces of supply and demand; the buyer can buy as much at that price as he can pay for, but he will be unable to buy any at all at even a slightly lower price. The butcher who buys broilers, for example, can buy all that he wants at 35 cents when that is the market price, but if he offered only 34 cents he would not be able to buy any at all.

3. In a perfectly competitive market each firm sells a homogeneous product; that is, the product of one firm is identical with that of all other firms, and the buyer, accordingly, has no preference for the product of one firm over that of another. The miller, for example, doesn't care whether the wheat he buys was raised by Farmer Black or Farmer White; the fact is that the wheat from many farms is dumped together in a grain elevator, and there is no way to distinguish the product of one producer from that of another. This requirement eliminates most of the products purchased by the ultimate consumer from the perfect-competition category. The rise of brand names and trade-marks in recent years serves to differentiate the product of one firm from that of another,

and, whether the products are in fact identical or quite different, great efforts are made by sellers to convince consumers that their products are superior to those of other firms. If these efforts prove successful, the firm achieves a degree of monopoly power; it has at least a limited range within which it can set its prices. The makers of Chesterfield cigarettes, for example, could raise the price of their product considerably above the price of competing cigarettes and some loyal Chesterfield smokers would undoubtedly pay the higher price in order to get their favorite brand. Some firms have, in fact, found it profitable to put the same product in two different packages and sell then under different brand names at different prices. None of this, of course, would be possible in perfectly competitive markets.

4. A perfectly competitive market is characterized by freedom of entry of firms into the industry and freedom of exit of firms from the industry. In some situations entry of new firms into an industry is restricted by license requirements or patent rights. In the public utility field a firm may be required to continue a service even if it can be demonstrated that the service is unprofitable. But in a perfectly competitive market firms may be expected to enter the industry if high profits make the industry attractive and to leave the industry when losses make it unattractive. This requirement is important, of course, in the consideration of the long-run behavior of firms.

Demand, Supply, and Price

The point has been made repeatedly that in a competitive market price is determined by the forces of supply and demand. In earlier chapters we have had a look at supply and demand, and several aspects of these important market forces have been analyzed in some detail. At this point we look at them from three different levels: supply and demand from the point of view of (a) the consumer, (b) the market, and (c) the firm.

CONSUMER DEMAND AND SUPPLY

In Chapter 2 it was pointed out that consumer demand implies a desire for a good plus the ability to pay for it plus the willingness to pay. Each of these components of demand contributes to the negative slope of the consumer demand curve. The intensity of the consumer's desire for a unit of a given commodity declines as the consumer acquires more and more units of the good. This is

FIGURE 25.1. CONSUMER DEMAND AND
SUPPLY—In a Perfectly Competitive Market

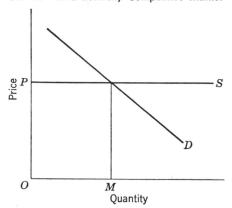

the essence of the law of diminishing marginal utility, which states
that after a point the additional utility derived from the consumption of successive units of a good becomes smaller and smaller.
The additional utility derived from the consumption of an additional unit of a good is known as marginal utility, and the marginal
utility of a good determines the maximum amount the consumer
is willing to pay for it. The family that is just willing to buy seven
quarts of milk per week when the price is 25 cents per quart will
not buy the eighth quart unless it can get each quart at something
less than 25 cents. And, of course, as the price falls the consumer's
ability to buy increases. All of this is reflected in the negative slope
of the consumer demand curve.

The consumer in a perfectly competitive market finds that he
can buy as much as he can pay for at the going price. That is to
say that the supply curve facing the consumer is perfectly elastic
and is represented by a horizontal line. The amount that the consumer buys is determined by the intersection of the negatively
inclined demand curve and the horizontal supply curve. This is
illustrated in Figure 25.1. If the price is established at *OP*, the
consumer will buy *OM* units. This situation corresponds very
closely with reality. For most consumer goods the supply is perfectly elastic, and the amount the consumer buys is determined
by price, that is, by the height of the supply curve.

MARKET DEMAND AND SUPPLY

Market demand is the summation of the demands of the consumers who together comprise the market. Since each of the con-

FIGURE 25.2. MARKET DEMAND AND SUP-
PLY—In a Perfectly Competitive Industry

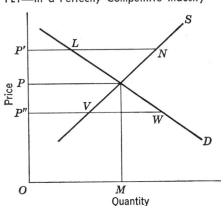

sumer demand curves is negatively inclined, the demand curve for the entire market will also slope downward from left to right. The market supply curve is the summation of the supply curves of the firms which comprise the market. As we have seen, the firm's supply curve is that part of its marginal cost curve which lies above its average variable cost curve, and this has a positive slope. Since each firm will supply more units of its product at a higher than at a lower price, the market supply curve is also positively inclined. Market price is determined by the intersection of the negatively inclined demand curve and the positively inclined supply curve. This is illustrated in Figure 25.2. The equilibrium short-run or market price is *OP* and the quantity sold is *OM*. At any higher price, as for example, *OP′*, the amount demanded, *P′L*, is less than the amount supplied, *P′N*, and competition among buyers and sellers will cause price to fall. At any price lower than *OP*, such as *OP″*, the amount supplied, *P″V*, is less than the amount demanded, *P″W*, and competition will cause the price to rise. It will be noted that more units will be exchanged at market price than at any other price; at price *OP′* fewer than *OM* units will be demanded, and at price *OP″* fewer than *OM* units will be supplied.

FIRM DEMAND AND SUPPLY

The firm in a perfectly competitive market can sell any part or all of its inventory at the going market price. This means that the demand curve facing the individual firm is perfectly elastic and is represented by a horizontal line at the level of the market price as established for the industry as a whole. The firm's supply curve is that part of its marginal cost curve which lies above the average variable cost curve, and it slopes upward from left to right. The firm maximizes its profits by producing to the point where its marginal cost equals price, that is, to the point where the positively inclined supply curve intersects the horizontal demand curve.

Output multiplied by price equals the firm's total revenue. Conversely, the firm's total revenue divided by output equals revenue per unit of sales, or average revenue. If a firm sells 1,000 units per time period at a price of $5 per unit, the firm's total revenue is $5,000. The total revenue, $5,000, divided by output, 1,000, gives an average revenue of $5, which is equal to price. The demand curve may, in fact, be viewed as an average revenue curve; it indicates for each output what the revenue per unit (price) would be.

Suppose that the perfectly competitive firm which is currently selling 1,000 units of output at a price of $5 decides to increase output by one unit to a total of 1,001 units. Total revenue will increase to $5,005. The additional revenue resulting from the production of an additional unit of output is called marginal revenue. In this case marginal revenue is $5, which is the same as average revenue or price. For a firm in a perfectly competitive market marginal revenue is always equal to price since the firm's total revenue will be increased as result of producing an additional unit by an amount equal to the price of the unit of output. Instead of saying that a perfectly competitive firm will maximize profits by producing to the point where marginal cost equals price, we may say, accordingly, that the firm will maximize profits if it produces to the point where marginal cost equals marginal revenue.[1]

The nature of the firm's demand and supply curves is illustrated in Figure 25.3. The left side of the figure indicates that market price has been established at *OP* and the amount bought and sold is *OM* when market demand is *D* and market supply is *S*. The price *OP* is a given datum to each firm in the industry, and its demand or average revenue curve is represented on the right side of the figure by a horizontal line at this level. To maximize profits the firm will produce to the point where marginal cost equals marginal revenue (price), and this will be at an output of *Om* for each firm. (The scale along the *x* axis is, of course, greater on the left than on the right side of the figure. If the in-

---

[1] In this form the rule is valid for all firms whether they sell in perfectly competitive markets or not.

FIGURE 25.3. DEMAND, SUPPLY, AND PRICE—Under Perfect Competition

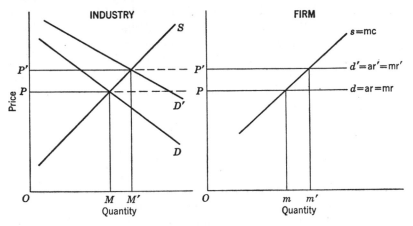

dustry were made up of 1,000 identical firms, OM would equal 1,000 Om.)

If market demand should increase to D', price would rise to OP' and the amount exchanged to OM'. Each firm's average revenue and marginal revenue curve would rise to the OP' level, and the output of each firm would increase to Om'.

The Equilibrium Conditions

In earlier chapters we have referred to market price as the equilibrium price, and we have analyzed in some detail the short-run and long-run equilibrium positions of the firm. In this section we will summarize the equilibrium conditions under three heads: consumer equilibrium, firm equilibrium, and industry equilibrium.

CONSUMER EQUILIBRIUM

As was pointed out in Chapter 1 the essence of economics consists in the fact that because of the scarcity of economic goods we must economize in the use of our limited resources. The consumer is confronted with virtually unlimited wants which he must try to satisfy with a limited income. Some wants, of course, can be only partially satisfied, and some will not be satisfied at all. The consumer's problem is to maximize his total satisfaction with his income and the prices of consumer goods as given. To do this the last dollar spent on each commodity must provide the same satisfaction as the last dollar spent on every other commodity. If the last dollar spent on commodity A, for example, provides more satisfaction than the last dollar spent on commodity B, the consumer can increase his total satisfaction by shifting some expenditure from B to A. The additional satisfaction derived from the consumption of the last unit of commodity A is the marginal utility of A. The marginal utility of A divided by the price of A is the additional satisfaction derived from the last dollar spent on A. The general rule for consumer equilibrium may, therefore, be put in the following form:

$$MU_a/P_a = MU_b/P_b = \cdots = MU_n/P_n$$

where MU_a is the marginal utility of A and P_a is the price of A.

This point may be demonstrated geometrically with the use of Figure 25.4. MU_a is the marginal utility of dollars spent on A curve, and MU_b is the marginal utility of dollars spent on B curve. The x axis for the right side of the figure reads in the conventional way from left to right and measures the number of dollars spent on A. On the left side of the figure the x axis is read from right to left and measures the number of dollars spent on B. Suppose that the consumer has a total of NM dollars to be spent on these two commodities. His income will be allocated to maximize his total satisfaction if he spends an amount on each commodity which will make the satisfaction derived from a dollar spent on A just equal to the satisfaction derived from a dollar spent on B. In this case he should spend OM dollars on A and ON dollars on B. The satisfaction from a dollar spent on A, MA, is then just equal to the satisfaction from a dollar spent on B, NB.

FIRM AND INDUSTRY EQUILIBRIUM

Little needs to be added to what has been said in earlier chapters concerning the equilibrium of the perfectly competitive firm. The firm is in short-run equilibrium as soon as it has adjusted its output to the point where marginal cost equals price (marginal revenue). At this point the firm's profits will be maximized, and no further adjustment is called for.

A word needs to be said about the firm as a buyer of inputs. Various combinations of productive factors might be employed to produce a given quantity of output, and the profit-maximizing firm will utilize the optimum or "least-cost" combination of inputs to produce any given output. The situation confronting the firm as a buyer of inputs is analogous to that facing the consumer as a buyer in final goods markets. If the firm produces with the least-cost combination of factors, the output resulting from a dollar spent on factor A must equal the output resulting from a dollar

FIGURE 25.4. CONSUMER EQUILIBRIUM—

$$\frac{MU_a}{P_a} = \frac{MU_b}{P_b}$$

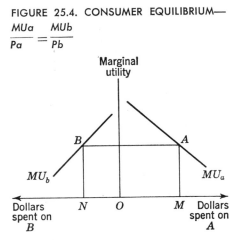

spent on factor B. If a dollar spent on A results in a greater output than a dollar spent on B, it would pay the firm to divert expenditures from B to A.

The equilibrium of the firm as a buyer of inputs can also be expressed in formula form. If we define the marginal product of a factor as the additional product resulting from the employment of an additional unit of the factor, it follows that the marginal product of a factor divided by the price of the factor is the additional product resulting from a dollar spent on the factor. The conditions for the least-cost combination may then be put in the following form:

$$MP_a/P_a = MP_b/P_b = \cdot \cdot \cdot = MP_n/P_n$$

where MP_a is the marginal product of factor A and P_a is the price of A.

The equilibrium of the industry is a long-run concept. The industry is in equilibrium when each of the firms which comprise it is in long-run equilibrium. Each of the firms will be making "normal" profits but no more than that. There is, accordingly, no incentive for new firms to enter the industry or for old firms to leave it. Each firm will be of optimum size since any less efficient firm would be operating at a loss. Each firm will be in short-run equilibrium, producing to the point where short-run marginal cost equals price. Each firm will be making normal profits, which is to say that short-run average total cost equals price, and long-run average cost also equals price. In short, optimum-sized firms are producing optimum output at a price which just covers total costs.

From the point of view of the consumer, who is presumed to

be sovereign in a private-enterprise economy, perfect competition is clearly the ideal market type. Any commodity will be produced if consumers are willing to pay the full cost of its production. This provides for the allocation of resources in accordance with consumer preferences. The consumer gains from the high volume of production and from low prices. Goods will be produced at the lowest possible costs, and maximum economic efficiency will be achieved. Since goods are homogeneous, these gains are enjoyed by the consumer without the utilization of scarce resources in sales promotion and advertising programs.

It seems appropriate to conclude this chapter with the reminder that the concept of perfect competition is not intended as a description of reality, or, for that matter, of utopia. The concept of perfect competition is an analytical tool. In evaluating the real-world situation it is frequently helpful to inquire as to what the situation would be if the market were perfectly competitive. Perfect competition serves as a frame of reference or a bench mark. It may not be too much to hope that as Americans come to understand the competitive model better they will interfere with the free workings of the price system with somewhat greater reluctance and resist with somewhat greater effectiveness public and private efforts to establish and maintain monopoly. In the next chapter we turn to a consideration of some of the aspects of imperfectly competitive markets.

26

IMPERFECT COMPETITION

In the previous chapter the model of a perfectly competitive private-enterprise system was set forth in some detail. This model, although admittedly (and purposely) based on "unrealistic" assumptions, is probably the most useful piece of analytical apparatus possessed by the economist—at least when he is dealing with microeconomics. By "useful" we mean that it aids greatly in understanding and predicting real-world situations. This it can do because it abstracts from the complex economic world certain key variables and carefully develops their consequences with regard to such matters as price, output, and the movement of resources between alternative uses.

During the 1930's, that hectic decade of depression which stimulated economists to try new paths in both macro- and microeconomics, the competitive model fell into disrepute in some quarters because of its unrealistic assumptions. Instead, rather elaborate models were constructed on the assumption of the omnipresence of monopoly in the economy. Joan Robinson in England published the *Economics of Imperfect Competition*, while Edward Chamberlin in the United States published *The Theory of Monopolistic*

Competition, both in 1938. These attempted reorientations of the theory of value have not succeeded in swallowing up the competitive analysis and, in general, appear to have less predictive usefulness than the purely competitive model. Nevertheless, they help one understand such real phenomena as advertising, trade names, and price collusion and consequently make a contribution to economic knowledge. The student should keep in mind, however, that *description* which strikes him as being realistic may not actually *explain* anything to him which he did not already know. A careful description of the orbit of a sputnik about the earth will not tell how it got up there or why it does not speedily fall to the earth.

Chapter 6 gave a general picture of the effects of monopoly in the sale of output. The present chapter applies more refined analytical techniques to this problem and deals also with "oligopoly" (where there are a *few* sellers of a particular commodity rather than just one seller or a large number of sellers). The nature and effects of cartels (which are monopolistic associations of sellers) are also considered in the present discussion of imperfect competition.

Alternative Demand Situations

The easiest way to distinguish sharply between the principal market situations is to consider the nature of the demand curve facing the firm. It was pointed out in the previous chapter that the individual firm under pure competition can sell as much as it wishes at the prevailing market price; that is, it is faced with a horizontal demand curve. A monopolist, on the other hand, is faced with a downsloping market demand curve since, by definition, he is the only seller of the good in question in that market. In both cases the demand curve "stays put" regardless of the price or quantity adjustments made by the firm.

OLIGOPOLY DEMAND

When only a few firms sell in a particular market, however, there is no single, determinate demand curve for any one of them. The situation of a small number of firms (but more than one) is designated "oligopoly" by economists. Under this market situation each seller is highly aware of his close rivals, and an important action by one is likely to cause a reaction on the part of the others. The concept of a demand curve for an oligopolist has significance only

FIGURE 26.1. RIVALS' REACTIONS—Affect
Oligopolists' Demand

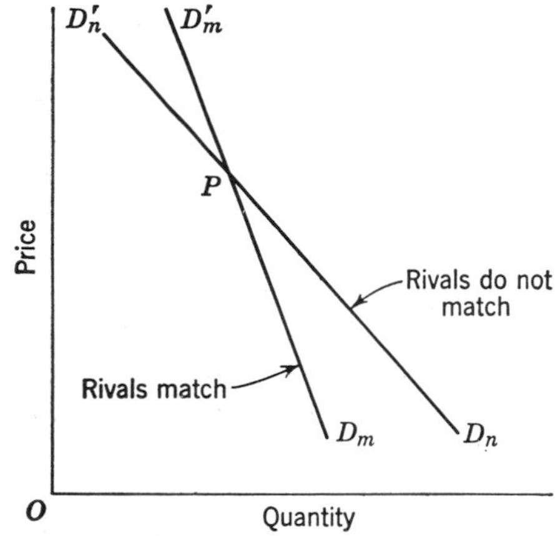

if there is an accompanying assumption regarding rivals' actions. For example, the demand for Plymouths depends a great deal on the price charged for Chevrolets, Fords, and perhaps certain other cars. Thus there is no unique functional relationship between the price of a popular automobile and its sales.

While the idea of a demand curve for the product of an oligopolistic firm has little meaning, the general situation facing such a firm can be made somewhat clearer with the aid of a diagram such as Figure 26.1.

Original price is assumed to be at point P. Curve PD_n indicates that there will be a substantial increase in sales if the firm under consideration cuts price below P but rivals maintain their prices unchanged. (Ford sales would probably be considerably stimulated if prices were cut $100 while Chevrolet and Plymouth declined to cut.) If rivals match a price cut below P, sales will increase, but less substantially, as indicated by PD_m. Many other demand curves could be drawn, however, since many other patterns of reaction by rivals are possible. (They may cut almost as much, may cut even more, one may match and others not cut, etc.)

The same sort of reasoning is applicable to a price increase above the level P. Segment PD'_m shows that a price increase matched by rivals will not bring so sharp a drop in sales as one which rivals do not follow. The latter sales drop is shown along PD'_n. A well-known construction known as the "kinked demand curve" is made up of the portions D'_nP and PD_m. That is, a rather common oligopolistic pattern is that close rivals will match any price cut (which threatens their sales) but will not react to a price boost (which is not a threat). The fear of this sort of situation is conducive to mainte-nance of the status quo with respect to price.

The "rivals match" and "rivals do not match" curves are likely to diverge more sharply for a small firm than for a large one. That is, rivals' reactions make a great deal of difference to a small firm while they may be less important for a large one. Also, the effect of rivals' reactions is less significant when the goods sold by the oligopolistic rivals are somewhat dissimilar. Monopoly can be con-sidered to be the limiting case of oligopoly when rivals' reactions make *no* difference to the sales of a firm. There is then a single, determinate demand curve facing the firm rather than the inde-terminate oligopoly situation. A powerful oligopolist whose sales are affected but little by what any rivals may do is in almost a monopolistic position. His "rivals match" and "rivals do not match" demand curves almost coincide. He is apt to be the "price leader" in the industry if there is either an overt or unwritten agreement among firms to agree on price rather than to follow more aggressive pricing practices.

Economics of the Monopolistic Firm

As has been indicated, the monopolist is not confronted by the horizontal demand curve which faces the purely competitive seller (*e.g.*, the small commercial fisherman) but by a negatively in-clined demand curve. He can increase the physical volume of his sales only by lowering his selling price, and unlike the perfectly competitive firm, he can raise price without losing all of his cus-tomers. This situation is directly traceable to the lack of perfect substitutes (in the opinion of some buyers).

In order to understand fully the way in which the monopolist can determine optimum price, it is necessary to introduce another in the economist's arsenal of "marginal" concepts, namely, mar-ginal revenue. Suppose the demand for a product of a monopolist is represented by the simple schedule in Table 26.1. The third column, total revenue, is found simply by multiplying each related price and quantity. Thus the column shows what the dollar sales of the monopolist would be at each of the alternative prices which he might choose. The marginal revenue column is then derived from the total revenue column; since "marginal revenue" means *additional* revenue, it is only necessary to record the difference in total revenue at each quantity. Thus a quantity of 2 units will sell for $8 per unit, yielding a total revenue of $16. At the next higher quantity (3 units) total revenue is $21; the addition to the monopolist's revenue would therefore be $5 if he increased sales from 2 to 3 units by cutting price from $8 to $7. Similarly, an increase in sales from 5 to 6 units would reduce his total revenue from $25 to $24; hence marginal revenue corresponding to a quantity of 6 is −$1 (a one-dollar reduction in revenue).

It should be noted that, except at the very top of the demand schedule where the two are equal, marginal revenue is always less than price. Why is this so? Suppose the monopolist is selling 2

Table 26.1. Derivation of Marginal Revenue

Price per unit	Quantity demanded	Total revenue	Marginal revenue
$10	0	$ 0	$—
9	1	9	9
8	2	16	7
7	3	21	5
6	4	24	3
5	5	25	1
4	6	24	−1
3	7	21	−3
2	8	16	−5
1	9	9	−7
0	10	0	−9

units at the price of $8 per unit. In order to sell the third unit he must price all units at $7. Thus he gains $7 in revenue by the sale of the third unit, but he takes in $1 less on each of the first 2 units (since he now sells each at $7 instead of $8). His marginal revenue, therefore, is $5 ($7 − $2). To the perfectly competitive firm, marginal revenue and price are identical because selling additional units does not affect price; to the monopolist, marginal revenue is below price because selling more units does depress the price of all units which could otherwise have been sold at a higher price.[1]

It should be easy to see from a combination of the foregoing and the earlier study of elasticity of demand that the monopolist seeking to maximize profit should never sell at a price which

[1] We are assuming that the monopolist follows a policy of selling to all buyers at a single price. Frequently, however, he practices "price discrimination," charging different buyers different prices. This more complicated case will be examined in Chapter 27.

FIGURE 26.2. OPTIMUM MONOPOLY
PRICE—When Marginal Cost Is Zero

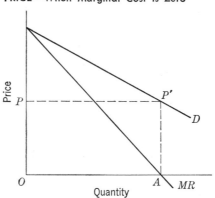

falls along the inelastic portion of his demand curve. Marginal revenue is negative whenever demand is inelastic; total revenue then
falls as price goes down, and negative marginal revenue reflects
this fact. If the monopolist, through error in judgment, sudden
change in demand conditions, or kindness of heart, is selling at a
price for which marginal revenue is negative, he can increase his
profit by raising price. This will usually help in two ways: (1) total
revenue will be greater at the higher price, and (2) total cost
normally will be lower because fewer units will be produced for
sale.

There are some cases, such as those mentioned in Chapter 6,
where cost of production is either zero or is not relevant to the
pricing decision (because, for example, the good is already on
hand in an excessive amount). In these cases, the monopolist has
only to decide at what quantity the dollar value of his product
will be greatest. In Figure 26.2, optimum price lies on the demand
curve directly above the point of zero marginal revenue and exactly at the point of unitary elasticity of demand. Marginal revenue
at this "best" quantity is zero. Sale of any additional units would
reduce the seller's income, since marginal revenue would be negative.

Normally the monopolistic producer is faced with a more difficult problem than that of merely selecting the quantity at which
the dollar value of sales is greatest. He must usually give active
consideration to the cost side as well as the revenue side.

Solution of the problem of optimum output under monopoly is
most clearly demonstrated through use of the concepts of marginal

FIGURE 26.3. MONOPOLIST MAXIMIZES PROFIT—
Marginal Cost = Marginal Revenue

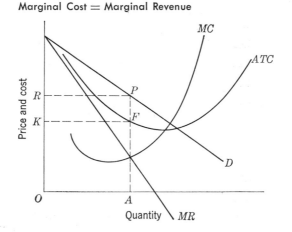

revenue and marginal cost. As already stated, marginal revenue is *additional* income resulting from the sale of a small additional quantity of a good. And, as shown in the earlier chapters, marginal cost is *additional* cost incurred in producing a small additional quantity of a good. It is quite obvious that it is advantageous to produce any unit which will add more to revenue than it adds to cost, *i.e.*, any unit for which marginal revenue exceeds marginal cost. It should be equally clear that it is *not* advantageous to produce any unit for which marginal cost exceeds marginal revenue. Therefore, the monopolist who is striving to maximize profit should try to carry on production at exactly the rate at which marginal revenue and marginal cost are equal. This optimum behavior can be viewed geometrically in Figure 26.3. Optimum output is *OA*, determined by the intersection of *MC* and *MR*. Optimum price *AP* is the highest price at which this quantity can be sold, as shown by the demand curve. Profit per unit is *FP*, determined by the difference between price and average cost of output *OA*. This is not the largest profit *per unit* which could be earned, but the area *KRPF* shows the largest total profit which can be secured.

A PRACTICAL EXAMPLE

The principle just described may be readily illustrated by the pricing of movie tickets in many small towns in the United States where there is only one theater or where all the theaters are owned by the same distribution company. In the determination of the "best" price to charge movie fans, the company will probably give

FIGURE 26.4. MONOPOLISTIC DETERMINATION
OF PRICE OF MOVIE TICKETS

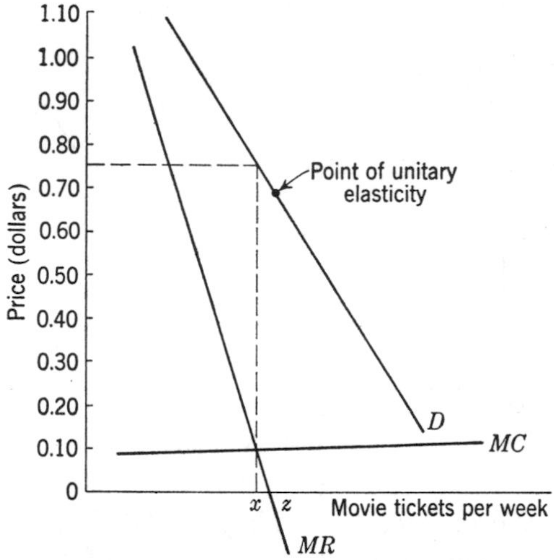

considerably more attention to demand than to cost. This is because a large share of the costs of film exhibition are fixed or "sunk"
in the short run (in rental charges for buildings, depreciation of
projection equipment, fire-insurance payments, etc.). The marginal (additional) costs of taking care of additional customers (up
to the limits of seating capacity) are relatively low. These would
be made up only of such items as the increased cost of usher
and janitorial services and additional wear on seats and carpets.
Geometrically, the situation might look like the hypothetical one
shown in Figure 26.4.

In this situation, the optimum price will be only slightly above
the price at which elasticity of demand is unitary, and the number
of movie tickets sold will be only slightly less than the quantity
Oz which would yield the maximum total revenue. The case is
not very different from the no-cost case, because marginal costs
are low. If the marginal cost curve were higher in relation to the
demand curve, optimum price for the monopolist would exceed
the maximum-expenditure price to a greater degree.

LONG-RUN MONOPOLY ADJUSTMENTS

In both the geometrical and the practical example given above,
we have been concerned exclusively with the short-run pricing
and output decisions of the monopolistic firm. We now turn to the
long-run adjustments which the monopolist will make. It will be

found that these are somewhat different from those made in the competitive case.

The monopolist, like the competitive firm, has a U-shaped long-run average cost curve; that is, if the firm is either too small or too large, its production cost per unit will be higher than if it is of optimum size. The size to which the firm will actually be built will depend on the anticipated demand for its output. This size may happen to be that for which cost per unit is at a minimum, but it is more likely that the firm will be either too large or too small to mimimize cost. The latter case is especially likely to occur if monopoly exists because the market is too small to support more than one firm (for example, a general store in an isolated town with a population of 200).

When the monopolistic firm is too *large* to be of maximum efficiency, it is probable that the market for its product is sufficiently large to support several, or possibly a great many, competing firms. In this case it would be socially desirable to have competition rather than monopoly. Competition would tend to force firms to be of the most efficient size in order to survive. This force is lacking to the extent that competition is absent.

In so far as new firms, attracted by monopoly profits, are able to produce close substitute products, the long-run adjustments in monopoly tend to be similar to those in competition. For example, a firm possessing a monopoly in the sale of a particular brand of lawn mower could not long remain in production at an inefficient (high-cost) scale of operations. Other firms, producing at lower costs and consequently selling their mowers at lower prices, would be able to drive the inefficient firm out of business. On the other hand, an inefficient gas company with an exclusive franchise to serve a city might be able to remain in business indefinitely, but the owners might have some incentive to increase efficiency in order to increase profits. We may conclude, therefore, that the same sort of pressures toward efficiency are present in monopoly as in competition. The difference is primarily one of degree rather than kind. All monopolists are faced with some competition, and the degree of efficiency of monopolistic enterprises is closely related to the degree of competition which exists.

Monopoly and Profits

It should not be assumed that monopoly power ensures profits automatically, although abnormal profits are always the motivation for attempts to secure a monopolistic market position. Many patented items are never produced because businessmen realize that demand-cost conditions would not permit profitable production. Even if original demand-cost conditions are satisfactory, profits made by early firms may be reduced or wiped out by the appearance of other enterprises which sell close substitutes. The first man to recognize the profit potential of a new site for a gasoline station, for example, may earn a good income only until others erect stations in the vicinity. It is quite possible that this enterprise and the others will then all earn for their proprietors even less than they could make by working elsewhere. The attraction of being at once president, vice-president, general manager, etc., of a firm, as well as the hope that conditions will improve, induces many small enterprisers to continue in business long after the more rational course would be to give up. There is a strong tendency for businesses which require little capital and experience to be overcrowded and chronically unprofitable for most firms. Examples are filling stations, gift shops, concrete-block plants, and small grocery stores. Ease of entry is a necessary condition to the existence of pure competition, but the entry of new firms producing close substitutes is often effective also in reducing the profits of firms which sell differentiated products. Where entry is extremely difficult because of the large investment needed, profits tend to be more dependable as long as national income is high.

Profits serve, therefore, the same function in monopolistic industries as in competitive ones. Profits tend to attract new firms producing more-or-less substitutable goods, and the subsequent entry of new firms tends to eliminate all or part of the profits. The major difference between monopoly and competition in this respect is the rate at which new firms can take away the abnormal or excessive profits of existing firms.

Oligopoly Price Policy

The monopoly analysis which has just been completed is based on the assumption that the demand curve is unaffected by the monopolists' own price policy. This assumption is justified either if substitutes are remote or if the firm in question is not sufficiently important to cause sellers of close substitutes to alter their policies in defensive actions. An electric power company or a telephone company are examples of monopolistic firms with only remote substitutes for their products. A lipstick producer may exemplify the second situation; each brand of lipstick is quite a close substitute for the others, but a firm may set its price on the assumption that its price policy will not affect the policies of other firms in the industry, since it supplies such a small part of the total market that it is not a great threat to other producers. In both of these types of situations, monopoly analysis is applicable.

In a great many industries, however, the number of firms is sufficiently small relative to the market to make each highly sensitive to the actions of others. This is the "oligopoly" situation, as already mentioned. Oligopolists may be selling either exactly the same commodity—for example, industrial materials such as steel, copper, sulfur, lime, pig iron, or cast-iron pipe—or differentiated products such as trucks, refrigerators, motel accommodations, or theatrical productions.

Oligopoly is frequently the ultimate outcome of a situation in which the optimum-sized firm is large relative to the market served. In terms of the long-run average cost curve, the lowest cost outputs often can be attained only by relatively large firms. In cities such as Nashville or Des Moines there are likely to be only two, three, or four major department stores. The market area served is not large enough to support more department stores of the size necessary to secure the full advantages of modern retail distribution such as a large variety of merchandise, delivery service, credit facilities, and advertising. Although such goods as typewriters, tractors, and automobiles are distributed on a national or international scale, the market is able to support only a relatively small number of firms of efficient size.

OLIGOPOLISTIC STRATEGY

The pricing problems facing firms in an oligopolistic situation become similar to those facing opposing generals in war or opposing players in a poker game. Action taken depends to a large degree upon a subjective estimate of what other sellers will do as a result of such action. As indicated earlier, the demand curve which is important for the decision-making of the firm is derived from specific assumptions concerning rivals' behavior. The essential point is that the demand curve which affects the oligopolist's decisions is not based solely or even primarily on the objective market facts but rather on his subjective estimates of his rivals' behavior; these estimates may or may not be accurate. Actual behavior depends in such cases in part on the types of personalities making the decisions. One predominant characteristic of oligopolistic markets is that the whole pricing structure can be significantly affected by individual business leaders. The pricing policies of the automobile industry and of the tire industry were for many years strongly influenced by Henry Ford and Harvey Firestone.

From time to time, competition among oligopolists results in "price wars" in which rivals continue to undercut one another until prices are driven far below usual levels. A warring oligopolist may even cut price temporarily below average variable cost if he is attempting to ruin one or more competitors to his own ultimate gain. In an all-out price war, the survivors are likely to be the firms with the most reserves, in the form, for example, of highly liquid assets and good sources of credit. Price warfare, or "cutthroat competition," is likely to occur only when productive capacity is large in relation to demand. Rate wars were chronic among the overbuilt American railroads during the last century. Similarly, cutthroat competition frequently breaks out in cities, especially during a depression, in such fields as dry cleaning and gasoline distribution.

In periods of general prosperity, oligopolistic rivals are not likely to engage in strenuous competition on a price basis. Instead, they are likely to reach explicit or tacit understandings regarding prices and to brand as a "price chiseler" any seller who fails to fall in line. There are various ways of causing a "chiseler" to change his policies—*e.g.*, by threat of a price war or through pressure exerted through his suppliers or sources of credit. Where oligopolists are strongly organized and firmly led, price may be approximately the same as that which a monopolist would set if he were in control of the entire productive capacity of the industry. This situation is especially likely if the various firms all produce identical or very similar commodities (*e.g.*, cigarettes) and if costs are nearly the same. To the extent that products and costs differ, the rivals will prefer different prices, and if a single price is maintained through collusion it is apt to be a compromise which may not maximize profit for any particular firm.

The trade association is an extremely common device for securing collusive action regarding price. Such associations perform certain desirable services for their members and the public, such as setting quality standards, standardizing specifications, and dispensing information regarding raw-material prices. It is probably fair to say, however, that their real importance rests in keeping member firms in continual contact with each other, thus permitting ample opportunity for agreements regarding price.[1] These agreements are far more likely to be in the form of a cocktail conspiracy than to take a written (traceable) form.

PRICE LEADERSHIP

When one firm in an industry is substantially larger than any other firm—a common situation, existing, for example, in the production of steel, "tin" cans, and corn products—the dominant firm is likely to be the price leader. This means that the company is usually the first to announce a price change, either with or without prior consultation with other firms, and that rivals quickly match the leader's move. Such a price leader generally makes a move in full anticipation of being followed; he can maximize his own profit by equating marginal cost with marginal revenue as related to the demand which will exist after followers have made the appropriate price and output adjustments. His task of choosing a profitable price is made far easier by the virtual certainty of being followed—a situation that does not exist in ordinary noncollusive rivalry among oligopolists.

To the extent that the price leader is acting not only in his own interest but in the interest of the industry as a whole (probably doing so under pressure from the others), he may purposely set the price at a level which is not the optimum for his own firm but which is a good compromise from the point of view of all the firms. This situation is more likely when no one firm is substantially larger than other firms in the industry. Usually a price leader is of substantial size, however, and possessed of particularly aggressive management. Like outright price agreement among oligopolists, price leadership is more common when the rival firms produce the same or quite similar commodities. When a company views its own product as distinctive (as in the case of patent medicines), monopoly pricing tends to prevail.

THE PRESSURE FOR SECRET PRICE CUTS AND NONPRICE CONCESSIONS

Whenever oligopolists maintain identical, or nearly identical, prices as a matter of policy—whether by outright collusion or through following the leader—there may be a strong tendency for individual firms to undercut the published price in subtle ways in

[1] Adam Smith observed in 1776: "People of the same trade seldom meet together, even for merriment and diversion, but the conversation ends in a conspiracy against the public, or in some contrivance to raise prices." *The Wealth of Nations* (New York: Modern Library, Inc., 1937), p. 128.

FIGURE 26.5. DIVERGENCE BETWEEN AGREED
AND OPTIMUM PRICE—May Lead to Secret Price-
reducing Arrangements

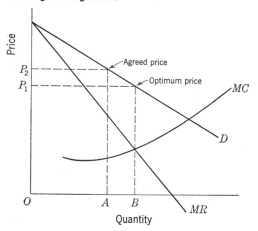

order to increase their shares of the market. The tendency for the
individual firm to cut the agreed-on price is especially strong in
periods of slack demand. In such cases individual firms are likely
to find that through adherence to the agreed-on price they are not
maximizing profits. Such a situation is depicted in Figure 26.5.

The oligopolist is confronted by the demand curve D as long as
his rivals adhere strictly to the agreed price OP_2. His marginal
revenue is then represented by MR and his marginal costs by MC.
The optimum price for this firm would, under these conditions, be
OP_1, but he has agreed to maintain price OP_2. He would like to
lower price but cannot do so without incurring the anger of managers of other firms and probably causing a reduction in the demand
for his own product as a result of retaliatory price cuts.

When this sort of difference exists between agreed-on and optimum price, the firm has an incentive to make hidden price cuts
in order to secure additional sales without unduly disturbing rival
companies. A very large number of practices which amount to secret price cutting are available to businessmen. These include re-
bates, favorable credit terms, "money-back" guarantees, engineering services, repair and maintenance work, liberal trade-in allowances, and lavish entertainment of the buyers. To the extent
that such practices are followed (wisely) by a firm such as the
one whose cost and revenue data are pictured in Figure 26.5 sales
can be increased toward the optimum OB. Rivals may, however,
engage similarly in such concessions: this would reduce the de-

mand (curve D) of the firm in question. Oligopolistic firms, especially the price leaders, frequently tire of the increasing concessions made by rivals and overtly lower the dollar price in order to
prevent a further creeping encroachment on their own sales. Completely effective collusion within an industry thus requires agreement not only as to the basic price but also with respect to a very
large number of ancillary matters pertaining to the terms of sale.
It is easy to see that effective collusion becomes increasingly difficult as the number of firms involved increases.

The term "nonprice competition" is frequently used by economists to cover the multitude of practices used in oligopolistic industries to attract sales when it is the industry practice not to
engage in outright price cutting. These include advertising and
other sales-promotion efforts in addition to the nonprice concessions mentioned above. Actually, it is frequently difficult to classify
a particular practice as either a price reduction or a nonprice action to gain sales. For example, more liberal credit terms may
involve a lower interest rate which actually reduces price to the
installment purchaser. But alternatively, the credit arrangement
can be considered as a separate commodity purchased by the
buyer; in that light the easier credit terms can be viewed as a
nonprice concession with respect to the commodity bought on
terms. Similarly, a higher trade-in allowance can either be considered as a reduction of price of the new article or as a nonprice concession to the buyer.

In the cigarette industry, competition among the big three—
Camel, Chesterfield, and Lucky Strike—is mainly on a nonprice
basis. Normally, instead of competing in price, the sellers of these
cigarettes advertise very heavily, each striving to increase its share
of the market and, less directly, to build up the total market for
cigarettes. Probably sales of any of these brands would fall off
substantially if its producer stopped advertising while the others
continued their heavy selling outlays.

The risk which oligopolists may run by maintaining price and
engaging instead in nonprice competition was forcibly shown during the severe depression of the 1930's when cigarette buyers were
of necessity more price conscious. Starting with almost negligible
sales in 1931, makers of "10-cent brands" increased their volumes
until they accounted for over 20 per cent of domestic cigarette
sales for a few months in the fall of 1932.[1] This caused the big

[1] As described in Neil H. Borden, *The Economic Effects of Advertising*
(Chicago: Richard D. Irwin, Inc., 1942), Chap. 8.

three to cut their prices in January, 1933, to the neighborhood of
10 cents a pack, and their sales responded quickly at the expense
of the regular 10-cent brands. In periods of higher national income,
however, the practice of nonprice competition may serve the interest of the large cigarette producers well.

Price Policy of Cartels

We have examined the tendency of oligopolistic firms to engage
in collusive practices in order to prevent competition on a price
basis. The understanding which is reached is frequently extremely
informal, constituting nothing more than a "gentleman's agreement" to maintain price or to follow any change made by the
leader. In other cases, oligopolists may systematically surrender
their price-determining power to a central agency which may also
be given additional powers such as the authority to allot exclusive
sales territories among the cooperating firms. The firms may then
be said to belong to a "cartel."

Cartels are perhaps even more common in industries where the
number of firms is large and where a substantial degree of competition could otherwise exist. This situation is due especially to the
direct governmental support of cartel arrangements in many areas
of the economy. Milk boards, for example, are governmentally
sponsored agencies which have the authority to set minimum retail prices on milk in a great many localities, effectively cartelizing
the sale of this highly essential commodity. In other cases, cartel
arrangements may be effectuated by private organizations such as
marketing cooperatives or professional societies (*e.g.*, bar associations). In the discussion which follows, we shall be concerned with
the operation of cartels in situations where the number of sellers
is large rather than with cartels in oligopolistic situations.

AN EXAMPLE OF CARTELIZATION

The principle of cartel price determination may be illustrated
by the pricing of barbershop services, since these prices are fixed
by such agreements in most American cities and towns. The individual barbershops surrender to the association, or "union," the
power to determine price. The association officials must evaluate
the total conditions of demand for barbershop services in the area
as well as the cost conditions and estimate the "best" price from
the point of view of the barbers and barbershop operators.

The determination of the price of haircuts may be depicted as in

FIGURE 26.6. CARTEL DETERMINATION OF
PRICE OF HAIRCUTS

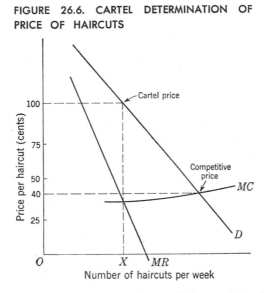

Figure 26.6. Curve *D* represents the total demand for haircuts in a particular town and *MR* the corresponding marginal revenue curve. It should be emphasized that these are "industry" demand and revenue curves and do not represent the curves which would face any individual barbershop. The curve *MC* represents the industry marginal cost curve. It is drawn so that marginal costs change slowly as quantity changes reflecting that many firms are included, and, therefore, a substantial change in the total number of haircuts sold in the city may take place without any one shop being overworked, *i.e.*, being placed in a high-cost operating situation. It may be seen from a glance at Figure 26.6 that the profit-maximizing price will be $1 and the number of haircuts *OX*.

For the individual barbershop proprietor, however, this may not be a wholly satisfactory solution. He may recognize that his best interest lies in going along with the dictates of the association, but he will be strongly tempted to make price cuts and to offer non-price concessions (*e.g.*, free scalp massages). His position would then be similar to that described for the oligopolistic firm depicted in Figure 26.5. The individual barbershop could increase its profits by cutting its prices, provided that it could be sure that the other barbershops in town did not do the same. If all other barbershops did cut price and if the price-setting power of the "union" were to vanish, the situation would approximate that of pure competition, with price falling to about 40 cents in Figure 26.6. (The particular prices shown have no special significance but have been chosen arbitrarily to illustrate the principle.) This pressure for price cuts makes cartel agreements always difficult to maintain unless severe disciplinary measures may be taken against violators.

DIFFICULTIES OF RESTRICTING ENTRY

In Figure 26.6, the cartel- or association-set price is substantially higher than the price which would prevail under competition. It is possible, however, that the industry might be made up of either more or fewer firms than would be operating in the competitive case. One of the major difficulties faced by such associations is their frequent inability to restrict entry into the industrial, occupational, or professional group. If, in our example, entry could be limited (with state and municipal support) by means of restrictive licensing, the number of barbers might be kept down and sizable monopoly profits retained by association members.[1] If, however, the association or cartel possesses the power to set price but does not have the power to restrict entry of firms into the industry, individual firms will gain little in the long run. For, attracted by apparent high earnings to be secured through the high price, many new firms will enter the industry. As new firms come in, old firms must share the market with them and hence lose sales. This movement may well continue until no firm in the industry is making more than a competitive rate of return on its investment. But each firm will be operating at far less than its lowest-cost output. Our barbershop example is a good one to illustrate this point. It seems likely that few barbershops, if any, make abnormally high profits. Yet most of them tend to operate at far less than the lowest-cost capacity. The position of a single firm (barbershop) may be illustrated in Figure 26.7. The firm would like to operate "at capacity," or sell *OB* haircuts per week, since at this sales volume the firm's marginal cost equals the cartel price. But there are so many barbershops in town that each one must operate at far less than its most desirable output. And since new barbershops can normally be opened without difficulty, the final position for a single firm is shown at output *OA*. At this position, average costs (including a normal rate of return on fixed investment and normal wages of management) are just covered, and no abnormal profits are present.

The social loss due to the cartel type of agreement is twofold: first, prices are higher than they would be under competition and,

[1] Certain professional groups, such as medical doctors, actuaries, and public accountants, have been notably successful in restricting entry.

FIGURE 26.7. SINGLE BARBERSHOP OPERATES
AT HIGH COST, LOW OUTPUT

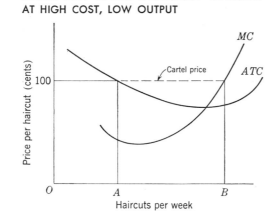

second, the many resources which are devoted to the production of
the cartelized good or service are underutilized. This problem of excess capacity is especially prevalent in those areas of the economy
in which firms can be set up without too much initial capital investment, *e.g.*, small retail establishments. With such excess capacity
present, once the cartel-like price agreements are broken, price wars
are likely to ensue. A good example is provided by the gasoline
price wars so often found among filling stations when a cartel-like
arrangement breaks down.

THE ECONOMIC SIGNIFICANCE OF CARTEL AGREEMENTS

The word "cartel" has been deliberately employed to define this
type of market situation, although it generally connotes a European
rather than an American type of monopolistic combination. It is
true that open price agreements of the cartel sort among large industrial firms have occurred largely on the continent of Europe,
particularly among German firms. The antitrust laws have fairly
effectively prevented this sort of agreement among large firms in
the United States. It is, however, precisely in situations like that
described by the barbershop example that the cartel restrictions are
most serious in this country, and these have too often been overlooked in considerations of the over-all monopoly problem.

The importance of such local monopolistic restrictions should not
be underestimated. In 1946, the nation's bill for barbershop services exceeded the aggregate amount spent for refrigerators, wash-
ing machines, and sewing machines, despite the postwar boom in
household-appliance sales. In that same year, considerably more

than one-half of personal-consumption expenditures in the United States were devoted to such items as rents, laundry, dry cleaning, locally produced foods, recreation, barbershop and beauty-parlor services, local transportation services, medical expenses, death expenses, and automobile repairs.[1] All these industries are outside the jurisdiction of the Federal antitrust laws, since these apply only to firms operating in interstate commerce. And in nearly all of these service types of industries, some sorts of cartel agreements are likely to be found. In many cases state and municipal governments actively support this type of monopolistic agreement through official price-setting commissions and boards. The Federal government also supports cartel-like agreements, especially among sellers of agricultural commodities. Competitive forces are allowed little or no influence in the setting of fluid-milk prices, for example. These are set by milk-marketing boards largely composed of representatives from both the producers and the distributors of milk.

[1] J. W. Markham, "The Effectiveness of Federal Anti-trust Laws: Comment," *American Economic Review*, Vol. 40, p. 169 (March, 1950).

27

PRICE DISCRIMINATION

The analysis of the previous chapter was based on the assumption
that the profit-maximizing action taken by a monopoly or a cartel or
by colluding oligopolists consists to an important extent in finding
the single best price at which to sell. Under many circumstances
occurring under conditions of imperfect competition, however, it is
both possible and profitable for a company to sell different units of
the same good at different prices, that is, to practice price discrimination.

Conditions Favorable to Price Discrimination

In order to engage in price discrimination a firm must find some
means of separating markets for purposes of differential treatment.
Also, the markets must be kept separate; otherwise those who buy
at the cheaper prices can resell at a profit in the dearer markets. If
a minor amount of resale occurs the price discrimination scheme
may still be workable, but if it occurs to a major extent the system
will break down. It is also important in price discrimination that
communication between customers who receive unlike prices be

poor, or that the information, when received, does not cause undue resentment against the seller.

QUANTITY DISCOUNTS

One of the most important bases for price discrimination is the quantity purchased by the individual buyers. "Block rates" are extremely common in the sale of electricity, with successive blocks of current purchased within a month being sold at lower rates. Here the discrimination is not directly against one buyer compared with another, since in theory all have an equal opportunity to secure the lower marginal rates on large purchases. Actually, some households —those of the relatively well-to-do—use much more current than do the poorer homes and consequently get a lower price per unit. Similarly, quantity discounts on food, soap, drug items, and other consumer goods are apt to discriminate against the poorer families who cannot afford to buy in large quantities and to carry the larger average inventories which this entails.[1]

INCOME OR WEALTH OF BUYER

A more direct discrimination between persons is often based on a separation of customers on the basis of apparent income or wealth. This is common in the case of surgeons, who may charge quite different prices for the same operation according to their estimate of the customer's ability to pay. (Moral: Don't brag about your stock-market successes to your surgeon.) This practice is not based entirely on the surgeon's desire to earn a high income, however, since it makes more feasible the handling of some cases on a charity, or near-charity, basis. That is, while persons of higher income may be discriminated against, persons in the lower brackets may be given unusually low rates.

Similarly, a lawyer may sell the same legal opinion for a higher fee to a wealthy client than to a poor one. Also, real estate brokers commonly charge a fixed *percentage* of the sales value of residential property for their services. While the amount of work involved in handling a more expensive property is greater than it is for a lesser transaction it probably does not increase in proportion to price. Consequently, the percentage fee is a common device for price discrimination. Publishers of magazines regularly provide lower subscription rates to new subscribers and to those who are

---

[1] If a quantity discount is no more than the saving to the seller inherent in passing part of the inventory burden onto the buyer, there is some question as to whether price discrimination can properly be said to exist.

slow to renew, and graduate students frequently may join professional associations at less than regular rates. Children are admitted at lower prices to theaters (in spite of the greater trouble and muss which they cause). Some of these types of price discrimination are based not only on income but also on the desire of sellers to instill habits and associations which will stimulate demand in the long run.

CONVENIENCE TO BUYER

Price discrimination is sometimes based on convenience to the buyer. A reserved seat may sell at a higher price than an equally well-located unreserved seat. The difference in price is a premium paid to avoid uncertainty and possible inconvenience, but it may well be higher than is appropriate and, in effect be based mainly on an ability to extract more money from those better able to pay.

TIME OF PURCHASE

Sometimes sellers are able effectively to discriminate on the basis of time of purchase. The same moving picture usually costs more in the evening than in the afternoon. Similarly, stores may be able to charge higher prices for the same merchandise before Christmas and Easter than after these holidays. These cases do not fall quite so clearly in the category of price discrimination as do quantity discounts, however, since even in purely competitive markets an increase in demand tends to raise price in the short run. The pre- and post-holiday price differentials are apt to be larger, however, if monopoly power is possessed by the seller.

PRESTIGE OF THE BUYER

An influential person such as a corporation president, important political officeholder, or university dean often receives an especially favorable price from a real estate developer. This is based on the tendency of junior executives, for example, to wish to live in the same neighborhood as the boss in order to enhance their own prospects through social or casual contacts. If the boss soon moves away —perhaps to improve his own social contacts—the followers are apt to be left languishing in a neighborhood which they do not really like.

DISCRIMINATION VIA TRADING STAMPS

Trading stamps, which have gained such importance in recent years, have both advantages and disadvantages from a social point of view. One important advantage is that they may provide an effective method of "chiseling" on a price established by means of tacit or overt collusion between sellers. Also (though the social advantage is less clear) they may provide the housewife with a sort of spending money for securing needed appliances which a parsimonious husband would not furnish her actual cash to buy. On the other side is the extra clerical labor which trading stamps occasion as well as the resources which they divert from other uses. For purposes of the present discussion we wish to emphasize that they also constitute a device for the exercise of a price discrimination.

To the extent that a buyer does not bother to accept trading stamps from a seller who uses them he in effect pays a higher price than is appropriate since presumably the cost of the stamps to the store is largely included in the prices which it charges. The buyer then pays for the stamps but does not take home his full purchase. Similarly, many of the stamps which are accepted by customers are never redeemed—to the advantage of the stamp companies. The nonredeemer is discriminated against in the same degree as the one who does not take home the stamps.[1]

Coupons passed out by soap companies and other firms may similarly result in virtually a two-price system. Those who are careful enough to present all available coupons receive the lower price while those who do not care to bring coupons—or who cannot remember to do so—pay the full price and hence are discriminated against.

A GEOMETRIC REPRESENTATION

In more analytical terms, price discrimination involves separating total demand into two or more submarkets for unlike price treatment. The height and shape of the separate demand curves then determine what prices will be most profitable to the discriminating monopolist.

This principle can be illustrated in a simple diagram if it is assumed for convenience that, like stadium seats, the good is already on hand so that cost need not be considered. Figure 27.1 shows separate demands D_1 and D_2 for a good which is already on hand in the amount OS. Curves MR_1 and MR_2 show corresponding marginal revenues.

The best quantity to sell in market 1 is OA, the amount for which

---

[1] It may be objected that some people do not care to bother with trading stamps and hence that they are not really discriminated against. However, this is not convincing if commodity prices actually include the price the grocer pays for stamps.

FIGURE 27.1. PRICE DISCRIMINATION—
When Good Is on Hand

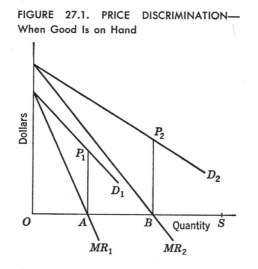

marginal revenue is zero. Similarly, the best amount to sell in the other market is *OB*. If amount available is *OS*, not all of this quantity will be sold (some seats will remain empty). Prices in the two markets will be AP_1 and BP_2, respectively. If the meaning of marginal revenue is kept in mind it is clear that no more than *OA* should be sold in market 1 since negative marginal revenue—a reduction in total income—would result. If *less* than *OA* were sold in the first market total income would be lower because additional units could be sold at positive marginal revenue, that is, would add to income. The reasoning is similar for market 2. If no other demand can be tapped, the stadium management will either have to let the seats remain empty or will have to give them away to the Boy Scouts, ladies, or other groups who may at a later date become cash customers.[1]

DISCRIMINATION VIA MULTIPLE PRODUCTS

In the examples used so far the discriminating monopolist has sold different units of exactly the same good at different prices—unless one considers that stadium seats in unlike locations are not

---

[1] The diagrammatic representation is quite similar, but somewhat more complicated, if the problem also includes determination of the best rate of output. This rate is determined by the intersection of the marginal cost curve and the marginal revenue curve applicable to *total* demand. Optimum sales in the two markets are quantities where the separate marginal revenues are at the same level at which marginal cost and total marginal revenue intersect. The geometrically minded student can profitably draw the chart for this more general case.

the same commodity. Actually, most price discrimination involves selling closely substitutable, but somewhat dissimilar, goods at price differentials which are not in line with cost differences.

Most firms produce numerous products rather than just one, and a leading reason for this practice is found in the desire to have available both the plain and de luxe versions (and perhaps several varieties in-between) so that those who are ready to pay more for pretty much the same thing will have ample opportunity to do so. Usually the plainer models are sold at smaller markups above cost, though exceptions can be found, of course. This is at least a partial explanation for the large number of different models of American automobiles in spite of the small number of companies in the field. It also helps explain the wide variety of life-insurance policies available from a given company, and the reluctance of most companies to sell term insurance (which is the plainest model).

SPATIAL PRICE DISCRIMINATION

The necessity for incurring freight charges in order to overcome the geographic separation of sellers and buyers provides numerous opportunities for the exercise of spatial price discrimination. This occurs when buyers in some areas are charged for more freight than is actually involved while others may be charged only for actual freight or possibly for less freight than is actually involved.

Basing-point pricing is the most important device for the exercise of spatial price discrimination, although the system is now used less than before it ran into effective Federal opposition. The "Pittsburgh-plus" system of pricing, used by the steel industry prior to 1924, is the most famous example of the practice. Mills all over the country calculated their delivered prices by adding to the Pittsburgh mill price rail freight from Pittsburgh to the buyer's location. Only if the steel actually originated in Pittsburgh would the freight charge included in the price coincide with the actual freight cost incurred. If the steel was actually shipped by rail a greater distance than if it had come from Pittsburgh the steel mill making the shipment had to absorb some of the freight cost. More frequently, however, "phantom freight" charges were paid by the steel buyer. This occurred whenever the purchase was made from a mill closer to the buyer than Pittsburgh. It could also occur when water shipment was used instead of rail shipment, even if the distance was greater than from Pittsburgh. For example, the Bethlehem Steel Company plant in Baltimore, Maryland, might ship through the Panama Canal to Los Angeles. Cost of such shipment would be less than rail freight from Pittsburgh to Los Angeles, but the latter city would not secure any price advantage from the water shipment. Discrimination against the economic development of entire regions of the nation was involved in this method of pricing steel.

The steel industry switched to a multiple-basing-point system in 1924 after the U.S. Steel Corporation was ordered by the Federal Trade Commission to abandon Pittsburgh-plus. Delivered price at any locality was then calculated by adding freight from the *applicable* basing point. Usually the applicable basing point was the one from which rail freight was the lowest.[1] However, not all steel mill cities were designated as basing points, so "phantom freight" was still involved in many shipments. The system was an improvement over Pittsburgh-plus but was still inequitable.

The portland cement industry was also a well-known and important user of a multiple-basing-point system. About half of the cement mills were designated as basing points in the 1930's. In 1948, however, the Supreme Court of the United States upheld a Federal Trade Commission order that the industry "cease and desist" from its basing-point system. As a result of this decision, both the portland cement and steel industries changed over to an f.o.b. mill system under which actual freight is charged from the actual source of shipment to the destination. As was pointed out in Chapter 7, basing-point pricing is one of the fields in which important victories have been won for society by the Federal government. However, basing-point pricing is still used by some industries.

Basing-point pricing, with Detroit as the base, was long used in the automobile industry, especially by Ford and General Motors. Spokesmen for the industry say that this system has now been abandoned.[2] Dealers were charged full transportation charges as if the car had come from Detroit even when it was assembled at a much closer facility. To the extent that dealers were able to pass on to consumers these phantom freight charges, car buyers near assembly plants, but remote from Detroit, were discriminated against. So far as dealers were forced to absorb some of the phantom freight in order to make sales they were discriminated against by the Detroit-plus system.[3]

[1] This was not always the case because of variations in mill prices. The lowest mill price plus rail freight determined the applicable basing point.

[2] "GM Says It, Too, Is Abandoning Use of Phantom Freight Charges," *Wall Street Journal,* February 27, 1956, p. 1.

[3] Each automobile manufacturer is a monopolist in the sale of new cars to its dealers. The dealer can buy from no one else and has a sizable investment in facilities which are quite specialized to a particular car or to a few makes of cars. This situation can lead to a price squeeze on the dealer, especially when business activity slows down.

BLANKET RATES

Freight rate structures themselves often create situations involving geographic price discrimination. A leading example is the use of "blanket" rates which permit shipment over a broad area at the same rate in spite of great difference in length of haul.

California oranges in carload lots may be shipped from any point of origin in that state to any point between Denver and the North Atlantic seaboard at the same total cost.[1] This type of rate discriminates against buyers located in Kansas City, for example, compared with those in Philadelphia. More resources are used up in bringing oranges to the latter city, but this is not reflected in price.

Socal Significance of Price Discrimination

The various types of price discrimination which we have examined in this chapter have different social effects, most of them bad. To the extent that they increase profits of monopolistic firms some redistribution of income from buyers to sellers is effected. When the basis for discrimination is quantity purchased by the consumer—as is usual for electricity—the pricing system has the effect of making the poor poorer.

Large firms often receive lower prices than small firms on materials and supplies. Although this is illegal in interstate commerce under the Robinson-Patman Act—unless the discount is in line with the actual cost saving—it is a difficult thing to prevent. The effect may be to throw an inappropriate cost obstacle in the path of small firms which are in competition with large ones. On the other hand. the social welfare is not furthered by preventing the larger firms from securing any price advantage which is due to the economies of large-scale buying.

Price discrimination which has as its purpose the extraction of more money from those able to afford it might be defended by many. The Cadillac, Lincoln, or Imperial owner who is charged more for similar repairs than the owner of a Volkswagen may be regarded by many to be reaping only just rewards for his tendency toward ostentatious display. However, this view seems inappropriate in that it is not the function of private sellers to attempt to redistribute income. To the extent that society deems a certain

[1] Kent T. Healy, *The Economics of Transportation in America* (New York: Ronald Press, 1940), p. 250.

degree of redistribution to be appropriate, agencies of government through such devices as the income tax and government expenditure can more properly effect the redistribution.

Spatial price discrimination tends to distort the economically appropriate patterns of location of industry. The existence of a material supplier in a particular city should be a factor promoting the nearby establishment of firms which utilize that material. If a basing-point system requires the payment of freight on that material from some fictitious source, the most economical location is not encouraged. Firms will tend to be established near basing points but not near all sources of supply. Different localities compete heavily for the establishment of new plants, and regional price discrimination by suppliers of key materials can convert this into unfair competition.

28

LOCATION OF ECONOMIC ACTIVITY

The main body of price theory—as reflected in an elementary way in this book—leaves out of consideration the whole problem of space and hence does not consider transportation costs. Instead, it is implicitly considered that buyers and sellers are at the same point. For most purposes this drastic simplification is justifiable and useful as a method of analysis.

A businessman seeking to find the best location for a new plant is unlikely, however, to find much help in theory which omits all mention of space. In order to have predictive usefulness for this sort of problem, theory must explicitly recognize transportation costs as a vital variable. Like theory relating to imperfect competition (Chapter 26), location theory is useful also in helping one understand how a private-enterprise system works; that is, it has value to the student even if he will never be faced with the problem of picking the best location for an industrial plant, store, or other facility.

Optimum Scale

One matter which immediately becomes easier to comprehend when transportation cost is allowed in the picture is the existence of a U-shaped long-run average cost curve for a plant. (This is described in Chapter 24.) It is not difficult to see that a plant becomes more efficient as it gets larger, but it is not always clear why it should again run into higher costs per unit as it becomes still larger. However, if it is remembered that a larger plant must ship its product a greater distance in order to dispose of it, the diseconomy of size becomes evident.

It is clear that it would not be efficient to have one huge brick plant located somewhere near the center of the United States, shipping its product to all corners of the nation. Transportation costs on the bricks would be so great that it would be easy for enterprisers all over the country to set up brick-making operations and undersell the centrally located plant in their areas. If the long-run average cost curve is considered to include both production and transportation costs, it will clearly rise sharply for a brick plant as it gets too large.

This point is less important if transportation cost on the final product is relatively small (or if "blanket" freight rates permit it to be shipped long distances at the same total cost). A bobby-pin manufacturing plant, for example, is unlikely to become significantly less efficient as it becomes larger because the transportation cost per unit of its product is low. In a great many industries, however, it is more economical for a firm to establish branch plants near population centers than to expand the main plant and ship long distances.

It is not difficult to see that improvements in transportation facilities are conducive to the establishment of a smaller number of more centrally located plants whereas increases in railroad rates, increased highway congestion, higher prices for trucks, and higher wage rates for truckers are conducive to the establishment of smaller, more decentralized plants. Firms which have their plants so located as to encounter especially heavy transportation costs are at as much competitive disadvantage as those whose manufacturing operations are relatively inefficient.

A correct discussion of the economics of plant location requires that both demand and cost be considered simultaneously.[1] This leads quickly into complicated formulations, however, and for present purposes the demand side will be largely neglected. That is, adequate demand will be assumed to exist at alternative loca-

[1] This is brought out especially clearly by Melvin L. Greenhut, *Plant Location in Theory and in Practise* (Chapel Hill: University of North Carolina Press, 1956), Chap. VI.

tions considered, and attention will be paid only to the cost side. Also it will be assumed that only one important material is used, and that only one product is produced by a plant. As has been emphasized before, this sort of simplification is often necessary to keep analysis manageable. Some important matters may thus be understood which might not otherwise be grasped at all.

A DIAGRAMMATIC REPRESENTATION

Assuming demand to exist, and leaving out personal considerations (such as the enterpriser's desire to remain in the home town), the objective in locating a manufacturing plant may be said to be minimization of the total unit cost of gathering materials, processing them, and distributing the product. The cost of the materials will obviously be lowest if the manufacturer locates his plant right at the material source. The cost of distributing the finished product is minimized if the operation takes place right at the market (which will be assumed to be at one place rather than at several). Processing costs may vary from place to place.

In Figure 28.1 line G shows the cost of bringing to a plant, at different locations between the material source and the market, enough of the principal raw material to turn out one unit of the finished product. Line G is lowest if the plant is located at the source of the material and rises as locations farther from the ma-

FIGURE 28.1. COST PER UNIT—Depends on Location

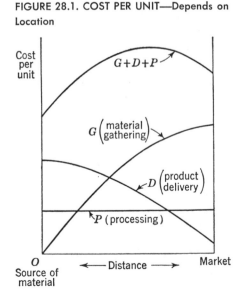

terial source, but nearer the market, are considered. The material source and the market are considered to be a substantial distance apart—say 500 miles—and distance is measured along the horizontal axis. The closer the plant is located to the material supply, the farther it is from the market, and vice versa. Line G does not include the mill price of the raw material, since presumably this would not change with the plant's location. Hence transportation alone is a locational factor.

Line D is the curve which shows for alternative possible plant locations the cost per unit of delivering the finished product to the market. It is lowest at the right-hand end of the distance scale, which represents location right at the market, and rises to the left as locations more distant from the market are considered. (The entire chart, like a long-run average cost curve, should be thought of as a planning device—a way of thinking about the plant location problem.) The D curve will be highest if location right at the material source should be selected. Processing cost per unit has been assumed for convenience to be the same at all points between the market and the material source. (Actually, it may vary from place to place.) This should be thought of as the average cost of production per unit in a plant of optimum size operated at its optimum output.

The top curve, labeled G + D + P, shows the total material-gathering, processing, and product distribution cost per unit for alternative locations. It is found by adding the three separate curves. Since this total curve is lowest at the extreme left it indicates the most economical location to be at the material source. The disadvantage of having to ship the final product a long distance is not so great as would be entailed in locating near the market and bringing the raw material a long distance to the plant. If it were lowest somewhere in between the two extremes, this would indicate the best location. This is more likely to occur if there is a dip in processing costs at some in-between point due to unusually low labor costs, cheap land, or some other special advantage.

An analysis of the curves G and D throws considerable light on some important factors of location. Both curves are concave downward, reflecting the lower rate per ton mile usually given for longer hauls compared with shorter ones. (This is a type of "quantity discount.") If a railroad, for example, gave an especially good distance rate on the raw material and a less favorable one on the finished good this would tend to promote location at the market. In terms of Figure 28.1 this rate structure would make the G curve bend downward more sharply than the *D* curve. This would tend to cause the total processing-and-transportation curve to be lowest at the market end.

Weight-losing Materials

In some manufacturing operations the principal raw material loses a great deal of weight in processing. This promotes location at the material source since it would clearly be uneconomical to incur heavy transportation charges on substances which are not incorporated in the finished product. An extreme example is gold ore, which is almost entirely discarded in processing. Gold refining consequently takes place right next to the gold mines. The same weight-losing property of the main material accounts heavily for many other locational decisions. For example, the paper industry is located near the forests, crab-meat processing takes place right where the crabs are caught, portland cement is made at the sources of suitable limestone, cotton is ginned near the cotton fields, and fruit juices are processed near the orchards. In some of these cases the material would deteriorate quickly if not processed, and this further increases the economy of location at the material source. In terms of the chart, the more weight-losing the material is, the greater the rise of the *G* curve from left to right and consequently the more likely it is that the total cost of production and transportation will be lowest at the material source.

Orientation to the Market

In other types of industries it would be more costly to transport the finished product a long distance compared with the principal material. In the manufacture of cans it is cheaper to ship the sheet metal a long distance than to ship the cans far owing to the more economical shape of the sheet metal for transport purposes. As a consequence, can manufacturing plants are found at the market, that is, near the plants which process food for canning. Some can manufacturing plants are located right next door to the food processors (*e.g.*, soup makers), and a conveyor belt between the buildings virtually makes the two assembly lines a continuous unit despite the separate ownership of the companies.

Bulky items such as farm machinery are manufactured near the market since the shape of the machinery makes it cheaper to transport the materials and components a long distance than to ship the finished product very far. If the finished product is markedly weight-gaining or volume-gaining, manufacture is likely to be market-oriented. An extreme example of weight and volume gain is found in the construction of a residential, commercial, or industrial building. In this case the "factory" is mobile and is moved to the very spot where the market exists. Building supplies are brought right to the market. The prefabricated housing industry utilizes large and stationary plants, but even these plants are market-oriented owing to the high cost of transporting the final product compared with the materials.

If the product is weight-gaining in nature, even though not particularly bulky, location near the market is likely to be economical. Sulfuric acid is an example of such a market-oriented product. Manufacture of this acid requires the addition of water and oxygen to the powdered sulfur. It would probably be unprofitable to produce sulfuric acid along the Gulf Coast for sale in the North despite the availability of sulfur deposits because this would mean incurring heavy freight charges for transporting water. The desirability of locating near the market is reinforced by the need to use substantial containers for the acid.

In terms of Figure 28.1, a high transport cost per unit for the finished product means a sharp rise of the D curve from right to left. This tends to cause the $G + D + P$ curve to be lowest at its market terminus.

Location at Either End

Some materials enter into the final product so fully that it makes little difference whether they are processed near their source or shipped a substantial distance to be processed near the market. Petroleum is an example. Refineries can be located economically either near the oil fields or near the large cities which are consuming centers for gasoline and other products. They are found, in fact, at both places. This is traceable to the completeness with which crude oil is processed into a number of products; it is not significantly weight-losing in nature. Also, there is no great difference in the cost per unit of transporting petroleum and gasoline.

Flour milling is also carried on economically either near the wheat fields or near the main markets. Wheat is not a great weight loser in the milling operation, and freight rates on wheat and flour are not greatly dissimilar, so the G and D curves rise about an equal distance at their extremities. Differences in processing costs are quite likely to swing the locational decision. A detailed study of the economics of plant location for the flour-milling industry would have to take into account the possibility of shipping to the East either by railroad or on the Great Lakes, the relative perishability of wheat and flour, the export market, and other factors. Frequently the locational forces are not nearly as simple as the above analysis may have suggested, especially when there are many important materials and markets. Yet many of the factors involved in the simpler analysis would enter importantly into the fuller analysis.

Land Use Pattern

An interesting attempt to evolve a theoretical picture of the type of economic activities which will take place at various distances from an important market, well isolated from others, was made by a German economist, von Thünen, in the nineteenth century. He considered a town in the middle of a large plain, with the land all of equal fertility. In this way he was able to concentrate on the effects of location in relation to the market. By assuming that the entire plain was well isolated by a wilderness from other areas of economic activity it was possible for von Thünen to avoid the complexity of having the value and use of some land affected by the possibility of serving two markets.

One conclusion from this model was that land located nearest the town would command the highest rent. The greater the distance from town the lower the rent would be; at a sufficient distance it would decline to zero. Optimum land use was closely related to rent. The most valuable land near the center would be used for producing such commodities as milk and green vegetables. A little farther away from the center, intensive cultivation of forest lands for building materials and fuel would take place. Grain and cattle would be raised at a still greater distance from town. The most extensive land use, for hunting and fishing, would take place in the most remote areas.

The basic idea in von Thünen's analytical scheme is that different types of commodities vary in their ability to bear transportation costs relative to rental costs. Fresh milk, for example, must be transported to town daily. Over a period of a year the total transportation cost would be great if it were not produced near the market. It is better for milk producers to pay high rental charges for close-in land than to be distant from the town. Cattle, on the other hand, would be sent to market less often (and may provide their own transportation) so cattlemen can minimize their costs by using distant, cheap land. Each land user should attempt to minimize the sum of his rental-plus-transportation costs, and this action not only determines land uses but also determines the rent on differently situated land.

Von Thünen's model still has significance, although it tends to become less descriptive of actual situations as a country develops. Milk production and truck gardening usually occur near the city. Cheese and butter are likely to be manufactured farther from the city since transportation cost is lower in relation to value. Land is unlikely nowadays to be cultivated intensively for fuel owing to the development of superior substitutes, but cattle grazing is still likely to take place quite far from the city.

Von Thünen's model helps make clear a basic function of land rent, whether the rent is based on differential fertility or on different locations with respect to market. This basic function is to allocate the land to the most economical use by shutting off inferior uses. That is, an enterpriser who attempts to use land in the downtown area of a city for a golf driving range will be unable to pay the rent from the proceeds of the business and will soon have to seek more peripheral land. The land will then be available for more appropriate uses such as hotels, banks, restaurants, and department stores. Both business and society will gain.

Locational Interdependence

A good many locational decisions are somewhat similar to oligopoly in that the reaction of rivals should be anticipated before a move is made. It may be better for a prospective motel owner to choose a location which is not the best presently available if this choice will make it impossible for another motel to be located on the same side of the road but in "front" of him with respect to the stream of traffic.

Sometimes a firm can profitably locate a branch plant to take advantage of a growing market but may have to consider whether a rival will also set up a plant in the territory. It may be that the move will be a good one only if a rival does not "match" his move into the new territory. Similar considerations may govern the location of retailers within a city.

The price policy of a firm is often related definitely to its location. A gasoline station located a few miles outside the city may attempt to cut prices just enough to coax a substantial number of city dwellers to drive there regularly for gasoline. A service station at the edge of a large swamp may take advantage of the situation by charging an unusually high price because of the absence of competitors over a long stretch. The swamp may help in two ways: motorists about to head into it may be afraid not to fill up first; and those who have just been through may be low on gas and afraid of getting into another swamp. A particularly aggressive entrepreneur may locate a filling station at each edge of the swamp and "take" the tourists both coming and going!

In general, the search for the best location for a plant involves the weighing of numerous factors, and the success or failure of an enterprise often depends on how well this is done. Nonspatial economic theory emphasizes such factors as the need to build plants of optimum size, to hire inputs in correct amounts and proportions, and to watch and anticipate the profitability of various alternative lines of business activity. In practice it is also necessary to pick a good plant site, usually from a bewilderingly large number of well-advertised alternative possibilities.

Demand, as well as cost, may depend on the location chosen. A furniture manufacturer may prefer to locate in and serve a small area where he has something of a monopoly than a much larger market where competition is intense. If he appears to be unusually prosperous, however, competitors are apt to move into the same territory in order to cut themselves in on the profit opportunity. Monopoly power, whether based on spatial or other considerations, is often only a temporary thing.

29

UNCERTAINTY, SPECULATION, AND HEDGING

One of the basic facts of life is that the future is uncertain. As a consequence, all holders of assets are necessarily speculators. The money value of any asset except cash itself may vary through time. And the value of cash in terms of goods for which it will exchange also varies. It has been noted that the value of money rises and falls with decreases and increases in the general level of prices. Fluctuations in security prices are constantly occurring and sometimes are of dramatic magnitude, as during the 1929 stock-market crash. Inventories, buildings, land, and other items of material wealth frequently change markedly in value in a short period of time.

Even the conservative individual who holds most of his wealth in the form of a deposit in a savings bank, in Series E government bonds, in shares of a building and loan association, or in life-insurance policies with cash surrender value is speculating (probably without realizing it), since the real value of his savings may be impaired by general price inflation or increased by deflation. Similarly, the profit position of a manufacturer may be affected more during a given year by changes in the value of his raw-material inventory than by his manufacturing and selling operations. Banks, insurance companies, and other institutions which hold large volumes of securities for purposes of earning interest are highly aware of changes in their market prices and are always ready to make portfolio adjustments which appear desirable.

Professional Speculation

Unlike the man who is only an inadvertent speculator, persons known as professional speculators buy and sell securities and commodities solely in the hope of selling at prices higher than those at which they buy. Their purposive speculative activity relates to *particular* price changes rather than to changes in the *general* price level, as is the case with the holder of cash or assets with a fixed cash value. Professional speculation is greatly facilitated by the existence of well-organized security and commodity markets such as the New York Stock Exchange, American Stock Exchange, New York Cotton Exchange, and Chicago Board of Trade.

The professional speculator who feels "bullish" about a particular asset (*i.e.*, expects its price to go up) will purchase the asset and hold it until he feels that the time to sell has arrived. His position during the interval between purchase and sale is known as a "long" one. His profit, if any, is the excess of the selling over the buying price, minus commissions and taxes.

In terms of asset preference, the speculator can be said to show preference for a security or commodity compared with money when he makes his purchases. When his desire for more liquid assets, his "liquidity preference," becomes sufficiently great, he converts the security or commodity into cash by selling it. The buyer, on the other hand, must prefer the security or commodity to cash at the price paid. A general increase in liquidity preference would clearly bring a wave of selling orders, which would lower security prices. This, of course, was the situation during the 1929 stock-market crash and in the early years of the great depression of the 1930's.

If a speculator feels "bearish" (*i.e.*, expects a fall in prices), he can, if correct, translate his expectation into a capital gain by taking a "short" position in a security or commodity. This means that he sells first at a specific price and commits himself to make delivery at a later date. He will profit if the asset falls in price so that he can subsequently buy it for less than the price at which he has already sold it.

In the security markets, the short seller first borrows the desired number of shares of the particular security from his broker. (Brokers regularly have possession of a considerable volume of securities which they are holding for the owners, and they cooperate with one another in making such shares available to short sellers.) Next he sells the security at the market price and receives a credit for the amount of the sale to his account with the broker. At a later date he must "cover" his sale by buying the same number of shares of the same security in the market, thus being able to return them to the broker. If his expectation of a price decline was correct, he profits by the transaction.

Dealings in commodities such as wheat, corn, cotton, and eggs are somewhat different, because of the quoting of "futures" prices as well as "spot" prices. Spot prices are simply prices quoted for immediate delivery of the commodity. (These are the only prices quoted for securities.) Those who actually want to buy commodities usually do so in the spot or "cash" market. Here the exact type and grade of commodity needed can be obtained. The "futures" market in the same commodity is quite separate from the cash market. Futures prices are presently quoted prices applicable to delivery at a future date. They are quoted in terms of a "standard" grade of the commodity and hence the futures market is usually not suitable for those who actually want to buy a commodity for processing or other use. For example, the spot price of a particular grade of wheat in the Chicago market might be $2.35 per bushel on November 1. On the same day the price of wheat to be delivered in December may be $2.38. March wheat may sell at $2.45, May wheat at $2.48, and July wheat at $2.47. These futures prices quoted on November 1 may be thought of as the spot prices then expected to prevail (on the standard grade) when those future dates arrive. Different persons, of course, have unlike expectations as to what spot prices will be, but the futures prices reflect a consensus of opinion determined by traders' buying and selling actions.

A grain speculator who possesses storage capacity and who entertains bullish expectations regarding prices can, if he wishes, buy spot grain and store it until a future date in the hope of selling it at a profit (even after paying for the storage services). If he does not possess the storage space, he may rent it. A simpler practice, however, is to make use of the futures market. If the speculator were confronted on November 1 with the price quotations indicated above, but believed that next July wheat would sell for more than $2.47 per bushel, he could *buy* July wheat, thereby contracting to accept delivery. If he acts on this opinion and it turns out to be right, he can profit by the difference between the $2.47 which he will pay and the higher price at which he can sell the wheat in July.[1] Conversely, if he believes on November 1 that the price in July will be below $2.47, he can *sell* July wheat. If this bearish position (similar to a short position in the stock market) is correct, he will profit by the price decline because he can buy July wheat in July (or perhaps earlier) and thus offset his earlier sale. He is unlikely actually to bother with wheat. Instead he deals solely in wheat contracts.

SPECULATION AND SOCIETY

Speculation has often been criticized, and it has been made the scapegoat by some politicians for depression, unemployment, inflation, and almost every other economic evil. Prices in the speculative markets (security and commodity) do depend to a greater degree on expectations than prices in other markets. For this reason, if a threat of deflation causes traders to become pessimistic (bearish), the speculative markets may aggravate the downswing, and security prices may fall sooner and faster than other prices. On the other hand, if inflation is in the offing, and this is anticipated by professional speculators, security prices tend to lead the general price increase and in this way make the inflation worse by creating unduly optimistic expectations.[2] The recession of early 1958 was reflected first in a stock-market decline which started in the summer of 1957.

It is clear, however, that the existence of organized security and commodity markets along with the activity of professional speculators serves a positive social function. Speculators in securities create a more active market which facilitates purchases and sales by individual investors. The availability of such a market tends to encourage the flow of personal savings into equity shares (common stocks). The social usefulness of commodity speculation is even more evident. First of all, it allows the rate of consumption of periodically harvested commodities to be regulated without governmental interference. Second, commodity speculation permits cer-

---

[1] Actually, the contract may change hands many times between November and July, finally coming into the possession of someone who actually wants to accept delivery of the wheat.

[2] The inflation following World War II was not characterized in this way. This inflation was prevented from becoming worse than it actually was by a sort of "depression psychosis" born out of the long depression of the 1930's.

tain types of business firms to remove some uncertainty by "hedging," which will be discussed later.

Regarding the first point, if it is to carry out its rationing function properly with respect to agricultural crops which appear at particular seasons, price must move in such a way as to retard consumption which is proceeding at too fast a rate and to encourage consumption if stocks are being used too slowly. Suppose the rye crop is being consumed too rapidly. Speculators, anticipating a price rise prior to appearance of the next harvest, can (1) buy spot rye and store it and (2) buy rye futures. Both actions tend to raise spot prices for rye. In the first case the increased demand directly raises spot prices. In the second case the increased demand raises futures prices, and this in turn, makes it more profitable for speculators to buy rye and store it, thus indirectly raising spot prices. Higher spot prices retard the rate of use of the existing stock. Thus speculators' vigilance, based on self-interest, promotes a more even utilization of supplies. A similar force operates to increase the rate of use of agricultural stocks when they are being consumed too slowly, spot prices being depressed by speculators' selling orders in the spot and futures markets.

PUTS AND CALLS

It is not even necessary to deal in actual stocks in order to speculate on the stock market. Instead, one can buy *options* on stocks which require less capital even than margin dealings in securities. These options are called "puts" and "calls." Formerly they were used in United States commodity markets but are now confined to the stock markets in this country. They are something of a substitute for a futures market in stocks.

A put is a contract under which the buyer has the option of delivering to the seller a specified number of shares of a certain stock at a specified price until a certain date. If he finds it advantageous to do so the holder of this sort of option can "put" the stock to the person who sold him the option. This action will be advantageous if the stock falls in price below that which was specified in the put contract.

Suppose one anticipates a fall in the price of copper and, consequently, a decline in Anaconda common. Instead of selling short, one might buy a 90-day put on 100 shares of this stock. This might cost $350, for example, and allow the owner of the option to deliver it to the seller (maker) of the option at $48 per share. If the bearish expectation regarding Anaconda is correct it would be worthwhile to exercise the option. Suppose it fell to $42 a share in the New York Stock Exchange. The option seller would have to pay $4,800 for stock which the option buyer could get in the market for $4,200. The put buyer would make a profit of $600 minus the $350 which he paid for the option and minus commissions and taxes. On the other hand, if the stock went up in price, he would not exercise the option and would lose his $350.

The purchase of a call option has the opposite motivation, namely, a belief that the stock in question will increase in price. The buyer of the call has paid for the privilege of calling the stock away from the option seller at a specified price. He will do so if the market value goes above the call price, and can make a speculative profit if the stock goes up enough to more than cover the cost of the option.

In the case of both puts and calls the sellers are usually large stockholders who can furnish the options as needed by the put and call brokers. Option sellers secure substantial income from these options at the expense of sacrificing possible capital gains on stocks. The seller of a call, for example, will have stock called away from him if it goes up in price. But the income received by selling options can do much to balm his feelings.

Hedging

As has been indicated, professional speculators are useful in making possible, in some lines of business activity, a pattern of action known as hedging. Hedging can be defined roughly as betting in two opposite ways on the same thing. Normally, however, this does not make sense, especially if the odds are the same on each bet. If, for example, the betting odds on an election were even, it would not make sense to bet $50 on the Republican and an equal amount on the Democrat. If, however, you were under some sort of outside compulsion to bet on one candidate—for example, if the Democrat were your prospective father-in-law—it might be wise openly to bet on him and surreptitiously to bet an equal amount on his opponent. Whoever won, you would break even, but at the same time you would be improving your chances of being considered a good catch—unless your hedge was discovered.

The above example illustrates a basic reason for hedging by businessmen, namely, to offset speculative positions which they are forced to assume as incident to carrying on their regular business activity. The purchase of insurance is a type of hedging. If a businessman owns a building and takes out fire insurance, he is, in effect, placing a bet that his building will burn down. Since the premium is relatively low, because of the small proportion of buildings which actually burn down during any given year, his asset position will not be drastically impaired whether or not the event insured against occurs. Similarly, the purchase of life insurance (which should really be called by the more sinister name "death insurance") is a hedge against loss of income to the family in the event of the insured's demise.[1] It is essentially a bet with the company that one will die within a certain period. (A heavenly hedge?)

The varieties of hedging which are of greatest economic interest consist of actions taken as protection against *unfavorable price changes*. A person of considerable wealth, for example, can hedge against unfavorable changes in the general price level by keeping part of his wealth in assets which are of a fixed money value (such as deposits in building and loan associations) and the rest in assets which can fluctuate in dollar value, such as common stocks and real estate. In a period of inflation his cash and other assets of fixed monetary value will decline in real value, but his real estate and stocks will probably maintain their real value or gain in this respect. In a period of deflation, the gain in real value of cash and similar assets will tend to offset the probable reduction in the dollar value of his other holdings.

HEDGING IN THE COMMODITY MARKETS

Hedging is frequently practiced in businesses where storage is a regular part of the operations. If a sizable inventory of eggs, wheat, cotton, or other commodities is held—or if substantial inventories of processed goods containing these materials are held—the businessman is in an inherently risky position since he will have to take a capital loss in the event of a price decline. In order to offset his risky "long" position in a commodity, the businessman must take a "short" position in the same commodity. This is done by selling the commodity in the futures market—thus committing himself to make delivery of a certain amount at a specified price during a specified future month.

[1] Insurance should not be bought against the life of (ordinary) children since, from an economic point of view, they are liabilities rather than assets. (Farm children are sometimes an exception.) This is not to say that it is necessarily unwise to buy a typical "insurance policy" which may actually embody more saving than actual insurance.

As a more specific example, many textile mills buy spot cotton early in the season as a raw material. Their business thus requires that they take a long position in cotton. To protect against a capital loss the mills sell cotton futures in roughly an equal amount. As orders are received for textiles (which in effect assures a definite price for an equivalent amount of cotton which is on hand) the corresponding futures sale is offset by a futures purchase of equal amount. If cotton has gone up in price, the price received for textiles would reflect this increase and, in effect, a capital gain will have been realized on the cotton. A roughly similar capital loss will have occurred on the cotton futures. The hedge will have turned out to be unfortunate (like the purchase of insurance if no calamity actually occurs). However, if the cash price of cotton falls, the hedge will prevent a capital loss, since cotton futures will fall roughly the same amount. A speculative profit in the futures market will roughly offset the loss on stored cotton reflected in the lower prices at which cotton textiles can be sold. As the mill works off its cotton inventory it makes futures purchases, providing protection over the necessary period.

AN OPPOSITE HEDGE

The textile mills in the above example had to sell short in order to protect long positions. Many businesses require entering the futures markets on the long side instead to protect a short position. A candy manufacturer, for example, may be asked in August to quote definite prices for candy to be delivered for the Christmas season. Once he makes contracts for such delivery he is "short" on candy. He can hedge by immediately buying November sugar in approximately the amount he needs. This is an offsetting long position. In November he will go to the spot sugar market in order to buy the sugar he needs for the Christmas candy. (While he could simply accept delivery on his November sugar futures contract, the spot market is where he is likely to get the exact type of sugar which he needs and where he needs it.) Then to offset the earlier purchase of November futures he sells November sugar futures in an equal amount. If the thing he feared in August—an increase in the price of sugar—actually occurred he may not do well on his candy sale because of increased costs, but he will have a profit in the futures market to improve his net income.

Or suppose a road-builder has contracted with a state to construct a particular stretch of highway for a certain price. He is "short on road." He can at least partially hedge by acquiring contracts immediately calling for delivery of materials at definite prices as he needs them. He can also acquire or rent necessary machinery immediately in order to have less worry about an increase in cost from this source. If his labor is unionized he can attempt to negotiate a contract calling for a definite wage rate over the road-building period.

HEDGING BY FINANCIAL INSTITUTIONS

The asset holdings of financial institutions such as insurance companies, building and loan associations, investment trusts, and commercial credit corporations are subject to value fluctuations; consequently, hedging is often vitally important to conservative management. The hedging process in this case does not involve the use of futures markets but consists rather in arriving at a pattern of asset holding which offers some protection against a decline in security prices.

Managers of financial institutions are constantly torn between two conflicting desires. On the one hand, they like to see interest rates rise so that they can secure a greater return on *new* funds placed in their care or on cash which becomes available when maturity dates are reached for bonds which they own. On the other hand, higher market interest rates mean lower market prices for bonds already in their portfolios. These paper capital losses would be transferred into actual capital losses if the bonds were sold.

In order to make this important point clear, let us consider a corporate bond with a $100 face value which pays $4 per year in interest. This indicates that if the bond were originally sold at par, the market rate of interest at the time of issue was 4 per cent for bonds with similar risk characteristics and maturity dates. Suppose the market rate of interest rises to 5 per cent. The bond which we are now considering must fall in market price; no sensible buyer will now pay $100 for it, since it pays $4 per year in interest whereas $100 used to purchase a newly issued bond will yield $5 per year. If the older bond had no maturity date (as was true of British "consols"), it would fall to $80 in market price ($C = \$4/.05$). If it had a very distant maturity date (say 1999), it would fall nearly that much in price. If, however, it was due to mature (*i.e.*, return the $100 face value) in the near future, it would fall only slightly in price. Financial institutions and other holders of marketable bonds are fearful of increases in interest rates to the extent that they hold bonds bearing distant maturity dates. At the same time, as we have just said, they favor higher interest rates in so far as they have new funds with which to purchase securities because of the favorable income effects.

Hedging on the part of financial institutions is inherently more difficult in nature than the variety, previously discussed, involving futures markets. The manager of the financial institution has available no clean-cut transaction which will neatly counterbalance an unfavorable price movement. He is forced by the nature of the business to take a substantial long position in bonds in order to secure interest income. But if he wishes to be conservative, he must keep a part of the company assets in the form of cash or short-term securities. The cash will not be affected in value by a change in interest rates, and short-term bonds will fall only slightly in market price if interest rates rise. (Also, if the latter are held for a short period until maturity, no capital loss at all need be taken if they were bought at par.)

Suppose the cash and bond holdings of a small financial institution (other than a bank) were as follows:

Cash	$10,000
Short-term bonds	20,000
Long-term bonds	50,000

No interest will be earned on the cash, a low rate of return will probably be earned on the short-term bonds, and a higher rate of interest will be earned on the long-term bonds. Some of the cash may be needed as a working balance to carry on current transactions, but the remainder and the short-term bonds should be considered a hedge against the possibility of a rise in interest rates (fall in bond prices). The cost of the hedge is the additional interest which could be earned if only long-term bonds were held.

Bullish or bearish sentiment, that is, expectations of increases or decreases in security prices, will also affect the pattern of asset preference. If bond prices are expected to rise, the desire to hold cash is diminished. If bond prices are expected to fall, the desire to hold cash will be greater.

Uncertainty and Profit

Uncertainty which cannot be turned into a definite cost by means of buying insurance or reduced in importance through other sorts of hedging provides the reason for the existence of profits (both positive and negative) in a competitive capitalistic society.[1] If uncertainty were absent the return on capital goods would consist only of interest. Quasi-rents received from the use of capital goods would exactly cover just depreciation and interest since there would be no surprises to cause excesses or deficiencies of supply in relation to demand. Perfect foresight would ensure just the right allocation of resources to each use.

In practice anticipation is imperfect, of course, so that firms usually are receiving either more or less than a normal interest return on invested capital. When this return is positive economists say they are making "profits," while "losses" are suffered if less than a normal rate of return is received.

This differs from the accountant's definition of profit because the economist includes a normal return as a cost of production while the accountant does not. The accountant designates as "profit" or "net income" the amount left over out of gross income after costs. However, his costs do not include any return on the capital secured through the sale of stock or the retention of earnings in a business. Interest is an accounting cost only if it is explicitly paid on capital borrowed from a bank, by selling bonds, or in a similar way. Also, the accountant does not enter the alternative earnings of a self-employed man (*e.g.*, one who runs his own filling station) as a cost. In economics this is a cost.

The distinction is of great practical importance because of the corporation income tax. If a corporation raises new capital by selling bonds, the interest paid on this loan is deductible as a cost before computing net income for income-tax purposes. If the same amount is invested in the corporation out of retained profits or from the sale of stock, no cost deduction may be made for normal interest on this amount of capital. As a result, corporations have in recent years been selling more bonds than stock. This creates a capital structure which tends to cause more business failures in a depression because bond interest, unlike stock dividends, cannot be skipped in lean years.

Determination of Market Rate of Interest

The interest rate which must be paid on bonds and other I O U's is also influential in determining how much firms will borrow. The

---

[1] The uncertainty theory of profit is due to Frank H. Knight and is set forth in his *Risk, Uncertainty, and Profit* (Boston: Houghton Mifflin Company, 1921).

FIGURE 29.1. SUPPLY AND DEMAND—Also
Determine Interest Rate

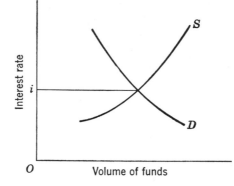

lower the interest rate the more investment projects will appear worth undertaking, because interest paid is a cost of undertaking investments whereas interest earned from them is income. Also, at lower interest rates consumers will be willing and able to borrow more and the same will be true of many governmental bodies.

The demand curve for loanable funds at any time is down-sloping from left to right when quantity demanded is related to the interest rate. The supply of loanable funds has a positive slope because higher interest rates will make it worthwhile for banks, insurance companies, and other lenders to supply more funds to the market. Figure 29.1 shows the demand and supply for loanable funds at a given time.

The interest rate Oi is the rate which equates the amount of funds demanded and the amount supplied.[1] This can most easily be considered to be the yield on Federal government bonds—a low yield due to low risk of loss. Interest rates on more risky loans will tend to move with this rate, but at a higher level. Since the usefulness of any theory is to aid prediction, what predictions does the loanable funds theory of the interest rate permit? For example, what effect would a recession have on the interest rate? The most significant effect of a recession would probably be a reduction in the demand for loanable funds owing to poorer investment prospects and, perhaps, to a cutback in installment buy-

---

[1] The supply curve should be considered to include the funds which creditors continue to supply by their willingness to hold old I O U's. Similarly, the demand curve includes funds which continue to be demanded by borrowers who have debts outstanding. For most purposes, however, the chart can be considered simply to show the supply and demand for new savings in a given time period.

ing by consumers. If supply is relatively steady, this will reduce interest rates. Bond prices may well rise in a recession, unless business becomes so poor as to threaten the ability of debtors to pay interest and repay principal. Actually, bond prices did increase in the early part of the 1957–1958 recession.

Federal Reserve actions such as decreasing the required reserve ratios will increase the supply of loanable funds and this will tend to cause interest rates to fall. An important new field for investment, such as may be created by new developments in the peaceful use of atomic energy, would increase the demand for loanable funds and hence would tend to increase interest rates.

A general increase in liquidity preference stemming from pessimism regarding the near-future outlook for business will reduce the supply of loanable funds; individuals with cash savings will have to be offered higher interest returns in order to be coaxed to lend any given amount. This decrease in supply may offset the decrease in demand for funds mentioned above as likely to occur in a recession. If the Federal Reserve System offsets the increase in liquidity preference by steps to ease credit, however, a business recession is very likely to cause interest rates to fall.

30

THE NATURAL MONOPOLIES

The public-utility industries, particularly those in the areas of transportation, communication, and power, have traditionally been considered in the United States as representing a unique industrial category in which competition is unworkable. Even those who have advocated vigorous antimonopoly policies in general have felt that monopoly in the public utilities is unavoidable, and it has often been argued that in many respects monopoly in this field is desirable. Public utilities are, it has often been said, "natural" monopolies. Utility companies often, for example, utilize the streets for street railway tracks, electric-light cables, or gas lines. Even if a city had very wide streets, probably not more than two street-car companies could lay their tracks down the principal avenues. If several gas companies had their mains buried under the streets, repairs to the lines would probably keep the streets torn up much of the time. Overhead power and telephone lines are unsightly at best, and if a community were served by several companies, the aesthetic offense would be unnecessarily multiplied.

In addition to the practical and aesthetic arguments advanced against the maintenance of competition in the public-utility area, it has been argued that there are significant economic reasons for setting up monopolies in this field. First, it is pointed out that frequently public-utility firms have very high fixed costs and relatively low variable costs. It follows, accordingly, that as the firm's output increases over a wide range, the cost of producing a unit of service is likely to fall. In railroading, for example, the firm has a tremendous investment in land, tracks, bridges, tunnels, rolling stock, freight and passenger stations, repair shops, and so on. The expense of maintaining these properties goes on largely independently of the amount of traffic hauled by the railroad. The marginal or "out-of-pocket" cost of hauling an additional barrel of flour, for example, may be pretty nearly zero, and even the shipment of an entire trainload of wheat may add relatively little to the company's total cost. As a consequence, within very broad limits, the more traffic the railroad hauls, the smaller will be the average cost (per ton-mile) of the service rendered. In similar fashion it may be argued that if four or five electric-power companies served the same community there would be an unnecessary duplication of expensive specialized capital equipment, and it is likely that no firm would be able to use its facilities at the minimum-cost output.

Furthermore, it has been observed that in many public-utility areas the economies of large-scale production are so great that, within limits, the larger the plant the lower are the average costs of production. Because of increasing returns to scale, a firm using a small plant would not be able to compete with a firm using a larger plant. It is concluded, therefore, that in the nature of things public utilities must be monopolies; public utilities are "natural" monopolies.

Second in significance to the monopolistic character of public utilities is the fact that they render services which are economically important. Modern economic life could not continue without fundamental change if an urban area were deprived of the services of electric, gas, water, railroad, telephone, or telegraph companies. For most of these services only unsatisfactory substitutes are available. Society has, accordingly, found itself in the dilemma of depending on private monopolies for certain important services. Unwilling, at least without a struggle, to pay monopoly profits to private concerns for rendering indispensable services, policy makers have usually resorted to the device of issuing exclusive franchises to public-utility companies and then subjecting the firms to regulation, usually by public-utility commissions. In this way it is hoped that the public can gain the advantages of large-scale production while avoiding the risk of exploitation at the hands of the private monopolies. It is with the strengths and shortcomings of this system that we are concerned in this chapter.

The Nature of Public Utilities

That public-utility companies are unlike department stores or the corner grocery in certain fundamental respects is undeniable. It seems clear that because of certain practical and economic considerations some public utilities must be operated as local monopolies, and, if they are monopolies, the public interest requires either that they be owned outright by the government—Federal, state, or local—or that they be subjected to public regulation. But it does not follow simply because public utilities are monopolies that there cannot be problems of excessive monopoly even in this area; and there is a hazard that industries which are not in fact "natural" monopolies will seek public-utility status in order to be rendered legal monopolies and thus escape the rigors of competition. If regulation were completely effective, *i.e.*, if utility companies were in fact deprived of all monopoly profits, this last point would be of little economic consequence. But, as we shall see, the regulation of privately owned public utilities poses real practical problems even when the theoretical issues are clearly understood by those charged with the responsibility of regulating rates and services in the public interest. And in numerous instances utility regulation in practice seems designed to protect the utility company rather than the general public.

It should be recognized that governments have not, in fact, limited their regulatory activities to the public-utility industries. The Federal and state governments have at various times and places imposed direct regulations on almost every type of industry, usually under the guise of claiming that the industry in question was "affected with a public interest." Whether or not a business was affected with a public interest has been the center of many a stormy legal controversy. Since 1934 court decisions have, however, made it clear that government regulation may be extended to almost any industry in the economy.

The regulation of industries which do not fit the public-utility category will not be discussed here. The dividing line between what is and what is not a public utility is legally obscure, but we shall confine our attention in this chapter to firms in the areas of communication, transportation, water, and power, where perhaps the only genuine cases of natural monopoly may be found. These public utilities are characterized as follows:

1. A public utility usually operates under an exclusive franchise granted by a governmental unit. An electric-power company, for example, receives from the city government the exclusive right to provide electric power to all buyers in the municipality. The power company is then not only a natural monopoly but a legal monopoly as well; there can be no competition from another power company for the life of the franchise.

2. A public-utility company usually has the power of eminent domain, *i.e.*, the power to take private property for public use after fair compensation. This is a power normally reserved for the government alone.

3. A public-utility company is subject to government regulation, usually by a public-utility commission, but it is entitled to reasonable compensation—a "fair" return.

4. A utility company is required to render adequate service to all comers.

5. A utility company is required to charge "reasonable" rates, and it is prohibited from discriminating among customers of the same class. "Reasonable" rates are presumed to be those which will provide the company with a "fair" return.

Economics of Public Utilities

Let us apply techniques of economic analysis to the problems of public-utility regulation in an effort to evaluate policies in this area. We shall first investigate the implications of the fact that utility companies enjoy increasing returns to scale of plant. It will be assumed in what follows that the firm has only a single plant and that no distinction need be made between economies of scale for plant and firm.

Because of certain technical factors many utility companies, particularly those in the fields of gas and electric power, are characterized by decreasing costs as the size of the plant increases. In most market areas the demand for electric power is insufficient to justify the construction of the optimum-sized production and distribution system. As was pointed out in Chapter 24, a company contemplating the building of a new plant is confronted with a choice as to scale. A relatively small plant, as, for example a_1 in Figure 30.1, would have higher average costs than a larger plant, *e.g.*, a_2. The optimum-sized plant would be a_5, which could produce

FIGURE 30.1. INCREASING RETURNS TO SCALE—May Create Natural Monopolies

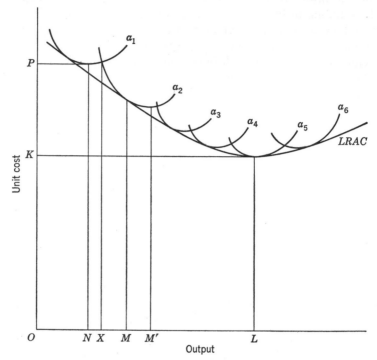

an output of *OL* at a cost per unit of *OK*. If the market is too small to justify a plant of this size, a smaller one will be constructed. If it is anticipated that less than *OX* units will be sold per time period, plant a_1 will be preferred to a_2. If the anticipated output is *OM*, that output can be produced by plant a_2 at a lower cost than by any other size plant.

Suppose that there are no restrictions upon competition and a market is currently being served by a firm with a plant of the a_1 size. If demand is sufficient and a new company builds a plant of a_2 size, it will be able to undersell the first plant; at any price below *OP* the first plant will be selling below cost while the larger plant will be able to sell at a price somewhat below *OP* and enjoy considerable profit. If competition is allowed to operate without restriction in this situation, either the first company will be forced out of business or the two companies will get together and agree on a price which will provide monopoly profits to one or both concerns. In neither case will the consumers' interest be protected by

FIGURE 30.2. DECREASING SHORT-RUN COSTS—
Characterize Long-run Equilibrium

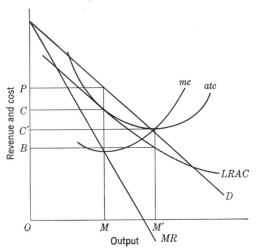

the competitive forces of the market. This is sometimes expressed by saying that decreasing costs and competition are incompatible.

Figure 30.2 represents the cost and revenue data for firm a_2 of Figure 30.1. *LRAC* is the long-run average cost curve. The firm's short-run average cost curve is *atc*, and its short-run marginal cost curve is *mc*. *D* is the market demand curve, and *MR* is the firm's marginal revenue curve. In the long-run equilibrium position the firm will operate to the point where *MR* = *mc* and *atc* = *LRAC*. At this output the price would be *OP*, the average cost would be *OC*, and the profit per unit of output would be *CP*. The following points should be noted:

1. This firm can produce the output *OM* at a lower cost than it could with a plant of any other size. This follows from the fact that the *LRAC* curve indicates the lowest cost at which any output can be produced, and at output *OM*, *LRAC* = *atc*.

2. Although this plant can produce an output of *OM* at a lower cost than any other larger or smaller plant, it can produce the larger output *OM'* at even lower cost, *i.e.*, *OC'* is less than *OC*.

3. Although this plant can produce *OM'* units at a lower cost than it can produce *OM* units, a larger plant could produce *OM'* units of output at a lower cost per unit than this firm can; *OB* is less than *OC'*.

Two conclusions follow from this analysis: (1) In an industry characterized by decreasing long-run costs each firm in the industry will, if it is in long-run equilibrium and is maximizing profits, operate under conditions of short-run decreasing costs, *i.e.*, to the left of the lowest point on the short-run average cost curve. (2) In an industry characterized by decreasing costs competition tends to become "cut throat" or "ruinous," with monopoly finally emerging.

To the extent that the assumptions made in this analysis correspond with reality in the public-utility field, the conclusion is that rates and services cannot be regulated by competition, but monopoly is the inevitable and "natural" state for these industries. The pressures for increasing output and thereby reducing costs, both in the short run and in the long run, will be so great that every effort will be made by firms to undersell competitors until all competition has disappeared. It is clear, however, that the advantages of increasing size are not without limit, and in recent years there seems to have been some tendency for plants of smaller size to be substituted for larger plants in the production and distribution of electric power.

As was pointed out in Chapter 6, the desire to hold some degree of monopoly power is universal among sellers, and managers of public-utility companies are no exception. It has been insisted by some writers, in fact, that the concept of a natural monopoly is largely a fiction invented to justify exclusive markets for public-utility companies.[1] On two points we can be reasonably sure: (1) Even if local monopolies of public utilities are necessary, and it seems that they are, it does not necessarily follow that public utilities should be national or regional monopolies. Except where hydroelectric resources can best be exploited by very large plants, for example, it does not appear that an electric generating and distributing system large enough to supply power to fifty communities has a significant cost advantage over a plant designed to serve a much smaller market. (2) Although we have assumed that when competition cannot be relied upon to maintain "fair" prices it becomes necessary for the state to regulate public utilities to protect the general interest, a number of industries have been regulated as public utilities for reasons other than the protection of consumers. Some firms, such as taxicab companies, have sought public-utility status because they have felt that the gains from exclusive markets outweigh the disadvantages of public regulation.

[1] See Horace M. Gray, "The Passing of the Public Utility Concept," *The Journal of Land and Public Utility Economics*, Vol. 16, pp. 8–20 (February, 1940).

In other cases, such as interstate motor trucks and vans, regulation was imposed not to protect consumers but to protect the railroads with which the trucks and vans compete. There is, of course, no simple formula for determining when an industry is so affected with a public interest as to make it a public utility, but the public interest requires that legal monopolies be no more numerous or extensive than is necessary. Since, as will be demonstrated later in this chapter, public regulation of monopolies is at best a poor substitute for competition, its scope should be restricted to those areas where competition is clearly unworkable.

RATE REGULATION IN PRINCIPLE

In regulating public-utility monopolies the courts have laid down the principle that the utility is entitled to a "fair return on a fair value." To allow more than a fair return would be to permit the firm to enjoy monopoly profits; to allow less than a fair return would be to deprive the firm of property without due process of law, and such a rate would be declared unconstitutional.

Let us suppose that Figure 30.3 represents the short-run cost and revenue data for a local utility firm. If the firm were allowed to operate as a private monopoly and it attempted to maximize profits, it would produce *OM* units of output and sell them at a price of *MP* per unit. A "fair" rate, on the other hand, would be represented by *OR*, since this is the rate at which price equals average total cost, on the assumption that average cost includes

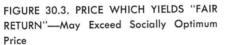

FIGURE 30.3. PRICE WHICH YIELDS "FAIR RETURN"—May Exceed Socially Optimum Price

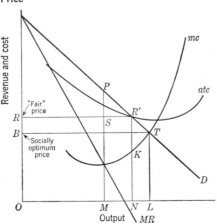

a "normal" or "fair" rate of return on capital investment. The output under such regulation would be *MN* units greater than under unrestrained monopoly, and the price would be lower by *PS*.

It should be noted, however, that while the regulated price, *OR* or *NR'*, is equal to average total cost, it is greater than marginal cost. Marginal cost at output *ON* is only *NK*, thus indicating that output is still too low in terms of the ideal allocation of resources. This follows from the fact that marginal cost represents the amount of additional resources required to put an additional unit of the service on the market; price represents the amount consumers are willing to give up in order to secure the additional unit. As long as price exceeds marginal cost, more resources should be devoted to the production of the service—consumers prefer an additional unit of this service to anything else the resources might be used to produce. The ideal price from the resource-allocation point of view would therefore be *LT*, and the ideal output *OL*.

It should be recalled from the analysis in earlier chapters that under purely competitive conditions price equals marginal cost, and the optimum allocation of economic resources is thereby achieved. But under conditions of perfect competition, price is also equal to average cost, so that in long-run equilibrium firms neither make abnormal profits nor incur losses. Rate regulation for public-utility companies poses, therefore, a policy dilemma. If prices are set at average cost levels (*OR* in our example), the output of the utility may be restricted below that which is socially most desirable in terms of consumer sovereignty. On the other hand, if price is set at marginal cost levels, the utility company may be unable to cover average costs and thus suffer losses, or it may make abnormal or monopoly profits. In our geometrical example, marginal cost pricing would cause the utility company to incur losses, since price falls below average costs. If, however, the demand curve were to intersect the marginal cost curve somewhere to the right of the lowest point on the average total cost curve, marginal cost pricing would allow the company to secure an abnormal return.

In actual practice utility commissioners have followed the rule of "fair" return and have made an attempt to keep prices at average cost levels. As a result, output in the utility industries may be below or above that which is socially most desirable. A simple example may be cited to illustrate the point. Suppose that a toll bridge is constructed. It is estimated that the annual cost of interest plus amortization charges on the original cost of construction is $100,000. It is further estimated that 100,000 vehicles will travel over the bridge each year. Average cost pricing of the bridge would require, therefore, that toll charges be $1 per vehicle. (The fact that this bridge normally would be owned by government rather than a private company makes no difference in our analysis.) But the actual cost of resources "used up" in moving an additional vehicle across the bridge may be very slight, perhaps 10 cents. Let us suppose that there are several ferryboats operating near this bridge, and a reasonably competitive price of 50 cents per vehicle is established. Now this 50-cent price pretty well reflects the additional cost of moving a vehicle across the river by ferry. Many motorists will travel by ferry and pay 50 cents rather than pay $1 to go across the bridge. But if they travel by ferry, they will actually use up 50 cents' worth of economic resources, whereas if they had traveled by bridge they would have used only 10 cents' worth. This indicates that the practice of setting toll rates at average cost results in restricting unduly the use of the bridge and promoting a socially undesirable utilization of the ferryboats. But unless average cost prices are charged, how can the bridge be paid for?

Presumably an all-wise socialist state could set prices at marginal cost levels, subsidizing some industries and taxing others, but a further problem is raised when long-run considerations are taken into account. If marginal cost pricing were adopted, the optimum allocation of resources would be achieved once the bridge was constructed. But how could the decision ever be made whether to build the bridge in the first place? About the only criterion available for such a decision is "will it pay?" And to make a project pay, average cost pricing is almost necessary.

We must conclude that the setting of utility rates by commission, no matter how wise and objective the rate-setting body happens to be, can rarely achieve socially optimum results. Such rate setting does serve the interests of consumers better than unrestrained private monopoly would, but at best commission regulation fails to utilize resources in full accordance with consumer preference.

Our theoretical model suggests one more shortcoming of commission regulation of public utilities. Since the company is legally entitled to a fair return, *i.e.*, a normal profit above costs, there is little incentive for the firm to attempt to cut costs. If by improving efficiency and curtailing all unnecessary expenses the firm is able to reduce average costs, the old rates will then provide a surplus above costs, and the firm will be enjoying monopoly profits. Since the company will be making more than a fair return, the logic of utility regulation would require that the rates be lowered. Since, in fact, rates are not adjusted frequently, an increase in efficiency may for a time increase the profits of the firm, and this may be sufficient inducement for the introduction of cost-reducing innovations. But clearly the same incentives for cost cutting do not exist in a regulated monopoly that operate in a highly competitive industry, and in some instances it appears that there is a premium on inefficiency in the regulated utilities. The difference between the strength of the incentives for greater efficiency in privately owned public utilities and those operated by a governmental unit probably is not great.

RATE REGULATION IN PRACTICE

We have so far examined some of the theoretical difficulties involved in the setting of utility rates by public authorities. There are, in addition, some extremely troublesome practical problems in utility-rate determination which deserve brief attention here. In the famous case of *Smyth v. Ames* (1898), the Supreme Court stated that railroads and other public utilities are entitled to a "fair return on the fair value" of property being used for the convenience of the public. The courts have had great difficulty in determining what is fair in both instances.

"Fairness" of a rate of return on capital depends in large measure on the riskiness of the investment. A return of $2\frac{1}{2}$ or 3 per cent may be appropriate on a United States government bond, while 20 per cent might be consistent with the risk of investing in a Central American oil property where the authorities might decide suddenly to expropriate all foreign-owned oil wells. In general, the riskiness of investment in the utility fields is low—at least where the industry is properly a regulated public utility—because close competition is, and should be, absent. On this account a relatively low rate of return should make it possible for utilities to attract sufficient working capital. Utility investors and officials are, of course, anxious to receive the highest possible rate of return on their investment. Administrative commissions and courts have no clear-cut criteria to follow in arriving at what constitutes a fair rate of return, and they must resort to largely arbitrary judgment, which is often influenced by the amount of pressure brought to bear by interested groups. Generally the courts have held that a return of 6 to 8 per cent was "fair," and in recent years a return of 5 per cent or less has sometimes been considered adequate. But if 5 per cent is a fair return, it is to be 5 per cent of what?

This raises the question of how to compute the "fair value" of utility property. The Supreme Court in *Smyth v. Ames* set forth a confused array of considerations to be taken into account by regulatory commissions, including: (1) original cost of construction, (2) the amount expended in permanent improvements, (3) the amount and market value of its bonds and stocks, and (4) the present as compared with the original cost of construction.

Of these several considerations which the Court said must be taken into account in determining the value of utility property, the market value of the company's securities is clearly the most inappropriate. The value of the company's securities might be helpful in determining the valuation of a firm's property for some purposes, *e.g.*, a valuation for tax purposes. But the market value of the company's stocks cannot properly be used to determine appropriate rates, since the value of the stocks depends upon the rates charged. Virtually any rate could be justified if the market value of the company's stocks were used to determine "fair value." If the commission sets very low rates, the company's earnings will be low, and the value of its securities will be correspondingly low; the low income represents a fair return on the low valuation. If, on the other hand, the commission sets very high rates and the firm's income as a result is high, the firm's securities will have a high market value; the high income represents a fair return on the high valuation. Since the value of the securities depends on the rates charged, it is circular reasoning of the most vicious sort to argue that the fair rate should be determined by the value of the securities.

Original cost (including improvements) and reproduction cost have both been frequently accepted by commissions and courts as appropriate capital values for rate-making purposes. The former has often been modified by the "prudent-investment" concept, according to which clearly improper expenditures—on poorly engineered projects, bribes, and unscrupulous promoters—are disallowed. Utility companies themselves have usually favored the reproduction-cost basis, since the long-term upward trend in prices generally makes reproduction cost higher than actual cost.

The concept of reproduction cost is inherently a vague one. If an existing railroad were actually reproduced at the present time, it would be necessary to provide plant facilities for turning out types of locomotives and cars no longer being produced. How can one reasonably estimate what such equipment would cost to build to-day? Further, what is to be assumed regarding obstacles to con-struction? It may have been necessary a hundred years ago when the railroad was actually built to cut down a forest where none exists today. Should the area be mentally reforested? Land values have risen greatly since the railroad-building era of the nineteenth century. Public land grants of tremendous size were made to some of the railroads by the United States government. Should the railroads now be considered to buy the land at today's high values (which in part are due to the existence and influence of the rail-roads themselves)? The same perplexing problems exist with re-spect to the notion of reproduction costs of electric-power com-panies, gas companies, etc., but they are generally less striking than in the case of the railroads.

Recent years have seen a new approach to the fair-return–fair-value problem. In 1944 the Supreme Court handed down the *Hope* decision, which, at least for the moment, ranks with *Smyth v. Ames* in importance in the public-utilities field. The Federal Power Commission had valued the property of a natural-gas company at $33 million after depreciation and allowed a return of 6½ per cent. The company insisted on a valuation of $66 million and a return of 8 per cent. In deciding against the company the Court did not take a stand in favor of any rate base. It was the view of the Court that if the end result is rates which enable the company to operate successfully, to attract capital, and to compensate its investors for risks assumed, those rates are sufficiently high.

The effect of the *Hope* decision is to relieve the commissions of the necessity of setting rates which provide a fair return on the present fair value of the utility property, as was required by the *Smyth v. Ames* decision. Instead, the fairness of the rates is judged primarily by their effects on the ability of the utility to furnish adequate service and secure needed financing. This judicial guidance is so vague that there is probably even more room than before for differences in opinion as to what rates are appropriate.

Summary

We have seen in this chapter that the public utilities, for both economic and non-economic reasons, often must be oper-ated as monopolies. In some instances the geographic extent of the monopoly has probably been greater than optimum, and in other cases firms have been made legal monopolies when actually a workable degree of competition could have been maintained. It has been established, however, that competition is not workable in some areas.

Unwilling to depend upon unrestrained private monopoly for the provision of important services, the American public has insisted that the utility firms be subjected to regulation, usually by public commissions. This has given rise to numerous theoretical and practical problems. The courts have for many years insisted that the utility companies are entitled to a fair return on a fair investment. What constitutes a fair return must be determined more or less arbitrarily, and the establishment of fair value has given rise to the rate-base controversy. The *Hope* decision seems to indicate that the Court has abandoned the rate-base approach to the valuation problem and substituted the idea of the "end result." It is clear that no satisfactory solution to the valuation problem has yet been devised, and it is doubtful that there is any real solution.

There is no way for a commission to provide a "fair return on a fair investment" and at the same time to allocate resources strictly in accord with consumer preferences. Commission regulation and consumer sovereignty are not completely compatible. Commissions, in fact, are not likely to concern themselves with the problem of efficiency of resource allocation even though their decisions have an important bearing upon how the economy's resources will be utilized.

Other practical problems harass utility commissions in their efforts to regulate rates and services. Commissioners are frequently poorly paid by the states, and in competition with the highly paid lawyers and engineers representing the utility companies they are often at a serious disadvantage. In addition it is frequently difficult to prevent a "community of interest" from arising between regulatory-commission employees and the companies regulated, especially since such employees often are either obtained from or are likely to move into the industry regulated. If the commissioners lack insight into the problems of the companies which they regulate, they may inadvertently handicap them in their efforts to provide good service at reasonable rates. The great difference in financial resources of the companies being regulated and the commissions has frequently worked out to the disadvantage of the public.

This has been a case study of an area where competition cannot be relied upon to protect the public interest. We have tried to contrast the complexities of regulation with the relative simplicity of the operation of the free market place. In spite of the difficulties, regulation has in many instances worked out rather satisfactorily to all concerned; during the last few decades electric power, for example, has been one of the few commodities steadily to decline in price. But regulation of private monopoly is inherently more complicated than competition, and the extension of the legal monopoly status to additional firms should be undertaken only when it is clear that competition cannot be entrusted with the responsibility of maintaining reasonable prices and adequate service. Some industries, such as trucking and taxicab service, now treated as utilities, might well be returned to a fully competitive status. The advantages of large scale in these industries are not so great as to make them appropriate fields for regulated monopoly.

31

PERSONAL INCOME DISTRIBUTION

The income received by a family usually depends primarily on the amount of labor which it is willing and able to sell during a period of time and on the price of that labor. Most of these services are sold to private or governmental employers, but significant amounts of real income are provided through self-employment—the housekeeping activities of the housewife and the yardwork of the husband are examples. Farmers, especially, are likely to have more income than dollar figures indicate because of the excellent possibilities of obtaining income in kind by eating some of the farm produce. As was indicated in the previous chapter the high income-tax rates now in existence make income in kind a particularly favorable sort of income from the point of view of the individual recipient.

A family's income is affected also by the amount of wealth which it owns and by the percentage yield which the family is wise enough, or lucky enough, to secure on such wealth. Again, it is especially favorable from a private point to view to secure income in a nonpecuniary form in order to avoid income tax. The family which rents a house and keeps $10,000 invested in corpora-

383

tion bonds will pay an income tax on the interest income from the bonds. If the $10,000 is invested in a house in which to live, interest income should still be received, but since it will be in the form of housing services, rather than in money, no income tax will have to be paid on this property income. Interest income is secured in the form of housing services enjoyed by the home owner just as an interest return is normally part of the income secured by the businessman from his capital goods.

Some Income Statistics

In spite of the problem of income in kind, it is instructive to examine some data on the distribution of money income. These have been collected by the Federal Reserve System and the University of Michigan by means of interviews of a "cross section" of American families. Regardless of the care with which such sampling is carried out it may involve considerable error in view of the small proportion of American families covered.

Table 31.1 shows the 1956 distribution of spending units according to the annual income received. It is a useful antidote to over-optimistic pronouncements of an "age of abundance" to note that

Table 31.1.   Distribution of Income, 1956

Annual income	Percent distribution of spending units
Under $1,000	9
1,000–1,999	12
2,000–2,999	12
3,000–3,999	12
4,000–4,999	14
5,000–7,499	24
7,500–9,999	9
10,000 and over	8
	100

Source: *Federal Reserve Bulletin*, August, 1957.

one-third of those interviewed had money income of less than $3,000 per year. According to the Federal Reserve analysts, those in the age groups 18 to 24 and 65 and over (constituting together one-fourth of all those surveyed) accounted for half of the incomes under $3,000 per year.

Among the spending units headed by persons 25 to 54, over half earned $5,000 or more in 1956. Only one-fifth earned less than

$3,000. It is apparent that the early and late years are the difficult periods from an income point of view.

Occupation as well as age is, of course, a vital determinant of income. Even apart from the differences in income between members of such remunerative occupations as the medical and dental professions and ordinary white collar and blue collar workers, there are marked differences between workers in different industries. The Commerce Department's *Survey of Current Business* for December 1957 shows average weekly earnings of $82.74 in all manufacturing in the United States. The highest reported average was $115.62 in petroleum refining, while the low of $43.85 per week was in laundries. Weekly wages are also low in knitting mills, textile mills, and apparel manufacturing. They are high in such fields as automobile manufacturing, railroad equipment manufacturing, and construction. In part these differences reflect the lower wage rates typically paid to female labor.

OWNERSHIP OF FINANCIAL ASSETS

The distribution of wealth, as well as income, is, of course, a matter of great social significance. Here the institution of inheritance is extremely important. A great many families have much more wealth than they have personally accumulated. As the percentage of the living population becomes a smaller percentage of the total who have lived, per capita wealth should increase (so long as war does not destroy large amounts of capital). Socially owned wealth (parks, highways, government buildings, etc.) should also increase on a per capita basis over time.

Significant data on total assets are difficult to compile. However, recent information is available from the Federal Reserve System on the results of 3,041 interviews made on a sampling basis in January and February, 1957. The purpose was to determine the holdings of "financial assets" per family. These assets were defined to include checking accounts, savings accounts, savings and loan and credit union shares, U.S. government bonds, state and local bonds, corporate bonds, and common and preferred stock. Currency was excluded because of the difficulty of getting reports.

As in the case of income, there is a marked relationship between asset holdings and age of the principal breadwinner. Only a few hundred dollars of financial assets per family were owned in the 18 to 24 age bracket, but holdings increased to an average of over $6,000 per family headed by a person 55 to 64 years of age.[1] Per-

[1] *Federal Reserve Bulletin*, August, 1957.

sons over 65 are usually in a better position with respect to wealth than with respect to income, when compared with those in the younger age brackets; they have had more time to accumulate and inherit wealth.

Government and the Redistribution of Income

As has already been pointed out in this book, resources tend to be paid according to their marginal revenue productivity to employers. This occurs in a purely competitive economy, but is true to a large extent in our own economy even though competition does not prevail fully. The major virtue of this sort of payment is that it is the only one which will provide incentives for owners to get resources into their most productive employments and for firms to employ inputs in their most effective fashion.

Though marginal revenue productivity payment is highly efficient from the point of view of total output, the resulting distribution of income may not be acceptable. If the whole national income were distributed on the basis of productivity, some individuals would be extremely rich while others would starve to death. Those owning specialized resources upon which the market evaluation was very high (for example, a rock-and-roll artist or TV comedian) would be paid high returns. Individuals owning no salable resources (the sick, the aged) would receive no income at all.

An additional undesirable feature of payment exclusively according to productivity is the tendency toward cumulative inequality in income and wealth. An individual's income position depends in large measure on the amount of economic resources (human and nonhuman) which he inherits. A high income received by a father usually serves to increase the future income of the son. This is true because, first, the wealthy father is able to provide his son with favorable environmental conditions during childhood, *i.e.*, better education, health, nutrition, etc., thus making him a more productive worker later in life, and second, the rich father may pass along to the son claims to nonhuman resources that yield income, *i.e.*, real property, stocks, bonds, cash, business connections, etc.

The undesirable features of productivity payment to resources may be largely eliminated, and yet the resource-allocation incentives of productivity retained, by a judicious use of the fiscal system. This is, in fact, accomplished to a considerable degree by the United States fiscal system. It is accomplished, however, without the redistribution of income as such being the avowed purpose; indeed, if policy makers (congressmen) were asked whether or not they approved a policy of income redistribution by the fiscal system, most of them would probably answer in the negative. Yet these same men would vote for old-age assistance, public housing, aid to the blind, grants to dependent children, etc., on the one hand and for sharply progressive income-tax rates on the other. The net result would be income redistribution.

Many governmental services are undertaken largely because of society's dissatisfaction with the prevailing distribution of income. At base, most of the agitation for improved housing, sanitation, nutrition, and similar services stems from a desire to improve the income position of certain groups. Public-housing projects are supported largely because slum dwellers do not have adequate incomes, not because they spend the income they do receive in what is considered a socially undesirable way.

A large share of the redistribution of income accomplished by the fiscal system arises not from the public expenditure but from the taxation side of the fiscal account. Popular ideas concerning the equitable distribution of the tax burden include the concept of progressive taxation. Even if government services were equally beneficial to all citizens, progressive taxation would ensure that real incomes—after taxes are paid and benefits from government are received—would be more nearly equal than before. Of course, not all individual taxes are progressive, but the major revenue producer, the personal income tax, clearly is progressive. Also, cumulative inequalities in income and wealth tend to be reduced by the estate, inheritance, and gift taxes. In total, considering all taxes and all government services, the fiscal system does serve to redistribute incomes substantially.[1]

It is important to realize that the fiscal system provides a way in which income redistribution may be changed without at the same time undermining the economic organization through direct

---

[1] The precise amount of redistribution of real income carried out by the fiscal system is extremely difficult to determine. An estimation requires that the real burden of each tax and the real benefit of each government expenditure be imputed to individual income receivers in a specific fashion. The most complete attempt to make such a heroic estimation is that of John H. Adler, "The Fiscal System, The Distribution of Income and Public Welfare," in Kenyon E. Poole (ed.), *Fiscal Policy and the American Economy* (Englewood Cliffs, N.J.: Prentice-Hall, Inc., 1947). Adler estimated that in 1946–1947 individuals in the lower-income brackets (under $4,000) gained from 3 to 60 per cent, while the upper-income individuals (above $4,000) lost from 4 to 23 per cent, as a result of the fiscal system (pp. 396–397).

interference with the price system. Individuals will continue to disagree on the amount of income redistribution actually desired. Some will want more than is now carried out; others will think we have already gone too far. The social decision will be a continuing compromise among conflicting opinions.

Although individuals may differ in their views concerning the amount of real income redistribution which it is desirable for the government to accomplish by means of the fiscal system, there should be general agreement on the desirability of public policy directed toward providing all individuals with a substantial equality of opportunity to earn income. The removal of inequalities in opportunity attacks the basic source of income inequality. Government action in the educational, health, nutrition, and sanitation areas may in many cases be best considered in this light rather than directly as income-redistribution measures. Here we find still another reason for the desirability of government action to keep markets free, *i.e.,* to encourage competition. For the maintenance of competition is one of the chief means of equalizing economic opportunity. As long as men are free to offer their services to any employer and free to enter any type of business, great pressure toward removal of severe income inequalities will be present. Monopoly, whether in the form of restrictive licensing arrangements, exclusive franchises, restrictions on entry into various occupations, or closed-shop provisos, tends always to prevent the equality of economic opportunity necessary to the smooth functioning of an enterprise system.

Redistribution via Inflation

One advantage of income and wealth redistribution via the fiscal system is that substantial control over its effects can be exercised by the taxing and spending authorities. The same is not true of the redistribution of wealth and income which occurs through movements in the general price level. During the past two decades, especially, this movement has been strongly in an upward direction. It is important, consequently, to examine the redistributive effects of inflation. An understanding of this matter can be of personal, as well as social, benefit.

It has already been pointed out that those who have relatively fixed incomes, such as clerical workers, retired persons, and graduate students receiving fellowships, are in effect subjected to an additional tax on their earnings as prices go up. Industrial workers in such fields as automobile and steel manufacturing and petroleum refining are not likely to suffer in this regard.

Another way to look at this problem—and in part it is a way which overlaps the above view—is to examine the redistributive effects of inflation on creditor versus debtor groups in the economy. Most people are at once both debtors and creditors, but seldom in an exactly offsetting degree. Consequently, it is instructive to classify groups of people broadly into predominantly debtor and creditor categories in order to arrive at some conclusions as to the effects of inflation on their economic status.

THE CREDITOR GROUPS

Among the creditor groups are those who have saved all or part of the sum necessary for receipt of a retirement pension from a private source. Most pension funds are invested wholly or mainly in Federal, state, and local bonds or corporate bonds. These yield a fixed dollar income per year, and a fixed number of dollars at maturity. The real value of the income from these bonds declines with inflation. Hence the real value of pension funds invested in bonds declines with inflation taking real wealth and income away from those relying on the fund. Some pension funds are now invested in part in common stocks and real estate in order to avoid this squeeze. This appears to be an excellent practice.

Similarly, persons who hold private and GI life-insurance policies have acquired a contingent claim to a fixed number of dollars, the real value of which has been eroded seriously in recent years by inflation. As is the case also with Federal bonds, it is unfortunate that the same government which established GI insurance as an important institution has failed to protect the real value of such claims through appropriate monetary and fiscal actions and through a uniform antimonopoly program. Similarly, the Federal government has established a system of insurance for bank deposits and building and loan association shares which encourages people to put their savings in these institutions. While the insurance is not objectionable in itself, it is unfortunate that the real value of such accounts is not better protected by their governmental sponsor.

Social-security recipients also constitute a creditor group in a sense since the fund out of which such payments are made is invested in government bonds. This case is less clear, however, since as retired persons come to constitute a more important voting group they will probably secure pension increases which will be, in effect, financed by the issuance of additional money by the Federal government. That is, the earmarked portion of the Federal debt will not really constitute the whole fund out of which social-security pensions must be met. A recent manifestation of this Congressional tendency was the speedy move to increase the period of unemployment compensation permitted under the Social Security Act as soon as a substantial number of persons approached the limit of time for receiving such compensation. Admirable though such consideration for human welfare may be, it is clearly conducive to inflation—which at the same time is harmful to other persons.

THE DEBTOR GROUPS

Despite the popularity of calculations of the Federal debt "per capita," the actual burden of this debt does not rest equally on each person but falls instead on people to the extent that they pay the additional taxes out of which interest payments are met. Taxpayers constitute a powerful, if not formally organized, debtor group who constantly work for tax relief regardless of the propriety of such relief from the viewpoint of fiscal policy or distributive justice. The principal creditor groups mentioned above are not so clearly aware of their potential losses through inflation and are consequently not a powerful contra taxpayer group. This relative political impotency derives from the contingent nature of many of the claims (*e.g.*, life-insurance claims) and from the fact that many will not be collected in the near future. Since immediate and certain losses to taxpayers are in conflict with more remote and less certain losses to the creditor groups, the pressure to obtain socially inappropriate tax cuts is likely strongly to influence our economic future.

The existence of greatly augmented corporate debt also contributes to inflation. Corporation executives typically are owners of common stock, and frequently hold valuable, or potentially valuable, stock purchase options. Corporate bonds are typically held by outsiders. Corporation officials thus have a stake in inflation since this tends to transfer real wealth from bondholders to stockholders.[1] The transfer takes place, essentially, through the fixity of interest and principal payments on borrowed funds in contrast with

[1] A statistical test of the effect of debtor and creditor positions on the firm is described by Reuben A. Kessel, "Inflation-Caused Wealth Redistribution: A Test of a Hypothesis," *American Economic Review*, March, 1956, p. 128.

the stockholders' ownership of assets which increase in value as prices go up.

It frequently appears that corporation executives in some key oligopolistic industries go along quite readily with union demands for pay increases when conditions are favorable for a compensating, or more than compensating, boost in prices of output. In part this seems to be explicable as constituting a way in which both labor and management can profit by transferring real wealth and income away from those who hold fixed monetary claims to corporate assets *i.e.,* away from the creditors.

In general, the importance of the whole debtor-creditor dichotomy has been increased in the past two decades with the great growth of Federal, state, and local debt, of corporate debt, and of insurance, pension funds, building and loan shares, and bank deposits. All debt must be owed by someone, or at least its burden must be allocable to some groups more than to others. The persons representing the creditor stake in the economy are in general possessed of less economic and political power than the debtor interest, in part because many of the claims are of a contingent nature. Taxpayers, business executives, and labor leaders are among the groups who tend to further the status of the debtor groups. Private pension recipients, actual and prospective life-insurance beneficiaries, shareholders in building and loan association, depositors in banks, and private owners of government and private bonds typify the less potent creditor groups. As a general forecast, it appears likely that the debtor groups will succeed in continuing to transfer real wealth from creditors to themselves.

Despite the distributive inequities produced by inflation, incomes in the United States are now much more evenly distributed than they were at the turn of the century. As a result, many mansions in the old resort centers such as Newport, Tuxedo Park, and Saratoga are now tourist attractions only. Few incomes are high enough to support the lavish form of expenditure which was represented in the maintenance of such establishments. On the other hand, the leveling up of the lower incomes has increased significantly the resources devoted to the production of commodities such as meat, dairy products, and Ford, Chevrolet and Plymouth automobiles.

Critics of the capitalistic system, especially those of the socialist and communist varieties, pay a great deal of attention to the unequal distribution of income which arises in such a system. As pointed out here, this need not be a valid criticism at all, for we possess the means whereby the distribution can be changed within wide limits to one which is more acceptable. But another point needs to be made in rebuttal to such criticism. This concerns the distribution of rewards in any social system, whether capitalistic or not. The socialist system in which the state takes over and operates large segments of the economy is likely to generate even more severe inequalities in the distribution of rewards than is the capitalistic system. For in any system where most economic decisions are made by political groups, the inequalities of political power are likely to be more dangerous than inequalities in economic power generated by a capitalistic system.

Part 2

POLITICAL ECONOMY

32

GOVERNMENT SPENDING

The possibilities of deliberately adjusting the level of government spending in order to accomplish economic stabilization objectives have been discussed in Chapter 19. There remains to be discussed government spending in the more traditional and more general sense, that is, as the means of financing certain specific public services.

Government Expenditure and Resource Allocation

A LIMITATION ON CONSUMER SOVEREIGNTY

In the early chapters of this book, we discussed consumer sovereignty as the great organizing principle of the free-enterprise economy. Purchases by individuals in the market were considered as votes for the production of goods and services. Businessmen seeking to make the greatest possible profit are attracted by these consumer purchases to combine basic resources for necessary production of the goods and services indicated as the most desirable in a pecuniary sense. As with many of our economic constructions, however, the economy guided solely by consumer sovereignty must be recognized as an oversimplified model. There are many limitations on the operations of the guiding principle of consumer sovereignty (including monopoly in all its forms), but perhaps the most significant in the United States of today is that limitation which is due to the existence of government as a major purchaser of goods and services. In developing the principles of resource allocation, we assumed, in effect, that no government existed. This was a reasonably realistic assumption, with reference to government's economic importance, until the last half century. For this latter period, however, one of the dominant characteristics of the American economy has been the increasing amount of government activity, in both an absolute and a relative sense. The degree to which this growth has taken place may be indicated by an illustrative glance at the facts. In 1900 only one out of every twenty-five employed workers in the United States was employed by some governmental unit. In 1950, one of every eight employees in the nation worked for the government. Government now owns one dollar out of every five dollars' worth of capital assets, whereas in 1900 only one out of every fifteen dollars' worth was government owned.[1]

Total government expenditures (Federal, state, and local) in the United States amounted to approximately 12 per cent of national money income in 1929, the last year prior to the great depression. In the peak spending year of World War II, 1945, this proportion exceeded 60 per cent. Since World War II, the ratio of total government expenditures to national income has never fallen below 20 per cent. These proportions serve to make clear the significance of government in the total economy and the limitation placed on the operation of the principle of consumer sovereignty. Government demand for goods and services becomes important in determining the pattern of resource allocation. The power of individuals voting in the market to call forth goods and services, to motivate production, is reduced, and the power of individuals voting in the polling places (or their representatives) to call forth economic goods and services is correspondingly increased.[2] Voter sovereignty replaces consumer sovereignty, carry-

---

[1] See S. Fabricant, *The Growth of Governmental Activity in the United States 1900–1950* (New York: National Bureau of Economic Research, Inc., 1953), for a careful presentation of these and many similar facts regarding the growth in governmental activity over the half century.

[2] For an excellent discussion of the encroachment on consumer sovereignty by government, the reader may consult George Hildebrand, "Consumer Sovereignty in Modern Times," *American Economic Review*, Vol. 41, pp. 19–33 (May, 1951).

ing with it all the imperfections of decision-making in representative democracies, the influence of pressure groups, voter ignorance, etc. It must be recognized that one of the most difficult problems of our times concerns the proper dividing line between these two great principles of economic control.

The Government as Purchaser

In carrying out many of its functions, the government enters the market and purchases real goods and services. For example, if the service is that which is to be provided by an additional nuclear-powered submarine, the government, via the Department of Defense, will enter into a contract with a private firm, or group of firms, for the construction of the ship. Thus, the government's dollars "vote for" the use of resources in shipbuilding and are as influential as are dollars of private expenditure (consumption or investment) in determining the pattern of resource use.

Business firms in combining productive inputs and transforming them into final outputs will respond to government demand. As a result, a significantly different pattern of resource use arises in any economy in which government is a large purchaser from that which would arise in an economy where the government is a small purchaser. The impact of government purchases tends to affect nearly all segments of the economy in greater or lesser degree.

INDIRECT EFFECTS OF GOVERNMENT SPENDING

The effects of government expenditure on the allocation of economic resources are not limited to those caused directly by the government's purchases of goods and services. The provision of government services may also indirectly alter the resource-use pattern. Government provision of education is a good example here. This makes up a major portion of state and local government expenditure. Direct effects of the sort discussed above are confined to the shifting of economic resources into such activities as school-building construction and the teaching profession. The indirect effects are far more important. Public education can best be considered as an investment in human resources. This is a type of investment which appears extremely productive in a social sense yet would be much less extensive if the function were left in private hands. This is true since the benefits from education are long-run in nature and are not fully concentrated on the private individuals who would be forced to undergo the costs. Society in the next generation will benefit a great deal more from the education of children in this generation than will the parents of the children. Left alone, parents would probably tend to undervalue educational investment. As a result, we would have more investment in capital resources, less in human resources, were it not for public activity in the educational field. Similar effects result from public provision of health facilities, sanitation, and safety regulation.

Important indirect effects upon the allocation of resources can be traced from almost any major government expenditure. To provide another important example, let us consider expenditure for highways. The direct effects would be concentrated primarily in the construction, machinery, cement, and asphalt industries. The indirect effects which stem from the provision of highways and streets are concentrated, on the other hand, in the automobile and petroleum industries. By having available better highways, individuals and firms utilize far more resources in the form of automobiles, trucks, and buses than would be the case with a less adequate road system.

A significant share of government expenditure is made without the government's purchasing real goods and services at all. These are called "transfer expenditures," the implication being that funds are transferred directly to certain individuals and firms. These tend to influence economic activity by their effects on the behavior of recipients. Important categories of this type of expenditure are interest on the government debt, old-age-assistance payments, subsidies to veterans, and unemployment compensation. Some of the recipient groups are likely to exert less productive effort as a result of the government transfer payment, but this does not appear to be an important effect. Perhaps a more important type of reaction is found in the change in the saving-spending pattern. As the government assumes more and more the burden of insecurity previously borne by individuals and families, the saving by families for future rainy days is likely to be reduced and current spending for consumption increased. While this might prove a desirable reaction during times of unemployment when less saving and more spending are needed, in the long run it is likely to result in a smaller rate of real capital accumulation.

Although transfer expenditures differ basically from production expenditures in that no direct impact on resource allocation occurs as a result of government purchase of real goods and services, the distinction may easily be overemphasized. In many cases the government faces a choice between transferring funds directly to recipients and purchasing real goods for their benefit. The case of free school lunches provides an example. If the government actually purchases the lunches and gives them to the children, this outlay is considered a production expenditure. If, however, the government gave the children the money with which they might purchase the school lunches, the outlay would be considered a transfer expenditure. For many of the welfare types of expenditures, this choice is a real one. If transfer payments are made directly to individuals, the pattern of resource allocation is modified on the spending side only to the extent that the private purchases of the recipients are shifted. If expenditure is made by government on tangible goods and services, the pattern of resource allocation is directly affected. A greater limitation is placed on the operation of the principle of consumer sovereignty in the latter case than in the former. In making decisions of this sort, great care must be exercised lest government officials begin to think that they are somehow better able to tell the people what they should want than are the people themselves.

THE REAL COST OF GOVERNMENT SERVICES

In our discussion of costs, we concentrated for the most part on money costs. This is appropriate when discussing the behavior of business firms, since business decisions are affected by money-cost considerations. However, when we discussed cost in a broader sense, we introduced the idea of alternative cost. The real cost of anything is not a money cost; money serves more or less as the unit of account in the estimation process. Real cost must be considered in the terms of sacrificed alternatives or opportunities.

This notion of alternative cost is extremely useful in considering the real costs of government services. The cost to society incurred by the government's provision of a particular public service is the amount of other goods or services which could have been produced by the economic resources that are used in the production of the public service. The cost to the United States of maintaining a large defense establishment is the goods or services which the labor and capital resources employed in the defense establishment (soldiers, workers in aircraft factories, physicists, iron, steel, etc.) might have produced alternatively, publicly or privately.

In this view, we may state that many of our post-office buildings, for example, were constructed at a very low or negligible real cost to society, even though the money costs may have been significant. This is true because many of these buildings were constructed during the great depression of the 1930's. At this time, many economic resources were unemployed and were not producing anything. Government employment of these resources allowed projects to be constructed which were essentially costless in a real sense, because little of value in the nature of alternatives was sacrificed. We may state that the real costs of government services, the production of which employs otherwise unemployed resources, consist mainly of alternative government services which might have been produced. The real costs of post-office buildings constructed in the 1930's are not represented by alternatives in the private economy but by the parks, swimming pools, etc., that could instead have been produced by government. In summary, for government services as a whole, the real costs are low in periods of depression because the private economy is not putting many resources to full use.

On the other hand, the real costs of government services in times of full employment are high. In real terms, it was much more costly for the United States to build aircraft carriers or housing projects in 1954 than it would have been in 1934, even though precisely the same amount of labor, steel, and other resources might have been used. During periods of high employment, the resource-allocation problem, or the problem of scarcity, comes into its full importance. The expansion of government services must utilize resources which would otherwise have produced something for the private economy. More tanks mean fewer private automobiles, more public housing means less private housing, etc.

THE BASIS OF GOVERNMENT SPENDING

Why does government spend? The answer to this question introduces immediately the whole issue of public versus private uses of economic resources. Why do people, acting in their capacities as voter-representative decision makers, choose to employ a large proportion of the total available resources in the pursuit of collective rather than private goals? What purposes or goals does government serve?

To discuss adequately such questions would lead us into considerations of political philosophy, an extremely interesting and important branch of scholarship, but one which we cannot explore here. Therefore, we can only touch on some of the points relevant to such general questions.

In the first place, certain services must, by their very nature, be enjoyed jointly by all members of the community. Hence, they must be publically produced if adequate investment is to be forthcoming. External defense is the standard example. Whereas it would rarely be advantageous for individuals acting privately to provide investment in a military establishment, it will almost always be advantageous to the people acting jointly through government. The deterrent threat represented by the Strategic Air Force benefits all citizens alike, and it is impossible for one citizen to purchase additional protection for his own family without the benefits spilling over to his fellow citizens. Goods and services possessing such characteristics are genuinely collective, and they must be produced, or provided, by government.

Many government services are not by nature "collective" in the sense discussed above, and it is difficult to explain their provision by government on other than historical or traditional grounds. When we look at the whole complex of governmental activity in the modern economy perhaps the wisest course, at this stage of our studies, is to learn something about the facts rather than the reasons.

The Federal Budget

The executive budget of the Federal government for fiscal 1959 amounted to approximately $74 billion. Some rough knowledge of the breakdown of this typical postwar budget into the various spending components will be helpful.

The first point to be noted is that 64 per cent of this total, or some $47 billion, was devoted to expenditures on national defense, including international aid. Although the percentage of total Federal expenditure devoted to national security expanded somewhat in fiscal 1959, the heavy concentration upon defense spending has been characteristic of the Federal budget during the whole of the post-World War II period, and especially so since the Korean War. There seems little chance that this item will be substantially reduced, and much chance that it will be significantly increased, as long as the Cold War continues. Despite the obvious stupidity, from a global view, of an international armaments race, the absence of some sort of international agreement forces each national participant in the race to devote economic resources to producing more and more terrible weapons when these same resources could alternatively be used to provide goods and services directly beneficial to citizens. The state of the international armaments race is likely to be a major factor determining the over-all size of the Federal government's budget over the foreseeable future.

The provision of benefits and services to veterans accounts for an additional $5 billion in Federal spending. For the most part, these expenditures take the form of "transfer payments," that is, the government does not directly purchase goods and services but, instead, pays out revenues directly in the form of pensions, educational benefits, etc. For some purposes, notably those concerned with evaluating the impact of Federal spending on the level of economic activity, transfer expenditures can best be considered as negative taxes rather than expenditures, reserving the latter category for so-called "productive expenditures," that is, those government outlays which do involve some direct purchase by government of real goods and services.

Federal expenditure on agriculture takes between $4.5 and $5 billion. The major share of this total is devoted to the various programs designed either to support prices of agricultural products above equilibrium levels or to provide income subsidies to farmers in return for their holding land out of production. As with veterans' benefits, this item in the Federal budget is relatively easy to attack on economic grounds but extremely difficult to reduce for political reasons.

Interest payments on the national debt amount annually to almost $8 billion. This is a major expenditure which is only subject to partial change. As economic conditions dictate shifts in monetary policy, the general level of interest rates will move upward and downward within limits. As these interest rate changes are reflected in the refunding operations of the Treasury Department, the over-all item for interest expenditure will move. If the debt is maintained at approximately $275 billion (its level in early 1958), the interest total may go down somewhat as the pattern of interest rates falls below the heights reached during the "tight money" period of 1955 to 1957. Additional changes in this interest item in the budget can, of course, be effected by shifts in the composition of the national debt. The interest payments could be completely eliminated, or nearly so, by Treasury action to refinance maturing issues of nonbank debt by new issues sold to the Federal Reserve Banks. On the other hand, complete refunding of all bank-held debt into long-term securities would substantially increase total interest payments. Drastic changes in debt composition of this sort do not seem likely to occur.

All proposed additional Federal spending accounts for something over $9 billion for fiscal 1959. This catch-all item includes expenditures for labor and welfare programs, national resources, commerce and housing, and general government.

The executive budget does not formally include items of Federal expenditure which are financed directly from trust funds, the revenues for which come from specifically "earmarked" sources. Yet these trust-fund expenditures are becoming increasingly important, and they must be included in any complete summary of Federal spending. The fact that the expenditures are made out of trust-fund receipts in no way changes the effect which these expenditures will exert on the national economy.

Estimated trust-fund expenditure for fiscal 1959 amounts to $16.4 billion. The single most important item in this total covers payments made under the Social Security program, estimated to be almost $9 billion in fiscal 1959. These payments are almost exclusively "transfers." The second major trust-fund item, and one which will assume increasing importance over the next fifteen years, is Federal payments in support of the recently enacted interstate highway program. A total Federal outlay of $2.5 billion for this purpose is budgeted for fiscal 1959.

State and Local Expenditure

Any consideration of public expenditures in the United States must reckon with three levels of government: Federal, state, and local. Owing to the expansion of the role of the Federal government in the depression of the 1930's and the subsequent World War II and Cold War periods, the importance of state and local government fiscal policy has tended often to be neglected. Public spending by these levels of government has, however, been increasing at a very rapid rate and amounted in the late 1950's to a total of approximately $50 billion. When these expenditures are added to the Federal totals there is, of course, some double counting since almost $4 billion of state-local spending is financed through revenues from the Federal government. State and local spending seems certain to increase substantially over the next decade, and a conservative estimate of $65 billion annually by 1965 has been made.

The single most important expenditure made by states and local units is for education. In fiscal 1956, this amounted to $13 billion, and with the population upsurge continuing along with the boost provided American education by Soviet scientific advances, a doubling of this total seems likely to occur within a relatively few years. Highway construction and maintenance comprise another significant item of state expenditures, but this function has, to some extent, been assumed by the central government, at least as regards the construction of an integrated interstate highway network.

The Public Economy

With Federal government spending amounting to more than $70 billion and state-local spending almost $50 billion, any discussion about the national economic organization must include considerable reference to the "public" economy. More than 25 per cent of the value of the Gross National Product is effectively channeled through some governmental unit. Colin Clark, a noted statistician, once used 25 per cent as the decisive or marginal figure for a bearable tax burden. He argued that if a nation attempts to tax away from its citizens more than 25 per cent of their gross income, regardless of the uses to which the revenues were devoted, inflation must result. While the general validity of this proposition may be questioned, and 25 per cent is certainly no magic figure, the dangers should be recognized. The United States, as a nation, has not by any means become fully adjusted to a public sector of the economy as large as that which has been experienced in the relatively few war and postwar years. Whether or not a satisfactory adjustment can be made remains to be seen.

33

TAXATION AND THE
ALLOCATION OF RESOURCES

During periods of high employment, the public or governmental employment of resources must involve some real cost to the society or, more correctly, to the individuals living within it. These real costs can be expressed in terms of the alternative goods and services which could be privately enjoyed if there were no public demands upon resources. Taxation may be defined as the process through which the group distributes these real costs among its individual members. A tax is analogous to a price in the private economy. The latter reflects the cost of acquiring a privately produced good whereas a tax reflects the cost of acquiring publicly produced or supplied goods and services.

From this approach, it becomes clear that taxation is necessary only in so far as there are real costs in providing public goods. Periods of deep depression, which are characterized by widespread unemployment of economic resources, may cause the real or opportunity costs of providing public service to be quite low or even negligible. Resources can be put to work in such situations when they would otherwise be idle. (This point was discussed in the preceding chapter.) In such periods, which do not seem likely to recur in the foreseeable future, no taxation would be required. Government purchases would be financed appropriately by printing money, or its modern equivalent, government borrowing from the banking system. In this case, the traditional function of taxation, namely, that of raising revenue, is not appropriate.[1]

In all periods of high employment, however, the traditional function of taxation is an appropriate one. To be sure, the government could also finance its purchases in boom periods by direct currency creation or by borrowing from banks. But this net addition to purchasing power would cause prices to rise, and resources would be drawn away from private employments. Real costs would be present just as in the more open method of taxation. Inflationary finance during periods of high employment is simply one means of taxation, and a particularly undesirable one because it is likely to be hidden or disguised.

Taxation and Consumer Sovereignty

The limitation on the exercise of consumer sovereignty represented by government's provision of services manifests itself also on the taxation side. Whereas government expenditures represent dollar votes calling forth production, taxation allows these government votes to be even more influential by reducing the expenditures of private individuals and firms. The power of individuals and firms to direct the flow of resources is reduced by taxation. Taxation withdraws income, thus potentially reducing both private spending and saving.

The more specific effects of taxation on the resource-use pattern depend on the way in which taxes are imposed. This involves two questions: first, who pays the taxes, and second, how the payment of the tax affects the taxpayers' economic behavior. The next step, then, is a discussion of the major types of taxes actually imposed by government, with the purpose of answering these two questions.

Personal Income Taxation

The most important single source of revenue in the fiscal system is the personal income tax. Revenues from this tax make up more than one-half of total Federal tax collections (about 38 billion dol-

---

[1] This discussion applies only to the Federal government, which alone possesses money-creating powers.

lars in fiscal 1959). This tax in general terms is perhaps the most acceptable of all taxes. First of all, it is paid directly by all individuals receiving incomes of more than a minimum amount. It is not imposed in a discriminatory fashion on a particular subgroup of individuals in the economy. The burden is general and, at the same time, recognizable. Second, it exerts perhaps a lesser effect on the organization of economic resources than any of the other major taxes. This is largely because of the generality of the tax. Since the tax is supposedly levied on all income recipients, it is difficult to escape payment by a shift of occupation or profession.

The behavior of some individuals is, of course, affected. The productive efforts of some, especially the high-income receivers, are reduced as a result of the high rates of the personal income tax. This results from the fact that the effective marginal rates of tax are very high for those individuals who receive high incomes.

The Federal personal income tax is highly progressive in its rate structure: the effective tax rate increases as income increases. Marginal rates of tax (the ratio between the additional tax liability and an additional increment of income) are higher than average rates. This tends to make the effects of the tax on productive effort more significant than would be the case if the tax rate did not increase with income. For example, a corporation executive (or any other high-income receiver) with an annual total income of $300,000 might pay a maximum of about $200,000 in taxes (at 1958 rates and depending on specific exemptions and deductions); thus his average rate of tax on his whole income will be 67 per cent. However, if his income is increased from $300,000 to $320,-000, with his authorized deductions remaining unchanged, his tax is increased from $200,000 to $218,000. The maximum marginal rate of tax is 91 per cent. Such high marginal rates may exert considerable influence on decisions of certain high-salaried individuals whether to play golf or to work harder, to take a Florida vacation or to stay home and work, etc. The personal income tax may also exert influence on the rate of real-capital accumulation through its impact on savings during periods of substantially full employment. The more progressive the rates, the greater the reduction in savings that is likely to result.

The characteristic features of the personal income tax may exert, however, as much or more influence on the pattern of economic activity than the rates themselves. The tax is levied on annual incomes and contains no provision for averaging out high and low incomes over longer periods. This requires, therefore, that the individual with a fluctuating or uncertain source of income pay a higher effective rate of tax on his income over the whole earning period than the individual with a more stable and secure income. This tends to discourage persons from entering occupations with fluctuating incomes and to place an undue premium on occupations promising income stability over time.

A second characteristic of the personal income tax which exerts important economic effects is the treatment of capital-gains income. The difference between the original purchase price and the sales price of an asset held more than six months is not treated as ordinary income. Only one-half of this gain need be reported as income, and this is taxed at a preferential rate if the individual's income is high. This provides a tremendous incentive for ordinary income to be converted into capital gains in order to secure this favorable tax treatment. One of the ways in which this may be done is for a corporation to plow back its earnings into investment rather than paying such earnings out to stockholders as dividends. As the investment is expanded, capital-stock prices rise; shareholders desiring to receive income may sell off shares and pay less tax than if dividends had been paid to them directly.

A third characteristic of the personal income tax which seems to exert an indirect effect on the economy lies in the withholding features. A large proportion (about two-thirds) of Federal personal income-tax collections is withheld from wages and salaries at the source of payment. This feature has the great advantage of administrative convenience to the government and the apparent advantage of easing the tax burden to the individual. This last is only an apparent advantage, however, for since individuals never "feel" the tax as such—it is removed before they look at their pay checks—they are likely to underestimate the real costs of government services. The economic effects of the withholding provision are likely to be that people will vote to have government provide more services and the private economy correspondingly less, even though, if confronted with the choice directly, they might vote the other way.

As the economy has adjusted to a permanently high-level rate of personal income taxation, mounting pressures have arisen for a revamping of specific features. Under the burden of the extremely high marginal rates of tax, individuals and groups have found it desirable and profitable to use all means to achieve legal avoidance of tax liability. Groups which have been politically powerful have been successful in introducing loopholes which effectively reduce tax liability. The largest of these is the capital-gains provision already mentioned. And beyond this, institutional features of the economy have gradually been modified significantly solely as a result of the tax. Business corporations have found it profitable to provide employees with real income in the form of expense accounts rather than direct salary payments. All sorts of payments of income-in-kind have been introduced specifically for tax avoidance purposes. It is now generally recognized that fiscal morality has been severely damaged by the high-level rates of the personal income tax. At this time there is considerable agitation for a rewriting of the personal income tax law with the view toward reducing top-level rates somewhat to bring nominal rates more into line with actual liabilities and at the same time closing up many of the now-existing loopholes.

Business Taxation

The second most important source of Federal-government revenue is the corporation income tax. Over 20 billion dollars, or about 27 per cent of total Federal tax collections, were obtained from this tax in fiscal 1958. This tax is levied directly on the net incomes of corporations. Corporation net income above a $25,000 minimum amount is taxed at 52 per cent. Although it will probably remain important as a revenue producer, this tax can never be considered an equitable one, since it disregards the structure of individual ownership of corporations.

There has been much controversy over the economic effects of the corporate income tax. Businessmen contend that the tax is considered as a cost of production and that it is passed on to buyers of products through higher prices. Economists have not fully accepted this view. Their reasons for not doing so may be appreciated by a review of the analysis of the behavior of business firms. If firms (corporations) make an attempt to secure maximum profits, they will produce and sell the output for which the difference between total revenue and total costs is greatest. A necessary condition for attaining this position is that marginal revenue must equal marginal costs. This is true regardless of the market position of the firm, whether it is monopolistic or competitive. It follows that the maximum profit output would be changed only by forces changing either marginal revenue or marginal costs. If output does not change, price is not changed, since presumably price reflects buyers' willingness to demand that output.

If the tax is placed on the true net profit of corporations, it cannot affect either marginal revenue or marginal costs, because it is imposed as a percentage of net income. If the firm was maximizing net income or profit before the tax is imposed, then a fixed percentage tax on this net income would still leave a larger residual than would be left out of a smaller total net income before tax.

On the basis of this type of reasoning, it is concluded that a tax on true profits cannot be passed on in the form of higher prices. Therefore, the burden must rest on the owners of the corporations. Since the corporation is such an important type of business organization, the effects of the tax tend to reduce the marginal product of capital throughout the economy.

The actual effects of the corporation income tax as employed in the United States appear to be some combination of that claimed by businessmen and that indicated by the use of theoretical analysis. There are perhaps two main explanations. First, economic analysis assumes that all business firms attempt to maximize profits. Actually, firms may be motivated by incentives other than profit maximization. This may be especially true for those corporations possessing some monopoly power. A monopoly firm may decide that reasonable profits are a more desirable goal, and more safe, than maximum profits. The monopoly firm may, accordingly, deliberately keep price below the profit-maximizing level in order to keep potential competitors from being too much attracted. In this situation, an increase in the corporation income tax would probably result in an increase in product price. The tax would serve to push the price up toward the profit-maximizing price.

The second reason that the corporation income tax is probably partially reflected in product prices involves a consideration of the tax base itself. If the tax were based on true net profit in an economic sense, the costs of the firm would not be affected. In actual fact, however, the corporation income tax is based on a more inclusive concept of profit. Included in profit are the total returns to the owners of the corporation, *i.e.,* the equity shareholders. Clearly, a portion of this return is cost in an economic sense. Economic profit is defined to exclude a normal rate of return (*i.e.,* what the capital could earn elsewhere) on invested capital. The inclusion of this element of cost in taxable income should not affect the short-run behavior of firms, but it may affect behavior in the long run. It serves to reduce the return to equity shareholders, and this in turn may tend to reduce the supply of equity capital for corporations relative to partnerships and proprietorships. This reduction in supply may tend to increase the difficulty of securing equity capital for corporate investment which, in turn, may eventually result in higher product prices.[1]

Excise Taxation

The third major type of taxation consists of excises levied on the manufacture, sale, or consumption of various commodities. This has been a relatively unimportant, although still significant, source of revenue for the Federal government, providing some $9 billion in fiscal 1958. But it is a major revenue source for state governments. Two basic forms of the excise must be distinguished and considered separately because of the differences in economic impact. First, a tax may be imposed on the sale of a single commodity with other commodities and services left untaxed or taxed at much lower rates. Second, a tax may be imposed at equivalent (or approximately equivalent) rates on the sale of all (or nearly all) commodities and services.

1. *Taxation of a Single Commodity.* The discussion of the case in which an excise tax is imposed on the sale of a single commodity allows us to utilize some earlier analysis exceptionally well. In treating the taxes actually imposed on liquor, tobacco, and gasoline it is best to employ the single-commodity assumption, because these commodities are taxed at considerably higher rates than other commodities.

An excise tax on a single commodity (or the differential between this and the normal rate of tax on all commodities) will tend to be shifted in large part to the consumers of that commodity in the form of price increases. Again we must make a distinction between the competitive and the monopoly case. If the industry is fully competitive and long-run average costs are constant, the whole of the tax will be shifted to consumers in the long run. As firms find that paying the tax subjects them to short-run losses, they will move out of the industry into nontaxed fields until the rate of return is again normal. This will result only when price has gone up by the full amount of the tax. This case may be shown in Figure

[1] For a comprehensive treatment of the corporation income tax see Richard Goode, *The Corporation Income Tax* (New York: John Wiley & Sons, Inc., 1951).

FIGURE 33.1. PRICE INCREASE EQUALS
TAX—In Constant-cost Industry

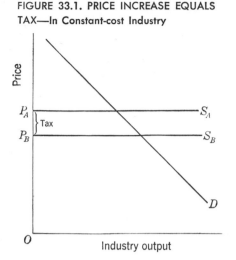

33.1. D represents the industry demand curve (which we assume to remain unchanged). S_B represents the long-run industry supply curve before tax, S_A the corresponding long-run curve after tax.

If the competitive industry is one of increasing costs, a portion of the tax burden will be shifted backward to the sellers of productive services. As firms leave the industry as a result of the losses caused by the tax, the demands for productive services peculiarly adapted to the taxed industry are reduced. This tends to reduce prices paid to the owners of the productive services. Thus, the tax burden is borne by both consumers of the product in terms of higher prices and owners of productive services in terms of lower input prices.

When an excise tax is imposed on the product of a monopolist, this will tend to be partially borne by the monopolist and partially shifted to the buyers of the product and in some cases to the sellers of productive services. This may be illustrated in Figure 33.2.

D represents the demand curve for the monopolist's product, MR the marginal revenue curve, MC_b the marginal cost curve before tax. The imposition of the tax on the monopoly firm will increase marginal cost by the amount of the tax, shifting the curve to MC_a after the tax. The monopoly firm will then tend to reduce output (sales) from OB to OA and increase price from P_b to P_a. It may be noted that the price increase is not so great as the amount of the tax. The exact proportion that will be shifted forward to consumers as a price increase depends on the relative

FIGURE 33.2. PRICE INCREASE IS LESS
THAN TAX—For Monopolistic Firm

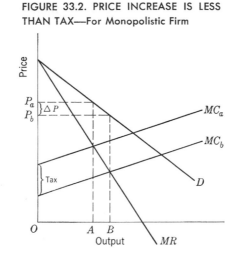

slopes of the demand curve and the marginal cost curve. The actual effects of the taxes imposed on tobacco and liquor may be estimated by using a combination of the competitive and monopoly analyses sketched above. Both the liquor and the tobacco industries are oligopolistic; hence they contain elements of both competition and monopoly. The high excise taxes tend to be borne by consumers in higher prices, by firms in lower oligopoly profits, and by owners of productive services (*e.g.*, tobacco farmers) in lower prices. Another characteristic feature of the cigarette industry is the extremely low responsiveness of quantity demanded to price changes. This tends to cause a greater proportion of the tax load to be passed on in higher prices than would otherwise be the case. This fact also indicates the productivity of the cigarette tax as a revenue source and thus its political popularity.

The liquor industry provides yet another example of the workings of competitive processes. The high tax during World War II and after has tended to push consumer prices very high. This high price has provided a strong incentive for firms to produce a closely competing but slightly differentiated product, namely, untaxed liquor, or "moonshine."

2. *General Excise Taxation.* The effects of a general excise (sales) tax imposed on the manufacture or sale of most or all commodities are considerably different from those of an excise imposed on the manufacture or sale of a single commodity. If a tax is imposed generally on all commodities, a greater portion of the tax is likely to be borne by the sellers of productive services in lowered

input prices than by consumers of final products in the form of higher product prices. Under given conditions of demand, the price of a product may be increased only if the quantity supplied is reduced. In the case of a particular excise tax, the egress of firms from the taxed industry does reduce quantity supplied. But if the tax is imposed on the products of most or all industries, there can be little egress of firms or resources from taxed industries; nothing could be gained in moving from one taxed industry to another. If such shifting is not possible, the resources devoted to the production of each product remain about the same after as before the tax. Thus output remains about the same, and product prices remain about the same. But the firms affected must pay the tax out of the same total revenue as before. Therefore, the demand for productive inputs will fall. And in order for the same amount of productive inputs to be employed, input prices must fall. The major share of the burden of a general excise tax then falls upon the sellers of productive inputs. It should be recognized that the so-called general excise taxes are normally not general in the sense that they apply equally to all products and services. Most states exempt major groups of commodities and services. The effects, therefore, are likely to be some combination of the specific excise and the truly general excise tax. As the taxes become more general, a greater share of the burden tends to fall on the owners of productive services.

Property Taxation

Local units of government depend for revenue primarily on one tax, the property tax. As it is actually administered, this is nearly limited to a tax on real property. A tax on real property is the one major tax which can be effectively imposed by local levels of government, for real property is the only economic resource which is relatively immobile and therefore cannot readily be shifted across local boundary lines to escape taxation.

This relative immobility explains, in part, the peculiar difficulties that arise when we attempt to trace the economic effects of the property tax. If real property were completely immobile and also completely permanent (not subject to depreciation) and fixed in supply, a tax levied on such property would be borne exclusively by the owner of the property at the time the tax was imposed. Future owners would bear none of the burden. The tax would reduce the expected net return of the property and the value of a capital asset is determined by the expected net return. So future purchasers would pay less for the property than they would have paid before the tax. Current owners at the time of the imposition of the tax would bear the full burden of the tax for all time by a reduction in the capital value. This process is called the "capitalization" of the tax. Renters of the property would never pay any share of the tax under these assumptions, since the supply is not changed as a result of the tax. The tax thus has no effect on the allocation of resources; it is levied on "pure rent."

Neither land nor other forms of real property, however, fit the assumptions of absolute permanency and fixity of supply. If real property can be produced and destroyed much as other assets, then changes in supply may result from the tax, and some of the burden may be shifted both to subsequent purchasers and to renters. A high tax rate would tend to reduce the investment in the development and improvement of real property. This would reduce the supply, and this in turn would tend to increase both market value and rental charges.

34

EXCHANGE RATES AND THE BALANCE OF PAYMENTS

In an earlier chapter it was demonstrated that a country as a whole will gain if it specializes in those commodities in which it has a comparative advantage and imports those things in which it has a comparative disadvantage. It was seen that this gain was of a mutual sort—each party to an international transaction is able to make more effective use of its resources and provide in the aggregate a greater total of goods and services for its consumers than would be possible without trade. Since both sides gain from international trade, the greater the amount of trade, the greater the total gain. It seems clear that the price of efforts at increased economic self-sufficiency is a reduced standard of living for consumers as a whole.

But proximately international trade is not between national economies; an individual or a firm in one country imports goods from an individual or firm in another country. If traders are to trade, there must be gains to them individually as well as to the economy as a whole. Even if it were generally understood that nations stand to gain from world trade, there would be no trade

416

between private-enterprise countries unless there were specific benefits to the importers and exporters directly engaged in international trade. It is appropriate, then, to see what the nature of these gains is and to determine why producers and consumers are interested in exchanging goods across national frontiers.

From the point of view of the producer, international trade appears to be advantageous in that it expands his market and, at least in the short run, increases his profits. If the demand of the foreign market is added to the demand in a producer's domestic market, the firm's profits are likely to be increased in much the same way that an increase in domestic demand resulting from an advertising campaign might increase its profits. And it may be that the foreign sales can be added at considerably smaller expense than would be required to effect a comparable increase in domestic demand. For firms in which decreasing costs are important— that is, where unit costs decrease as output increases—export sales may be particularly profitable; indeed, they may be necessary if the firm is to avoid losses. For example, an industry characterized by high fixed costs, such as the steel industry, in which the optimum-sized firm is very large could not operate in the Grand Duchy of Luxembourg unless it could sell in export markets.

The increase in profits to the firm resulting from adding foreign markets is sufficient explanation of why firms sell goods for export. If international trade did not increase profits, it may be presumed that firms would not engage in the export business. But why do consumers buy from foreigners? The answer to this question is somewhat more involved than the other, and the reasons are varied.

Some commodities are imported because they cannot be produced domestically, and, if they are to be consumed, they must be imported. The United States, for example, imports all of its supply of crude rubber, tin, coffee, raw silk, carpet wool, jute fibers and burlap, diamonds, cacao (used in chocolate), bananas, tea, spices, manila fiber, crude chicle (used in chewing gum), quebracho (used in leather tanning), and cobalt (used in cutting tools and paint). Ninety per cent or more of the following commodities has in recent years been imported: nickel, tung oil (used in quick-drying varnishes), high-grade manganese ore (used in steel alloys and batteries), asbestos, and chromite (used in stainless steel and heat-resistant wire). The list of commodities for which domestic production is insufficient to satisfy domestic requirements is extensive. Even the United States, which, as compared with other nations, is relatively self-sufficient, depends upon the rest of the

world for many of the commodities which we consider to be a part
of the "American way of life." For a number of other countries it
is a matter of "import or die."

In addition to the commodities which are imported because they
cannot be produced domestically, there are many goods which
are imported because for one reason or another they are not
produced domestically even though technical considerations would
permit their production. In some cases the quality of the imported
commodities is considered by consumers to be superior to that of
the domestic products. Such commodities as English woolens,
Scotch whiskies, French laces, and Italian wines are often considered by American consumers to be superior in quality to comparable domestic products, and they are imported even though
there may be a considerable price differential between the domestic
and the imported goods. A number of years ago, when the ownership of a Stutz Bearcat was the dream of all American boys—and
many of their fathers—the United States was a leader in the production of sports cars. Then, until recently, for reasons which are
not quite clear, if an American bought a sports car it had to be a
British MG or Jaguar, a French Bugatti, an Italian Ferrari, a German Mercedes, or some other foreign make.

Probably more important than either of the reasons just given
for the purchase of foreign goods is that imported goods can often
be bought at a lower price than similar domestic goods. If an Amer-
ican-made watch is priced at $75 and a Swiss watch of comparable
quality is available at $60, most American consumers will prefer the
Swiss watch. It is because some goods can be produced abroad and
sold more cheaply in domestic markets than they can be produced
and sold at home that domestic producers often demand from the
government "protection" from foreign competition, usually in the
form of a protective tariff. If, for example, a tax of $20 is levied on
the imported Swiss watch, the American watch will be less expensive to American purchasers although it was more expensive to
produce.

The Rate of Exchange

The price of $60 for the Swiss watch represents, of course, the
price in the American currency. The costs to the Swiss firm which
produced the watch, however, were incurred in terms of Swiss
francs—payments made for labor, materials, and interest on capi-

tal. We may assume that the cost to the Swiss watchmaker of producing the watch, including his profit, was 120 Swiss francs. If the watch was shipped to this country on a Swedish freighter, we may assume that transportation and insurance costs were 25 kronor. We may suppose that the markups of the American middlemen and the retailer totaled $25, and we have assumed that the tariff was $20. Then it appears that

$$120 \text{ Swiss francs} + 25 \text{ kronor} + \$25 + \$20 = \$80$$

It is clear that francs and kronor and dollars cannot, in fact, be added without being converted to some common denominator. This is effected by use of the rate of exchange, which may be defined as the price of one currency in terms of another. Let us suppose that the Swiss franc is worth 25 cents and that the krona is worth 20 cents in the foreign-exchange markets. The cost of the $80 watch may then be broken down as follows:

Cost of production to the Swiss firm (120 francs)	$30
Transportation and insurance (25 kronor)	5
American dealers' markups	25
American tariff	20
Total	$80

As long as the price remains unchanged, the American consumer is likely to buy the $75 American watch rather than the $80 Swiss watch. But now suppose that the exchange rate for Swiss francs falls from 25 cents to 20 cents. The 120 francs, which is the cost of production of the watch in Switzerland, is now the equivalent of $24 instead of $30, and if the other prices and the tariff remain unchanged, the watch will be sold in the American market for $74 instead of $80; it is now less expensive than the American watch in spite of the "protection" of the American tariff.

In comparing domestic and foreign prices, three prices rather than two have to be taken into account: (1) the price of the domestic commodity in terms of the domestic currency, (2) the price of the foreign commodity in terms of the foreign currency, and (3) the price of the foreign currency in terms of the domestic currency. The prices of the domestic and foreign commodities are determined in accordance with the principles developed earlier in this book. There remains the problem of how the price of one currency is determined in terms of another currency, *i.e.*, how the exchange rate is established.

SUPPLY AND DEMAND FOR FOREIGN EXCHANGE

In the absence of government intervention, which has been common in recent years, the rate of exchange is established in a highly competitive market. There are many buyers and many sellers, and no one of them is sufficiently important to affect the rate of exchange. Importers, tourists traveling in foreign countries, and American investors in securities of foreign companies are typical of the American demanders of foreign exchange. The demand curve for foreign exchange, like other demand curves, slopes downward from left to right. If British woolens were priced in England at one pound sterling (£1) per yard, for example, and if the price of the pound were $3, the price of woolens to the American buyer would be $3 per yard. If the rate of exchange fell to $2.80, however, the price of woolens to an American buyer would fall to $2.80 per yard. At the lower dollar price Americans would buy more woolens, and since each yard of woolens costs £1 in England, Americans would buy more pounds sterling. As the price of British pounds falls, the quantity demanded increases.

Similarly, the supply curve for foreign exchange may be assumed to slope upward from left to right. The supply of foreign exchange arises from payments made to Americans by foreigners for American exports. Since the amount of purchases of American goods by foreigners will increase as the price of foreign currencies increases (*i.e.*, as the dollar becomes cheaper), the amount of foreign currencies offered for dollars in international money markets will increase as the rate of exchange rises as long as the foreign demand for American goods has an elasticity of more than one. The rate of exchange is determined by the intersection of the demand and supply curves; in Figure 34.1 the "exchange rate on London," *i.e.*, the price of pounds in terms of dollars, is *OR*, and the number of pounds sterling bought and sold per time period is *OM*.

Suppose now that the American demand for British goods increases without a corresponding increase in the British demand for American goods. In Figure 34.2 assume that the original demand of Americans for a particular British good is represented by *D* and the supply of the good by *S;* the price of the good is $3 (£1) and the quantity exchanged is 18 units. Now assume that the demand increases from *D* to *D'*. The number of units of the British good now demanded by American buyers (and supplied by British exporters) is 30 instead of 18. In order to pay for the greater quantity of imports from England American buyers will have to acquire more

FIGURE 34.1. EXCHANGE RATE ON LON-
DON—Determined by Supply of and Demand
for Pounds

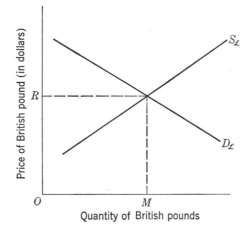

pounds sterling, *i.e.*, the demand for pounds will increase, raising
the price of the pound, say from $3 to $3.25. But the rise in the rate
of exchange has the effect of increasing the cost of the British goods
to American buyers. This is represented in Figure 34.2 by a shift of
S to S'. Originally, 18 units of the British good would have been
supplied by a British producer for £1, which was $3 in the Ameri-
can currency, and 30 units would have been supplied for £1⅓,
which was $4. Since we have assumed that the rate of exchange has
risen to $3.25, the 18 units, which are still supplied by the British

FIGURE 34.2. INCREASE IN UNITED STATES
DEMAND FOR A BRITISH GOOD—Raises Its
Price to American Consumers

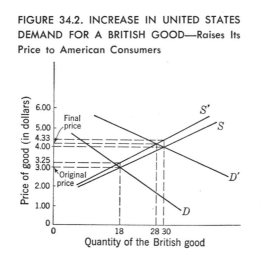

seller for £1, would now cost the American buyer $3.25 per unit, and 30 units would cost $4.33 each. The new supply curve S', accordingly, passes through the points 18 units—$3.25 and 30 units—$4.33.

The intersection of the new American-demand-for-British-goods curve D' and the new supply-of-British-goods curve S' indicates that Americans will now buy only 28 units instead of 30, and, as a result, the price of the British good to the American buyer will be somewhat less than $4.33 and the demand for pounds will decrease slightly, causing the exchange rate to be somewhat less than $3.25. (This slight further adjustment in the exchange rate is not reflected in the chart.)

In addition, the effect of the change in the rate of exchange from $3 to $3.25 (which from the British point of view is a *fall* in the exchange rate, *i.e.*, dollars are now cheaper in terms of pounds) is to make it possible for Englishmen to get $3.25 worth of American goods for their pounds instead of only $3 worth. This will make American goods cheaper to British buyers than they were before and, quite possibly, cheaper than similar British goods. The increased purchase of American goods by British buyers which would result could be represented graphically by a shift of the supply-of-pounds curve in Figure 34.1 to the right, and this would also tend to lower (from the American point of view) the rate of exchange below the $3.25 level. The new equilibrium rate would be established somewhere between $3 and $3.25.

This analysis indicates that an increase in the American demand for foreign goods will normally raise the dollar price of the foreign goods in essentially the same way in which an increase in demand raises the price of domestic goods. When the transaction involves two currencies, the process is somewhat more complex because of the interjection of the exchange rate, but basically the prices of foreign goods expressed in terms of the domestic currency respond to changes in demand in the same way that the prices of domestic goods react to demand changes.

ARBITRAGE

When exchange rates are free to fluctuate without intervention by government, the rates are likely to change several times a day, and, when trading is brisk, the changes may come so fast that it is with difficulty that traders in foreign exchange keep up with them. This gives speculators opportunity to ply their trade, and fortunes have been won and lost in this way. One aspect of speculation in foreign exchange which deserves special mention is known as *arbitrage*. Arbitrage consists of buying and selling a commodity in two different markets at the same time in order to take advantage of a momentary price differential in the two markets. Suppose that in New York the price of pounds sterling is $3, and in London the rate is $2.99. The arbitrager can make a profit by simultaneously selling pounds for dollars in New York and buying pounds for dollars in London. He may contract to sell £100,000 in New York for $300,000 and simultaneously buy the £100,000 to "cover" the transaction in London for $299,000. The $1,000 difference between the selling price and the buying price represents the arbitrager's gross profit (see Table 34.1).

Table 34.1. Arbitrage Transaction Illustrated

New York	*London*
£1 = $3.00	£1 = $2.99
Sell £100,000 for $300,000	Buy £100,000 for $299,000
The $300,000 covers the London transaction with a gross profit of $1,000	The £100,000 covers the New York transaction

The effect of the sales of pounds by arbitragers in New York will be to cause the rate to fall to something less than $3; the effect of the purchase of pounds in the London foreign-exchange market will be to raise the price of pounds to something more than $2.99. In a very short time—a matter of a few minutes—the discrepancy in the prices in the two markets will have been eliminated, the rate in each country probably settling in the neighborhood of $2.99½. The economic effect of arbitrage is, accordingly, to eliminate discrepancies in exchange rates in markets throughout the world. Since the arbitrager knows at what price he can buy in one market and at what price he can sell in the other, the whole transaction can be carried out at no risk to him. Arbitrage has, in fact, been described as betting on a sure thing.

EXCHANGE CONTROLS

During the last two decades exchange rates have been subject to a considerable degree of control by many foreign governments and have not, in most countries, been determined by the forces of supply and demand in free markets. The purpose of exchange control has been in general to "peg" the domestic currency at a higher rate than that which would obtain in free markets. The higher value of the domestic currency in terms of foreign currencies has the effect of increasing the volume of goods which can be purchased from abroad with a given quantity of the domestic currency. Conversely, by making the domestic currency expensive in terms of foreign currencies, the artificially high value of the domestic currency discourages the foreign purchase of domestic goods.

Although the governmental pegging of exchange rates clearly serves certain political objectives, such as stockpiling critical imports in anticipation of war or speeding up reconstruction following a war, it should be observed that this sort of interference by governments destroys much of the normal rationing function of price which characterizes free markets. The pegging of the value of the domestic currency at a high rate will have the effect of making the quantity of domestic currency demanded less than the amount supplied at the pegged rate, or, what is the same thing, it will make the amount of foreign currencies demanded greater than the amount supplied at the legal rate. The setting of the price of foreign currencies below equilibrium levels creates a rationing problem and makes necessary some direct allocation of the scarce currencies among prospective users. This has given rise to what is commonly called the "dollar shortage"; the interference by foreign governments with the free market for foreign exchange has had the expected result of converting the normal scarcity of dollars into a problem of dollar shortage. (This is the same type of effect that was noted in Chapter 4 in relation to rent control.) Exchange-control policy is given further attention in the next chapter.

Balance of International Payments

The U.S. Department of Commerce publishes annually what is known as the United States balance of international payments. This is a list by main categories of transactions which have given rise during the year to (1) payments by foreigners to Americans and (2) payments by Americans to foreigners. An understanding of the balance of payments and its implications will serve as the basis for an evaluation of policies which would have the effect of restricting international trade, a topic which will be explored more fully in Chapter 35. Receipts from foreigners for "exports" are referred to as *credits* in the balance of payments, and payments to importers for "imports" are known as *debits*. It is important, first, to understand why each item in the balance of payments is listed as a credit or a debit.

The principal items comprising the balance of international

payments are indicated in Table 34.2. Most of the entries are probably self-explanatory. It seems reasonable enough in view of the definitions given above, for example, to list payments made to Americans for merchandise sold to foreigners as a credit and the value of interest payments made by Americans to foreigners as a debit. But why is the amount borrowed by Americans from foreigners a *credit?* And why are American gold imports a *debit?*

As a rule of thumb, we may observe that *any transaction which gives rise to a demand for American dollars is listed in the United*

Table 34.2. Principal Items in the American Balance of Payments

Receipts from foreigners for "*exports*" *(credits)*	*Payments to foreigners for* "*imports*" *(debits)*
1. Value of merchandise exports sold to foreigners	1. Value of merchandise imports bought from foreigners
2. Value of freight and shipping services sold to foreigners	2. Value of freight and shipping services bought from foreigners
3. Value of foreign tourists' expenditures in U.S.	3. Value of American tourists' expenditures abroad
4. Gifts made by foreigners to Americans	4. Gifts made by Americans to foreigners
5. Interest and dividend payments made by foreigners to Americans	5. Interest and dividend payments made by Americans to foreigners
6. Value of American gold and silver exports	6. Value of American gold and silver imports
7. Amount borrowed by Americans from foreigners	7. Amount loaned by Americans to foreigners
8. Amount of repayment to Americans of sums previously borrowed by foreigners	8. Amount of repayment to foreigners of sums previously borrowed by Americans

States balance of payments as a credit; any transaction which gives rise to a demand for a foreign currency is a debit.[1] To test the rule, let us see what happens when Americans export merchandise to foreigners, a transaction which is clearly a credit item in the balance of payments. Suppose that an American exporter has shipped cigarettes to a British importer. The exporter wants payment in dollars, but the importer makes payment in pounds sterling. The for-

[1] The rule may be stated more generally as follows: Any transaction which gives rise to a demand for dollars or a supply of a foreign currency is a credit item in the United States balance of payments; any transaction which gives rise to a demand for a foreign currency or a supply of dollars is a debit. This is true since a demand for dollars implies a supply of a foreign currency, and a demand for a foreign currency implies a supply of dollars. It follows, accordingly, that an increase in a credit item in the balance of payments tends to cause the rate of exchange (the dollar price of foreign currencies) to fall; an increase in a debit item tends to cause the exchange rate to rise.

FIGURE 34.3.

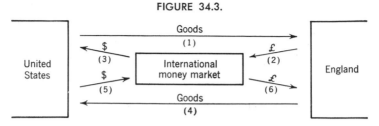

eign-exchange transaction, therefore, involves a supply of pounds and a demand for dollars. This classifies the merchandise export as a credit from the American point of view.

If we can imagine a mythical "International Money Market" located in the middle of the Atlantic Ocean, where the currency of one country is exchanged for that of another, and if we can determine whether for each transaction there is a demand for dollars or a demand for a foreign currency, we shall be able to classify the transaction as a credit or a debit.

Suppose that an American has exported wheat to England (step 1 in Figure 34.3). The British importer takes pounds to the International Money Market (step 2) and *demands dollars* in order to pay the American importer (step 3). Since the foreign-exchange transaction involves a supply of pounds and a demand for dollars, the export of merchandise is a credit in the American balance of payments.

If, on the other hand, an American imports goods from England (step 4 in Figure 34.3), he must take dollars to the IMM (step 5) and *demand pounds* to make payment for the merchandise received (step 6). The foreign-exchange transaction this time represents a supply of dollars and a demand for pounds, and this classifies the American import as a debit item in the balance of payments.

In similar fashion, each of the items in Table 34.2 can be analyzed to determine whether it is a credit or a debit. If a foreigner buys shipping services from an American firm, he must take his currency to the International Money Market and demand dollars in order to make payment. If a foreigner travels in this country, he must take his currency to the IMM and demand dollars to spend here. If a foreigner wishes to make a gift of money to an American, he will take his currency to the IMM and demand dollars. If an American receives a dividend check from a foreign corporation, he will take it to the IMM and demand dollars. If a foreigner wishes to buy American gold, he will take his currency to the IMM and demand dollars in the same way that he would in order to pay for any other American export. If an American firm wishes to borrow money from foreigners, it will probably do it by selling bonds to foreign buyers. The foreign bond buyer will take his currency to the IMM and demand dollars with which to buy the American bonds. If a foreign firm wishes to repay an old debt to Americans, it will take its currency to the IMM and demand dollars with which to make payment. All of these transactions are credit items in the American balance of payments since they represent a demand for dollars, *i.e.*, payments to Americans. In similar fashion, each of the debit items in Table 34.2 could be shown to represent a demand for foreign currencies.

BALANCE OF PAYMENTS MUST BALANCE

The next point to be made is that the balance of payments must always balance. The balance of payments is not to be confused with the balance of trade. The value of American merchandise exports may be more or less than the value of merchandise imports during any given time period. The value of *merchandise* exports minus the value of *merchandise* imports is called the balance of trade, and it may be positive, negative, or zero. A plus balance is usually referred to as a "favorable" balance of trade, and a minus balance is called "unfavorable," although there is nothing necessarily favorable about a "favorable" balance or unfavorable about an "unfavorable" balance of trade. But taking into account the entire balance of *payments*, "invisible" as well as "visible" items, the total credits must equal the total debits. This is rather curious since decisions as to what and how much to import and how much to export, and how much to borrow and how much to lend, are made by millions of different individuals, and it would appear to be sheer coincidence if the total debits happened to equal total credits. But the totals must be equal, and a simple illustration will make the reason clear.

Suppose that in a given year Americans have exported $1,000 worth of merchandise to foreigners, and no other item appears on the credit side of the balance of payments statement. We may suppose that during the year Americans have imported $600 worth of merchandise. Americans have a "favorable" balance of trade of $400, and the partial balance of payments would take the form of Table 34.3. We know that this is only a partial balance of payments statement, since this is a list of *payments;* the credit item of $1,000 would not have been included if the goods had not been paid for.

We know that foreigners paid for $600 worth of the Americans' exports by shipping goods of that value, but Table 34.3 leaves $400 of the payment unaccounted for; there must be $400 worth of debits not yet included.

Table 34.3. Partial Balance of Payments

Credits	*Debits*
Merchandise exports........$1,000	Merchandise imports.........$600

Suppose that during the year Americans bought $100 worth of shipping services from foreigners and American tourists spent $200 traveling abroad. This provided foreigners an additional $300 with which to pay for their imports from the United States, but we are still $100 short in accounting for the means of payment for the full $1,000 worth of merchandise which they actually received and paid for. We may suppose that the last $100 worth was paid for with money which foreigners borrowed from Americans. The balance of payments would then take the form of Table 34.4.

Table 34.4. Balance of Payments

Credits		*Debits*	
Merchandise exports........$1,000		Merchandise imports.......$	600
		Shipping services..........	100
		Travel expenditures........	200
		Loans from Americans......	100
Total...................$1,000		Total..................$1,000	

The debit side of the balance of payments may be looked upon as the source of the dollars which foreigners used to pay for the goods received by them from this country. And since the dollars paid by foreigners to Americans must equal the dollars received by Americans from foreigners, the total of the credit items must equal the total of the debits.

BALANCE OF PAYMENTS ANALYSIS

We are now ready to analyze the balance of payments statement and determine what insight into international commercial policy may be obtained through its study. Table 34.5 is a hypothetical American balance of payments statement for a given year.[1] The balance of trade (item 1 minus item 8) is seen to be +$5,400 million, and the balance of payments balances at $16,300.

---

[1] The Department of Commerce does not publish the actual balance of payments data in a form which is adaptable to the simple type of table used in this chapter.

Table 34.5. Representative United States Balance of International Payments

(In millions of dollars)

Credits		*Debits*	
1. Merchandise exports......$12,300		8. Merchandise imports......$ 6,900	
2. Freight and shipping services sold to foreigners..........	1,100	9. Freight and shipping services bought from foreigners	1,000
3. Foreigners' travel expenditures in U.S..............	300	10. American tourist expenditures abroad............	700
4. Interest payments to Americans by foreigners........	1,300	11. Interest payments made by Americans to foreigners....	300
5. Gold exports.............	100	12. Gold imports............	200
6. Amount borrowed from abroad..................	400	13. Amount loaned by Americans to foreigners........	5,000
7. Repayment of old debts to Americans by foreigners....	800	14. Repayment of old debts to foreigners by Americans...	2,200
Total...................$16,300		Total...................$16,300	

Suppose now that we are interested only in net figures. We have seen that merchandise transactions were on balance a net credit of $5,400 million. Similarly, freight and shipping services show a net credit balance of $100 million (item 2 minus item 9), and interest payments are on balance a credit of $1,000 (item 4 minus item 11). All of the other accounts show net debit balances. It will be noted in Table 34.6 that, just as the original balance of payments balanced, so does the balance of payments when stated in net terms only.

Table 34.6. Consolidated Balance of Payments

(Net figures, in millions of dollars)

Credits		*Debits*	
1. Merchandise............$5,400		4. Travel.................$ 400	
2. Freight and shipping.....	100	5. Gold..................	100
3. Interest...............	1,000	6. Loans.................	4,600
		7. Repayment of loans......	1,400
Total.................$6,500		Total.................$6,500	

It is possible to take the consolidation one step further. Suppose that we combine in one entry all goods and services items and in another all capital and interest items. The goods and services items are 1, 2, 4, and 5 in Table 34.6; items 3, 6, and 7 may be classed as capital and interest items. Item 1 plus item 2 minus item 4 minus item 5 shows a net credit balance of $5,000 million; item 3 subtracted from item 6 plus item 7 shows a net debit balance of $5,000 million. This is indicated in Table 34.7.

Since in Table 34.7 goods and services are a credit entry, capital and interest must be a debit; if there are only two items in the balance of payments statement, one must of necessity be a credit and the other must be a debit since, as we have seen, the two sides must balance. There are at least two conditions under which goods and services might be a credit item: (1) If large-scale loans were made by Americans to foreigners during the year so that the amount of the loans was greater than the amount of the interest paid by foreigners to Americans during the year, capital and interest items would be a net debit, and goods and services would, therefore, be a credit. (2) If Americans were paying large sums of interest to foreigners or paying off old debts to foreigners, capital and

Table 34.7. Condensed Balance of Payments

(Net figures, in millions of dollars)

Credits	*Debits*
Goods and services..........$5,000	Capital and interest.........$5,000

interest items might be on balance a debit, with goods and services a net credit.

In recent years the United States has maintained a favorable balance of trade largely as a result of situation 1 above. Lend-lease and other public and private loans to foreigners have been very large, and this has made possible the net export of American goods to foreigners; fundamentally, Americans have been making loans of goods to foreigners. But the more money that is loaned to foreigners in one year, the greater will be the interest payments in subsequent years, and if a favorable balance of trade is maintained by making loans, eventually the interest payments, to say nothing of the repayment of old loans, will represent a bigger payment to Americans than the amount of the annual loans by Americans to foreigners. When that happens, the capital and interest items will on balance be a credit from the American point of view, and goods and services must, therefore, be a debit. That is to say, if foreigners are to pay Americans the interest which they owe and eventually repay the principal sums borrowed, the United States must have an unfavorable balance of trade. But American commercial policy in the past has called for payment by foreigners of their debts to us while at the same time we have attempted to maintain a favorable balance of trade. Such a policy is inherently inconsistent and impossible of accomplishment. Either we must have a net debit balance for goods and services items, or we must expect foreigners to default on their obligations to us.

Americans could, indeed, export more than they import without restriction if the exports were to be given away. If the sole objective of American foreign-trade policy were to maintain full employment at home, the production of goods and giving them to foreigners might be defended on the grounds that it would create jobs. Lending money to foreigners with which they can buy American goods and then forcing them to default on their obligations is, of course, tantamount to giving the goods away. But it should be noted that producing goods and dumping them in the Atlantic Ocean would have the same effect on American employment. Since we cannot produce as many goods in the aggregate as Americans would like to consume, the gift of goods to foreigners or the destruction of goods to maintain employment cannot be defended as a long-run policy. More economic solutions to the problem of unemployment have been suggested in earlier chapters, and the effect of trade restrictions on American standards of living will be discussed in the next chapter.

35

INTERNATIONAL COMMERCIAL POLICY

Two points which are basic to a consideration of international commercial policy were made in earlier chapters dealing with international economics. It was pointed out in Chapter 20 that, although all countries gain from foreign trade as a long-run matter, any change in a country's pattern of international trading may generate extremely difficult short-run readjustments in the domestic economy. Substantial liberalization in international-trade policy would tend to revamp the entire organization of the economy, increasing the demand for some products and some factors and reducing the demand for others, increasing the output of some goods and reducing the output of others, raising some incomes and lowering others. This suggests that while from the point of view of the consumer free international trade is beneficial since it contributes to higher standards of living, there may be producer groups in the economy which are adversely affected by extensions of foreign trade. Those whose sales will be reduced if foreign goods are made available to domestic consumers will look upon imports as an evil, and they are likely to foster restrictive policies which will make it difficult or perhaps even impossible for certain foreign goods to compete with domestic products in the domestic market. The first

432

fact to be kept in mind in evaluating international commercial policy is that any change generates a conflict among the interests of economic groups within the country. A policy of expanding trade with foreigners will help some but hurt others; a policy of restrictionism will benefit some at the expense of others. Policy in this area, as in most, consists in large part of determining what groups are to be helped at the expense of other groups. Since producer groups are likely to be more vocal and more powerful politically, the interests of domestic producers are likely in practice to be protected against the interests of domestic consumers.[1]

A second point of significance in evaluating international commercial policy was made in Chapter 34. Here it was pointed out that the balance of payments must balance. A policy which calls for payment by foreigners to Americans of old debts and interest on old debt is inconsistent with a policy which provides a net export balance for goods and services items. Both policies cannot be carried out at the same time. Either Americans must import more than they export under such conditions, or foreigners will be forced to default on their obligations to Americans. Policy makers in the field of international trade must, therefore, first determine what groups are to be helped at the expense of other groups, and, second, they must determine whether a given policy which they are proposing will make impossible the carrying out of another policy to which they are also committed.

The determination of appropriate policy in situations in which one group stands to gain at the expense of other groups poses some of the most difficult problems in political economy. Policies of this sort in the area of international economics would include the following:

1. Proposals which would benefit the world as a whole but might help some nations and injure others.

---

[1] If one accepts Adam Smith's view that the interests of consumers and the general welfare are identical, the case against trade restrictions appears to be conclusive. Smith said: "Consumption is the sole end and purpose of all production; and the interest of the producer ought to be attended to, only so far as it may be necessary for promoting that of the consumer. The maxim is so perfectly self-evident that it would be absurd to attempt to prove it." Adam Smith, *The Wealth of Nations* (New York: Modern Library, Inc., 1937), p. 625. A similar view was expressed by Professor Simons: "All the grosser mistakes in economic policy, if not most manifestations of democratic corruption, arise from focusing upon the interests of people as producers rather than upon their interests as consumers. One gets the right answers usually by regarding simply the interests of consumers. . . ." Henry C. Simons, "Some Reflections on Syndicalism," *Economic Policy for a Free Society* (Chicago: University of Chicago Press, 1948), p. 123.

2. Proposals which would benefit the nation as a whole but might help some groups and injure others.

3. Proposals which would benefit some groups but would injure the nation as a whole.

Those who advocate restrictions on international trade seldom claim that their policies fall in category 1. Trade restrictionism is usually advocated as a frankly nationalistic policy. American tariffs are supported because it is alleged that they benefit American business. Argentine exchange control was imposed in the belief that it helped the Argentine economy. British cartels are given government support because it is thought that they help British industry. Arguments which suggest that the aggregate world production would be greatest under free trade usually make little impression on those who advocate restrictionism; their objective is not world welfare but national well-being. Whether this is a proper objective for public policy is a matter which need not concern us here, but whether trade restrictionism is injurious or beneficial to the nation is a matter upon which economic analysis can throw some light.

Protective Tariffs

The device resorted to most frequently by American policy makers in an effort to restrict the free flow of goods into the country is the protective tariff. By levying a tax on goods coming into the country the government can make imported goods more expensive than comparable domestic goods, which, of course, are not subject to the tax. If the tariff is sufficiently high, American consumers will find the imported goods too expensive to buy; if they consume the commodity at all, they must buy the domestic good.

The most obvious effect of the protective tariff is that it raises the prices of commodities protected by it; if it did not raise prices, it would afford no protection. The increase in prices represents a gain to domestic producers, at least in the short run, and a loss to consumers. The higher price for the product is likely to mean a greater income for producers and a reduction in living standards for consumers. The reduction or perhaps elimination of foreign competition secures the domestic market for domestic producers and tends to make them look with favor upon the protection of a tariff when the threat of competition from foreign sellers is significant.

Under conditions of full employment, if the price of a commodity is increased as a result of the enactment of a tariff, domestic producers of that commodity are likely to expand production, drawing labor and other resources from other industries, some of which may come from export industries. This means a reallocation of resources, taking them from industries where the country has a comparative advantage and adding them where the country is at a comparative disadvantage. As in the case of all monopolistic malallocations of resources, the real value of the aggregate output of all industries is less than if resources were allocated by the competitive forces of the free market, and the productivity of factors of production, *e.g.*, labor, is less than if employed in industries where comparative advantage is greater, with the result that the compensation to factors, *e.g.*, wages, is reduced.

The kinds of adjustments which restrictions on the free flow of goods in international trade bring into being depend upon the particular circumstances obtaining in a given case. Since no thoroughly satisfactory generalization is available to explain the repercussions which will follow from any possible interference with the normal currents of world trade, we shall analyze three different models, each making different assumptions with reference to the basic facts of the case.

CASE I. TARIFF EXCLUDES SOME IMPORTS BUT NOT ALL: CONSTANT
WORLD SUPPLY PRICE

Let us consider first a situation in which a part of the domestic supply of a commodity is produced domestically and a part is imported. The wool industry in the United States typifies this case; some sections of the country are well adapted to wool production, but the amount of wool which can be produced in these areas is not sufficient to meet the total domestic demand. In Figure 35.1 D_d and S_d represent the domestic short-run demand and supply schedules. In both the world and domestic markets the commodity is assumed to be sold under conditions of perfect competition, and the world price is assumed to be OW, which is unaffected by changes in the volume of American imports.

With a world price of OW, domestic producers will be willing to supply Os units, and domestic demand will be Od units. The difference between the quantity demanded by domestic consumers and the quantity supplied by domestic producers will be imported; in Figure 35.1 this is sd units.

Suppose now that a tariff equal to WW' is levied on all imports of this commodity. The price to domestic consumers will rise by the full amount of the tariff to OW'. At the higher price resources which were more productive in other employments before the enactment

FIGURE 35.1. PRICE INCREASES BY AMOUNT
OF TARIFF—When World Supply Price Is
Constant

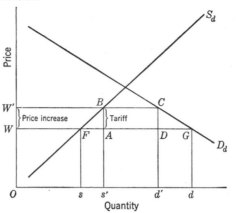

of the tariff will now be attracted to this industry, and the total
quantity supplied by domestic producers will be Os', an increase
of ss'. At the higher price, however, domestic consumers will take
fewer units of the commodity, the total quantity demanded at price
OW' being Od', a reduction of $d'd$ units. Imports will, accordingly,
be reduced from sd to $s'd'$.

What is the nature of the short-run gains and losses resulting from
the tariff? Domestic-producer income has clearly increased. Before
the enactment of the tariff, domestic wool producers received
$OWFs$ for the Os units produced; now they receive $OW'Bs'$ for
Os' units, an increase equal to $WW'BA + sFAs'$. On the presumption that the additional inputs could earn an amount equal to
$sFBs'$ in alternate employments, the net gain to domestic producers
in the short run would be $WW'BF$. This is sufficient incentive for
producer groups to favor the tariff. If price OW' is high enough to
provide short-run abnormal profits, these would tend in the long
run to be eliminated through the entry of new domestic producers
and the encouragement of substitute products.

Consumers are injured by the tariff, especially in the short run.
The price has gone up by the full amount of the tariff, from OW
to OW'. Since in the particular case represented by Figure 35.1 the
elasticity of the domestic demand between prices OW and OW'
is less than 1, the total expenditure at the higher price, $OW'Cd'$, is
greater than at the lower price, $OWGd$; that is, after the tariff consumers actually spend more for the smaller number of units than
they previously spent for the greater number.

Since imports after the tariff are equal to $s'd'$ and the central government collects a tariff of WW' on each unit imported, the total amount collected by the government as a tariff is equal to $ABCD$. This may be considered as a gain to the tariff-levying country, but it should be noted that consumers pay an amount equal to $WW'CD$ more for the Od' units than those units would have cost in the absence of the tariff, and this exceeds the amount collected by the government by $WW'BA$.

The income of foreign producers from sales in this market has been reduced by the tariff from $sFGd$ to $s'ADd'$, a reduction equal to $sFAs' + d'DGd$. This will cause a loss of export sales to the country levying the tariff. If the tariff-levying country were, for example, the United States, the dollar balances of foreigners would be smaller and the foreign demand for American goods would be reduced. This means that the export industries would decline, and the long-run effect of the tariff would be to shift resources out of export industries, where the nation has a comparative advantage, to import industries, where resources could be used less effectively.

CASE II. IMPORTS AVAILABLE UNDER CONDITIONS OF INCREASING COSTS

Let us consider as our second model the case in which imports are available to the tariff-levying country under conditions of short-run increasing costs. Suppose, for example, that the United States produces a part of its supply of a given commodity and imports a part, but that all of the imports come from Canada. That part of Canada's output which she would be willing to sell to the United States would be represented by a positively sloping curve. In Figure 35.2, S_a is the United States domestic short-run supply curve, D_a is the domestic demand curve, and S_{a+c} is the domestic supply plus the quantity available from Canada.

In the absence of restrictions on international trade, the price OP will be established, and Americans will buy Od units, Os from domestic producers plus sd from Canadian sellers. Suppose now that a tariff equal to HC is levied on imports from Canada. This will have the effect of shifting the S_{a+c} curve to S'_{a+c}, and price will rise to OP'. At this price American consumption will fall from Od to Od', domestic production will increase from Os to Os', and imports will decline from sd to $s'd'$.

Let us assess the short-run gains and losses in this case. Again the incomes of domestic producers have been increased. Before the tariff was enacted, the total income received by American suppliers was $OPFs$; after the tariff it rose to $OP'Bs'$, an increase equal to

FIGURE 35.2. PRICE INCREASES BY LESS THAN
TARIFF—With Rising Supply Price

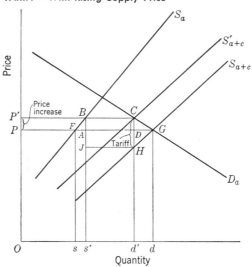

$PP'BA + sFAs'$. On the presumption that alternative employment
of resources would have provided domestic producers with an income equal to $sFBs'$, their net gain resulting from the tariff is
$PP'BF$.

The price paid by American consumers has gone up from OP to
OP', but the increase in price, PP', is less than the amount of the
tariff, HC. This results from the fact that a part of the tariff is
shifted backward to the foreign producers. The total amount which
American consumers pay for imports is equal to the area $s'BCd'$.
Of this amount the area $JBCH$ is collected by the American government as a tariff. The net income to foreigner producers is, accordingly, $s'JHd'$, and the price per unit realized by Canadian
producers is equal to $d'H$, which is less by the full amount of the
tariff than the price received by American sellers.

The income received by Canadian sellers in the American market after the tariff is less than that received by them before the
tariff by an amount equal to $sFAs' + d'DGd + JADH$. This means
that Canadians will have fewer American dollars with which to
buy American goods, and there will be a shifting of resources in the
United States out of the export industries, where resources can be
utilized more effectively, into import industries, where they can be
used less efficiently, with the result that total product and real income in the United States will be reduced.

CASE III. TARIFF STRENGTHENS DOMESTIC MONOPOLY

A tariff strengthens the monopoly position of a domestic firm. We shall briefly consider three cases: (1) a domestic monopoly which has no competition from foreign producers, (2) a domestic monopoly which must compete with foreign producers in the domestic as well as in the foreign market, and (3) a domestic monopoly which is protected by a high tariff on imports.

1. In Figure 35.3, d and mr represent a monopoly firm's demand and marginal revenue curves; mc is the firm's marginal cost curve. If we assume that the firm sells only in the domestic market and that there is no competition from foreign sellers, it will maximize profits by producing to the point where marginal cost equals marginal revenue. Monopoly price will be OP, and output will be OM.

2. If we now assume that this firm's product is sold in the world market under competitive conditions and that the world price OW is not affected by this firm's actions, the domestic firm, in the absence of a protective tariff, will have to sell at price OW instead of price OP. At the lower price, ON' units will be demanded in the

FIGURE 35.3. A PROTECTIVE TARIFF—Increases Monopoly Power

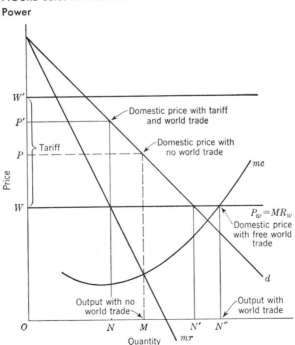

domestic market. The total output of the firm will now be ON'' since at this point marginal cost equals marginal revenue in the world market (MR_w) which is equal to world price; $N'N''$ units will, accordingly, be sold abroad. Whereas the firm would be a monopolist in a closed economy, it is placed in a competitive position under free international trade. This model points up the difference between competitive price and output and monopoly price and output, and it indicates that an effective way of preventing domestic monopoly and encouraging competition is the adoption of free trade.

3. Now suppose that a high tariff, *e.g.*, a 100 per cent duty, is enacted. In Figure 35.3 the tariff, WW', is equal to OW, the world price. The effect of the tariff is to keep foreign competition out of the domestic market while retaining the world market for that part of the firm's output which it can sell abroad to better advantage than it can sell at home. Under these conditions the firm will sell no more than ON units in the domestic market; for any output greater than ON, the marginal revenue resulting from sales in the world market will be greater than if they were sold in the domestic market; (*i.e.*, mr lies below MR_w). The firm will, therefore, sell ON units at a price of OP' in the domestic market and NN'' units at price OW in the world market. But OP' is an even higher price than the monopoly price OP which would prevail in a closed economy. The tariff in such cases not only maintains monopoly but may cause domestic monopoly price to be higher by making it possible for the monopolist to discriminate between domestic and foreign buyers.

EVALUATION OF TARIFF

In each of the three models analyzed the conclusion was that certain domestic-producer groups made short-run gains at the expense of the nation as a whole. These cases may be taken to be representative though not exhaustive. It is possible, in fact, if other nations do not retaliate with tariffs of their own and if the demand of foreign countries for the products of the tariff-levying country is sufficiently inelastic, that the tariff may improve the country's terms of trade, *i.e.*, the amount of imports received in exchange for a given amount of exports. In periods of less than full employment a protective tariff may increase total spending on domestically produced goods and services. The tariff serves to shift domestic demand from foreign to local goods and, by reducing the supply of foreign exchange available to foreigners, to shift foreign demand from domestic to foreign markets. Whether or not total spending on domestic goods will be increased or decreased by such a policy depends upon the elasticity of demand of Americans for foreign goods as compared with the elasticity of foreign demand for American goods. Spending, and hence employment, will be increased only if Americans will, as result of the tariff, shift more aggregate demand from the foreign to the domestic market than foreigners will shift away from the domestic market. Conversely, if the respective elasticities are in the proper relation to each other, a tariff may serve to reduce inflationary pressures in domestic markets. Despite the possible favorable effects which a tariff might have on income and employment, it is not to be recommended as appropriate policy. The fact is that other nations can and will retaliate, and, if all countries follow a tariff-raising policy, the volume of world trade will decline and all nations will suffer.

The economist's chief charge against the tariff is that it brings about a misallocation of resources. In the long run, even domestic producers may not gain. If the tariff results in abnormal profits and if competition prevails in the domestic market, new firms will enter the protected industries until profits disappear. The effect is similar to that observed in connection with such other government interferences with price as the fair-trade laws, marketing agreements, and unfair-practices acts. These give rise to a shift of resources from areas where resources can be utilized more efficiently to areas where they can be used less efficiently. But when the tariff is up for revision, Congress unfortunately is not likely to have the problem of efficient allocation in mind at all. Instead, each congressman is apt to be thinking of what will happen to certain firms, owned by and employing constituents of his, if the protection of the tariff is reduced.

In spite of the understandable pressures for higher and higher tariffs in this country, the last decades have seen considerable progress in the lowering of trade barriers, and it seems that the business community understands more clearly than ever before in our history the necessity of reducing restrictions on international trade. The Smoot-Hawley Act of 1930 provided the highest average rates of any tariff in our history, and this remains the basic tariff law of the land. But in 1934, largely as a result of the efforts of Secretary of State Cordell Hull,[1] Congress passed the Reciprocal Trade Act which permitted, among other things, the reduction of tariff

[1] See William R. Allen, "The Trade Philosophy of Cordell Hull, 1907–1933," *American Economic Review*, Vol. 43, pp. 101–116 (March, 1953).

rates up to 50 per cent. By the end of the first decade about half of
the duty reductions had been for the full 50 per cent. In 1945 the
President was authorized to reduce the rates prevailing at that time
up to 50 per cent, so the rates on commodities which had taken the
first full 50 per cent reduction could now be reduced to 25 per cent
of the 1934 level. Since that time multilateral agreements have
been worked out with several countries with the result that the
average tariff rates imposed by the United States are now lower
than they have been in several decades.

Big business concerns which have become large importers as
well as exporters have to an increasing extent seen the difficulties
which tariffs and other trade restrictions have been responsible for,
and some of them have taken a firm position in favor of tariff reductions.[1] Many local, regional, and national groups have in recent
years announced that they favor a policy of tariff reduction. Although the tariff on many commodities remains so high that the
volume in which they are imported is low, the situation has shown
marked improvement in recent years, and the prospects for the future appear to be better than most economists thought possible a
short time ago.

International Cartels

Although high tariffs have been the chief device employed by
the United States to restrict imports, other measures which have
similar restrictive effects have been employed from time to time.
Other countries whose record on the tariff is better than that of the
United States have worse records than ours with respect to other
forms of restrictionism. The ideal of free multilateral trade requires that all barriers to the movement of goods between countries
be removed. We shall briefly consider a number of these restrictive
devices, beginning with international cartels.

An international cartel is an agreement, formal or informal, entered into by firms situated in different countries and doing business across international boundaries when the purpose of the agreement is to increase profits by reducing competition. The term *cartel*
has been used in this book to denote sellers who surrender their
price-setting and related powers to a central association. These

[1] See, for example, "General Motors Overseas," *Fortune,* November, 1945,
pp. 125 *ff.*, and "Import and Prosper," *ibid.*, pp. 113–114. In an Associated
Press dispatch for February 17, 1953, Henry Ford was quoted as favoring immediate repeal of the 10 per cent tariff on automobiles and "the most rapid
possible elimination of all tariffs."

sellers may be numerous or relatively few. For the most part, our previous discussions of cartels have assumed that a large number of sellers are associated. International cartels, however, are typically combinations of oligopolistic sellers situated in different countries and doing business both domestically and beyond national boundaries. The cartel arrangements make possible extremely effective oligopolistic collusion to the benefit of the producers and the detriment of consumers. Cartel-determined prices are likely to approach closely those which would be charged by a single firm operating in international markets. Like domestic cartel arrangements, international cartels frequently have the outright support of government.

Numerous devices are employed by cartels. The members may enter into a single agreement to maintain prices. They may allocate markets geographically among the members of the cartel, or they may assign sales to an international trade association which maintains a joint sales agency for the members of the cartel. They may exchange patents and secret processes. Or the member firms in the cartel may be owned by the same group of men through an exchange of stock, a holding company, or other monopolistic devices. Since American antitrust laws prevent the kind of price agreements which firms in other countries may freely enter into, those cartels which include American firms usually attempt to utilize the patent in the hope that their actions will not be illegal.[1]

Frequently cartel agreements are sponsored by governments. During the 1930's government schemes to control the international output and price of wheat, sugar, coffee, tea, tin, and rubber were entered into by the leading exporting countries. The first international wheat agreement, which became effective in 1933, may be taken as representative. The governments of Argentina, Australia, Canada, and the United States, the principal wheat exporters, agreed as an antidepression measure to restrict the export of wheat during the next two crop years and to allocate exports in accordance with an assigned quota arrangement. Other wheat-exporting countries, including Russia, also agreed to reduce their exports, and thirteen wheat-importing countries, including France, Germany, and England, attempted to prevent an expansion of domestic production. Upon the expiration of the first wheat agreement, new

[1] A list of international cartel agreements in effect in 1939, which was prepared by the U.S. Department of Justice, showed that 109 of the 179 agreements included American firms. Corwin D. Edwards, "International Cartels as Obstacles to International Trade," *American Economic Review,* Supplement, Vol. 34, p. 330 (March, 1944).

agreements were entered into and by 1949 an International Wheat
Council was established to administer a plan whereby the importing nations agreed to purchase guaranteed quantities of wheat over
a five-year period and exporters agreed to sell those quantities,
totaling 500 million bushels, at a fixed schedule of prices.[1]

Even older than intergovernment arrangements to control commodity prices and output are the unilateral governmental control
schemes designed to restrict exports in order to maintain high monopoly prices. In 1910 the German government established a compulsory cartel to regulate domestic and foreign sales of potash, of
which Germany had a virtual world monopoly. Before the development of synthetic nitrogen the Chilean government sponsored
cartel arrangements for the sale of sodium nitrate, of which Chile
was the world's sole producer. Since 1918 the Japanese government
has had a world monopoly of natural camphor. The Dutch East
Indies government for many years restricted the sale of cinchona
bark, the source of quinine. In 1928 the Italian and Spanish governments established a bilateral cartel to regulate the sale of mercury
throughout the world; the cartel allowed 40 per cent of the world
market to Italy and 60 per cent to Spain.[2]

But more important than government monopolies or intergovern-
mental commodity agreements have been voluntary cartel arrangements entered into by firms from different countries. The potential
power of a cartel to raise prices is indicated in the case of tungsten
carbide. A cartel arrangement between General Electric and Krupp,
a German firm, raised the United States price from $50 per pound
to more than $450.[3] Cartels are usually less interested in quality
than in price, and the formation of a cartel agreement is likely to
reduce a firm's interest in quality improvement; sometimes the cartel makes it possible for a firm to dispose of inferior goods which
otherwise could be sold, if at all, only at a price discount. Under a
cartel arrangement between du Pont and Nobel, a British firm, a
market was maintained for a relatively unsatisfactory military pow-
der produced by Nobel, since du Pont was required by the cartel

[1] J. B. Condliffe, commenting on this agreement, says: "It was made clear
by this action that although the negotiation of such an agreement contravened
the spirit if not the letter of the International Trade Charter, there was enough
political influence in the hands of organized farm groups to put through a series
of international commodity agreements if agricultural prices should decline at
all sharply." J. B. Condliffe, *The Commerce of Nations* (New York: W. W.
Norton & Company, 1950), p. 788.

[2] George W. Stocking and Myron W. Watkins, *Cartels or Competition?*
(New York: The Twentieth Century Fund, Inc., 1948), pp. 69–76.

[3] Edwards, *op. cit.*, p. 332.

arrangement to refuse the business of Nobel's dissatisfied customers.[1] Cartels not only restrict output of existing plant but sometimes also attempt to limit construction of new capacity. Edwards reports: "In the case of magnesium, American productive capacity was limited by agreements between the Aluminum Company of America, Dow Chemical Company, and I. G. Farbenindustrie, which provided for the closure of the Aluminum Company's plant in the United States in order to give Dow a monopoly, the exclusion of new competitors, a maximum limit upon Dow's production, and prices so high that even this maximum could not be attained." One can almost hear the "Heil Hitler!" in the background.

Exchange Control

A third device which has been used frequently in recent years to control the amount and direction of international trade is exchange control. Like international cartels, exchange controls have assumed a variety of forms and have been used to accomplish several purposes. During periods of war most nations have made some use of exchange controls, and totalitarian nations have made elaborate exchange-control systems a permanent part of their programs.

Under conditions of free world markets in both commodities and currencies, an exporter sells his goods in a foreign market and usually receives a foreign currency in payment. He is free to use the foreign money in any way he chooses; he may invest his funds in the foreign country, he may buy goods for import, or he may exchange his foreign balances for the currency of his own or another country. An importer, in the absence of controls, may buy foreign currencies with his own money and buy goods in any part of the world he chooses. The prices of one currency in terms of others are established in a highly competitive free market, and consumers are able in this way to get the best quality and the lowest prices which the markets of the world provide. The effect of the imposition of exchange controls is to substitute the decisions of a government agency as to what and how much will be imported for those of firms and individuals trading in free markets. When exchange controls have been invoked, a seller in foreign markets is required to turn his foreign balances over to a government bureau, and he will receive from them the "equivalent" in terms of his own currency. An importer will have to buy foreign exchange from the government agency at a rate set by law. The government reserves

[1] *Ibid.*

the right to refuse to sell foreign currencies to domestic importers except to pay for imports of goods which it has determined should be imported, and it may require a license before goods can be exported.

The nature of exchange controls may be illustrated by a brief description of the British exchange-control system. This arrangement is based on the Exchange Control Act of 1947, and it requires that all payments made by Britons to foreigners and by one foreigner to another be channeled through special bank accounts. The use which can be made of balances in British banks depends mainly on the residence of the holder of the balance. There are three major classes of sterling accounts:

1. *Resident Accounts.* These include the accounts of persons living in Britain and the Commonwealth, except Canada and a few other countries including the British colonial and mandated territories. Transfers from one resident account to another may be freely made without restriction.

2. *American Accounts.* These include the accounts of persons living in the United States, Canada, the Philippines, and most of the northern countries of Latin America. These balances arise primarily from exports from the dollar area, and they may be used to buy any other kind of sterling, or they may be transferred into dollars. Other sterling, however, cannot be transferred to an American account except by permission. The object of this arrangement is to induce those who have claims on dollars, which are in short supply, to hold sterling with the understanding that they can transfer from sterling to dollars at will.

3. *Transferable Accounts.* These include the accounts of persons living in all other countries. Balances may be transferred freely from one transferable account to another, and much of the world's trade is financed in this way.

The Bank of England maintains the dollar price of sterling within narrow limits around the dollar-sterling parity of $2.80, but transferable sterling is permitted to fluctuate over a somewhat wider range.[1]

Import Quotas

The last of the restrictive devices to be considered in this chapter is the import quota. Introduced in France in the 1930's as an anti-

[1] Stephen Enke and Virgil Salera, *International Economics* (Englewood Cliffs, N.J.: Prentice-Hall, 1957), 3rd ed., pp. 183–185.

depression measure, it became a significant part of the international commercial policy of most European nations until the outbreak of World War II, affecting in some instances a major portion of the country's imports. In some respects the effects of import quotas are similar to those of a protective tariff, but in general it may be argued that import quotas introduce rigidities in the price structure and isolate the economy from changes in the rest of the world to a degree which make quotas even more offensive, from the point of view of the optimum allocation of resources, than protective tariffs.

The points of similarity and difference between quota restrictions on imports and a protective tariff may be observed in Figure 35.4. D_d and S_d represent the domestic demand and supply for a commodity. OW is assumed to be the world price of the commodity, and conditions are assumed to be the same as in the first tariff case discussed earlier in the chapter. If there are no restrictions on imports, Os units will be produced domestically, Od units will be demanded, and sd units will be imported. Suppose now that an import quota equal to BC is imposed. The domestic price will rise to OP, and at this price Os' units will be produced domestically, Od' units will be demanded, and imports will be $s'd' = BC$. The quota has resulted in an increase in domestic producers' income equal to $WPBF$, assuming that resources have been shifted from uses in which they previously earned $sFBs'$. Price to consumers has increased by WP; foreign producers' income from sales in this country has decreased by an amount equal to $sFAs' + d'DGd$; and importers will make an additional profit of AB per unit on the smaller number of units imported.

If, instead of an import quota, the government had levied a tariff equal to WP, the effect on price, quantity of imports, exports, production, and consumption would have been the same. The only difference would have been that the $ABCD$ additional profits received by importers under the quota arrangement would have been paid to the government under the tariff (compare Figures 35.1 and 35.4). But now suppose that the domestic demand increases from D_d to D'_d without any change in the quota. Price would now rise to OP', domestic production would increase to Om, and imports would be mn, which is equal to $s'd'$. Consumers are now injured to a greater extent than they would be with a tariff. Price cannot be forced by a tariff to rise by more than the amount of the tariff, but there is no upper limit to the price increase which can result from a quota. The increase in demand under the quota arrange-

FIGURE 35.4. IMPORT QUOTA—Is More
Harmful Than Tariff

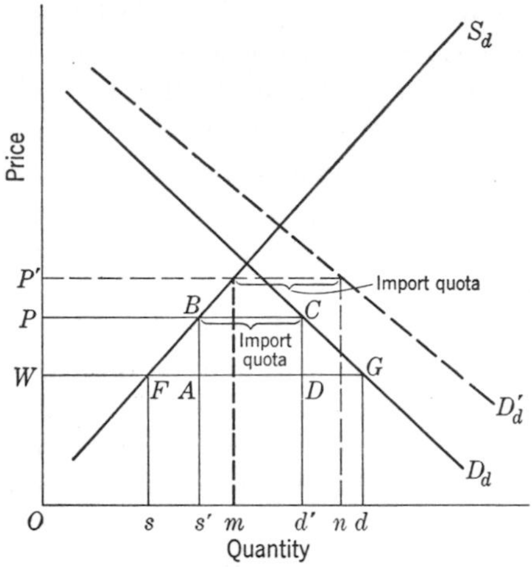

ment has resulted in an increase in domestic production with no change in imports; under a tariff the increase in domestic demand would call forth a greater quantity of imports with no change in domestic production, which makes the quota system more protective than a protective tariff. A decline in the world price, moreover, would not help domestic consumers if a quota system had been established, whereas, under the assumptions of the model, any fall in world price would be reflected in a reduction in domestic price under a tariff.

Summary

In conclusion we may observe that international-trade restrictions reduce the amount of world trade and, consequently, the gains which would result from the free movement of goods throughout the world. From the point of view of a single country, it is possible that restrictive legislation may benefit the nation at the expense of the rest of the world to a limited degree and for a short time. But since other nations can, and in practice do, retaliate, gains to the country as a whole resulting from restricting trade are not permanent. Both as between nations and within a single country, trade restrictions benefit some and injure others. The United States has traditionally followed a high-tariff policy designed to help certain domestic producers at the expense of consumers. In recent years, however, tariff rates have been significantly lowered

in this country, and there seems to be hope that the downward revision will be continued. With respect to other forms of trade
restrictionism, *e.g.*, international cartels, exchange controls, and import quotas, American policy has been less objectionable than that
of many other countries, but the ideal of free multilateral trade requires that all restrictions be eliminated in order that resources may
be allocated in accordance with the principle of consumer sovereignty.

There are, of course, considerations which may in certain situations outweigh the strictly economic factors, and an economy may
rationally pursue policies which would result in a reduction in
living standards. Adam Smith observed, for example, that defense
is of much more importance than opulence. Is it not true that in
these days of international security menaced by the constant threat
of atomic warfare that certain materials should be produced domestically whether we have a comparative advantage in their
production or not and, if necessary, that domestic producers be
provided the protection of a high tariff? The answer to this question
is that a high tariff has not, in fact, made us independent of other
countries for war materials. During World War II, in spite of many
years of high-tariff policy, a long list of critical materials had to be
imported. A tariff cannot make us militarily or economically independent of the rest of the world. Furthermore, if there are industries which are so vital to national defense that they should be
maintained without regard to efficiency considerations, it should be
observed that a tariff is not the only, and certainly not necessarily
the best, method of maintaining such industries. A direct subsidy
from the public treasury might be less expensive to the taxpayer and less detrimental to the interests of consumers than a
tariff. In addition, government stockpiling of a critical imported
material will sometimes serve as a satisfactory substitute for domestic production of the material under tariff or direct subsidy
protection. Finally, if we deliberately reduce our living standards
by imposing trade restriction, for whatever purpose, we should
understand that we are in fact lowering standards of living, and
that should be reckoned as a part of the cost of the policy being
undertaken.

36

ECONOMIC AID FOR
UNDERDEVELOPED AREAS

The foreign-aid program of the United States has gone through three stages since the close of World War II. Immediately after the war the nations of Western Europe were confronted with a tremendous job of reconstruction and development. During 1947 the American public engaged in a great debate concerning our foreign economic policy, the outcome of which was the Marshall Plan and grants of about $16 billion over a four-year period, most of which went to the countries of Western Europe. Partially as a result of the economic assistance provided by the United States, reconstruction took place at a faster than anticipated rate; by the end of 1951 European industrial production was 40 per cent above that of 1938 and 65 per cent above that of 1947.

During the year before the Korean War the American public expected foreign grants to be reduced, and the Secretary of Defense recommended that the military budget be cut from $14 billion to $13 billion. The war brought a quick change in these attitudes. The military budget was increased from $14 to $60 billion, and a second program of foreign aid was undertaken. From 1951 to 1954

United States government grants and loans totaled about $23 billion. Whereas the grants under the Marshall Plan had largely assumed the form of economic assistance, the expenditures made after 1951 were essentially defense and security measures.

Currently we are engaged in a third phase of the foreign aid program. There is widespread agitation for extensive and protracted aid to underdeveloped countries. This aid is to take the form of economic development assistance. To date this aspect of our foreign-aid program has been relatively small, representing probably not more than 5 per cent of the $60 billion we have expended on foreign-aid programs since the war.[1] It seems likely that Russia's recent demonstration of her progress in the area of rockets and guided missiles together with a stepped-up foreign-aid program of her own will provide incentives for more extensive American aid to underdeveloped countries.

Wealthy as the United States is as compared with the rest of the world, she does not, of course, have limitless resources. Economic development does not progress at a uniform and rapid rate even within her own borders. During the years 1955 to 1957, for example, the growth in output of physical goods and services averaged only about 1.4 per cent per year. For the decade before that it averaged about 3.7 per cent. It is clear that the United States can put all of its resources to work improving the lot of her own people. She has slums that could be cleared, highways that could be built, schools that could be replaced and expanded, teachers that could be trained and more adequately paid, research programs in medicine, technology, and science that could be carried out, and many other projects of unquestioned merit. Many of these programs, too, are important from the point of view of national security. The issue of foreign aid boils down to the basic economic problem: the alternative uses of scarce resources.

There can be little doubt that American funds, properly used, can be of genuine benefit to nations that are trying to accelerate their rate of economic development. A recent study of American assistance to Greece closed with these words:[2]

If trends of the last ten years continue for the next twenty, then most of the internal problems that now make Greek life so precarious will have

[1] The order of magnitude of the foreign-aid program is indicated by the fact that the total amount of development assistance appropriated for 1957 was $250 million.

[2] William Hardy McNeill, *Greece: American Aid in Action, 1947–1956* (New York: The Twentieth Century Fund, Inc., 1957), pp. 224–225.

sunk to insignificance, and Greek society will be able to confront the rest of the world internally stable and strong. Luck and tact, patience and wisdom, on the part of the Greeks and on the part of the greater nations of the world, will be needed if this result is to be achieved; but the changes that can bring such a happy solution to Greece's recent troubles are under way. This was not true ten years ago or even eight years ago. Greek and American effort has made the difference. It is no mean achievement; it is one in which both nations may properly take pride.

Motives for Foreign Aid

If Americans elect to devote a part of their resources to a continuation and expansion of the foreign-aid program, what motives may be expected to lead them to this decision? What incentives will impel Congress and the taxpayers to curtail domestic programs in order to provide economic assistance to underdeveloped countries?

There are, of course, opportunities for private investment in the underdeveloped countries that may be expected to be undertaken because they are profitable on strictly business grounds. Since the end of World War II American private investment abroad has averaged about $1.5 billion, and in recent years the rate has been somewhat higher. Much of this money has been invested in Europe, Canada, and other developed countries. Nearly $400 million per year has gone to Latin America, and some $200 million has gone to Asia, Africa, and the Middle East, the bulk of this to Middle Eastern countries that produce oil. Private investment has undoubtedly played an important role in supplying initiative and organizing ability, in transferring skills, encouraging modern marketing procedures, broadening local capital markets, improving commercial attitudes in the countries concerned, and generally promoting the benefits of an economy less dependent on government finance, government initiative, and government management.[1]

But how are we to justify the appropriation of funds for grants and loans to underdeveloped countries for projects and programs which, at least in the short run, will not meet the criteria for business investment? And if we are to expand our foreign-assistance program, how much money will be required to achieve such ob-

[1] The American Assembly, *International Stability and Progress: United States Interests and Instruments* (New York: Columbia University Press, 1957), p. 518.

jectives as we set for ourselves? And for how long a period of time will grants of this sort be needed?

The chief incentives which have led the American people to undertake a foreign-assistance program may be classified as humanitarian, economic, and security, and, if the program is to be continued and expanded, these appear to be the motives which will guide us.

Humanitarian considerations have been important in the past in causing Americans to extend foreign aid. In time of disaster such as floods and famine American generosity has become legendary. Americans have set up Roberts College in Istanbul and the American Universities in Beirut and Cairo. The Rockefeller Foundation has established health and agricultural programs in Latin America and elsewhere. The Ford Foundation has contributed some $15 million a year in the Middle East and Southern Asia. The willingness of the American people to help eliminate the evils of poverty throughout the world should not be discounted. Benjamin Fairless, former chairman of the board of the U.S. Steel Corporation and a member of a citizens' advisory committee which toured the world to determine the effectiveness of our foreign-aid grants, made these comments for the benefit of the critics of our assistance program:[1]

I wish some of these critics could have accompanied us as we travelled around the world, seeing and hearing evidence that not all U.S. expenditures are wasted or mismanaged.

In Iran, they would have heard of a tribesman who lived in a squalid village, almost as primitive as it had been in the time of Cyrus the Great. Animals were stabled in the living quarters of the villagers' houses. What few latrines there were drained into the central water ditch, and the people and livestock alike drank from this same polluted ditch.

Some years ago, the tribesman had reported to visiting Americans that he had had nine sons. "All," he added, "die from sickness." Then came the "point Four" technical-assistance program to teach the ways of sanitation. Another son was born, and this one lived. When the infant was several months old and strong and healthy, the father made a journey of several days to tell the nearest American health-mission director: "You be godfather this boy!" The name of the child—Point Four Mohammedi!

The second basis for support of a foreign-assistance program is the economic factor. The Marshall Plan was undoubtedly under-

[1] Benjamin F. Fairless, "Foreign Aid Is Good Business," *Look,* July 23, 1947, p. 43.

taken in the belief that it was in the economic interests of the United States to do it. The persistence of foreign aid at a rate of $4 to $5 billion dollars per year has undoubtedly helped to make world trade, in spite of many barriers which remain, much freer than under the prewar system. There is a widespread conviction, right or wrong, that the prosperity of the United States is insecure in a world where half the people are ill-clothed and ill-fed. By helping backward countries develop, it is argued, we are strengthening potential customers and improving the ability of suppliers of raw materials to produce for our industries. And as these nations develop, new markets are opened up for American capital.[1]

Undoubtedly the most important consideration in our decision to extend foreign aid is the security factor. Economic assistance to underdeveloped countries is a part of our total foreign policy, and here political considerations are likely to outweigh economic factors. Mr. Fairless has made the point in these words:[2]

You cannot weigh foreign-aid expenditures in the same manner that I, for instance, might consider an investment by United States Steel. Uncle Sam is not out simply to turn a profit. He is trying to preserve the peace, strengthen our allies, hold the line against communism, and help maintain conditions in which other nations of the free world can remain independent. To accomplish these objectives, we must consider political and military, as well as economic and engineering, factors.

Much the same point was made by Professor Jacob Viner, a distinguished economist:[3]

The only factor which could persuade us to undertake a really large program of economic aid to the underdeveloped countries would be the decision that the friendship and alliance of those countries are strategically, politically, and psychologically valuable to us in the cold war, that economic aid on a large scale can be relied upon to assure such friendship and alliance to us, and that the cost to us of a greatly enlarged program of economic aid would not be an excessive price to pay for these strategic gains.

It seems abundantly clear that the incentives for an extensive economic foreign-aid program are mixed. It is impossible, as a matter of fact, to determine how much of sums already spent should be classified as economic assistance and how much should

[1] For an evaluation of the humanitarian and economic arguments for foreign aid see Edward S. Mason in the American Assembly, *loc. cit.*, pp. 63–69.
[2] Fairless, *op. cit.*, p. 45.
[3] Quoted by Mason, *loc. cit.*, p. 65.

be called military aid. Even if it could be demonstrated that the short-run economic gain to the United States would be greater if the foreign-aid funds were spent at home, it would not necessarily follow that the foreign-assistance program should be curtailed or eliminated since the political and security factors may very well outweigh the strictly economic considerations.

Changes Come to a Static World

Perhaps the most important single point in this connection is the fact alluded to in Chapter 21: in many parts of the underdeveloped world a cultural and social revolution is under way. Whereas for centuries the life of the son has been in all essential respects identical with that of his father, the idea of progress has been wholly lacking, the basis for hope of a better life has been absent, and, indeed, the awareness that other people have achieved higher living standards has been wanting, knowledge of and a longing for the Western way of life have recently developed in these regions, and it seems clear that much in the traditions and taboos of these people will shortly be discarded and something else substituted in their place. That significant changes are about to take place seems abundantly clear; since about half of the world's population is directly affected by this revolution, the extent of the economic growth of these areas and the direction in which they move are matters of real concern to us and the rest of the world. There is no assurance that as the economic lot of these peoples improves they will embrace democratic, private-enterprise institutions. There is, in fact, no assurance that if we provide them with assistance in their efforts to improve their status they will model their economies after ours. But a hands-off attitude on our part might be followed by a trend in the affairs of the world which would make it more difficult for us to develop along lines that are congenial to our traditions and aspirations. Foreign aid may be motivated in part by humanitarian considerations, but in the final analysis foreign aid is considered necessary by many economists out of consideration for our own interests. This would be true even if the Russian threat were not present; the strenuous efforts of the Soviet Union to direct the development of the underdeveloped countries in directions suitable to her purposes has caused most Americans to consider our participation in this program highly important. But there remains widespread disagreement among students of this problem as to what should be done, how it should be done, how much should be done and for how long, or whether anything at all should be done.

Some Unanswered Questions

The process of developing an underdeveloped country is almost certain to be slow and painful. Repeated disappointments and failures are sure to be met by the underdeveloped countries themselves and by those who attempt to aid them. Judged on the basis of short-run achievements, much of the money spent on economic assistance will prove to have been "wasted." And there remain many unresolved issues which need to be settled. Professor Schelling has raised the following questions to which there are no universally accepted answers:[1]

Is the aid-giving relationship a healthy one? Is the aid-giving program merely an instrument for transferring resources to other countries; or is it also a desirable and influential relationship between us and the recipient countries?

To what extent can we insulate economic development assistance from the rest of our foreign policy, if we wish to? Do recipient countries want development assistance insulated from the rest of our foreign policy and, if not, can they prevent insulation?

Should aid to economic development be without "strings"?

What should be the criteria for the allocation of aid among countries? Should we give deliberate preference to countries allied with us or cooperating with us in our strategic plans?

Should military and economic assistance programs be separated in concept, in administration, and in the budget and appropriations? Can we separate economic development assistance from other kinds of financial assistance?

What attitude should we take toward the "aid" activities of the Soviet bloc?

Where and how does the process of economic development impinge on American objectives in an underdeveloped country?

What impact on the rate of development can an assistance program have? What is the proper magnitude and duration of development assistance? What kinds of loans or grants are appropriate to development assistance?

Will government loans defeat their own purpose by reducing private foreign investment in the underdeveloped countries?

[1] Thomas C. Schelling in the American Assembly, *loc. cit.*, pp. 131–167.

Should American aid be related to individual projects, or to some over-all program of development for the country?

Should our assistance to economic development be conducted through multilateral channels, such as the United Nations or the World Bank?

Should development-assistance be put on a long-range basis, with permanent legislation or the establishment of a separate "fund"?

Should we move ahead piecemeal or try to develop an integral whole program?

The answers to these and other questions must be found. The determination of what we should attempt to do is in itself no simple matter. The implementation of our policy once it has been established will certainly be difficult. Americans are famous for their propensity for doing things in a big way and as quickly as possible. This has undoubtedly been an important factor in their own rapid economic development. But this trait may work against Americans in their efforts to help other countries achieve economic development, because here patience in unbounded quantities will be necessary. Even if we are helped by a number of junior-grade miracles, the development of the underdeveloped countries of the world will be a slow and tortuous project.

37

FREE MARKETS AND FREE MEN

A few generations ago it was customary for fiction writers occasionally to digress from the main theme of the story and to address a few words to the "gentle reader." We have for the most part resisted the urge to chat with the reader. But we have come a long way together as we have explored the mysterious realm of economic analysis, and, as is often true of distant travels, perhaps the happiest part of the trip is its ending. As we complete the expedition, a few words to those who are still with us seem appropriate. Let us discuss where we have been and what we have seen, with perhaps a word about where we go from here.

The first chapter really gave us a forecast of what the book attempts to accomplish. This purpose is to show the way in which our economy, organized on the free-enterprise, or competitive, principle, solves those fundamental economic problems which must somehow be solved by any economic system. We have attempted to answer such questions as the following: How does this system of organization allow consumers' choices as to what is to be produced to make themselves meaningful? How does it get the proper goods and services produced if men are permitted freely to choose among occupations and among different lines of business? How are the various inputs combined to produce the desired outputs? How is the distribution of the fruits of all the economic effort carried out? We know that all these things are done; we knew this before we began to study economics. It is hoped, however, that the reader now possesses a fuller understanding of the leading role which prices play in the solution of the fundamental economic problem of scarcity and how they organize our extremely complex and interdependent economy.

This book has been designed in large part to show how the competitive economy does allow this miracle—for it is no less than a miracle—to take place. In order to demonstrate the efficacy of the cooperative process which is generated by free markets, it was necessary for us to concentrate on the efficiency aspects of the allocation of resources. We have shown that a system of free markets not only will get goods produced but will do so in a highly efficient manner. The real income of society will be maximized by a system of purely competitive markets.

But this suggests the first complicating problem which we encountered. What do we mean by "maximizing real income"? Heterogeneous goods and services cannot be added together except in value terms. But the prices which enter into values are affected by consumers' effective demand for goods, and these demands are largely determined by the distribution of income. So when we say that the social real income would be maximized under pure competition, we must be understood to be taking the distribution of income as given. Wants are satisfied by the competitive system in proportion to the purchasing power of individuals and families.

This raises an ethical question. Is the distribution of income which arises in a competitive economy a desirable one? We have shown that the distribution of income is determined in the input markets. The forces of competition tend to reward the owners of the most productive inputs. This sort of input pricing does serve to channel productive services into the spots where they are most efficient, to the advantage of both the individual and society. But is the resulting distribution of rewards equitable? On this question we may disagree. To the extent that the productivity of one's labor depends upon personal effort both in acquiring the necessary training and in performing the job well and faithfully, a certain appropriateness seems to attach to distribution according to marginal revenue productivity. To the extent that a high value of the labor and capital services over which one has command is due to luck, health, or inherited characteristics or wealth, the appropriateness of income distribution according to productivity is much more questionable. Most people will agree that some departure from competitively determined incomes is desirable. If we did not admit this, we would be contending that those individuals who are completely unproductive should receive no income at all; this would include many of the aged, the ill, and the disabled. Unless one is willing to embrace a Spartan philosophy of liquidation of the least useful members of society, one is forced to concede that the free market distribution of income must be modified somewhat in the direction of greater equality. But if we admit this, do we not also have to admit that we do not desire free markets? Not at all. For we may without difficulty separate the problem of income distribution from that of resource allocation. We may agree to modify the distribution of income and wealth as we will, but once we have done so, we may allow free markets to secure an efficient allocation of resources within the accomplished distribution.

While examining the allocative efficiency of the economy, we encountered a second problem of major proportions. This is the problem of monopoly. Upon investigating the way in which our system actually operates, we found that the pure competition of our theoretical model is a rather imaginary conception. Competition is actually a tremendous force in our economy, but sellers of both outputs and inputs are constantly striving for, and in some measure securing, monopoly power. Our analysis demonstrated that departures from competition generally serve to distort the allocation of resources and thereby to make the economy less efficient. Monopolists tend to restrict the flow of economic resources into certain areas of production. In this way they prevent the equalization of returns at the margin, that is, the equalization of the value of the marginal product of like resource units in different employments, and thereby lower the social product.

We were also forced to admit that yet another ugly problem exists in the real world—a problem which we were temporarily obliged to ignore in order to concentrate adequately on resource allocation. This is the problem of stabilization of the general level of economic activity. If large-scale unemployment of labor and capital exists, we cannot so easily acclaim the efficiency with which the employed resources have been allocated among alternative uses. Or if full employment is accompanied by inflation with its attendant impact on the distribution of income, our economy is not functioning in a wholly admirable fashion. It was necessary, therefore, for us to examine in some detail the determination of national income and aggregate employment of resources. Fluctuations in national money income were shown to be dependent on the spending decisions of individuals, firms, and government. The instability of the total stock of money was cited as a factor which amplifies economic fluctuations in both directions. And it was pointed out that the existence of all sorts of rigidities in the structure of prices generally means that real national income will fall when there is a decline in national income measured in dollars. This spells unemployment, the most severe of all varieties of economic waste.

In our analysis of the economy, we found, therefore, that there are three major problems connected with the working of the free-enterprise economy. First, there is the problem of income distribution; second, the ubiquitous problem of monopoly; and third, the problem of general economic instability. These clearly suggested our third step, which was to examine the way in which these problems may best be faced. This involved us in a consideration of the government's role in the economy—a matter which we had largely neglected earlier. Government, particularly the Federal government, is the only agency equipped to deal with the problems of distribution, monopoly, and stabilization. A good share of our discussion was devoted, therefore, to certain aspects of "political economy," a study of the economic impact of government.

The question of the role of government in combating general economic instability was considered. We observed that there is reason to believe that proper monetary and fiscal policy can do a great deal to prevent both drastic deflation and inflation. There are difficult problems relating to the amount and timing of government action, however, and politics plays a part which students of economics should not overlook.

When we came to the monopoly problem, the conclusions as to what the Federal government both should do and can do were not so clear. The vexatious problem is just "how much" competition constitutes workable competition, or obversely, "how much" monopoly we can put up with. Government has not been very successful in its attempts to prevent monopoly in output markets, but neither can its attempts be written off as a complete failure. The main protector of the public interest is the good old force of competition itself. Monopoly, including labor unionism, would not be nearly so troublesome if it did not so often receive a helping hand from government. This is so serious a threat to our economy that we devoted considerable space to a discussion of some of the many ways in which government action has established and encouraged monopoly rather than restricting or prohibiting it. Thus we discussed such measures as resale-price maintenance, farm subsidies, building codes, and tariffs. We must admit, of course, that there are some segments of the economy where competition can never be expected to work. These are the "natural" monopolies, where government ownership or private ownership and government regulation must be resorted to. We outlined some of the pricing principles which are involved in this area.

It should not be overlooked that our whole analysis has been conducted within a static framework—wants, resources, and technology were held constant in order to keep the analysis manageable. This is an especially important reminder in connection with the monopoly problem. Ours is a dynamic, growing economy, and this reduces considerably the threat imposed by monopoly. Technological change, especially, is apt to bring into existence new productive methods and new products which can, at least in part, be substituted for inputs and outputs which are monopolistically priced.

We spent little time on the problem of income redistribution. We emphasized only the essential fact that the fiscal system provides us with a way in which income may be redistributed without disturbing too greatly the operation of the market mechanism. Some of the economic effects of taxes and public expenditures were analyzed, but we did not go into the extremely difficult problem of determining the most desirable distribution of income, which is essentially a matter of ethics rather than of economics.

Where has all this analysis led us? Have we described the way in which the United States economy works at mid-twentieth century? Clearly the answer is no. But this has not been our purpose. Had it been, we would have found it necessary to present several hundred more pages loaded with figures, tables, charts (and even pictures), plus an overwhelming amount of historical and factual comment. And still we should have failed. An adequate description of the economy simply cannot be accomplished within the confines of two hard covers. If not to describe, what has been our purpose? It has been to provide a framework of analysis with which one may make sense out of the descriptions he meets elsewhere. As a businessman, you will face problems of the XYZ industry; you will know from experience the factual background of that industry much better than anyone could tell you in a textbook. So this book, instead of providing factual data concerning many industries, is designed to provide you with a systematic *way of thinking* about the problems of the XYZ industry and its relationship to the total economy. As a congressman, you will know from experience the industrial potential of your district much better than a textbook in economic geography could tell you. So this book is designed to provide you with a systematic *way of thinking* about the problems of your district in its relation to the total economy. As an ordinary citizen, you know the particular background of your job better than any college professor knows it. So this volume is designed to provide you with a systematic *way of thinking* about problems beyond those of your particular job— a way of thinking, for example, about national, state, and local governmental policies which are, and must continue to be, concerns of everyone.

An unlimited number of problems are certain to arise in the years ahead; we have no way of knowing when these will arise, where they will arise, or what will be their nature. The analysis has been designed to provide a rather simple kit of tools which may be applicable to many problems. Ths student who has learned economic analysis may be likened to the mechanic who leaves the garage to repair a broken-down automobile without knowing in advance exactly what is wrong with it. He carries a set of tools which may fit several possible situations. So with economic analysis. The mastery of it should enable you to predict the results of a proposed unfair-trade-practices act in your state, a merger of the main department stores in your town, the closing down of an established plant, an increase in the general wage level, an increase in the interest rate, a decrease in the price of pickles, and a multitude of other possible changes that may occur in the economy, any or all of which may affect you directly or indirectly.

This has been one purpose of this book. But it has not been the only one. Perhaps a more important, albeit less direct, purpose has been that of providing the reader with an appreciation of the free-enterprise, or competitive, system as a means of solving society's economic problem. We believe that the best approach to a genuine appreciation of the free-enterprise system is through an understanding of the manner in which it operates. This book has indicated that the free-enterprise system can operate efficiently and effectively if government is careful to fulfill its proper role, which involves positive action in some areas and deliberate refusal to act in others. And the private-enterprise system operates without restricting individual economic freedom. Free enterprise means essentially the freedom of anyone to set up any enterprise. People freely choose in the market place among goods and services; people choose the work they do; firms choose what, how, and how much to produce.

This broader aspect of the free-enterprise system now requires our attention. It is conceivable that a completely socialist state, in which all or most economic decisions would be centrally made, could prove as "efficient" in practice as the free-enterprise system. (We do not think this would be the case, but let us assume that it might be.) The case for a private-enterprise system would still be strong. The socialist state or other type of centrally planned economy (*e.g.*, the fascist states of Hitler and Mussolini) secures such efficiency as it achieves only at the cost of freedom of the individual. Freedom to change occupations, to move from one area to another, and to establish new firms is certain to be restricted in a socialist or fascist state. The free-enterprise system is the only one that guarantees a maximum degree of freedom for the individual along with a high degree of productive efficiency.

Ultimately, therefore, the essential defense of the competitive system lies in its political as well as its economic aspects. It solves the economic problem without undue governmental direction of individuals or firms. It largely removes the whole area of economic decisions from government, allowing such decisions to be made instead by millions of individuals, families, and business units. The competitive system is a scheme of decentralization, a means of removing from the hands of government officials the multifarious economic decisions relating to what, how, and for whom goods are to be produced. As a means of decentralizing economic control, the competitive system can be considered one of the major bulwarks of political democracy. Democracy in the sense of participation in the governing process by the whole body politic can function effectively only if the area of governmental decision is severely restricted. A government that is required to make most of the economic decisions cannot long remain effectively democratic in any meaningful sense. As government becomes more powerful in economic affairs, legislators and administrators are increasingly subjected to pressure by organized groups seeking economic gain. Democratically chosen officials who wield great economic power are especially unlikely to be champions of the rights of the people as a whole. In a fundamental sense, therefore, the competitive economy may be considered a necessary condition for the maintenance of political democracy.

This is so important a point that it should make one highly skeptical of efforts to impose authoritative price, wage, and production controls except under conditions of all-out war. Wherever indirect governmental controls are adequate to the task at hand, they should be employed in preference to direct controls over prices, inputs, and outputs. Monetary and fiscal measures have the great advantage of interfering to a minimum extent with the market mechanism, allowing the shifting forces of supply and demand for particular commodities to be reflected in appropriate price adjustments.

There is meaning in the principle of gradualism as applied to government intervention in economic affairs as well as to other spheres of government activity. By pursuing short-run will-o'-the-wisp policies indicated to be desirable by considerations of expediency while neglecting the longer-run effects, we may act to jeopardize the fundamental values of our society. Many ill-conceived economic experiments have a way of leaving quite permanent flaws in our social fabric.

APPENDIX

FUNDAMENTAL QUANTITATIVE RELATIONSHIPS

Much of economics is concerned with quantities and their relationships. In many instances these relationships can best be understood if they are treated mathematically. Simple geometry and algebra have been used in the body of this book in an effort to clarify numerous problems. Even this much mathematics could have been avoided, but in many instances that would have required lengthy and cumbrous explanations which would have made the text more difficult (unless the book were deliberately kept simple by the omission of all the difficult problems). By a greater use of mathematics, some of the points discussed in the text may be made more precisely, and, for those who have some knowledge of mathematics beyond algebra and geometry, these matters can more readily be understood if the relationships are expressed in mathematical terms. The purpose of the Appendix is to provide simple mathematical formulations of topics which either were developed in the text in nonmathematical language or were not treated in detail at all. Students with an interest in mathematics and a knack for quantitative analysis should find these notes of considerable help. Even those whose experience with grade-school arithmetic and high-school algebra has (unfortunately and foolishly) convinced them that they do not have "mathematical minds," if they apply themselves to the task with the same determination and energy with which they might approach, say, the learning of a new dance step, may discover that the mathematics required for an understanding of the economic principles developed here is well within the grasp of normal garden-variety human beings.

1. Functional Relationships

Frequently in analyzing economic data it is discovered that one magnitude depends upon another. The total cost of producing automobiles, for example, depends upon the number of automobiles to be produced: the greater the output, the greater the total cost. The two magnitudes—output and cost—are referred to as "variables." As one magnitude varies, the other also varies. It is often convenient to consider one variable as *independent* and the other as *dependent*. We may assume that the output of automobiles is the independent variable and that the cost is the dependent variable. If the output is 1,000 units, the total cost will be, say, $2,000,000; if the output is 10,000 units, the total cost might be $17,000,000. For every output there is a corresponding total cost.

When magnitudes are related in this way, it is said that one variable is a "function" of the other. The total cost of producing automobiles, for example, is a function of output. If we let C stand for total cost and O stand for output, the statement that total cost is a function of output may be written in this form:

$$C = f(O)$$

The symbol f simply stands for function. The equation does not mean that O is multiplied by f; it is read simply that C is a function of O. The equation does not even tell us whether C and O move in the same or opposite directions. It merely says that for every value of O there is a corresponding value for C.

While it is true that the total cost of producing automobiles is a function of the number of units produced, it is also true that total cost depends upon numerous other factors. A change in the wages paid to laborers in the automobile plant or a change in the price of steel would affect the total cost of automobiles at each output level. We may, accordingly, say that the total cost of automobiles is a function of the wages paid to the plant's employees, and this may be written in symbols as follows:

$$C = g(W)$$

where W represents the wage rate. The symbol g is here used for function instead of f to indicate that the functional relationship between cost and wages is different from that between cost and output.

The fact that total cost is a function of the price of steel may be represented as

$$C = h(P_s)$$

where P_s represents the price of steel. The h symbol indicates that this functional relationship is different from that between either cost and output or cost and wages.

The dependence of cost on all three variables—output, wages, and the price of steel—may be expressed as follows:

$$C = F(O, W, P_s)$$

and this is read: "Cost is a function of output, wages, and the price of steel." If we concentrate on just one functional relationship, *e.g.*, $C = f(O)$, we assume that all other variables, *e.g.*, W and P_s, remain constant. The device of assuming other things unchanged is referred to as the *ceteris paribus* (abbreviated *cet. par.*) assumption. Since in reality the "other things" often do not remain the same, this kind of assumption introduces an element of unreality into the picture. One advantage of the application of mathematics to economic problems is that frequently several variables can be treated simultaneously, whereas without the use of mathematics keeping track of more than two or three variables at a time requires an intellectual endowment that is denied most of us.

DEMAND AS A FUNCTIONAL RELATIONSHIP BETWEEN PRICE AND QUANTITY

We may say that the quantity of commodity X demanded is a function of the price of X. This may be expressed in symbols as $D_x = f(P_x)$. But we know that the amount of commodity X which consumers will take at any price is affected by factors other than its price. Changes in the prices of substitute and complementary goods will affect the consumer's demand for commodity X. Changes in the consumer's income or tastes will also affect his demand for X. All this may be put in the equation:

$$D_x = f(P_x, P_a, P_b, \ldots P_n, Y, T)$$

where $P_a, P_b, \ldots P_n$ represent the prices of other goods, Y is income, and T represents tastes.

When we say that $D_x = f(P_x)$, we are making the *ceteris paribus* assumption that everything else remains the same. But, clearly, if the price of X falls, *everything* cannot remain the same. If the prices of other commodities and the consumer's money income have remained the same, his real income has increased as a result of the decline in the price of X, or, if his real income is held constant, his money income must have fallen or other prices must have increased.

This is not, of course, to argue that, since all other things cannot remain constant as the price of X varies, it is useless to look upon the amount of X demanded as a function of the price of X. But it is important to keep in mind that a change, for example, in money income will change the functional relationship between price and quantity; for each level of assumed income there may be a different quantity demanded at each assumed price.

Particular functional relationships between two variables can be represented graphically. If three variables are used, the graph becomes quite complex, and for more than three variables the graphic technique breaks down completely. Geometry serves us, accordingly, only when the number of variables is restricted and "other things" are assumed to remain constant. More complex problems require the use of the calculus and other more powerful mathematical tools.

Fortunately, many problems in economics can be solved with the use of two variables and the *ceteris paribus* assumption, and they therefore lend themselves to graphic treatment. Let us suppose that the demand of a consumer for commodity X is indicated in the "demand schedule" given in Table A.1.

Table A.1. Demand Schedule

Price	Quantity demanded
$12	0
10	1
8	2
6	3
4	4
2	5
0	6

FIGURE A.1.

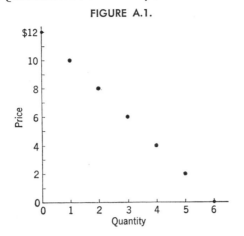

The demand schedule indicates that for each price listed there is a specific quantity which the consumer would buy during a particular time period. Each set of price and quantity represents alternative combinations.

The data of Table A.1 are plotted graphically in Figure A.1. The quantity demanded is measured on the horizontal or x axis, and the price is measured on the vertical or y axis. Each price-quantity combination in Table A.1 is represented by a dot on Figure A.1. To indicate that if the price of the commodity were $6 the consumer would buy 3 units, we move from the *origin* (the point of intersection of the two axes) to the right (*i.e.*, in the x direction) 3 units and then up 6 units. That locates the point $P = \$6$ and $Q = 3$. Each of the other points representing combinations of price and quantity is similarly plotted.

From the data given in Table A.1, this is all we can do. There is a temptation to draw a smooth curve through the several points and in this way present the "demand curve." But this would assume that, since the consumer would take one unit at a price of $10 and 2 units at a price of $8, he would take 1½ units at a price of $9. This may seem to be a reasonable assumption. But the table does not tell us that it is true. The data in the table are given in *discrete* units, and the graphic representation of the table must, therefore, also be in discrete units.

But suppose that in place of Table A.1 we are given the information that the consumer will buy commodity X on the basis of the equation

$$D_x = 6 - y/2$$

where y = price and D_x = quantity demanded. We can then draw up a demand schedule for any value of y with the corresponding value for x. By assuming various values for y we may derive the demand schedule shown in Table A.2.

Table A.2. Demand Schedule
$$D = 6 - y/2$$

Price	*Quantity demanded*
$12	0
10	1
8	2
6	3
4	4
2	5
0	6

It will be noted that this demand schedule is identical with that of Table A.1. The difference is that the second schedule represents points on a continuous curve. By substituting $9 for y in the equation, we see that the quantity demanded is 1½. By making the appropriate substitution we could determine the quantity demanded at any price, *e.g.*, at $8.98. All of the points representing combinations of price and quantity would lie on the straight-line demand curve which has an *intercept* at $12 on the y axis and an intercept of 6 on the x axis. This is shown in Figure A.2.

If we assume a value of $14 for y in our demand function, we find that x has a value of -1. Or, if price is assumed to be $-$2,

FIGURE A.2.

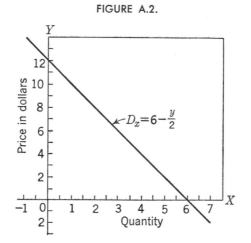

the quantity demanded would be 7. But since it is unrealistic to assume either that the consumer will buy less than zero units or that the price will be less than zero, we ignore as irrelevant all portions of the demand curve except those lying in the quadrant in which both x and y values are positive.

2. Average, Total, and Marginal Relationships

We have seen that the equation

$$x = 6 - y/2$$

may be viewed as a demand function if x is the quantity demanded and y is price. By multiplying both sides of the equation by 2, we get

$$2x = 12 - y$$

This may be written

$$y = 12 - 2x$$

In this form we are saying that $y = f(x)$, whereas in the original equation we had expressed x as a function of y. Table A.2 and Figure A.2 represent the data for the new expression as well as for the old. When we say that y is a function of x, we are saying that the price which the seller can get for the commodity depends upon the number of units he sells per time period. The price per unit sold represents to the seller his *average revenue;* if he sells three units at $6 each, his revenue per unit is $6. If we measure average revenue on the y axis, we may write the equation for average revenue as follows:

$$AR = y = 12 - 2x$$

where AR is average revenue. When plotted, the average revenue curve is seen to be the same as the demand curve in Figure A.2. Demand and average revenue, then, are the same thing from slightly different points of view.

Suppose that we are interested in knowing what the total revenue would be at any price. If we know the revenue per unit (price) and the number of units that can be sold at each price, we can determine the total revenue by multiplying average revenue by the quantity sold. In this way the total revenue column of Table A.3 is determined.

It will be noted that the total revenue starts at zero, increases

Table A.3. Average and Total Revenue

Average revenue	Quantity demanded	Total revenue
$12	0	$ 0
10	1	10
8	2	16
6	3	18
4	4	16
2	5	10
0	6	0

for a time as average revenue (price) decreases, reaches a maximum of $18 when price is $6, and then decreases as price decreases.

Since total revenue is average revenue multiplied by quantity sold, and since the quantity sold is x in the equation, total revenue is x times average revenue. Since average revenue is $12 - 2x$, total revenue is given by the equation

$$TR = x(12 - 2x)$$
$$= 12x - 2x^2$$

where TR is total revenue. By substituting values from zero to 6 for x in this equation, it will be seen that the total revenue will be that indicated in Table A.3. The total revenue and average revenue functions are plotted in Figure A.3.

The determination of marginal revenue introduces a complexity

FIGURE A.3.

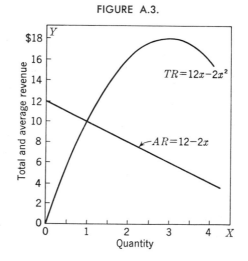

FIGURE A.4.

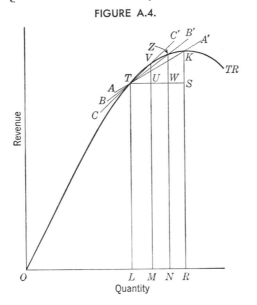

which we have not previously met with in this section. Marginal revenue has been defined in the text as the additional revenue resulting from the production of an additional unit of output. If, for example, we are currently selling two units of commodity X per time period, the average revenue function tells us that each unit can be sold for $8, and our total revenue will, accordingly, be $16. If we now wish to increase sales to three units, the price will have to be lowered to $6, total revenue will be $18, and marginal revenue will be $2. But marginal revenue might just as well have been defined as the reduction in total revenue resulting from selling one less unit per time period. If sales were reduced from two to one, price would be $10, total revenue would be $10, and marginal revenue computed in this way would be $6. Either method is only an approximation which may be close enough for most purposes, but it is possible to measure marginal revenue precisely at any output, as will be demonstrated below.

In Figure A.4, TR is the total revenue curve. If the quantity sold is OL, total revenue is LT. Suppose that sales are now increased to OR; total revenue will be RK. The increase in sales LR has resulted in an increase in revenue of SK. The marginal revenue, then, is $SK \div TS$ ($TS = LR$). If the increase in total revenue is represented by ΔR (the symbol Δ—pronounced *delta*—means simply a change, an increase if positive and a decrease if negative), and if the in-

FIGURE A.5.

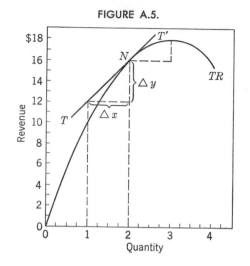

crease in total quantity sold is represented by ΔQ, marginal revenue is represented by $\Delta R/\Delta Q$. The line AA' is drawn through the points T and K. This means that the slope of AA' (slope is defined as $\Delta y/\Delta x$—in this case, SK/TS) is equal to marginal revenue as output increases from OL to OR.

Suppose now that output is increased by a smaller amount, from OL to ON. Marginal revenue would then be $WZ/TW =$ slope of BB', which is drawn through points T and Z. Similarly, if output is assumed to increase from OL to OM, the marginal revenue is equal to the slope of CC'. It will be noted that as the increase in sales (ΔQ) is assumed to be smaller and smaller, marginal revenue is equal to the slope of a line which approaches nearer and nearer the tangent to the TR curve at point T. We may say, therefore, that the marginal revenue at any output is equal to the slope of the tangent to the total revenue curve at that output. In Figure A.5, the marginal revenue at output 2 is the slope of TT', which is tangent to the TR curve at N. The slope of $TT' = \Delta y/\Delta x = \frac{4}{1} = 4$. The difference between this measure of marginal revenue and that which would result if marginal revenue were measured between discrete units may be indicated by noting that if output were assumed to increase from one to two, total revenue would increase from 10 to 16, *i.e.*, marginal revenue would be indicated as 6.

The general relationship between marginal, total, and average revenue can be indicated by the use of the calculus. Marginal revenue represents the *rate of change* of the total revenue as x increases,

FIGURE A.6.

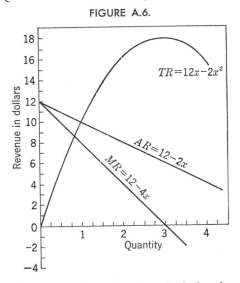

and the marginal revenue function is called the *first derivative* of the total revenue function. If the total revenue function is

$$TR = 12x - 2x^2$$

the rules of the calculus tell us that the marginal revenue function is

$$MR = 12 - 4x$$

Total, average, and marginal revenue are plotted in Figure A.6. It will be noted that at any output marginal revenue is less than average revenue. This must always be true when average revenue is decreasing; in order to "bring the average down," marginal must be less than average. Marginal revenue is equal to zero at the output where total revenue is at a maximum; when marginal revenue is positive, total revenue is increasing, and, when marginal revenue is negative, total revenue is decreasing.

The relationship between average revenue and marginal revenue can also be demonstrated with the use of elementary geometry. In Figure A.7, *DD'* may be viewed either as the average revenue (demand) curve and *TT'* as the tangent to the average revenue curve at *S* or *TT'* may be assumed to be a linear (straight-line) demand curve. If *TT'* is the demand curve, it may be demonstrated that the line *TL* drawn through *T* and bisecting any horizontal line drawn from the *y* axis to the demand curve is the corresponding marginal revenue curve. If output is *OM*, price will be *OP*, and total revenue will be indicated by the equation

$$TR = OP \cdot OM = OPSM$$

FIGURE A.7.

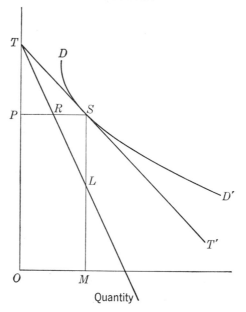

But total revenue is also equal to the area under the marginal revenue curve (the sum of the revenues added by all the units sold will equal total revenue). Total revenue is, therefore, equal to

$$TR = OTLM$$
$$\therefore OPSM = OTLM$$

But
$$OPSM = OPRLM + RSL$$

and
$$OTLM = OPRLM + PTR$$
$$\therefore RSL = PTR \text{ in area}$$

But
$$\angle TPR = \angle RSL$$

and
$$\angle PRT = \angle SRL$$
$$\therefore \angle PTR = \angle RLS$$

and
$$RSL \cong PTR$$
$$\therefore PR = RS$$

We may generalize by saying that if the average revenue curve is linear, the marginal revenue curve will also be a straight line beginning at the intercept of the average revenue curve on the y axis and bisecting any horizontal line drawn from the y axis to the average revenue curve. If the average revenue curve is nonlinear (*e.g.,* *DD′*), the marginal revenue *at any output* can be determined by drawing a tangent to the curve at that output and treating the tangent as if it were the average revenue curve. In Figure A.7, the marginal revenue at output *OM* is *ML*. To determine the marginal revenue at any other output (assuming that *DD′* is the average revenue curve), a tangent to the curve would have to be drawn at that output and the process repeated.

3. Price Elasticity of Demand and Supply

By the elasticity of demand is meant the percentage change in quantity demanded divided by the percentage change in price. If, for example, a 1 per cent drop in price is followed by a 1 per cent increase in the quantity demanded, elasticity of demand is equal to 1; if a 1 per cent drop in price is followed by more than a 1 per cent increase in the quantity demanded, elasticity is greater than 1; and if a 1 per cent drop in price is followed by a less than 1 per cent increase in the quantity demanded, elasticity is less than 1.

The elasticity formula for a linear demand function may be put in the form of the following equation:

$$E_d = \frac{\Delta x/x}{\Delta y/y}$$

where E_d is elasticity of demand, x is quantity demanded, and y is price. Through the use of Figure A.8 the formula may be simplified as follows:

$$E_d = \frac{\Delta x/x}{\Delta y/y} = \frac{MN/OM}{VH/MH} = \frac{MN}{OM} \cdot \frac{MH}{VH} = \frac{VS}{OM} \cdot \frac{MH}{VH} = \frac{VS}{VH} \cdot \frac{MH}{OM}$$

$$= \frac{PH}{PT} \cdot \frac{MH}{OM} = \frac{OM}{PT} \cdot \frac{OP}{OM}$$

$$= \frac{OP}{PT}$$

$$= \frac{T'H}{HT}$$

$$= \frac{MT'}{OM}$$

The elasticity of demand at any price is indicated by *OP/PT;* the elasticity of demand at any output is indicated by *MT′/OM.* If *P* falls midway between *O* and *T,* $E_d = 1$; at any higher price elastic-

FIGURE A.8.

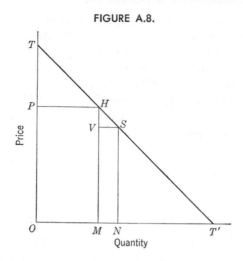

ity is greater than 1, and at any lower price elasticity is less than 1. It will be noted that a straight-line demand curve, such as TT', will have a different elasticity at every price. And any straight-line demand curve with an intercept at T on the y axis will have the same elasticity as TT' at any given price regardless of the relative slopes of the two curves. By referring to Figure A.6, it can be seen that, when $E_d = 1$, marginal revenue is zero and total revenue is at a maximum.

A general formula for elasticity, which applies to nonlinear as well as linear demand curves, substitutes the symbol d for Δ: $\dfrac{dx/x}{dy/y}$. The symbol d represents a change which is infinitesimally small.

The formula for elasticity of supply (E_s) may be developed with the use of Figure A.9.

$$
\begin{aligned}
E_s &= \frac{\Delta x/x}{\Delta y/y} = \frac{MN/OM}{VR/MW} = \frac{MN}{OM} \cdot \frac{MW}{VR} = \frac{WR}{OM} \cdot \frac{MW}{VR} \\
&= \frac{WR}{VR} \cdot \frac{MW}{OM} = \frac{PW}{PT} \cdot \frac{MW}{OM} = \frac{OM}{PT} \cdot \frac{OP}{OM} \\
&= \frac{OP}{PT} \\
&= \frac{AW}{TW} \\
&= \frac{AM}{OM}
\end{aligned}
$$

FIGURE A.9.

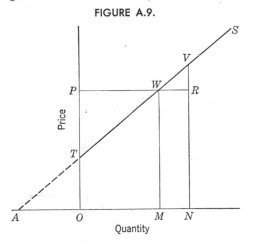

If the supply curve has a positive intercept on the y axis, as in Figure A.9, E_s will be greater than 1. If the supply curve has a positive intercept on the x axis, as in Figure A.10, E_s will be less than 1. If a straight-line supply curve passes through the origin, as in Figure A.11, E_s will be equal to 1 at any price. If either the demand curve or the supply curve is nonlinear, elasticity at any price can be determined by drawing a tangent to the curve at that price, extending the tangent to the y axis at T, and measuring elasticity at that price as OP/PT. If the curve has a negative slope, *e.g.*, a demand curve, elasticity will be negative, and if the curve has a positive slope, *e.g.*, a supply curve, the elasticity will be positive. For most purposes, however, the algebraic sign of the coefficient of elasticity

FIGURE A.10.

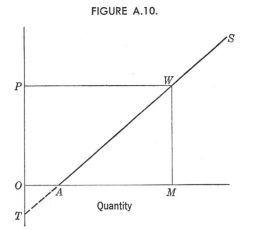

FIGURE A.11.

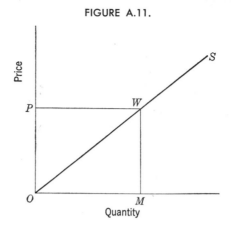

of a curve is ignored; *e.g.*, an elasticity of demand of −4 is considered to be greater than an elasticity of −3.

The relationship between elasticity of demand and the retailer's markup can be shown with the use of Figure A.12. If we let *e* stand for elasticity of demand, then

$$e = \frac{OP}{PT} = \frac{MK}{KL} = \frac{MK}{MK - ML}$$

Let *p* = optimum (profit-maximizing) price (*MK*) and *m* = marginal cost at optimum output (*ML*).

FIGURE A.12.

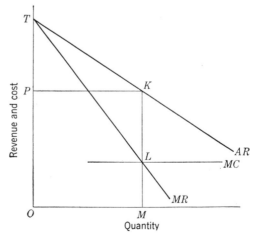

Then

$$e = \frac{p}{p - m}$$
$$e(p - m) = p$$
$$ep - em = p$$
$$ep - p = em$$
$$p(e - 1) = em$$
$$p = \frac{em}{e - 1}$$
$$p = m \left(\frac{e}{e - 1} \right)$$

If elasticity of demand is 2 in the relevant range, profit-maximizing price is

$$p = m \left(\frac{2}{2 - 1} \right) = 2m$$

That is to say, if the retailer's rule of thumb says to apply a 100 per cent markup to his cost price, the rule assumes that elasticity of demand is 2; if elasticity of demand is not 2, a 100 per cent markup is not the appropriate markup to maximize profits. In this way merchants who know nothing about the concept of elasticity implicitly make use of it nonetheless.

Figure A.12 may also be used to show that a firm with positive marginal costs will always sell at a price at which elasticity of demand is greater than 1. Let m this time represent marginal revenue (*mr* and *mc* are equal when profit is maximized).

Then

$$e = \frac{p}{p - m}$$
$$e(p - m) = p$$
$$ep - em = p$$
$$- em = p - ep$$
$$m = \frac{ep - p}{e}$$
$$m = p \left(1 - \frac{1}{e} \right)$$

If $e = 1$, marginal revenue (and therefore marginal cost) at profit-maximizing price is zero. If $e < 1$, marginal revenue (and marginal cost) is less than zero. These relationships may be confirmed by reference to Figure A.6. If a firm sells at a price at which elasticity of demand is less than 1, it could increase profits simply by reducing output and thereby increasing total revenue.

4. Profit-maximizing Output

Suppose that a given firm has the total revenue function given by the following equation

$$TR = 12x - 2x^2$$

and the total cost function indicated by

$$TC = x^3 - 4x^2 + 8x + 4$$

where x is output. It will be noted that the firm's total cost at output zero would be 4; this is the total fixed cost. The rest of the cost function, $x^3 - 4x^2 + 8x$, represents total variable cost; it assumes a different value for each value of x. The total revenue and total cost functions are plotted in Figure A.13.

If the firm's object is to maximize profits, it will operate at the output where the difference between total revenue and total cost is a maximum, *i.e.*, where the vertical distance between the TR and TC curves is a maximum. This appears from inspection to be at output 2. It will be noted that the tangent to the TR curve at output 2, TT', has the same slope as the tangent to the TC curve at that output, tt'. But the slope of the tangent to the total revenue curve is

FIGURE A.13.

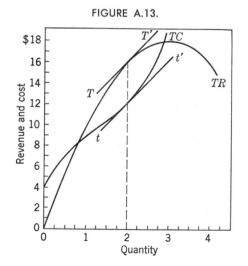

equal to marginal revenue, and the slope of the tangent to the total cost curve is equal to marginal cost. Since the slope of TT' equals the slope of tt', marginal revenue equals marginal cost, and profits are therefore maximized at an output of 2.

The same result follows if we analyze the problem in terms of average and marginal functions. We have seen that if total revenue is equal to $12x - 2x^2$ the equations for marginal revenue and average revenue will be given by the following:

$$AR = 12 - 2x$$
$$MR = 12 - 4x$$

Similarly, if the total cost function is $x^3 - 4x^2 + 8x + 4$, average total cost and marginal cost will be

$$ATC = x^2 - 4x + 8 + 4/x$$
$$MC = 3x^2 - 8x + 8$$

The average revenue, marginal revenue, average total cost, and marginal cost curves are plotted in Figure A.14. It will be noted that the most profitable output, *i.e.*, where $MC = MR$, is 2 units. The average cost per unit at this output is $6 and the selling price is $8, which provides a total profit of $4. This confirms the conclusion reached in connection with Figure A.13, where, with an output of 2 units, total revenue was $16 and total cost was $12.

A third, and still more general, solution of the problem of determining the output providing maximum profit may be indicated algebraically. We know the marginal revenue function and the marginal cost function, and at the maximum profit output these two will

FIGURE A.14.

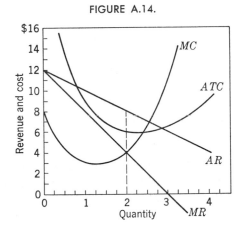

be equal. We may then set these equations equal to each other and solve for x:

$$MR = MC$$
$$12 - 4x = 3x^2 - 8x + 8$$
$$3x^2 - 4x - 4 = 0$$
$$(3x + 2)(x - 2) = 0$$
$$x = -\tfrac{2}{3}$$
$$x = 2$$

Since output cannot be less than zero, profits will be maximized when output is 2.

5. National-income Concepts

National income may be considered from either of two points of view. If we are interested in the source of national income, we may say that it is the result of expenditures on consumer goods and expenditures on investment goods. Since all goods are classified either as consumer goods or investment goods, we may write

$$Y = C + I$$

where Y is national income, C is expenditure on consumption goods, and I is expenditure on investment goods. We may, on the other hand, wish to indicate how income recipients dispose of their incomes. Since saving means not spending, the consumer has the choice of spending or not spending, *i.e.*, saving, and we may write

$$Y = C + S$$

where S represents saving. But since

$$Y = C + I$$

and

$$Y = C + S$$

it follows that $S = I$, *i.e.*, the amount actually saved must equal the amount actually invested.

When a consumer receives additional income, he will spend a part and save a part of the additional income. We may write

$$\Delta Y = \Delta C + \Delta S$$

where the Δ sign indicates the amount of the increment of each magnitude. The ratio of additional consumption to the additional income is called the marginal propensity to consume, and it may be written

$$MPC = \frac{\Delta C}{\Delta Y}$$

Similarly, the marginal propensity to save may be written

$$MPS = \frac{\Delta S}{\Delta Y}$$

Since $\Delta Y = \Delta C + \Delta S$, it follows that

$$\frac{\Delta C}{\Delta Y} + \frac{\Delta S}{\Delta Y} = MPC + MPS = 1$$

When a new investment is made, the investment expenditure generates additional income. The ratio of the additional income to the additional investment is called the income multiplier. If we let M represent the multiplier, we may write

$$M = \frac{\Delta Y}{\Delta I}$$

If we assume that the change in income generates no secondary repercussions on investment, this equation may be simplified as follows:

$$M = \frac{\Delta Y}{\Delta I} = \frac{\Delta Y}{\Delta Y - \Delta C} = \frac{\Delta Y/\Delta Y}{\Delta Y/\Delta Y - \Delta C/\Delta Y} = \frac{1}{1 - MPC} = \frac{1}{MPS}$$

If, for example, $MPC = \frac{9}{10}$, $M = \frac{1}{1 - \frac{9}{10}} = 10$; *i.e.*, for each dollar of new investment national income would be increased by \$10.

A more general formulation which takes into account possible income-induced changes in investment may be shown as follows. If ΔI_p represents the primary or initial change in investment and ΔI_i the induced change in investment,

$$M = \frac{\Delta Y}{\Delta I_p}$$
$$= \frac{\Delta Y}{\Delta Y - \Delta C - \Delta I_i}$$
$$= \frac{1}{1 - [(\Delta C + \Delta I_i)/\Delta Y]}$$
$$= \frac{1}{1 - MPX}$$

where MPX represents the marginal propensity to spend. If ΔI_i is zero, this formulation is identical with that given above.

INDEX

INDEX